THE ART OF DRAWING

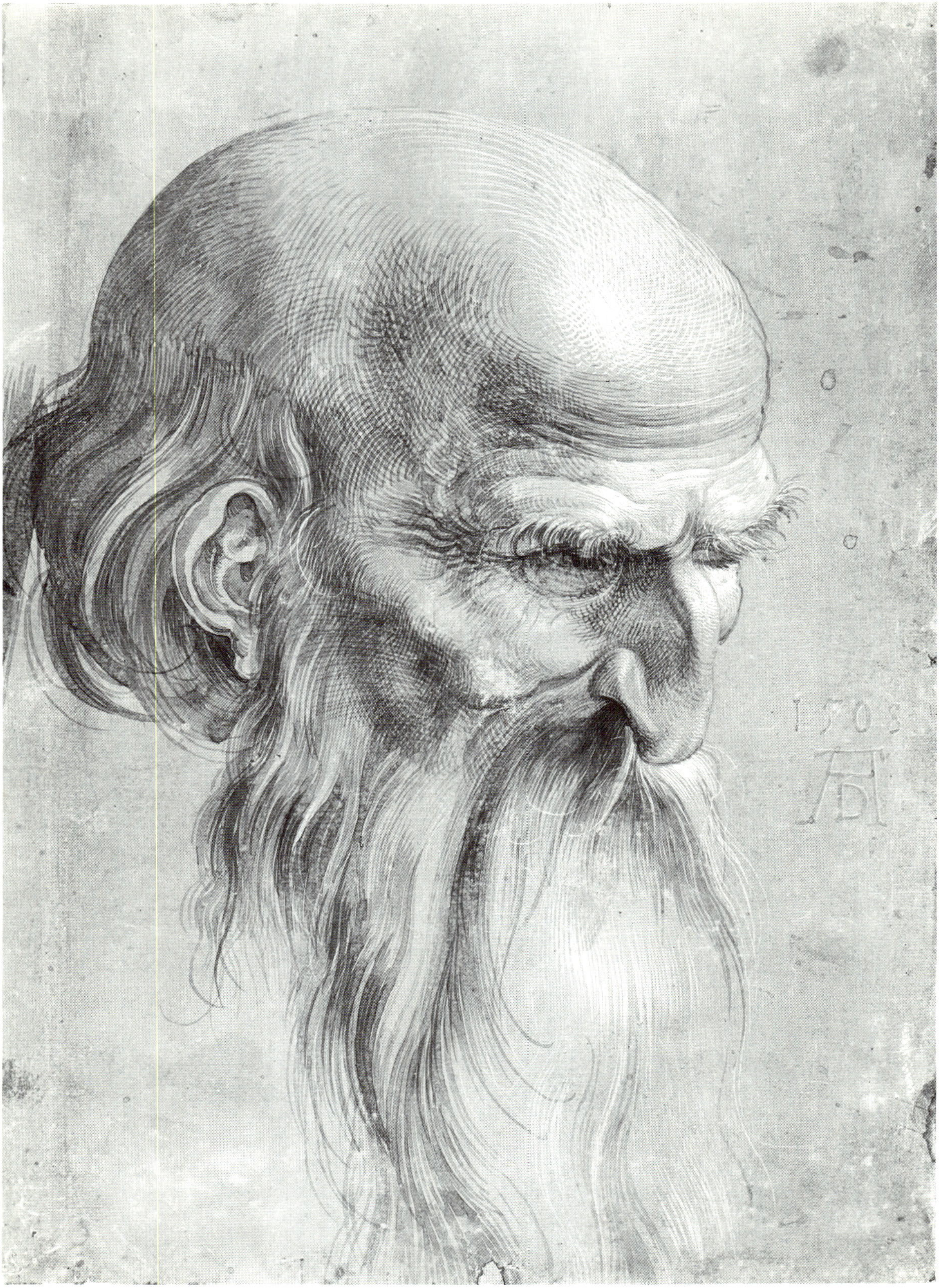
1508

Philip Rawson

THE ART OF DRAWING

AN INSTRUCTIONAL GUIDE

Macdonald & Co
London and Sydney

Unless otherwise stated, drawings are by Philip Rawson, except for illustrations 57 and 79 which are also by Piers B. Rawson.

Frontispiece: Albrecht Dürer, *Head of an Apostle*, 1508.

This book was designed and produced by
John Calmann & Cooper Ltd, London

First published in Great Britain by
Macdonald & Co (Publishers) Ltd
London & Sydney

A member of BPCC plc

ISBN 0 356 09500 2

Filmset in Great Britain by SX Composing Ltd
Printed and bound in Great Britain by The Pitman Press

Macdonald & Co (Publishers) Ltd
Maxwell House
74 Worship Street
London EC2A 2EN

Contents

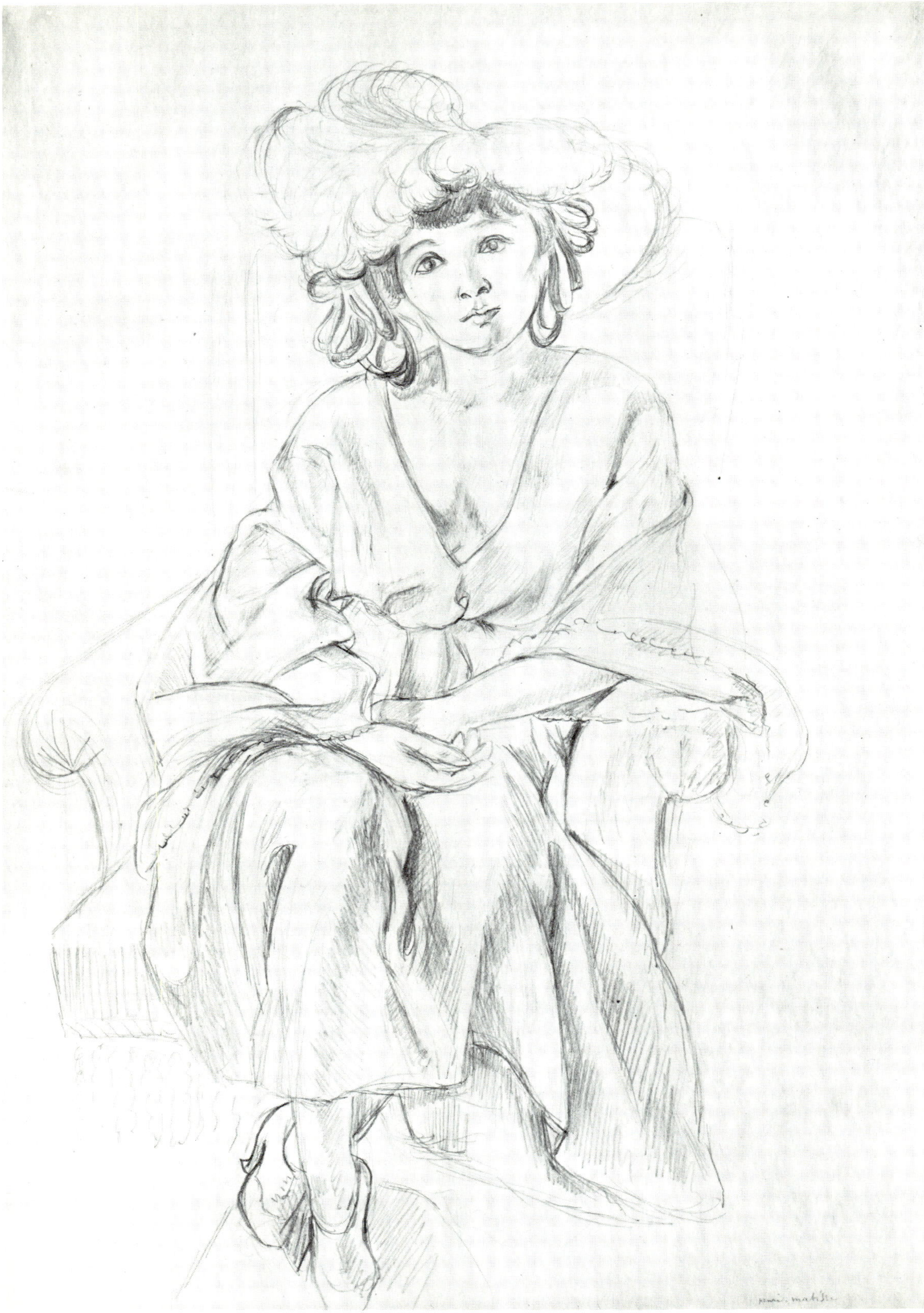
henri matisse

Introduction

Drawing embodies a genuine and independent way of thinking. Someone who draws actually sees more and knows more of the world he or she lives in than someone who does not draw. Even though it is probably the most fundamental and direct of the arts, drawing needs very little in the way of equipment. You can do it with virtually anything that will leave a mark.

Drawing is fundamental because you need to be able to draw before you paint or make sculpture. Yet it is not just a preliminary to those other arts; it is an art in its own right. If you have ever tried to work up a painting from a drawing you will know that you cannot just transfer an original drawing into paint. You will probably lose most of the vital lines you made during the process of laying out the drawing, even though you may preserve some general outlines. Of course, you may compensate for this loss by colour and brush-work. But what you lose may be those special qualities that made your drawing good in the first place.

Drawing begins with lines. To make the smallest mark, a dot even, you have to drag or twirl your drawing-point a little. Marks and lines are, therefore, records of movements that took time to make and each line is individual and specific. What an artist chooses to do with these marks defines his or her style.

Drawing is direct because it can reflect immediately the impulses of your imagination as your arm and hand respond to them. Remember the feeling of drawing with your finger in sand or earth? Many artists have drawn with their fingers dipped in ink. Some Chinese artists even used to keep one of their finger-nails long and specially trimmed to draw with. But anything you hold in your hand can act as an extension of it and leave traces of unrepeatable feelings and thoughts.

Most good drawings leave the marks from which they were built exposed, not covered by layers of afterthought. They thus preserve that special time-quality which is unique to the art of drawing. Also, when you read a drawing you actually need to take time to follow out the lines and sequences of lines that compose it, re-enacting them in your mind. So the drawn image can suggest far more about the world than the facts it depicts. Artists draw their lines for you to read; so read them carefully and sympathetically. And when you yourself draw, you will then be able to make your own marks interesting in similar ways.

1 Henri Matisse: 'The Plumed Hat', 1919. A careful drawing from the model, using overlaps and hatching.

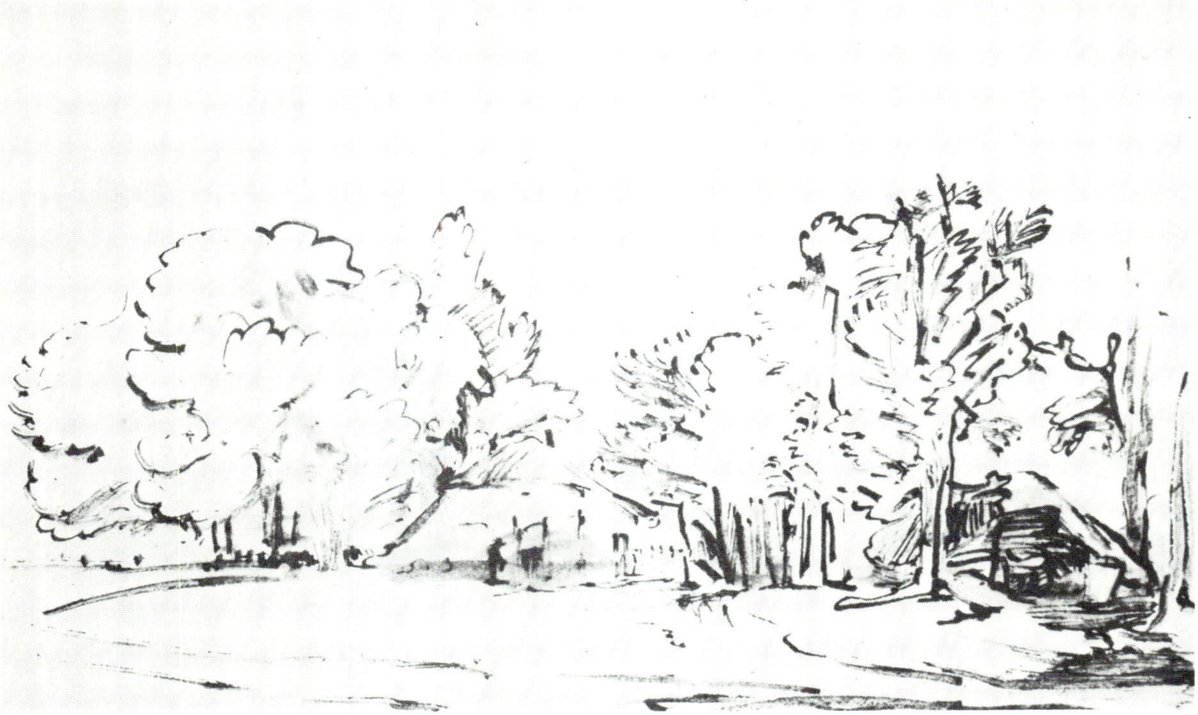

2 Rembrandt van Rijn: 'Cottages Beneath High Trees in Sunlight', 1657–8.
3 Leonardo da Vinci: 'Star of Bethlehem'. A study of a plant defining its spiral development in space.

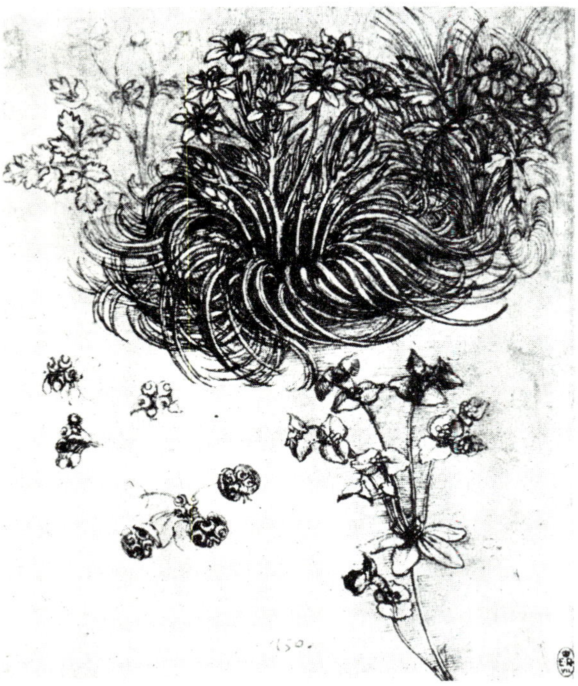

A drawing such as Rembrandt's *Cottages Beneath High Trees* is not simply an illustration of cottages and trees. Even though it is 'representational', the drawing as a sheer object does not look in the least *like* trees and cottages. It looks *like* any other sheet of paper covered with pen squiggles. To understand what it *represents* you need to read the language of the marks, rather as you read the words on this page. What the drawing actually tells you is something unique, which can only be conveyed by these particular marks, arranged in this particular way.

As you look at a drawing the marks will, so to speak, 'jump together' or 'click' in your mind as you grasp the image. You gather the meaning by reading over the marks to find what they seem to connect with in your own remembered experiences. Even the original artist would have to do the same if he picked up his own drawing to look at it a few weeks later. Understanding how this connecting process works can lead to fascinating insights. You need to learn to follow out the traces the artist made with a special kind of sympathy, a skill best developed by drawing yourself. You can then feel your way into an attitude of mind that encourages your memory to bring up a whole series of responses to marks, to lines, to groups of marks, and to the image that unifies them. The meaning of any drawing can only be a combination of what its marks can mean to you the viewer. And when you yourself draw, your marks will always mean something to somebody else who can read drawings.

Most children draw. Far too many stop drawing as they get older. Some seem to be put off by feeling that they cannot compete with the art they see around them – especially advertising art, which uses all sorts of mechanical aids. But nowadays more and more people are realizing that it is a great disadvantage not to develop one's artistic 'literacy'; and that to understand and create any art it is not enough simply to be able to imitate the surface effects of one variety of modern art or another.

There are many ways of learning to draw and of developing your present drawing style. In this book I shall discuss, one by one, various methods that you can use. You can never use them all at once, and each particular method is only one of the possibilities that you can take up or reject. Each artist normally builds his individual style out of a particular group of methods. To some extent we recognize a good draughtsman by his wealth of resources.

This does not mean that you should know in advance what your drawing is going to look like. Precisely the opposite. Good drawing involves two complementary processes: first, search and discovery; secondly, consolidation of the results into a unity. Without the second the first is uncoordinated and pointless. Without the first the second has nothing to work on. The first continually challenges the second and keeps it alive. As we explore each method we need to keep this dual aspect in mind.

You should study each section as you come to it by actually doing what it talks about, with as much rhythmic commitment and verve as you can. Then you can look at what you have drawn with a critical eye, modify it, and then perhaps do it again more clearly. Gradually the various techniques will become unconscious and natural, and when you read other people's drawings you will be able to appreciate them and understand them more fully.

One further point: after the first half of the book (Sections 1–21) it is not essential to follow through the sections chronologically, although it would certainly be helpful to do so at least once. The order in which the sections are laid out represents logical connection, not just a learning sequence, and so occasional references forward and back will be necessary.

4 Edgar Degas: 'Mounted Jockey', 1882–6. This quick sketch captures the characteristic lively movement of a horse and rider.

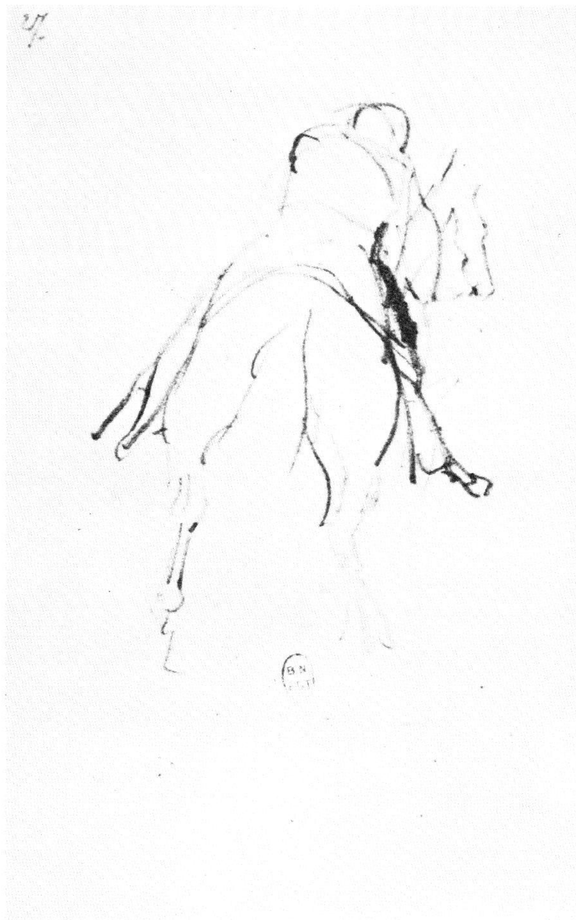

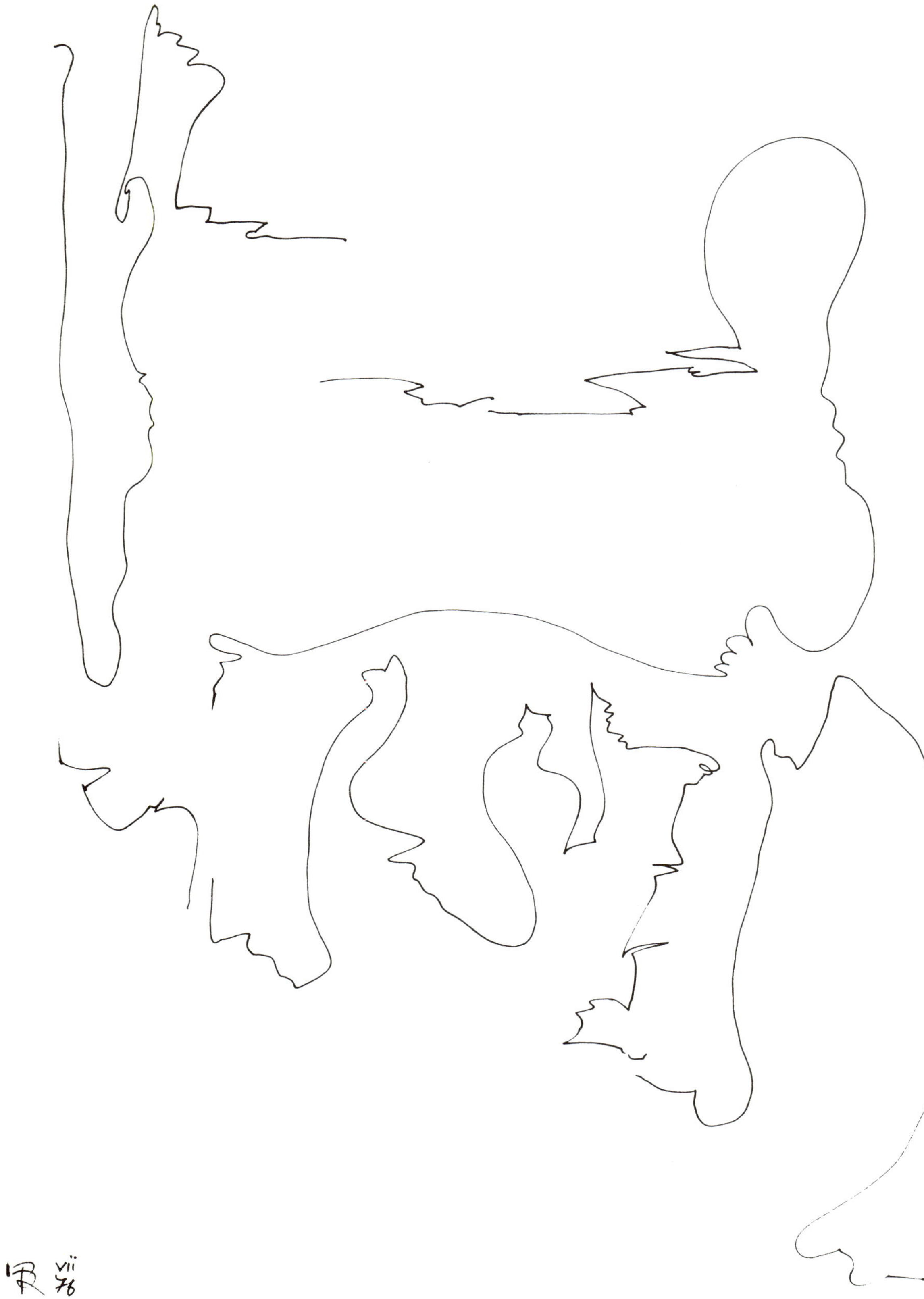
vii
76

I

Mark, Line and Structure

We shall begin by working with the basic marks, lines and structures upon which the strength and value of any drawing depend. We shall examine how they are the primary resource for building both non-figurative and figurative imagery; and how drawings need to work at the level of linear inflections and rhythm, and through their relations with each other and the format, as a basis for all further developments.

Section 1
Marks on the Ground

There are two ways of thinking about the marks and lines you make in drawing: the mobile 'following-along' way, and the 'static plan' way. The difference between them may have something to do with the functions of different areas of the human brain.

Here is an analogy. Imagine yourself following a guide on a route by boat through winding lagoons. You will be able to learn the route for yourself by following the twists and turnings, but you may not understand how the lagoons lie in relation to one another. Your journey back along the same route may seem quite different. Then imagine flying over the same lagoons in a helicopter – you can see at once how your route belongs to an overall plan. The first experience is a kinetic experience of movement, speeds and changes of course. The second is a structured plan-view which is fixed and static; once you know the pattern you could even take other routes through it. This may change your attitude to the route. Events on the journey may not seem to happen purely *in sequence* any more; they may appear as features of the fixed plan.

5 Rhythmic movements of the point produce lines on the surface.

In a similar way, lines can create journeys full of incident; but they can also lay out intelligible ordered structures. The same lines, or bits of line, can be read both ways. In different styles one or other of the functions may predominate, but again and again we shall meet this dual function of lines in drawing.

Section 2
Lines

Let us begin our study of marks and lines with the idea that they are traces of movement. Pick up any drawing point and begin to draw lines with it on pieces of paper, watching carefully how each line records the movements of your hand. Then draw a long continuous line over the surface of a whole sheet of paper.

Feel how the impulses come down your arm; and allow your hand to be paced by those impulses. Above all, try to avoid repeating standardized shapes, seek to introduce as much variety as you can into the lengths of straight sections, and emphasize the projection of angles and curves. You may be surprised to discover how few shapes you make to begin with; and you must look quite critically at what you do, because this is where the

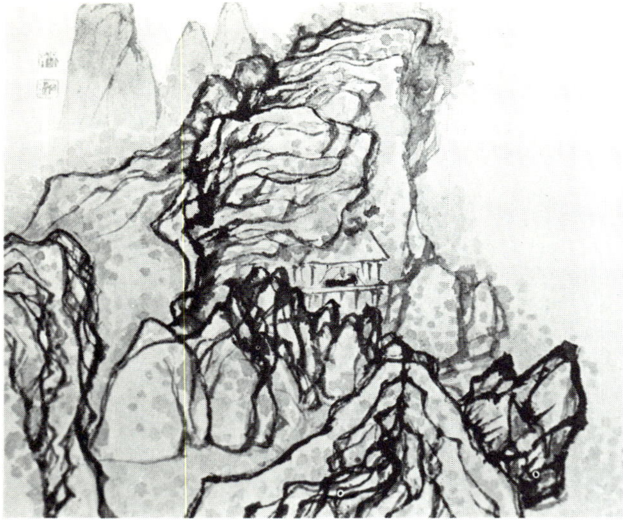

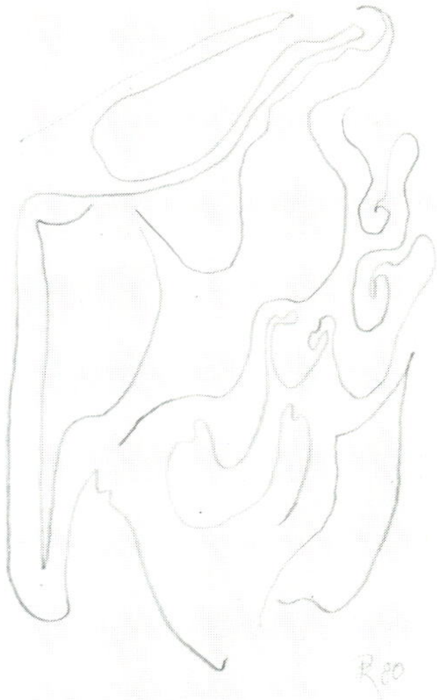

6 *Tao Chi: Landscape. Currents of movement drawn by the brush in ink and colour suggest veins through rocks.*

7 *Pencil drawing based on markings in a polished stone.*

8 *Jackson Pollock: 'Untitled', 1950. A free action drawing.*

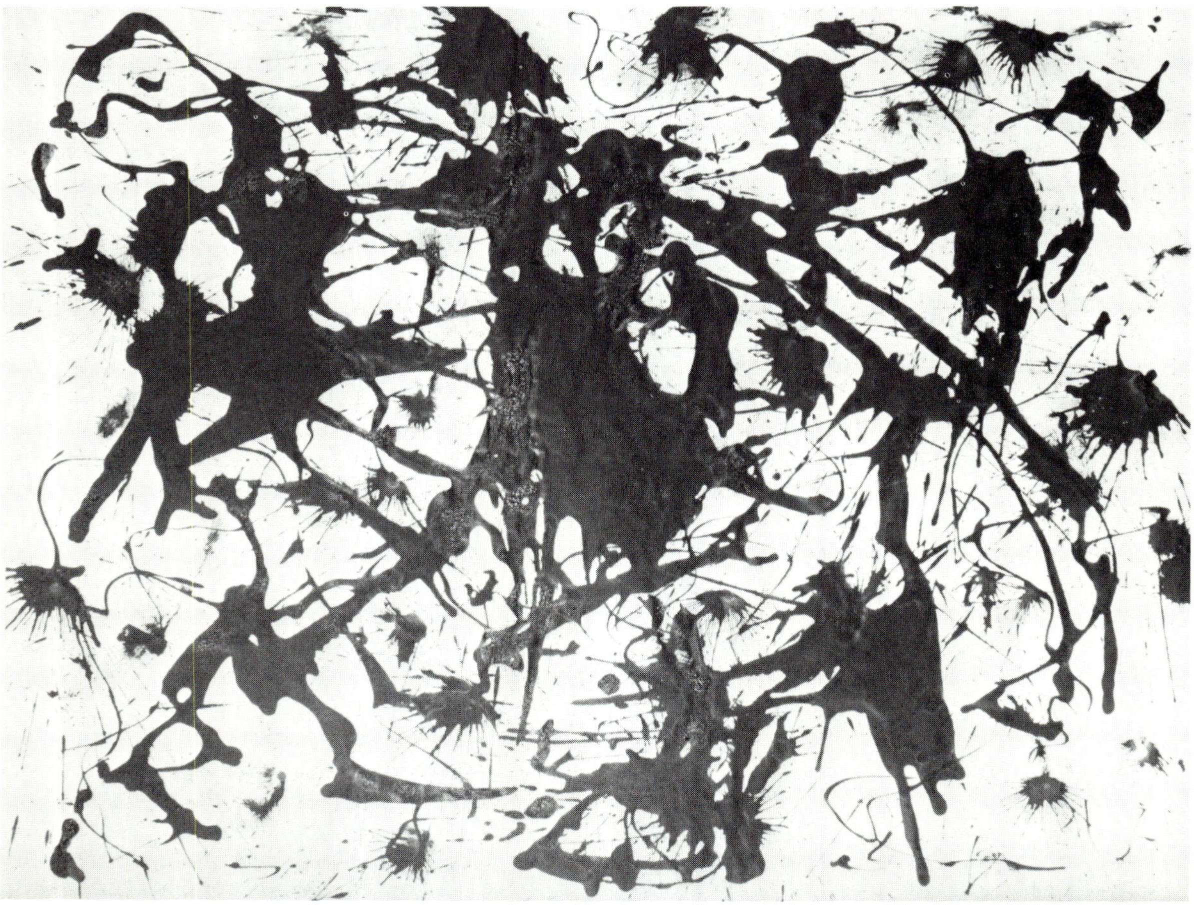

process of search and discovery begins – in reaching continually beyond the limits of what you already do. You can use all sorts of things to give
7 you ideas. For example, the veins in stones or the cracks in tree bark.

You will need lots of paper, preferably big (and cheap) sheets, and a variety of different drawing implements – hard and soft pencils, felt tips, pens and Western or Far Eastern brushes to use with ink. You will find many different points used in the illustrations to this book.

Using a variety of materials, try making a whole series of different lines on your paper – some long, some short; some fast, some slow; some stabbed, some scratched; some done by bouncing a brush, or by splashing and dripping with it; different kinds and shapes of dots; swerving lines, smooth lines, rising and falling lines; rows of splashed dots – all the kinds you can imagine. Make your lines run in many directions. This means moving your hand in quite unaccustomed ways, which will certainly challenge your invention.

9 Free brush calligraphy.

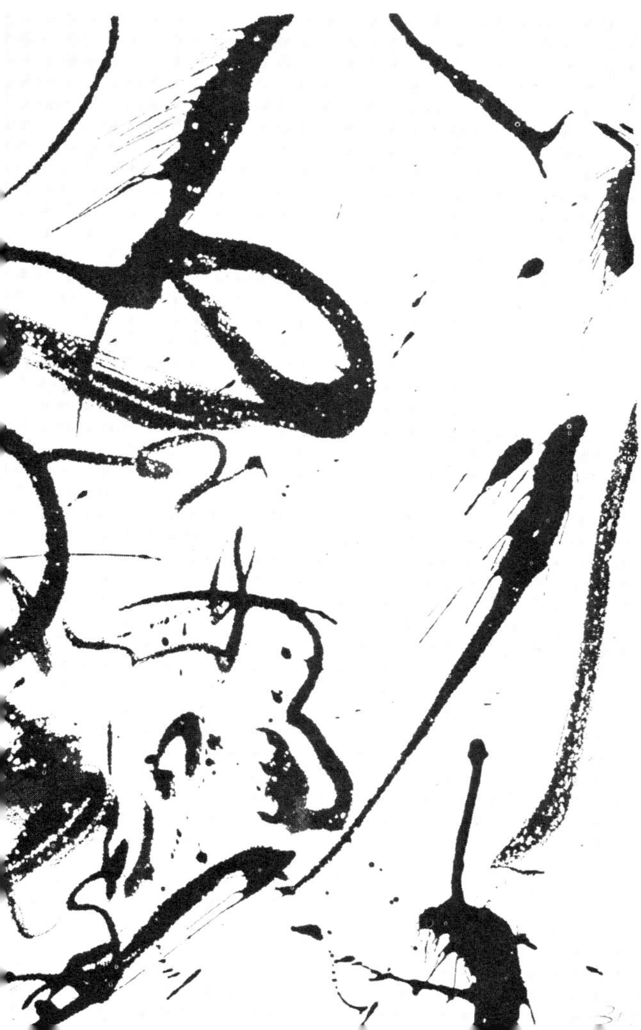

Draw reflectively some of the time, watching how your point moves and trying to make each kind of line a different shape, and thus more certain and definite. The rest of the time try to set your hand free; and you may be lucky enough to get into a state of mind where your hand seems to act without your consciously directing it. Gradually you should be able to build up a sort of balance between thoughtfulness and freedom, which will help you to get those two processes of search and consolidation working together. Above all, try and connect specific feelings with the different kinds of lines as you do them (see also Sections 7–9).

The art you are now creating is the basis of Abstract Expressionist calligraphy. You have come face to face with the fundamental element of graphic art.

When you begin to push yourself into making different lines do different things, you will probably discover that the normal way you hold the point for writing is too confining. It may help if you take your hand off the paper and begin to move your arm freely. People often feel that this is bound to make their lines uncertain and 'inaccurate', but this only matters if you are trying to define things in the same minute detail as, say, the letters of your handwriting. In art one does that very rarely. You can always rest your little finger on the paper. But the gain in fluency, if you can draw with your whole arm free, is immense. It will lead you away from cramped habits of thinking, and towards 'overall' drawing. Most important, it will make sure you always take your cues for building up your image from lines you have already drawn. This will help you to transmit your feelings not only into the shapes of the lines, but into the composition as a whole.

When you are reading drawings, all the characteristics of lines are important. Quite small inflections of touch and tone, and variations of speed and quality, may be vital clues to what the artist meant to say. Everything about a good drawing tells you something.

Section 3
The Expression of Lines

You have been drawing lines. But what defines the different shapes lines have? What makes one line able to suggest one kind of feeling, another a different kind?

First of all, there is an obvious difference be- 11a
tween straight lines and curves. Straight lines – depending on how much they predominate – give any drawing a sense of clearness, hardness, and sometimes rigidity. As you draw one, you set off in one direction and carry on until you stop, without changing your mind. If lines are vertical they connect naturally with the vertical of the standing human being; if horizontal, with the visible horizon. These two fundamental human factors are reflected in the edges of the common rectangular sheet of drawing paper.

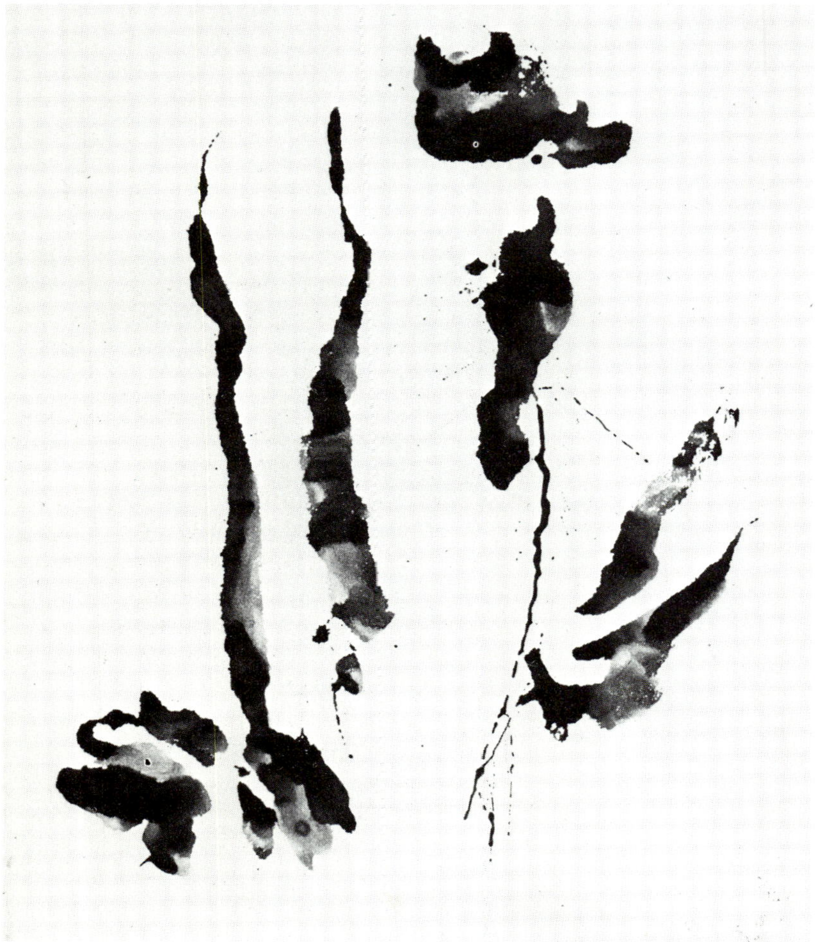

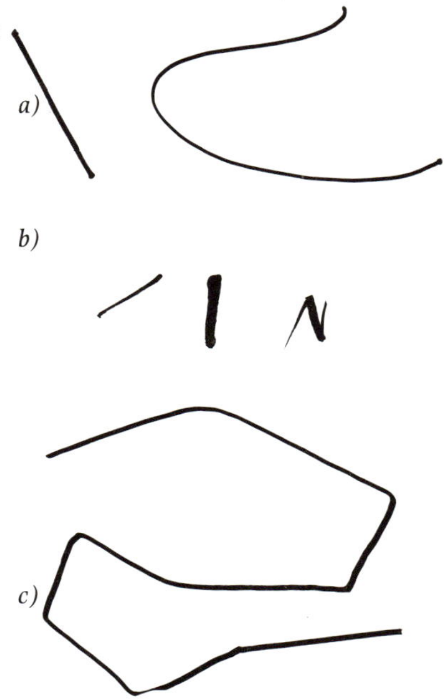

10 Brush calligraphy generates an overall image.
11 a) Contrast between a straight line and curve; b) straight lines drawn in different ways; c) a longer line composed of straight sections.

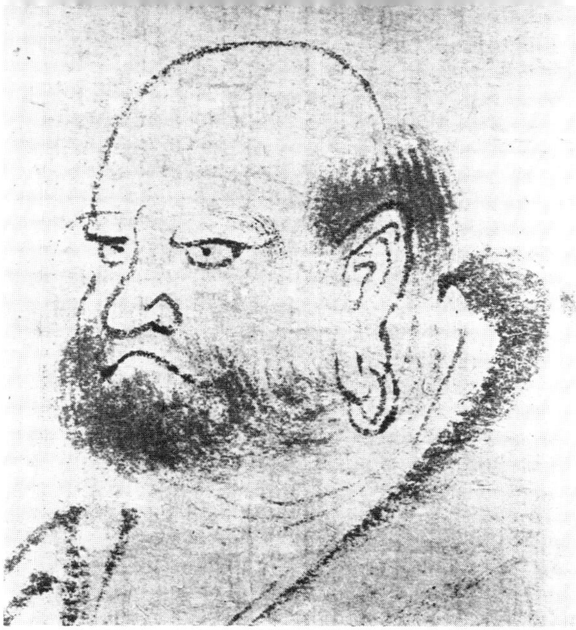

12 Unknown Chinese artist: 'Head of Bodhidharma', 14th c. Different kinds of lines convey the different qualities of parts of reality: loose folds of skin, wispy hair, crumpled flesh of the ear, and smooth dome.
13 a) A quickly drawn brush line; b) a line constructed of segments; c) lines drawn with care for the transverse relations across their directions.

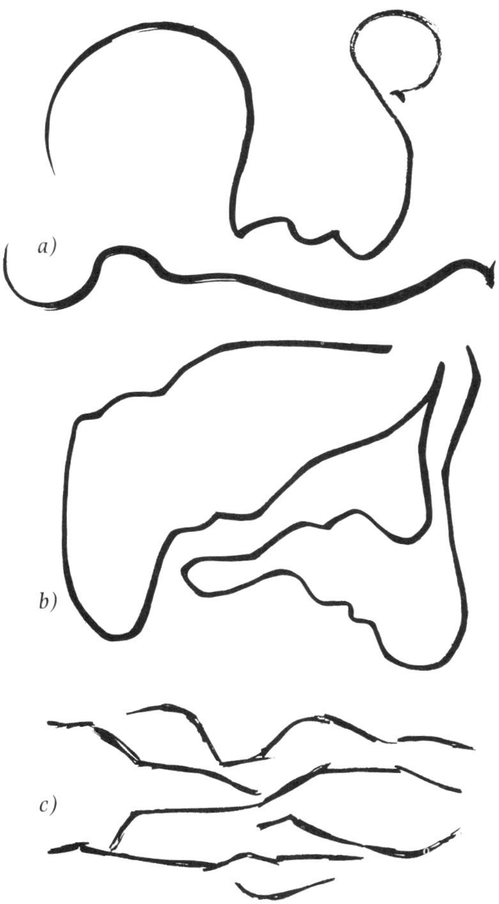

Until quite recently, ruled lines were rather rare in drawing, save in architectural or engineering designs and hard perspective images. A ruled line has an abstract, intellectual quality. It does not matter which direction you read it in. But there are in fact a surprising number of ways 11b
in which you can draw freehand something that has the artistic value of a straight line. Sometimes you can even tell which direction the line was drawn in, and which end is the head and which the tail. This can be important when you come to include straight lines into more complex combinations of line. You can string lengths of straight line together to make longer lines. Then, each of the straight segments serves as an element in the rhythmic structure of the longer line they together create. Paul Klee pointed out that a well-made 11c
line has this feeling of being strung out by a series of basic units of pull, which has a rhythmic function. In his own drawings he even emphasized this aspect of rhythm along the line in deep curves.

This leads us to an important difference between kinds of line, which by now you should be able to feel. First, there are those which are the result of moving the point quite fast and continuously. 13a
Your invention and your hand keep pace with each other. Any curve you make is the result of a curved movement of the hand.

This is the way Chinese and Japanese artists drew. Their long-breathed lines are images of long- 22
breathed movements of the mind and hand running along together. In fact this kind of drawing is often called 'cursive'. Usually the 'running' is so swift that there is no time for you to take much account of what lies on each side of the line. It is the line as a sweep of time that matters.

Secondly, there is the kind of line Klee was 13b
referring to. We can call it the constructed line. You can build it up carefully, revising it, going back over its segments, perhaps to reshape them to correspond with other lines and the areas and spaces on both sides. But the curves, angles and rhythms you construct out of the strokes do not individually correspond with complete gestures. You also have the time to take account of what is 13c
happening on either side of your line (Section 8).

In practice, any curved line that you draw (except for an arc) is bound to have some inner segments or 'quanta' of direction and length in it which make it different in character from any other line and which must be stressed to ensure that it is interesting. This helps to explain why pure arcs can be disheartening in a drawing. An arc contains no rhythmically shaped or identifiable units of direction, and so your eye is not free to look *across* it to see how its 'connection' with neighbouring lines is changing. This sort of connection is an important topic which we shall come to in a moment (Section 8).

Now I suggest you draw some lines with straight sections and curves in them. Try to differentiate the curves by varying the lengths of the different quanta of direction in each one; keep your overall sense of pulse and rhythm alive by remembering that all lines are the traces of your human gestures.

Section 4
Scale of Directions

When you start thinking in terms of quanta or units of pull along certain directions, the question at once arises: *which* directions? You vary your lines not only by varying the lengths of the straight sections but also by varying the directions in which they run. However, in any single drawing you will rarely use more than a certain number of directions across the paper. You will actually use a set of directions. So it seems sensible to make sure you are using a good one, and using it well.

Any set of directions should act rather like the fixed notes in a musical scale, giving your invention something to work with. It should make sure your lines are neither haphazard nor boring, but truly 'melodic'. It can also help you to check in the course of your work why one part of a drawing may seem dead, or not to fit with the rest. You may discover that a drawing becomes weak if its set of directions is not decisive enough or has become too limited. To pursue the musical analogy, a drawing can come to resemble a shapeless howl or a banal repetition of two or three notes. Conversely, good drawings are like interesting melodies, partly because they embody clear and varied scales. How they do it, with what kind of expression, is up to you. It does no harm to draw one of these little direction-notes in a corner of the sheet you are drawing on, to remind yourself of the scale you are using.

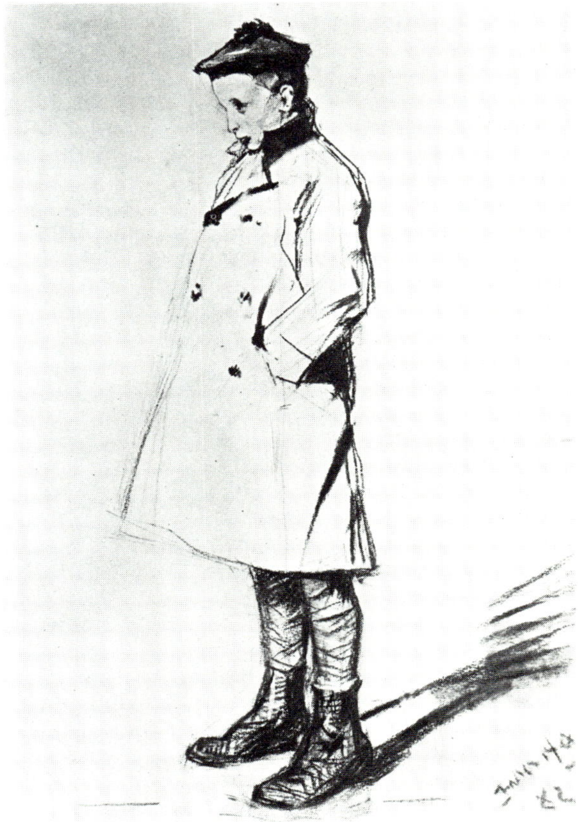

14 Henri de Toulouse-Lautrec: 'Odon Tapié de Celeryan at the Age of Ten'; drawn with a clear scale of directions.

You will find that you can make your scale of directions contribute to your drawing in quite important ways. You can, for example, choose one which leaves out one sector and stresses another; 15a
or you can use one that includes a group of right-angled relationships among its components

a)

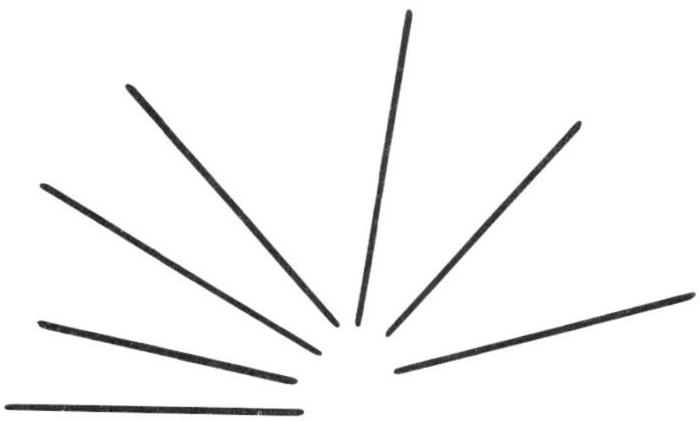

b)

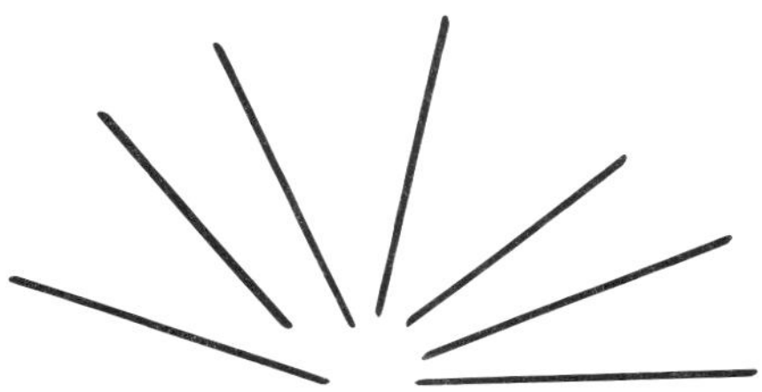

c)

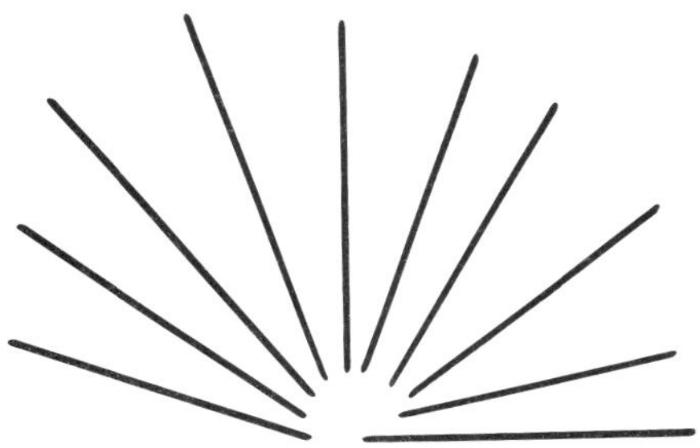

d)

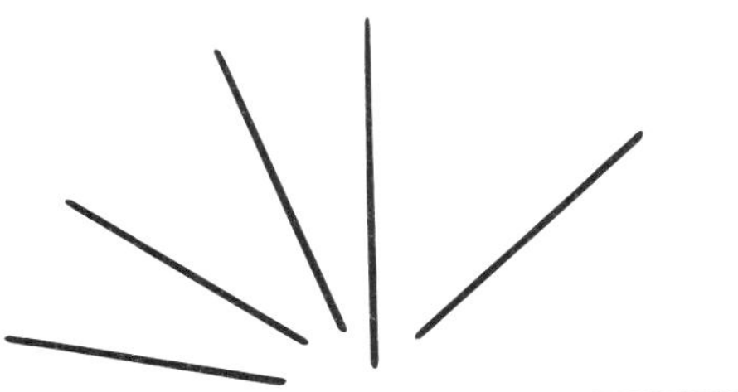

15 Diagrams of scales of directions: a) has several close directions on the left; b) has an even spread including some at right angles; c) has a large number; d) has few directions including a vertical and a horizontal.
16 The upper line (a) moves with smooth transitions, the lower (b) with angular.
17 Composition based on a leading line that states the main directions of a scale.

(Section 8); you can decide to use a lot of direc- 15c
tions; or only a few, well-chosen ones. The way 15d
lines pass from one direction to another also contributes to the expression. A line may pass
smoothly from one direction to the next one to it; 16a
then the next; or it may jump abruptly at an
angle to a direction far away on the scale; then on 16b
to another distant direction.

Here is a kind of rule of thumb you can use while you are laying out your drawings. Make sure that you set down all the directions of your scale somewhere in the design as soon as possible. You can even set down a leading line which itself contains them all; you do need to be careful, though, that this does not become a fixed habit.

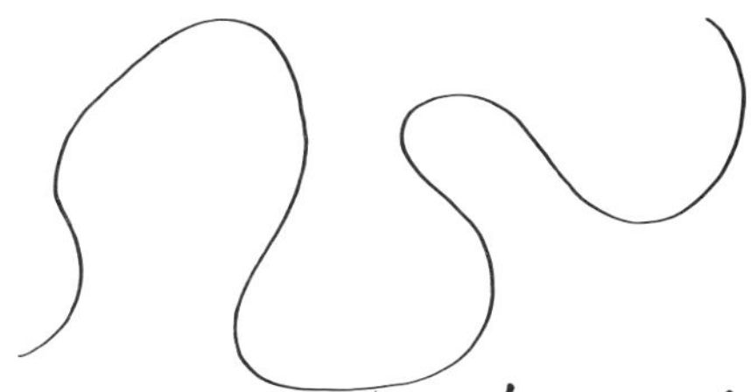

a)

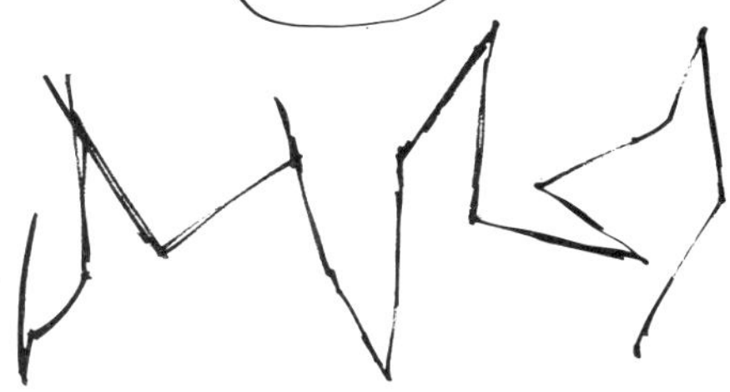

b)

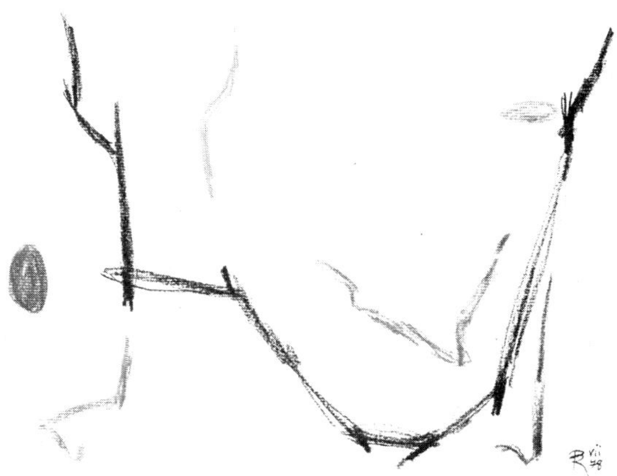

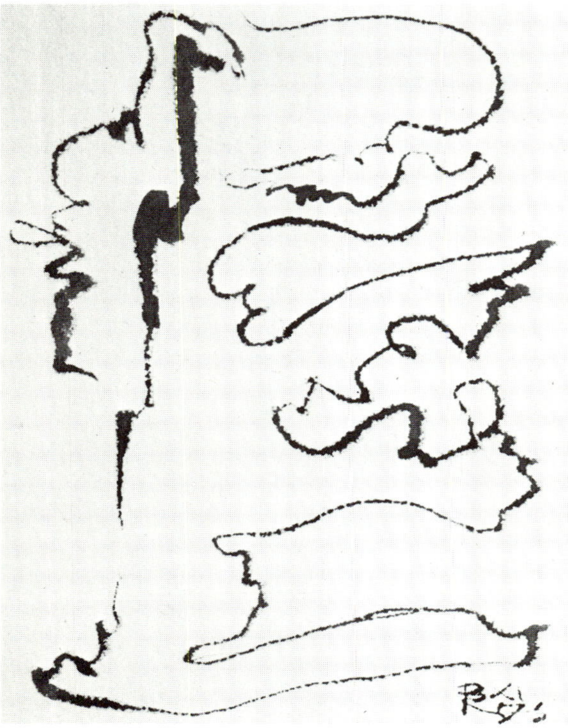

18 Rhythmic brush drawing, relating deeply curved rhythms to more abrupt angular ones.

Section 5
Rhythm

Rhythm is one of the most important factors in the whole of drawing. It is the root from which all our expression arises. Many of the drawings you have already done will have been imbued with rhythm. This does not mean that all drawing has to be so strongly linear. There are other kinds of rhythm out of which you can weave your work.

All our experience is shaped by rhythms. Our bodies are filled with all sorts of pulses, contractions and relaxations, heartbeats and breathing, and muscular squeezes; over these lie the rhythms of walking, expressive gesture and work, the pacing rituals of life such as domestic or office routines; then the larger outward framework of the times of day, the calendar and seasons which link us to the world we live in. They are both subjective and objective. In music and art rhythm can be measured quite objectively; but it can also affect our feelings profoundly. It is in rhythm that design and life meet. Maybe this is why many artists like to work to music.

When you begin a drawing it is a feeling for rhythms in the subject, for rhythmic spacing across the paper, that sparks your imagination. You build connections and expressive variations out of rhythm. Your sense of gracefulness, solemnity, ease, excitement and so on are all conveyed by qualities of rhythm. When a figurative artist first reads across a subject he is going to draw – a landscape, say – the first thing he naturally grasps are the rhythms in its spacing and connection. It is these that must be set down with the earliest strokes.

If you lose your sense of rhythm while you are drawing, the work can become awkward and heavy or fall apart. Without rhythm there are no real shapes. Rhythm shows you time laid out as measured space, in which you participate almost physically. It is also something you have to develop by an inner sense. No description can do it justice. All I can do here is point out the different forms it can take, so that you know what to look out for in other people's drawing. This will help you to find points of development in your own.

Rhythms can be 'carried' by all sorts of elements: brush-strokes, the edges of objects, the movements of lines, shadow patches, hatching, even scribbling.
They appear in the measures of space across the 14
surface that the eye scans as it surveys an image. Generally speaking, we can distinguish between those rhythms which are carried along the flow of lines and those which bridge the spaces between marks. While you were drawing all those varied lines you were actually studying your own feelings in relation to rhythm along the direction of flow, and training your hand to respond freely to them.

The basic element in all rhythm is some kind of repeated pulse or beat that counts off distances or spaces. Along an undulating line a rhythm can be

conveyed by crests and troughs; along a more
40 angular one by segments of straight line. The measure can be mechanically regular; or it can be organic, with slight variations which result from the 'phrasing' of a larger shape lying over the basic beat. It can be so small and finely textured that you are scarcely aware of it, like the weaves in a tapestry, or it can be very broad and uneven, as in many Expressionist drawings. When you are drawing well your mind may be unconsciously 'counting beats' and making sure your rhythms are varied and lively, without losing the unity of the design.

Some artists use sets of mathematical proportions
08 to make their rhythms interesting, generally in relation to some overall plan (Section 6). But shaping that is lively can actually stretch the measure of its beat. Good draughtsmen make sure that their series of pulses can be read individually as well as collectively. This is one of the reasons why it may not be advisable to work over a drawing again and again, when you may have lost the feeling for your original rhythms.

Piet Mondrian made two drawings of the same church, four years apart. In the second one, he extends rhythmic measures derived from the original subject-matter both to the open space around and to the inner shapes of the building. The rhythms here are made up from short strokes spaced out parallel to each other. We can think of them as resembling drum-beats in music. Try to do the same kind of thing yourself, marking off spaces that have different pulses, and develop different patterns of rhythm out of them.

Rhythmic feeling can obviously be captured in lines along their direction of movement. Undulations, loops and curves can express a wide variety of rhythmic patterns. Many of the illustrations so far have embodied purely linear rhythms; and your own drawings will have done so too. Pulses and phrasing emerge not only through the lengths of sections of line going first in one direction then another, and in the spacing, but also in the traces of altering hand pressures that are revealed, for example, by the rhythmic spreading and thinning of a brush.

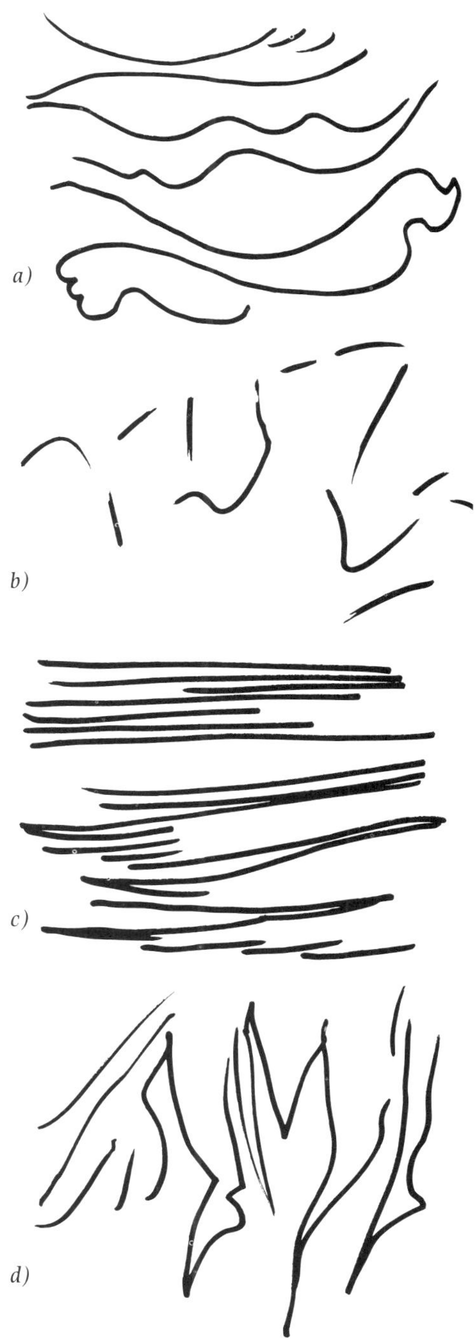

19 Variety of rhythmic patterns in drawing groups of lines.

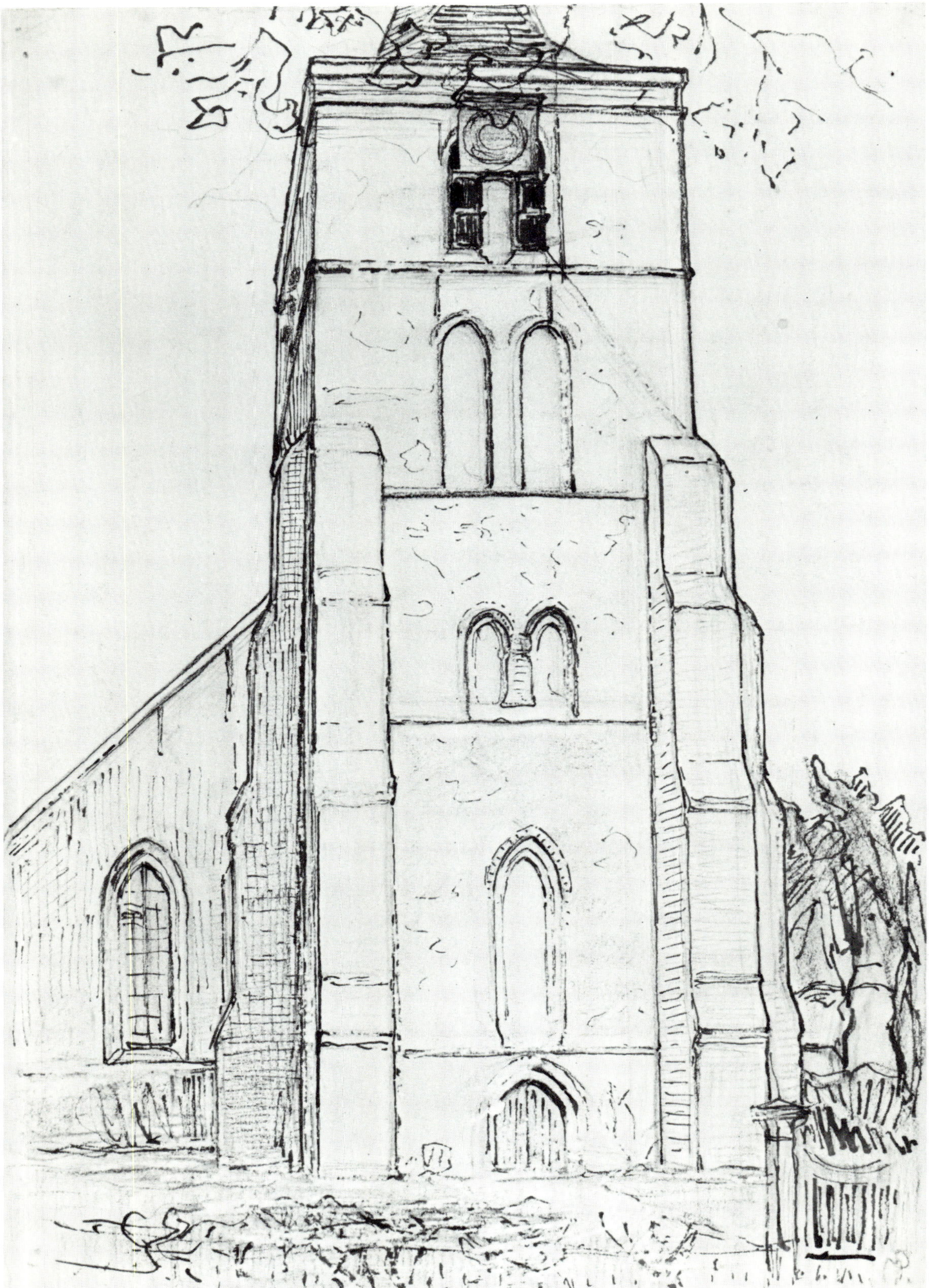

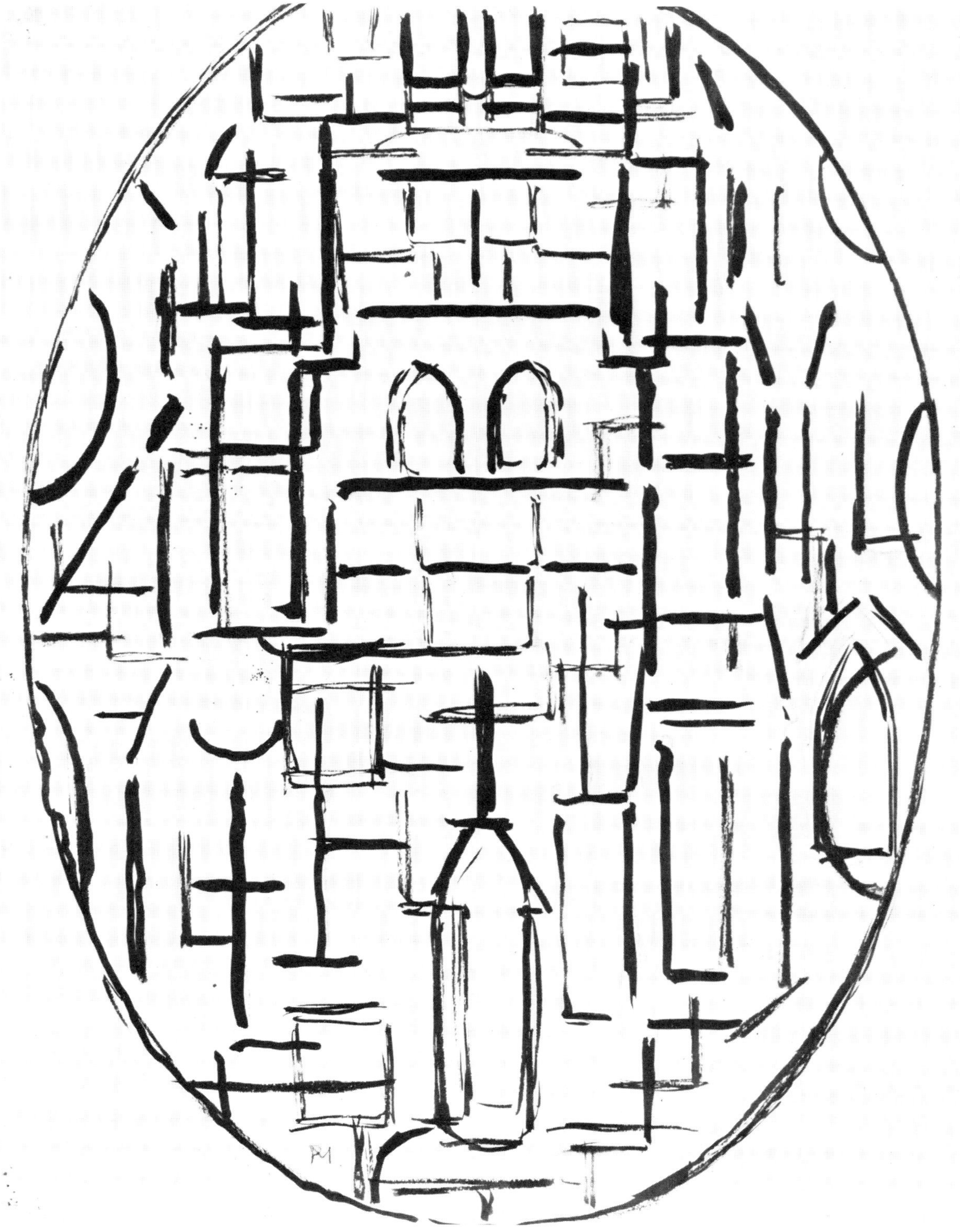

20, 21 Piet Mondrian: crayon drawings, the first of a church in Domburg (1909), the second (1914) a rhythmic design of intervals based upon drawings of the same church. Vertical and horizontal strokes are almost all that remain.

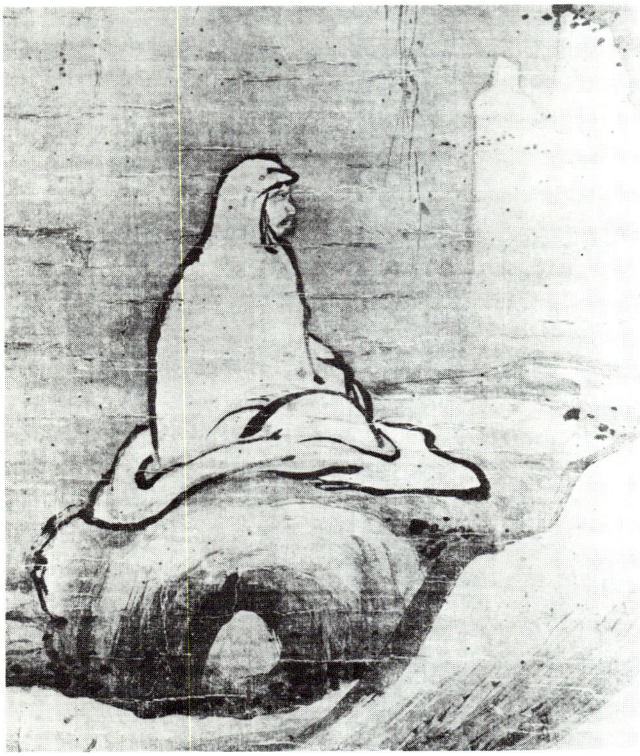

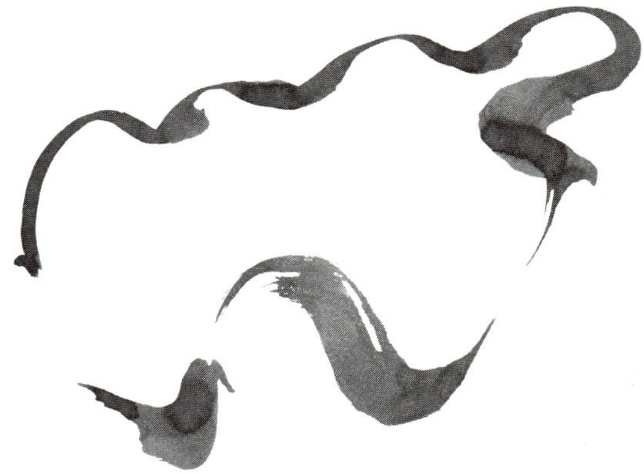

22 Unknown Chinese artist: brush drawing of the Zen master, Bodhidharma, 14th c. Its lines embody many types of rhythmic relationship. The folds of the robe cascade down the front to the ground; the curves above the knee link the curved hollow of the rock to the body, the contour in the foreground reflects the front contour of the figure.
23 Each individual brush stroke has a unique character.
24 Joan Miró: pencil drawing on a page of a calendar. Its rambling, looping rhythm is in great contrast to the harsh, angular rhythm of Picasso's 'Head of a Woman'.

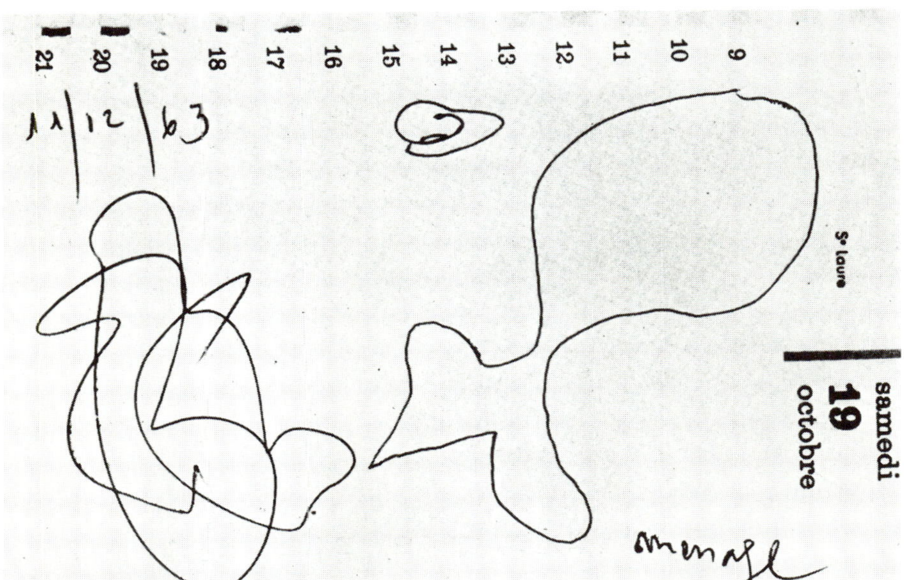

The next thing you can try is making sets of mobile *lines* which also express and incorporate transverse space-rhythms.

Of course, in actual drawing you do not need to follow a horizontal line across the page as some of the diagrams here do (or even only the horizontals and verticals as Mondrian did). You can work diagonally across the surface following your scale of directions, to develop interlocking series of spaced rhythms. But even there the pacing of your pulse will keep the different elements unified. It is probably Cézanne who has made the most sophisti-
8 cated use of interlocked space-rhythms across the drawing-surface. However, also compare the drawing here by Miró with Picasso's drawing, pl. 166, and feel your way into the different senses of rhythm they contain. The difference is not only in the apparent content or reference of the forms, but also in the pacing of the artists' lines.

Rhythm is the shaping principle of graphic forms. Unvaried rhythm is a dry, abstract thing.
5 It only conveys feeling when it takes on expressive variety – variety built upon unifying pulses of rhythms. We must always look at how we can make our rhythms interesting.

Section 6

Format

Most sheets of paper are rectangular: they have right-angled corners, so their sides are usually vertical and horizontal; and one pair of sides is usually longer than the other. The relative proportion contributes to the design; so to draw on a square sheet poses special problems. The outline of the shape is called the format. This contributes powerfully to any drawing.

Formats *a* and *b* in the illustration shown here are used most often by Western draughtsmen, who neglect *c* and *d*. Japanese Ukiyo-e artists often used format *c* for their 'pillar prints', which were meant to be stuck on the supporting posts of a Japanese house. This format can create fascinating effects by, for example, suggesting a half-open door that gives only a cut-out glimpse of some scene. Format *d* can be used to suggest a wide-ranging landscape view. Chinese artists extended it to 40 feet (*c.* 12 metres) or more in their hand scrolls, usually of landscapes. Such a scroll is meant to be unrolled gradually, so your experience

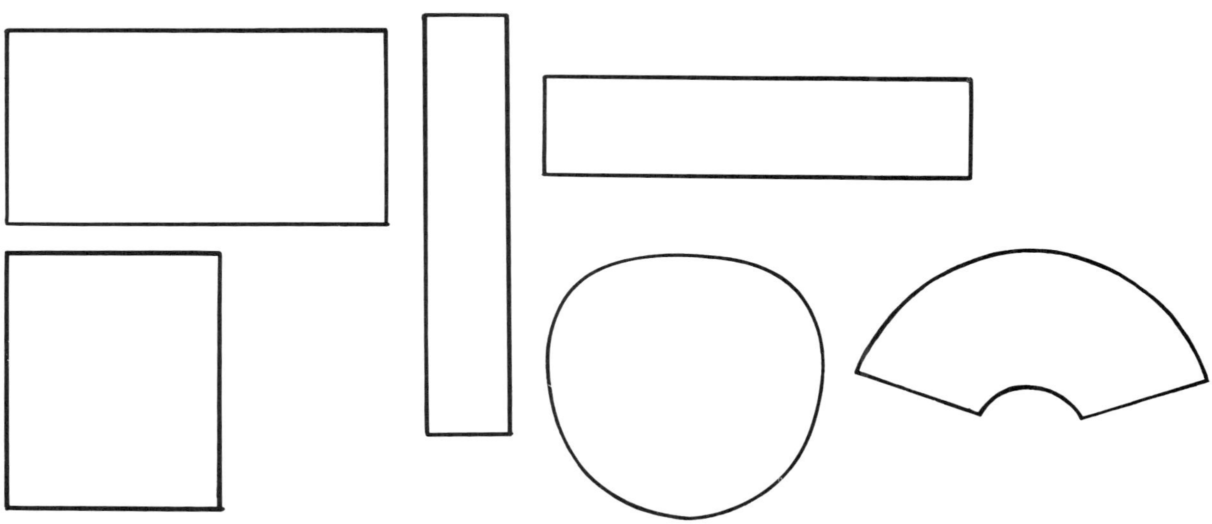

25 *Most common formats of drawing sheets.*

of the image becomes sequential, as if you were passing through a countryside, or seeing a panning shot in a movie. For almost any landscape format *d* is a sensible shape.

Formats do not even have to be rectangular. When you have begun to work freely you can try shapes as varied as some of the ones shown here. Far Eastern artists have used formats *e* and *f*,

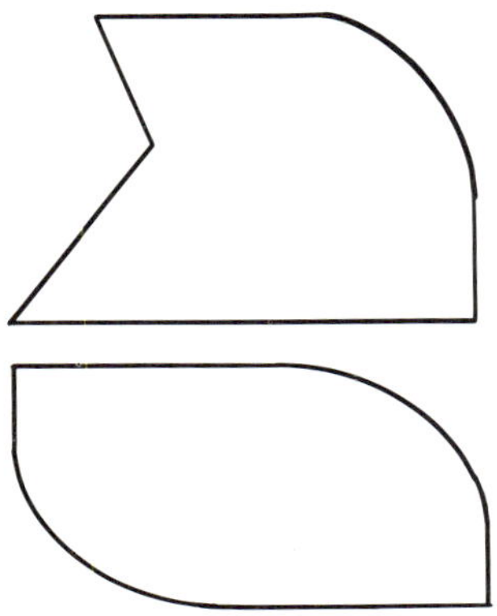

26 Unusual formats of drawing sheets.
27 Cretan pot, c. 1500 BC: the loops encircling the eyes of the octopus are two-dimensional versions of the loops encircling the whole pot, and echo the shapes of the handles.

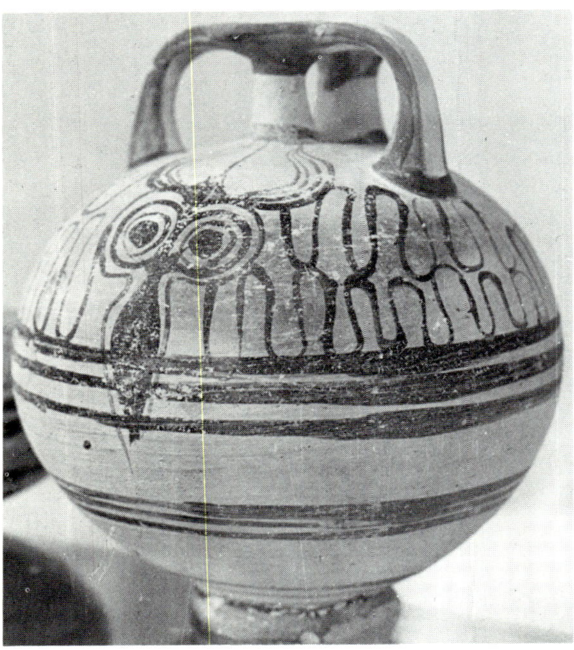

which are the shapes of Oriental fans. But there is no reason why you should not invent other formats for yourself. Very few artists have explored this kind of invention.

Your format does not even have to be flat. Quite a number of artists nowadays work on surfaces that have a good deal of three-dimensional movement. If you are a potter, for example, you will naturally draw your decoration on curved, three-dimensional surfaces. This can produce extraordinarily complex spatial images. It brings us to another important aspect of the way we interpret the format and its surface.

As you look at a really good drawing, the drawn marks seem to alter the surface. Drawing opens the surface up as a kind of space. The material carrying the marks does not disappear, but is transformed by our imagination into a second reality in which the things drawn seem to exist. A pot's surface becomes a strange three-dimensional curved space. Some of man's earliest drawings provide beautiful examples of this. Around 15,000 BC early hunters scratched several hundred figures of animals on the walls of a cave called the Font de Gaume, at Les Eyzies in the Dordogne region of France. In one place there is a long fissure running down the rock. One artist scratched the figure of a reindeer beside it, its head down as if it were drinking from the fissure, which therefore comes to represent a river. The rock donates its own reality to the image drawn on it. Exactly the same thing happens with the paper in any good drawing, as in the one by Titian illustrated here.

In this work there are recognizable figures; but a good piece of non-figurative work also creates its own field out of the format. Such a field must refer to time as well as space. First, because every drawing takes time to make, and we need time to read it. In addition, anything that appears in the drawing is meant to continue in existence, not simply to disappear in a flash. The quality of endurance is one of the important distinctions between reality and illusion. So the objective persistence of rock, metal, fibreglass, paper, contributes to the image you lay on to the substance.

28 Titian: 'The Bloody Deed of a Jealous Husband'. This pen drawing uses complex hatching.

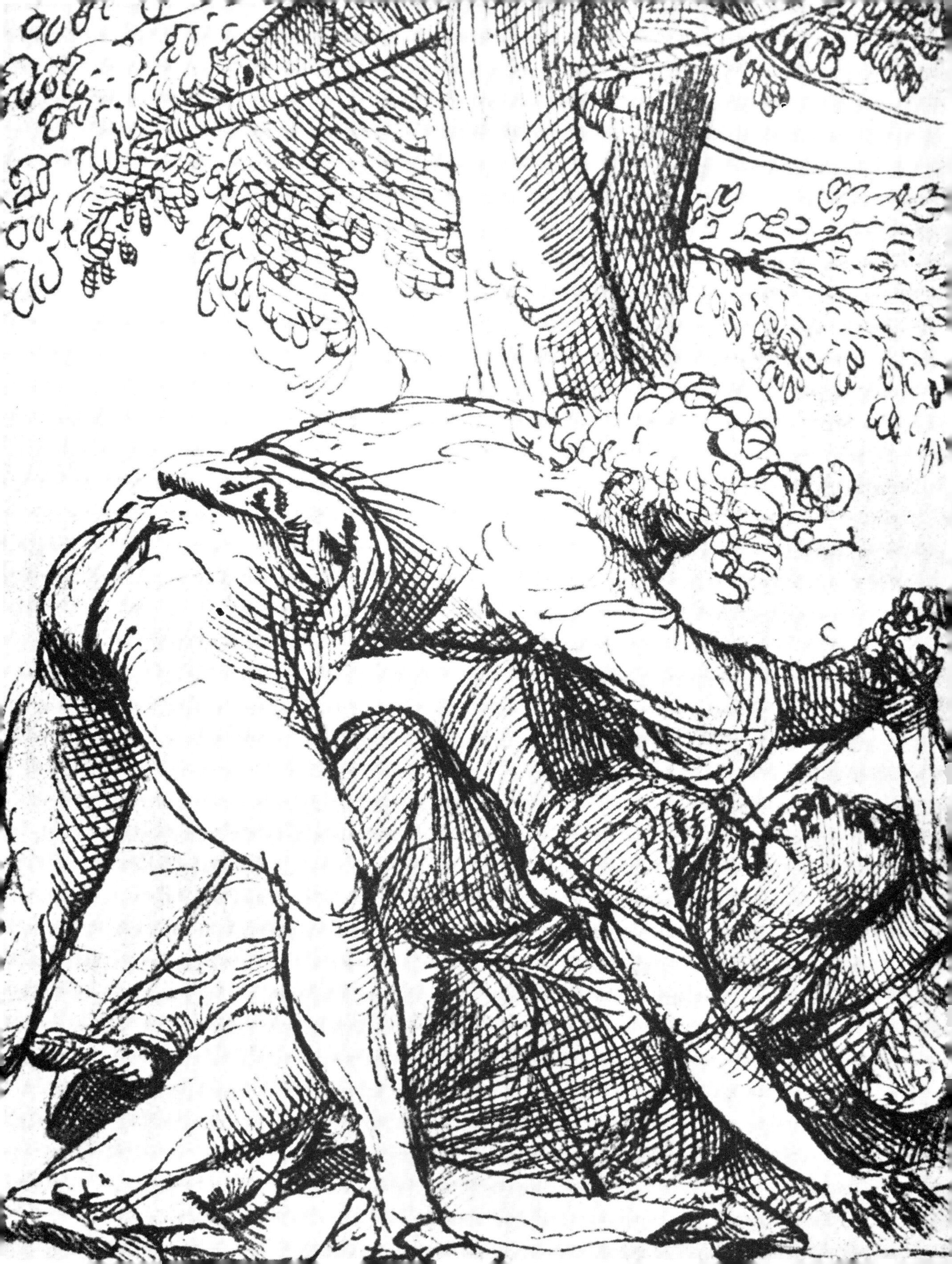

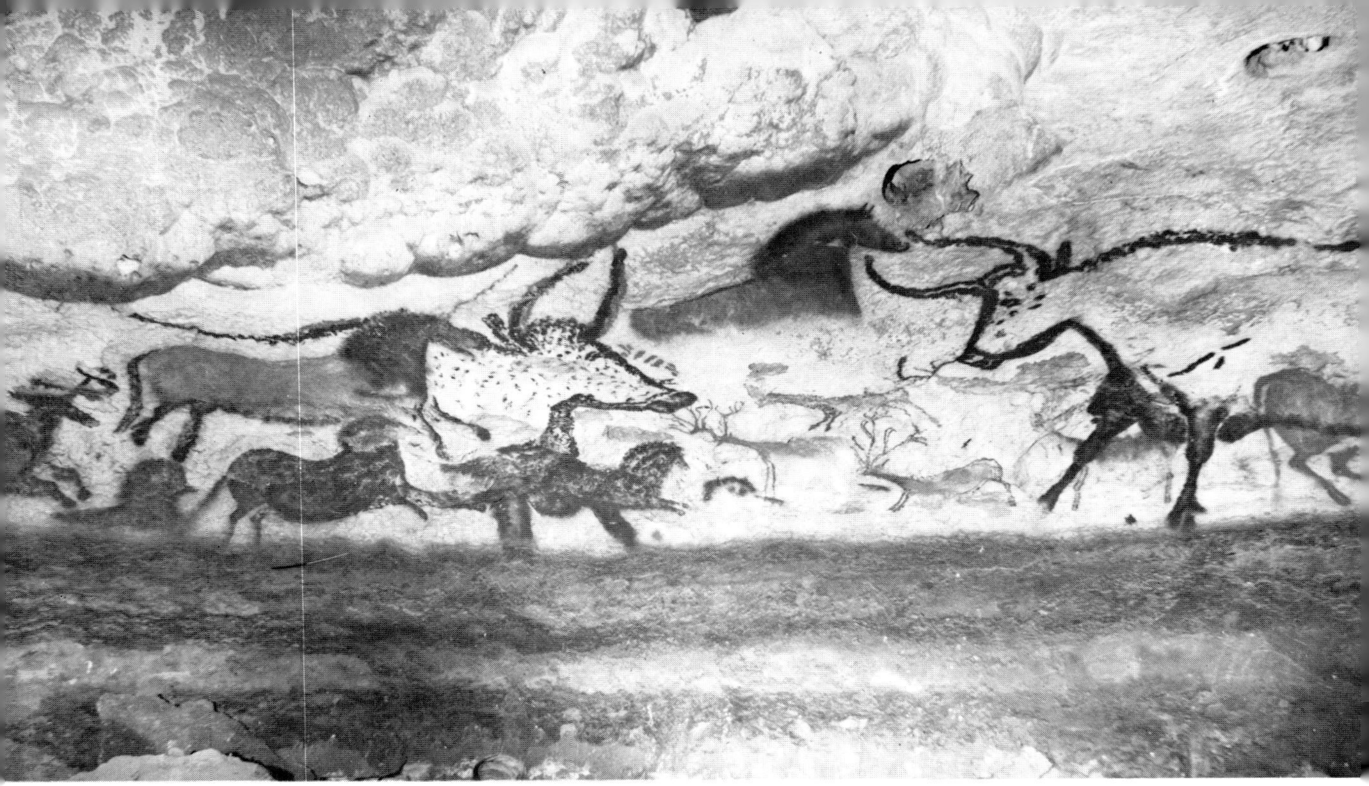

29 Palaeolithic painting in the caves at Lascaux, France, c. 20,000 BC.

Cave artists worked without a closed format: their surfaces were not framed by shaped edges. The whole rock-surface opened out for them into that second imagined reality. But nowadays rectangles organize our world. Houses are built primarily in rectangular shapes. And we even tend to think of 'visual organization' as naturally implying right angles. But we do not *have* to think that way. It can be quite refreshing to leave our framework for a moment for the more open imaginative world of stone-age man.

Section 7
Format and Expression

However, our Western artistic tradition has grown up within the rectangles of manufactured paper formats, and most of our great drawings have been made that way; so we are obliged to take the right-angled format very seriously. To show how much it matters, let us investigate how the expression of lines depends on the way they move around in relation to the edges of our standard paper sheets.

Think of your own responses to the way the lines in the diagram here move in relation to the four edges and corners. For me *a* droops violently, *b* floats, *c* attacks the edge and returns, and *d* drives down into the format, and checks.

Take some smallish pieces of paper, and try making some lines of your own with fairly distinctive kinds of movement. Then turn them upside down, and see how this changes their meaning. In a figurative drawing one can similarly interpret the way a single human figure, or a group of figures, relates to the format.

An important part of the expression of these lines comes from their movement from left to right, or right to left. Whether one is left- or right-handed is determined by which side of the brain has taken on certain functions. This implies there are psychological factors involved in how one feels about lines moving into or across the field of the image from the left or the right.

Another important factor is the direction we normally write in, for drawing has quite an intimate connection with writing. Most people who write Western languages have the feeling that to move from left to right is, somehow, to

30 Expressive movement of lines in a format; brush drawings.

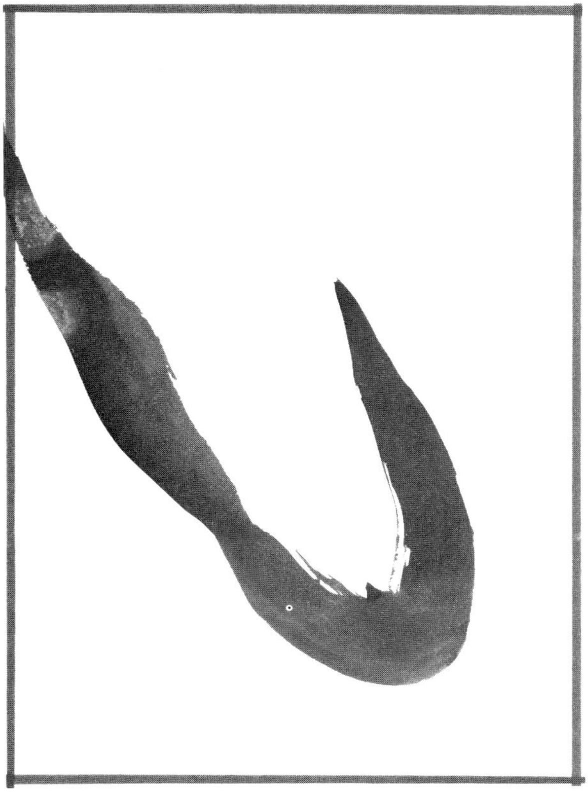

a)

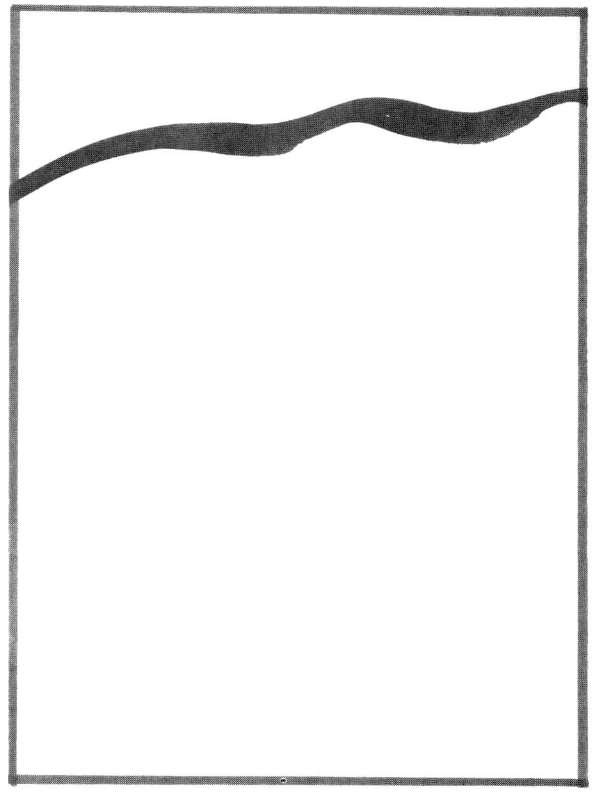

b)

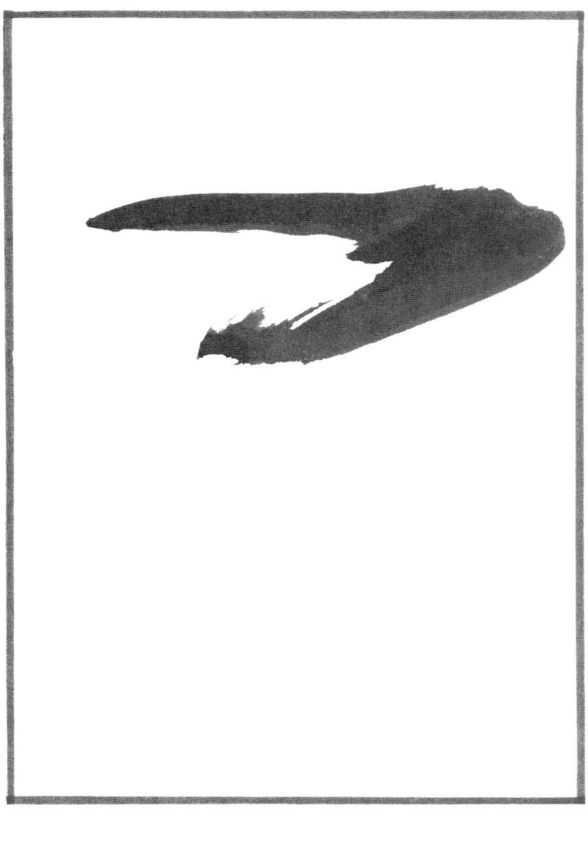

c)

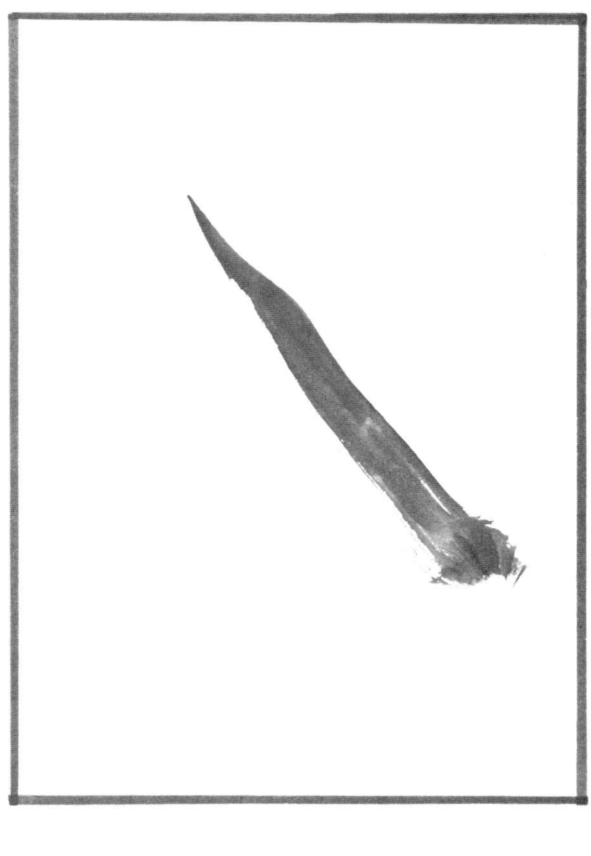

d)

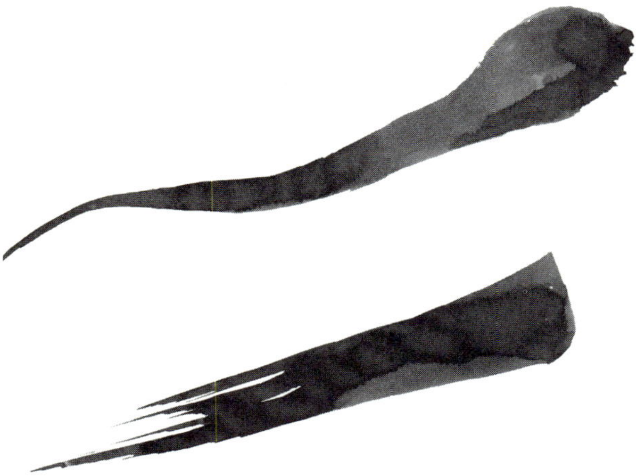

31 Line moving right, and line stabbing to left; brush drawing.

'advance outwards'; whereas to move the other way is somehow to 'retreat inwards'. So you may feel that a line which thickens as it 'moves' right is driving away, out of the format. Something standing on the right-hand margin you may therefore experience as a strong obstacle. You may experience an emphatic line crossing the other way, from right to left, as an act of violence inward, a stab to the heart almost.

Some cultures write in different directions. Muslims, for example, write their scripts from right to left, pushing the pen, not pulling it, and you should take account of this. Some of their beautiful leftward-moving, 'down-under and up' loops they feel are deeply affecting, in delicate and profound ways.

The Chinese and Japanese write in vertical columns from top to bottom, arranging the columns from right to left. This again has great importance in the expression of their drawing, so you must take it into account, especially in reading work on the long vertical formats so often used in the Far East. The direction of reading matters because you may be expected to have seen and interpreted one feature in the drawing before you get to another one. In such a long vertical drawing, for example, the lower parts of a mountain, where it runs down into the valleys, may just disappear. Unless you have understood the mountain tops, and the way their shapes interrelate, you may not be able to make sense of the bunches of lines where they fade out on the slopes and terraces.

It can be a very interesting imaginative exercise to try 'writing' various non-representational lines. You can call it 'written music'. You can also try feeling your way into the position of someone who writes in a different direction.

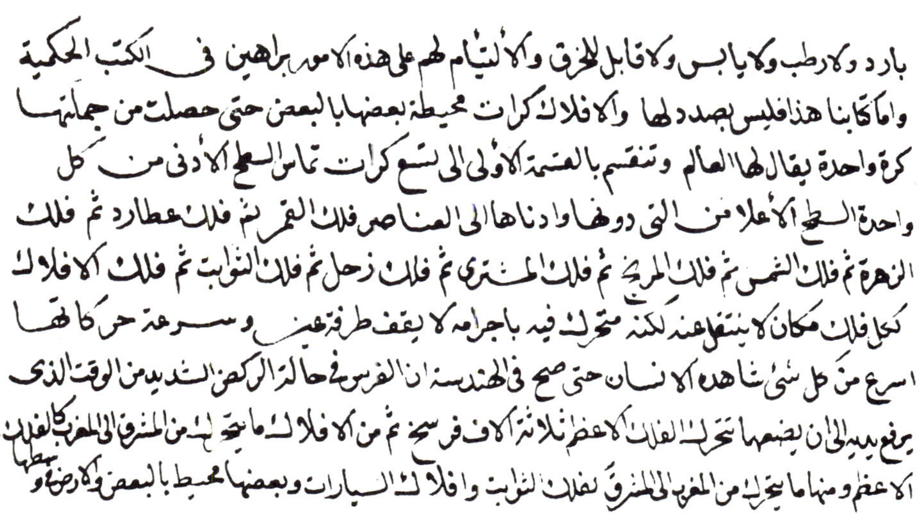

32 Muslim calligraphy, Persian, by Jalayrid, c. 1400, written from right to left with a reed pen.
33 Huang T'ing-Chien: Chinese calligraphic script of a poem in brush and ink.
34 Written music; brush drawing.

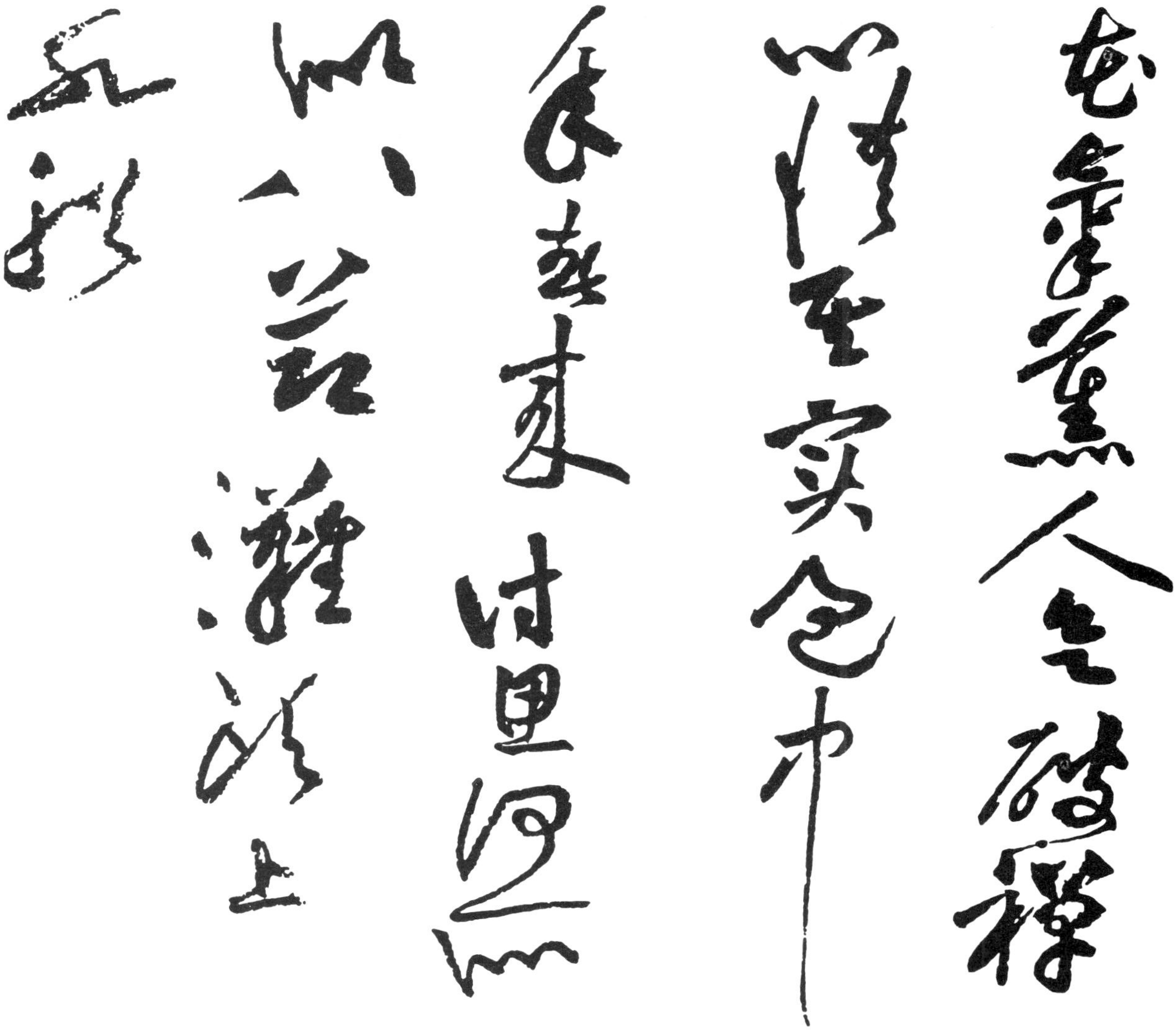

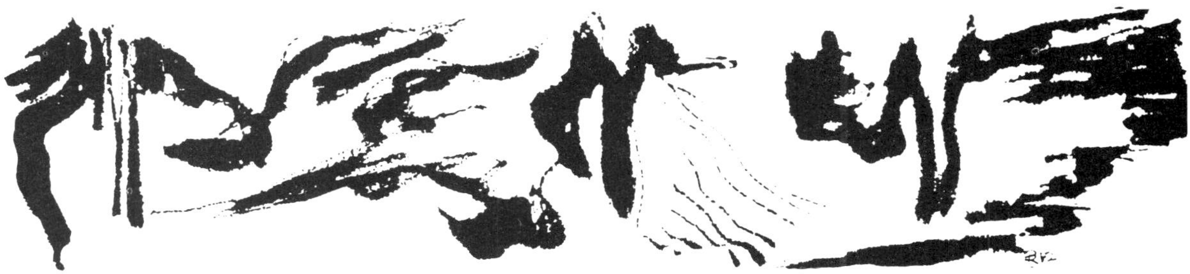

In the Middle East, until the fourth century AD, Greek was written first one line from left to right, the next one from right to left, and so on. It was called 'Boustrophedon'. You can try that too.

Here is a drawing which uses placings in the format as an absolutely vital part of its expression. It turns the paper into an open arena of space, with suggestions of opening and closing.

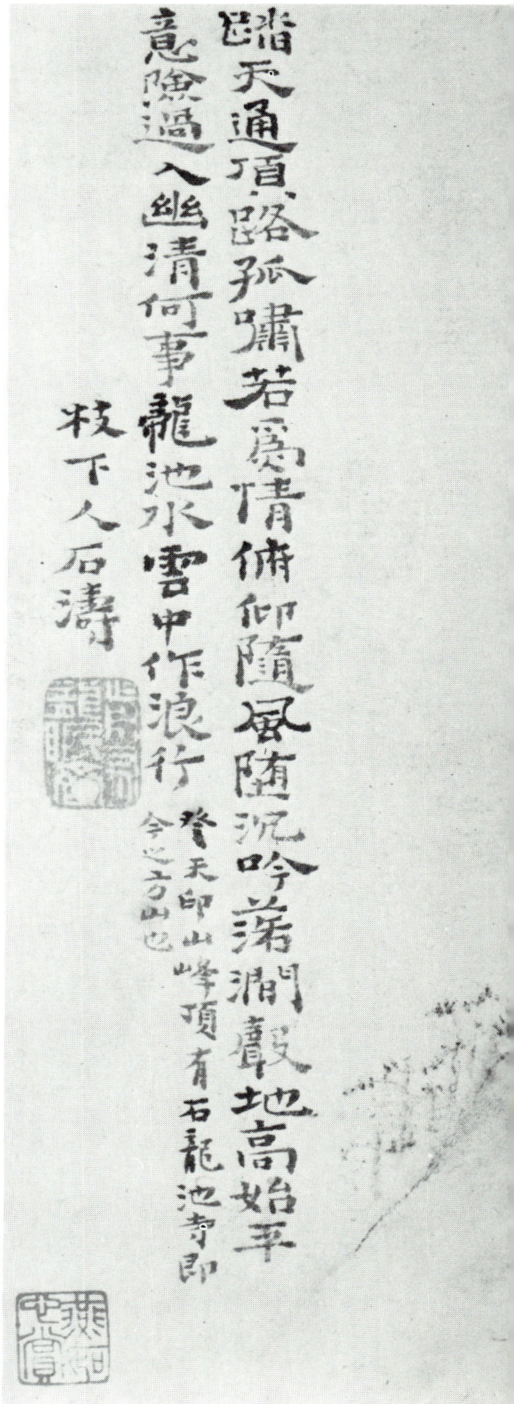

35 Abstract calligraphy 'Boustrophedon'; brush drawing.

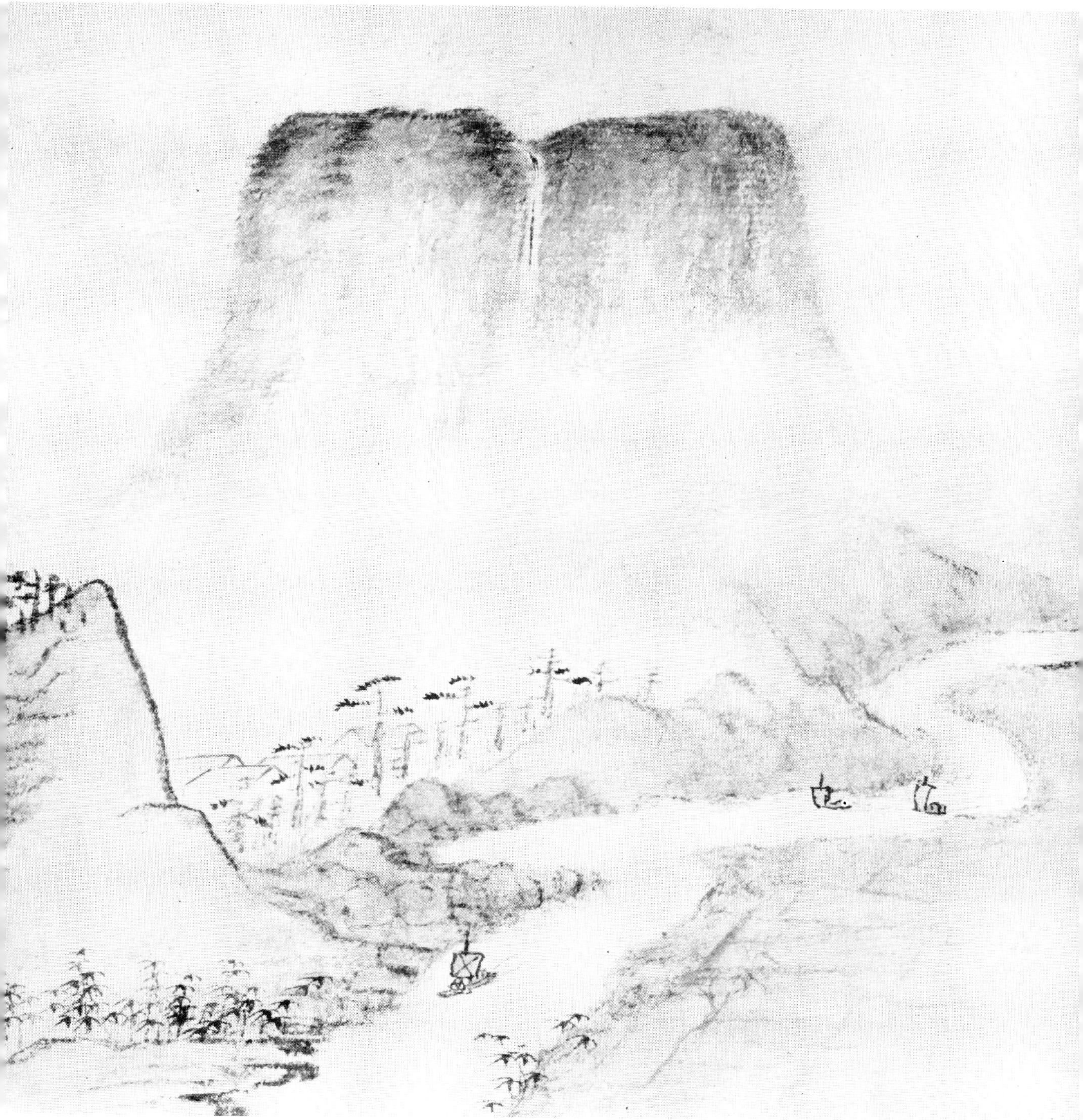

36 Tao Chi: brush drawing of an imaginary landscape, 16th–17th c., read from upper right to lower left and completed by the writing.

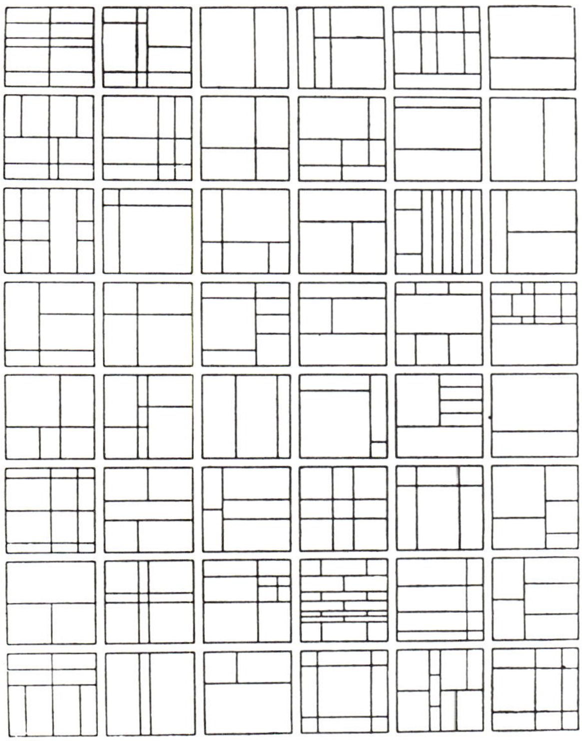

37 Le Corbusier: page from 'The Modulor', 1954, illustrating possible subdivisions of a square.
38 Diagrams of the Golden Section, expressed in areas (above) and as the lengths of a curved line (below).

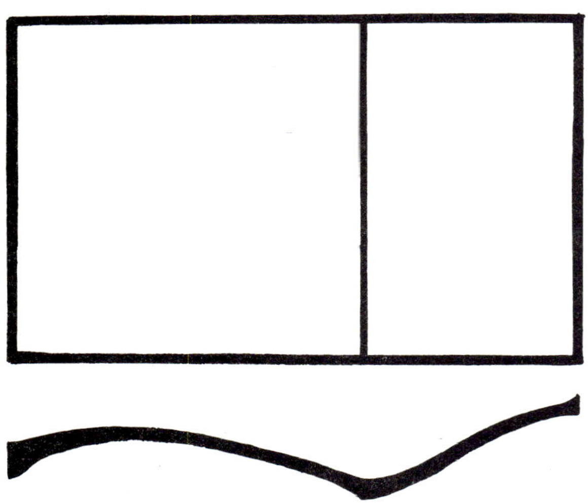

Another factor that makes a format expressive 37
is its proportions. Mondrian based all his later art upon dividing the format. He divided it with straight lines which follow the right angles of the edges. In this kind of work everything depends on the proportions in which the format is divided. These can be based upon relatively simple mathematical proportions such as 1:2, 1:3, 1:4, 1:7, or upon more complex formulae. One of the commonest is the Golden Section. It is defined mathematically as the proportion where $a:b = a+b:a$. No one knows why it is so aesthetically effective; it just is.

Section 8
Connection between Lines

We are now ready to look at the ways in which lines, as structures, can connect with and relate to each other both along and across their flow. Those two linked factors of direction and rhythm (Sections 4 and 5) are involved. Here a few simple illustrations are worth pages of text. Try making several versions of each of the kinds of linear relationship, keeping your work as lively and rhythmical as you can.

The first illustration shows how one line may 39
pick up the direction in which another is moving, projected across an intervening space. We can use a mathematical term to describe this projection: linear vector. There may even be a step or offset in the pickup.

The second shows how several linear vectors 39
may be gathered into or branched off from a single continuing line. Japanese drawing is full of these.

The third shows how lines may be connected 39
by the way they stand at right angles to each other. Rembrandt often used this technique, as in *Child Learning to Walk*.

The fourth shows how lines may seem to be 39
doing specific things in relation to each other. We understand this mainly by reading across from one line to the other as we follow their movement. It is phrasing in terms of direction and rhythm that plays the vital part.

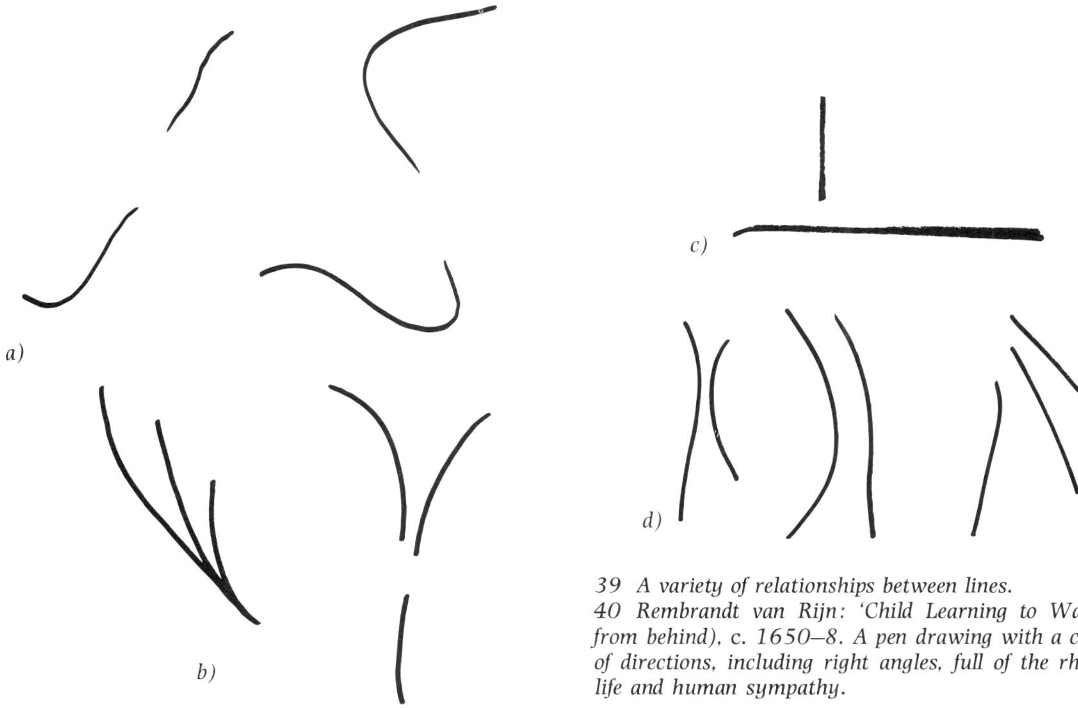

39 A variety of relationships between lines.
40 Rembrandt van Rijn: 'Child Learning to Walk' (seen from behind), c. 1650–8. A pen drawing with a clear scale of directions, including right angles, full of the rhythms of life and human sympathy.

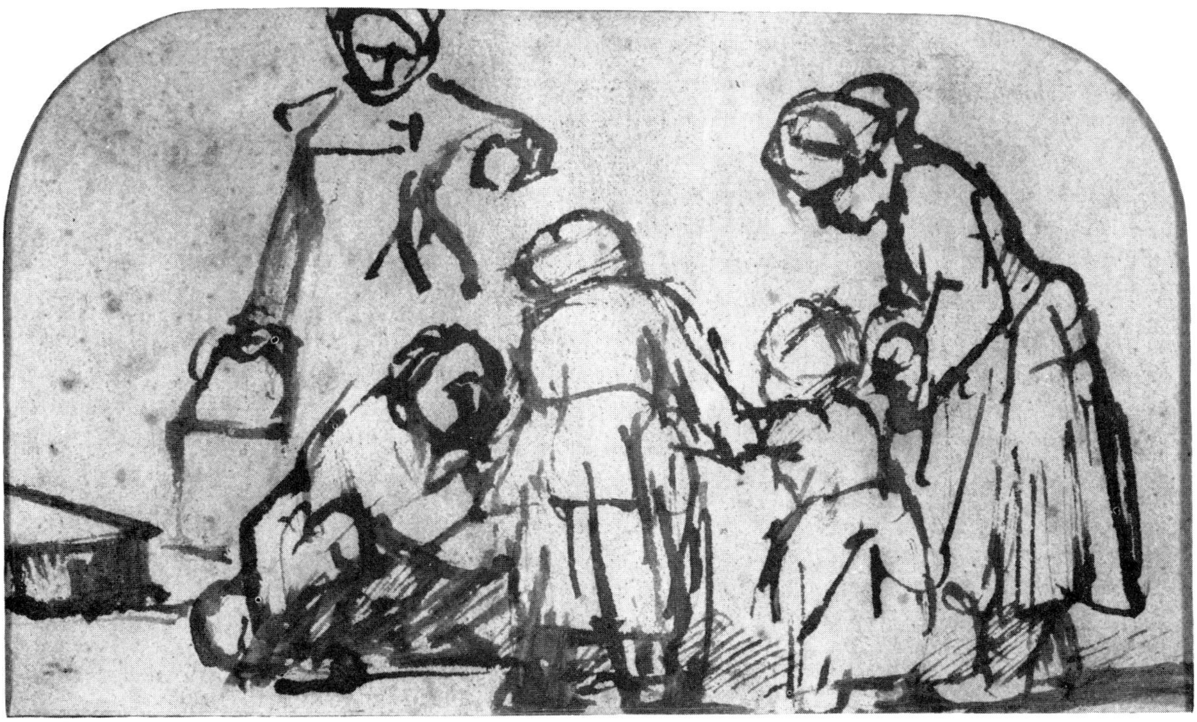

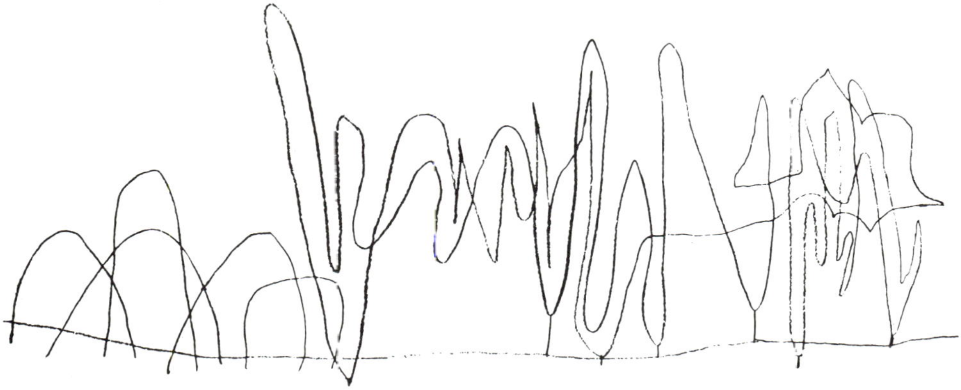

41 Paul Klee: pencil drawing. The principal forms are arcades, but the small linking lines from the bottoms of the curves to a ground line suggest that the artist was interpreting them as trees.

42 a) The lower shape represents a linear phrase related to the upper row of marks which expresses the fundamental unit of measure; b) a set of lines, each of which is related to each of the others in a different way.

43 Brush drawing illustrating both linear and crosswise relationships.

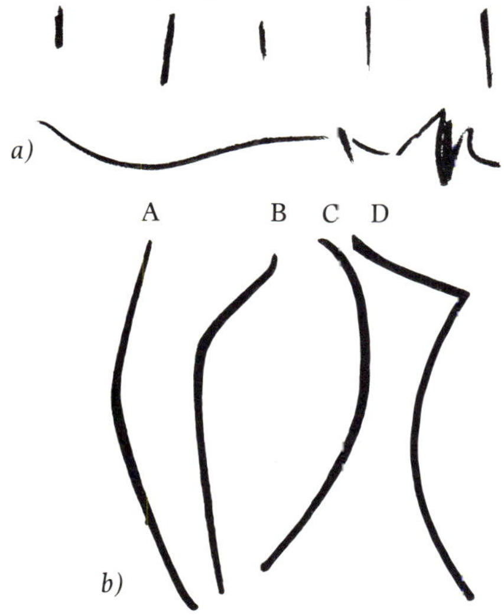

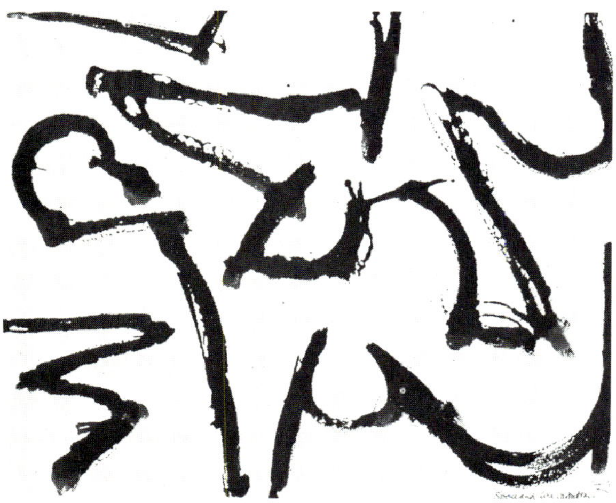

This drawing by Klee illustrates how one line may twine about another without keeping too strictly to the relationships of direction. At the same time a second line can develop a different relationship of rhythm both to the original line and to itself.

The next illustration shows how a linear 42 direction may be converted into, or picked up by, a transverse rhythm.

The next relationship is perhaps the most 42 interesting of all. It happens when several lines relate to each other in different ways at the same time. In the diagram here line A relates to line B in one way to produce a specific effect, whilst it relates to line C on the other side in another way; then to line D across and including line B in yet another way; while line C relates to line D in yet another. And so on. This can be beautifully worked out in figure compositions.

Illustration no. 43 shows an image in which many different kinds of relationship are woven together. See if you can disengage them from the whole.

The final pair of diagrams shows kinds of 44 relationship which work *across* the directions of lines, but still depend to some extent on our sense of their direction of movement for their expression. The second is particularly interesting because it is easy to read the pair of lines as enclosing between themselves a rounded volume. This kind of relationship between inflected lines is very important in all kinds of figurative drawing.

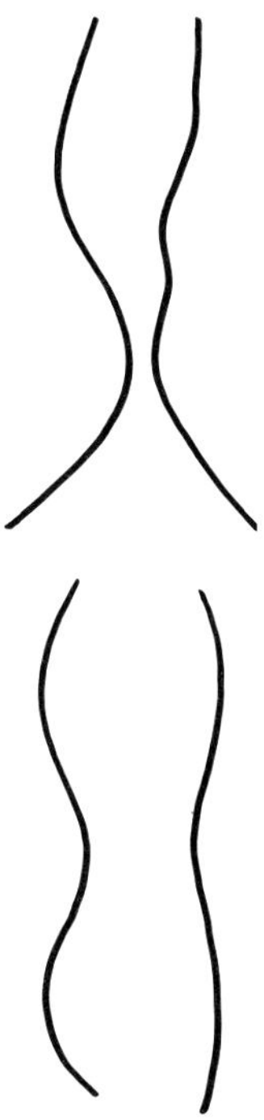

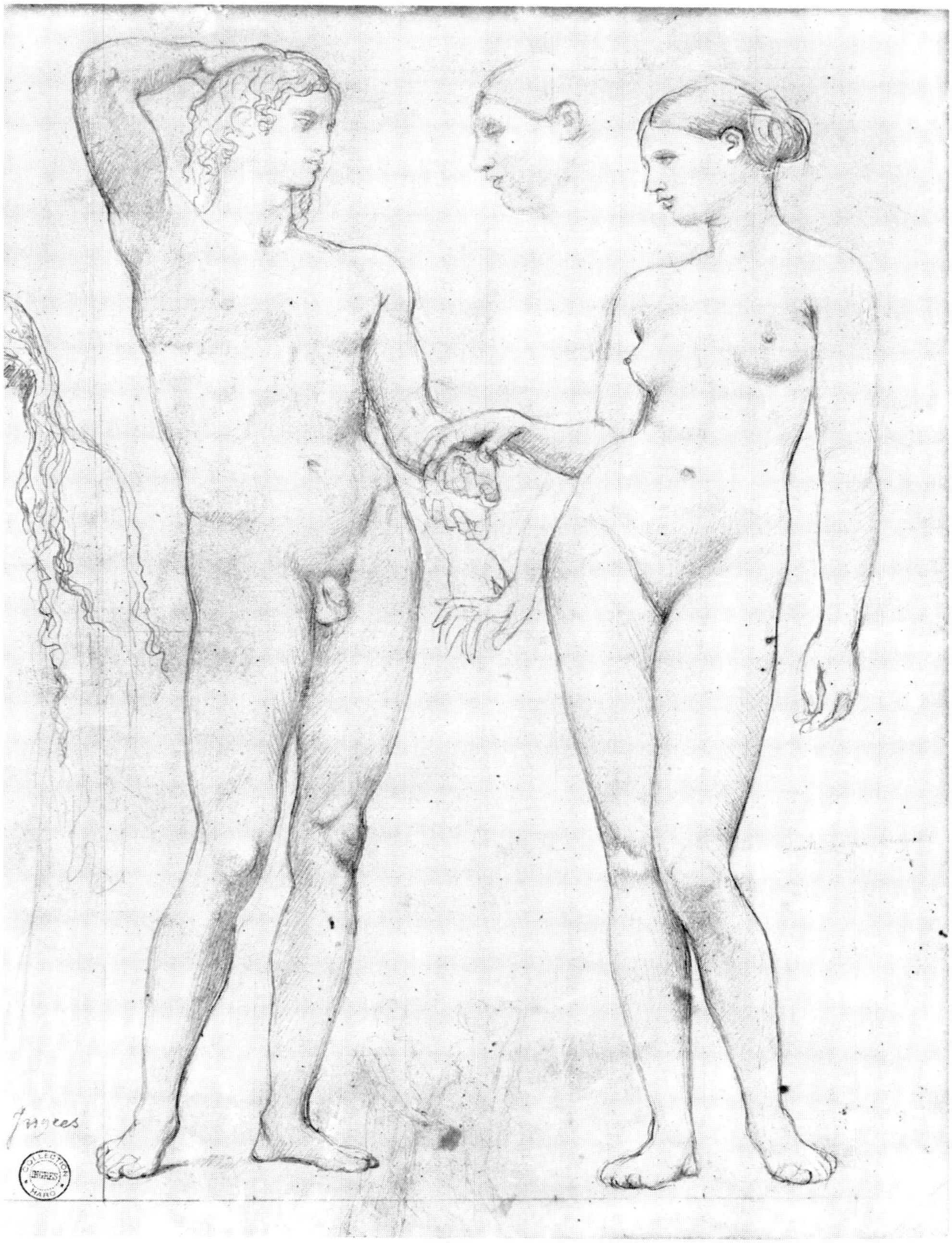

44 Lines whose relationship with each other suggests contained volumes.
45 Jean A.-D. Ingres: 'Two Nudes, Study for the Golden Age', 1842. A chalk drawing whose sinuous contours are worked up to suggest volumes contained within them.

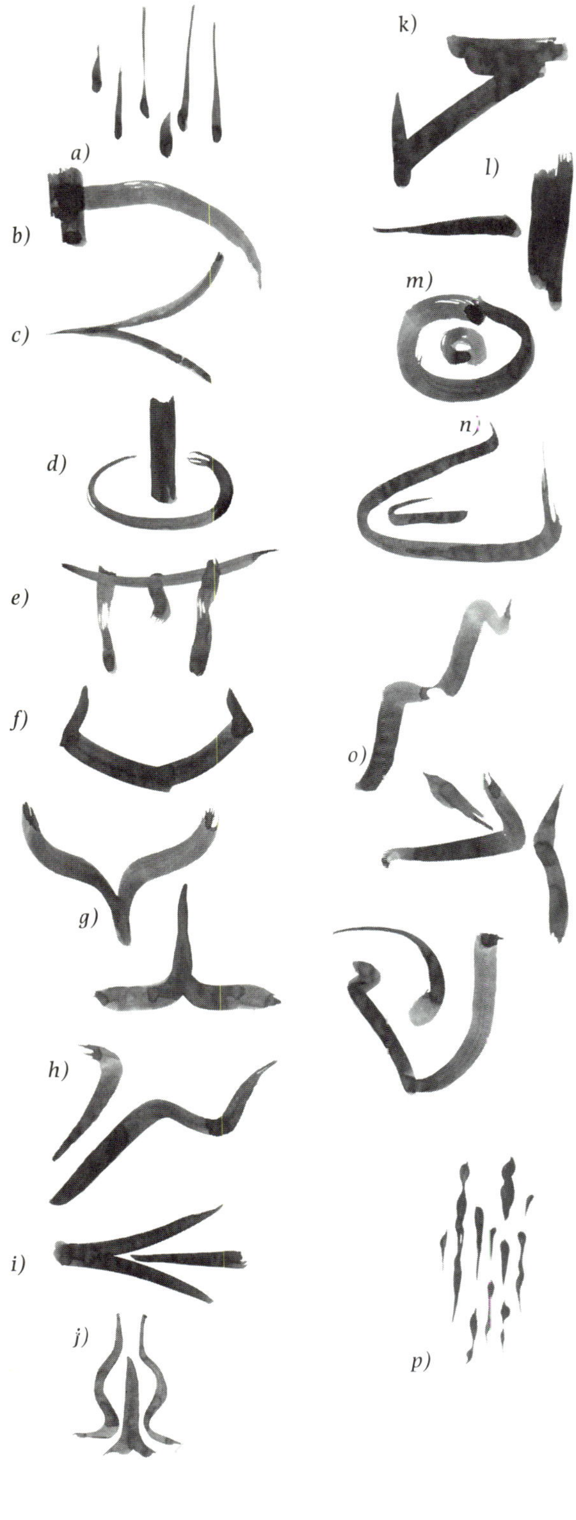

46 Diagrams of lines in action.

Section 9
Activity of Lines in Combination

There is one very important aspect to the expression of lines: it is the ways they 'act' in combination with each other. Some of these we can define in words; some we cannot. Many of them are connected with, or abstracted from, human gestures and actions. Even those we cannot easily name may be echoes of human actions – for which we normally have no names. Some may even suggest a kind of dynamic imagery we usually associate with the science of mechanics. For instance:

a) drip
b) droop
c) open out
d) wrap around
e) hang
f) straddle
g) spread out upwards (growth)
or downwards (pressure)
h) offer
i) split
j) penetrate
k) cantilever
l) obstruct
m) contain
n) enclose or embrace
o) what do these three 'do'?

You can work out an infinite number of versions of action and interaction; and you can vary their expression by making them operate in different directions. But some, you will discover, work because they imply the effect of gravity. If you change their direction they may either not work at all or they may look very strange indeed. Raining up- 46p
wards, for instance. Or is it?

Most of the groups of lines work because they somehow evoke memories of events or actions, whose *shapes* were the same but which did not involve the same things each time. For example, you might have seen a cat jump into a cypress tree with all its legs and claws spread. The 'shape' of that event could resemble very closely the shape of, say, a leafy branch or some seaweed falling into water. Such memory-shapes are perfectly real, though we may not have words for them. They may be stored in our memory in an abbreviated form. Your line drawings can capture the essence of these 'shorthand' images of action.

To generate these images in drawing you need to develop that special skill we mentioned earlier which involves looking into your own inner sense of movement; you should feel almost as if your body were full of dancing movement, which can then run down your arm into your hand. When you focus inwards to capture it you may come to feel almost as if you are in a trance.

Section 10
Humanity and Expression

You may have heard it said that a really good musician plays his instrument so that it 'sings' far more expressively than any human voice actually could. Similarly, in good art the lines suggest movements of the human body that are far more expressive than anything a real body can perform. Dancing and art do have a genuine connection. The Chinese recognize this quality in their artistic handwriting. Genuine imitation in drawing has as much to do with reading one's own inner bodily sensations as it has to do with recording external likenesses. So if, for example, you want to create an image of a 'hand grasping', you may find it helpful actually to grasp something

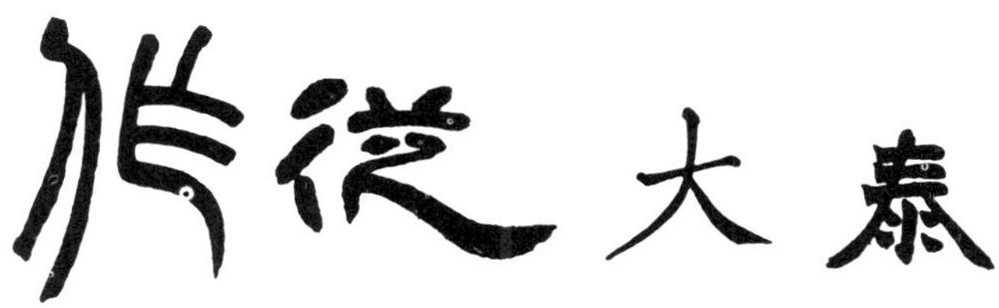

47 Examples of Chinese calligraphy that suggest bodily movement; brush and ink.
48 Brush drawing with dance expression.

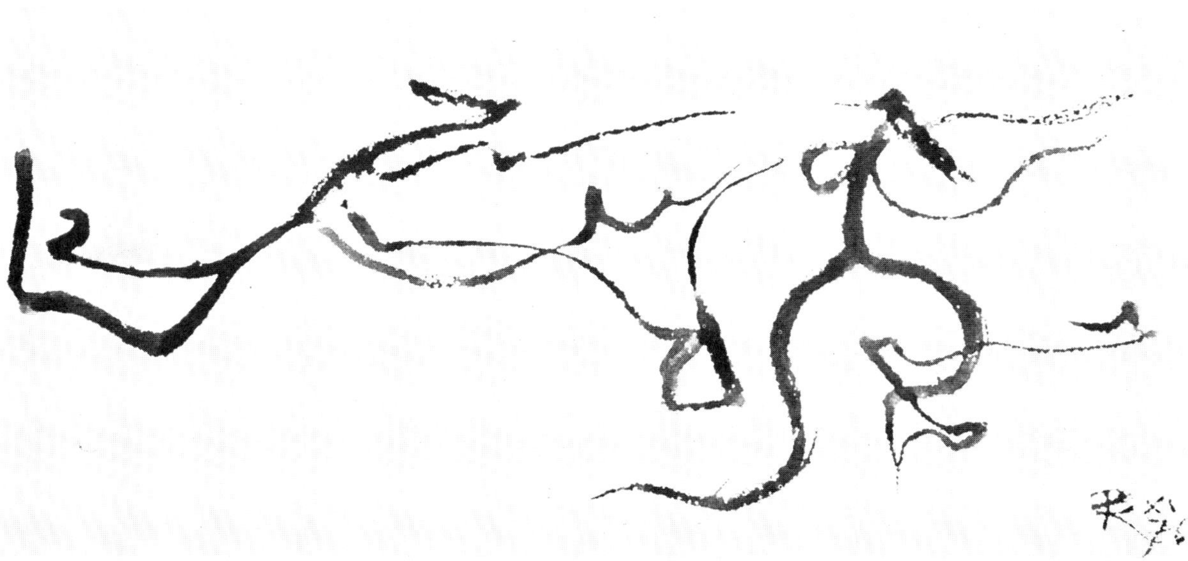

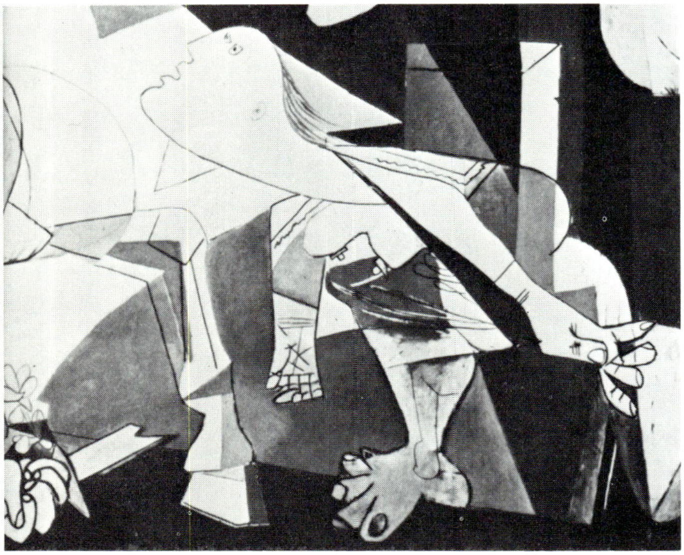

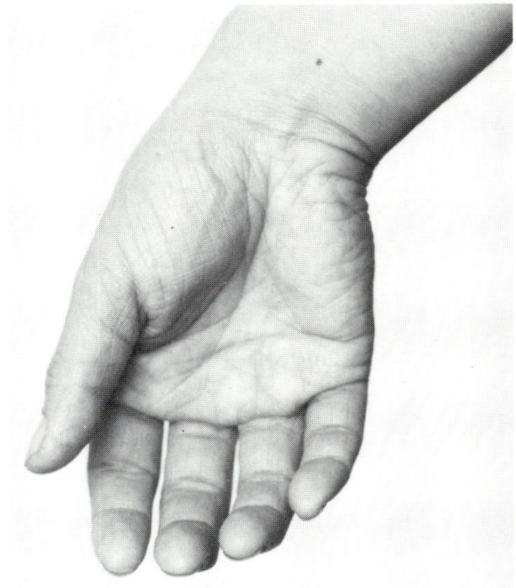

49, 50 Pablo Picasso: detail of the painting 'Guernica', 1936, illustrating a variety of hand-shapes; and photograph of a hand. They show how an artist can give expression to parts of the body far more effectively than a photographer can.

yourself, and then consult your memory of the shape of the gesture. Then you can produce an image of how your own hand felt in action.

Although Picasso's image may not 'look like' a photograph of an extended hand, it may be far more truthful to our experience of active reality than the photograph's more superficial and static resemblance.

This is where the old conflict between figurative and non-figurative art is resolved. A good figurative artist is able to do both things at once: to draw convincing kinetic short-hand imagery, conveying the artist's inner feelings about each part, which is also convincing as purely visual appearance. A figurative subject provides a powerful incentive to develop that imagery, and acts as a focus for it.

You can easily pick out many varied dance-like suggestions in figurative drawing such as the examples by Rembrandt shown here. These kinetic forms are unified by the overall image to which they contribute, even though they do not look like things we can easily recognize.

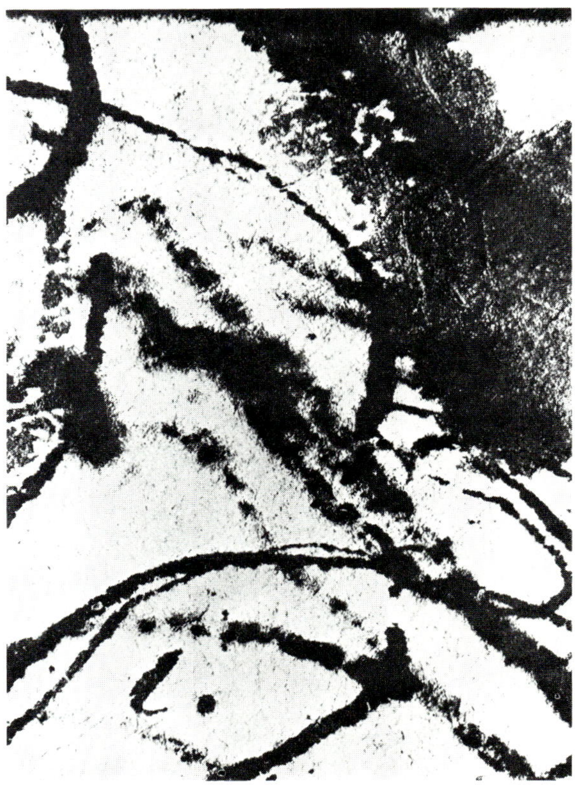

51, 52 Rembrandt van Rijn: two details of pen drawings, enlarged, to illustrate basic kinetic forms or glyphs.

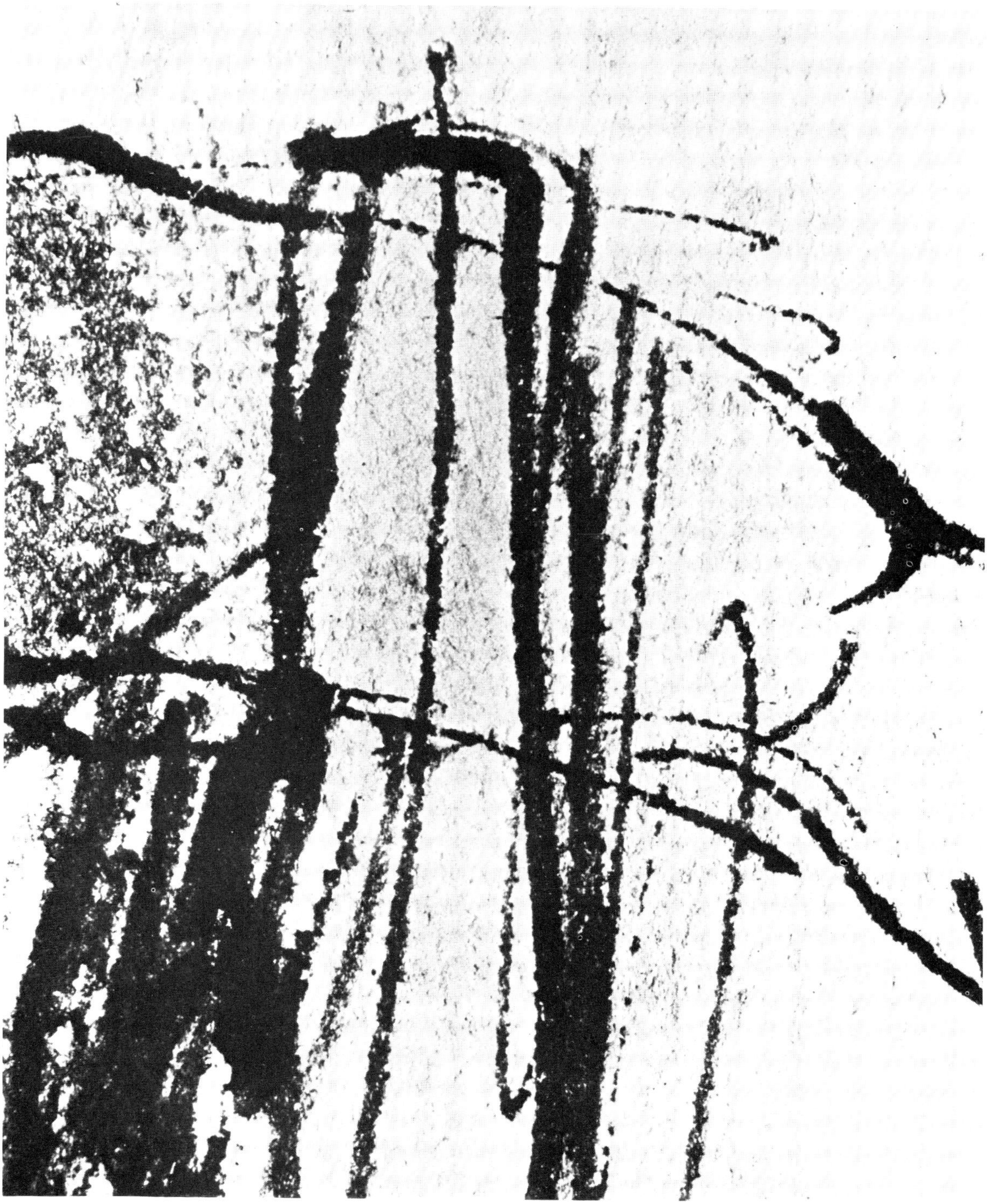

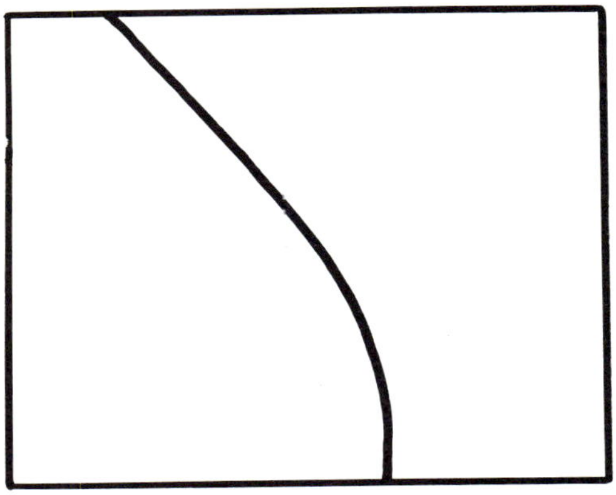

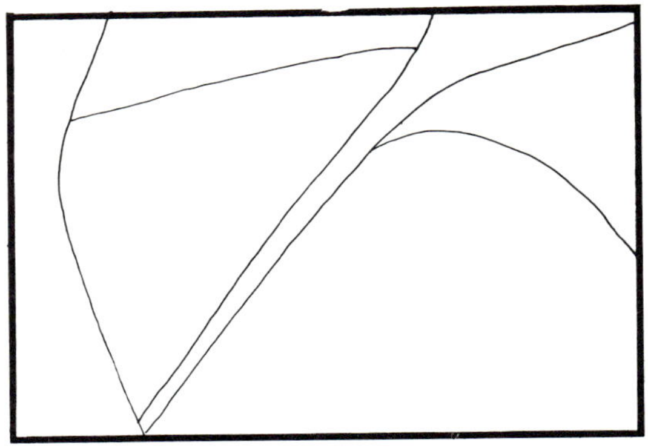

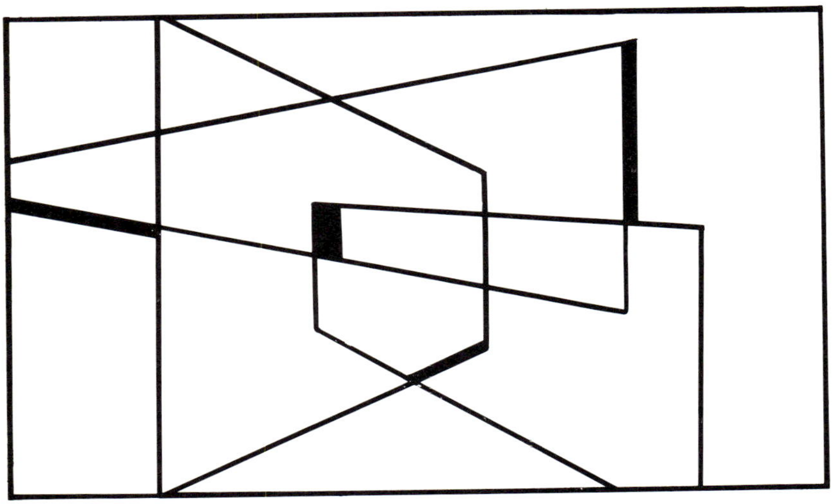

Above and left

53 Two diagrams of simple divisions of a format into enclosures; diagram of enclosures with perspective implications.

Below left

54 Architectural plan of the bazaar at Kashan. The different spaces are carefully calculated to allow for a very wide variety of uses and circulation patterns. The main direction of flow is through the passage marked with arrows.

Below right

55 Diagram of loops of line making enclosures.

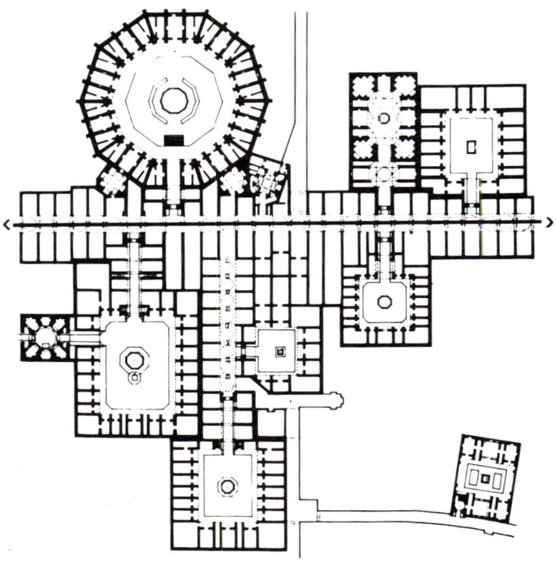

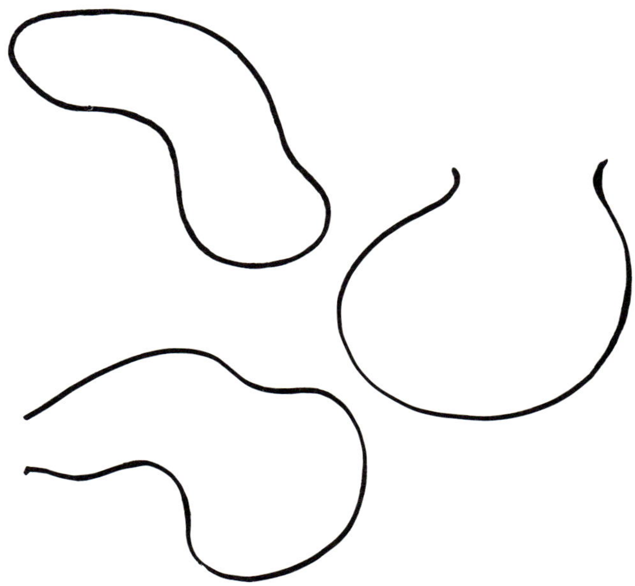

II

Area and Surface

Here we shall analyse the different ways in which parts of the drawing surface may be enclosed and treated, so as to play their part in the meaning of the whole work. These fall into two main groupings. First are enclosures in which the contour is all-important; second is a variety of 'activity-techniques' which can be used on the surface.

Section 11
Enclosures

The shaping of areas and enclosures is one of the most important methods in the art of drawing. Because drawings are done with a moving point, enclosures can be thought of as being derived in one way or another from lines. It is true that some artists try very hard to eliminate any linear feeling from the shapes they draw, expecting the viewer to perceive each shape as a unit. This is something we shall have to consider as well.

We shall start with a basic fact: one of the principal functions of lines is to separate. They may then turn into outlines. Outlines cut off sections of the drawing surface from each other. You can draw a line more or less straight across
3a your sheet. It will divide the sheet into two areas; each of them will be enclosed by the line and the edges of the sheet.

It is possible to make even this simplest of
20 procedures give interesting results. Rhythmic
21 proportions, which we have discussed in connec-
37 tion with Format (Sections 6–7), matter a lot. You can draw a few more such lines that connect up with the edges and each other, lines which do not claim much attention by any vigour or vital expression. You may then find you can read the
3b enclosures in terms of their shapes, proportions and relative 'pressures', rather than for their outlines alone. Some you may even begin to read figuratively, in terms of perspective, as suggesting 53c
plane surfaces – walls, open doors or cliff-faces.

It is, of course, the outlines and their relationships which are fundamentally responsible for the effects of the shapes they enclose. You immediately change the effects when you change the characters of the outlines.

Let us look at the ways lines set up a sense of area and enclosure. To start with, remember that even a line which makes a very strictly shaped enclosure actually records an act of the mind in time.

Even the outlines on, say, a draughtsman's 54
ground-plan of a building have a kind of time-sense built into them. Once you have scanned them and got hold of their spatial meaning you may not be able to tell, and it may not matter very much, which way round the lines were drawn or where the draughtsman's imagination started and stopped. But it is not impossible that a sense of live linearism, with beginnings and ends, *does* actually get through from a really good architect's designs into his buildings.

A line can make open and closed loops of dif- 55
ferent shapes and sizes with special relations to the format. All of them will have different expressions. Try making versions of your own, following these examples.

Clearly, a closed loop implies that everything inside it is part of a definite unit. On the other hand, an open loop can imply motion: what is outside can still get in or out, either like air into a balloon so that the enclosure can swell or shrink, or like people flowing in and out of a room of fixed size and shape.

Section 12
Enclosure Types: Organic

There is a special kind of distinction one can set up among types of outlined enclosure; they are often – and inexactly – called 'organic' and 'inorganic'.

56a The organic enclosure tends to have wavy, fluent outlines without many sharp angles. It is called organic mainly because it resembles the kinds of shape taken by soft-bodied creatures enclosed in a membrane, such as sea-slugs, anemones and microscopic water-animals. The contour resembles the membrane responding to varying inner and outer pressures – whose presence it also suggests. It thus makes us feel that the interior and exterior of the outline are fluid, balancing actively against each other.

You can even make organic enclosures which
56b seem to 'press up' against the edges of the format in interesting ways. Others may seem to be 'cut',
as if they had actually been made as *papier coupé* 56
(Section 17). You can make such enclosures by using masking tape to get clean-cut edges. If you stick tape along the edges of your intended shapes, you can brush on your tone quite freely, even on to the tape. When you pull it off you will be left with a sharp clean edge.

All these enclosures are most effective if you can make the outlines rhythmically interesting, and the shapes, curves and angles of all the inlets and promontories different. To do this is quite a challenge to your artistic invention. It is another of the ways in which your senses of life, rhythm and order can complement each other. Here you ought to refer back to Section 5, which deals with the rhythmic phrasing of lines.

It is true that there are plenty of organic shapes
which *do* display points and angles. Some may also 56
suggest natural processes involving fluid membranes; others may relate to crystalline and inorganic structures.

A radical difference appears between convex- and concave-sided enclosures. The convex-sided seem 'full'; the concave-sided seem to be borne in upon by the outside environment. You can make quite expressive drawings which combine these two aspects in single extended forms, so that

56 a) Organic 'membrane' enclosure; b) enclosures balancing inner and outer forces; c) enclosures with 'cut' edges; d) enclosure with prominent points.

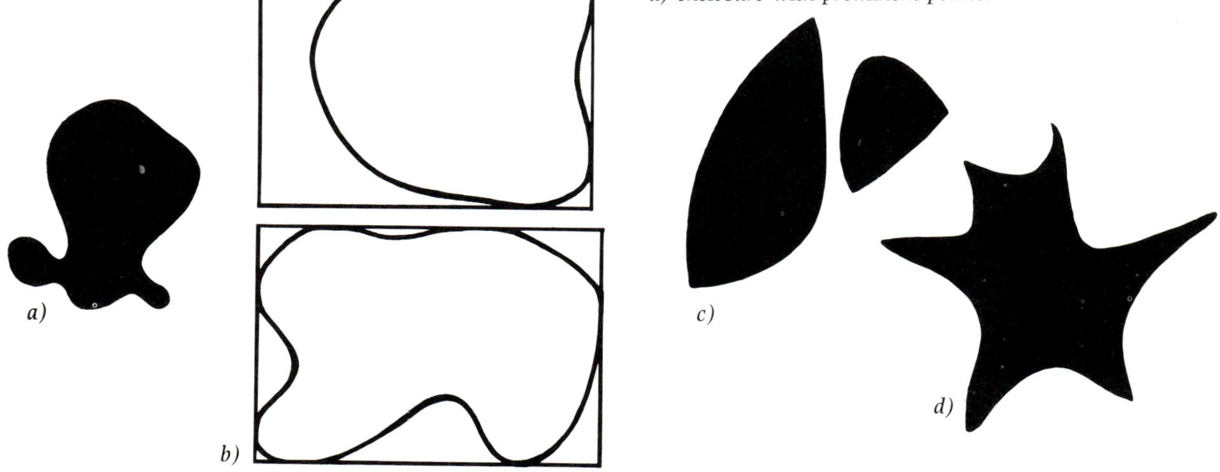

they counterpoint each other: soft against hard, pressure *out* against pressure *in*.

The points suggest places where inner thrusts are advancing outward without rupturing the outline. If we connect the points of thrust at the angles by *straight* lines, rather than curves, we suddenly enter a new realm of meaning: the geometric.

Section 13
Enclosure Types: Geometric

Geometry is based upon straight lines, the base-units for measurement. A straight line is 'the shortest distance between two points'. This implies movement between those points, though in geometry its direction is not stated. In art it may be. 'Geometric' shapes are mostly compounded from straight lines that 'run' in different directions, or 'act' in different ways upon a plane – in our case the drawing surface. A few geometric shapes are derived from the circle. A number of basic geometric shapes are so familiar to us that, the moment we spot them among lines, we recognize them. We are able to classify them without needing to run our eyes all the way round them, even though they have been drawn by means of outlines. This may be one of the reasons why geometrical shapes can seem static (rather than dynamic like linear or organic shapes) and why they may seem somehow to be independent of their outlines. This links them firmly to the structural plan-aspect of drawing (Section 1).

A triangle consists of three straight lines running together at their ends.

A quadrilateral consists of four straight lines running together at their ends. Special quadrilaterals are the square, with equal sides and right-angles; and the parallelogram, with parallel pairs of sides. A diamond or lozenge shape is an equal-sided parallelogram.

A circle is described by one end of a straight line moving while the other end remains on the same point.

An ellipse appears where two circles intersect.

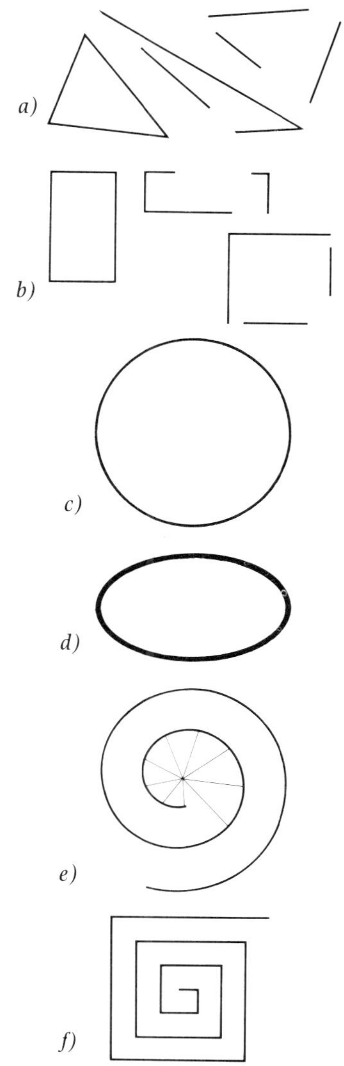

57 Geometric enclosure types.

A spiral is described by one end of a straight line moving while the other end remains on the same point, and while the straight line increases in length. 57e

A spiral can have a 'square' conformation as well. Spirals may actually have the value of enclosures. 57f

There are other straight-sided geometrical enclosures which have increasing numbers of
107 sides: the pentagon five, the hexagon six, and so on. But, purely from the point of view of their shapes, each can be interpreted at once by the non-mathematician in terms of rectangles and triangles added together.

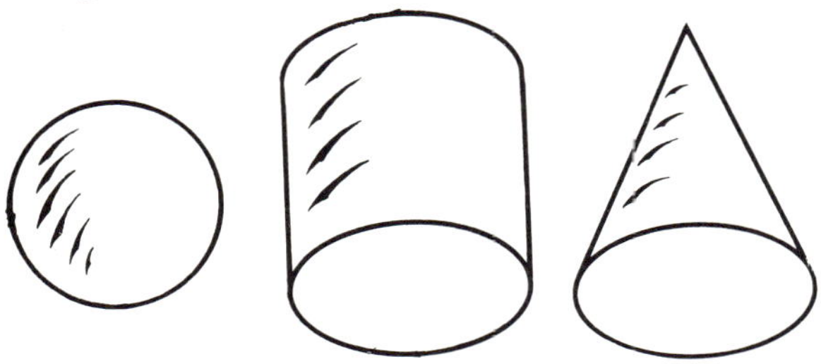

58 Sphere, cylinder and cone.

59 Kasimir Malevitch: 'In Suprematist Space', 1920. Rectilinear enclosures generate mysterious cosmic space.

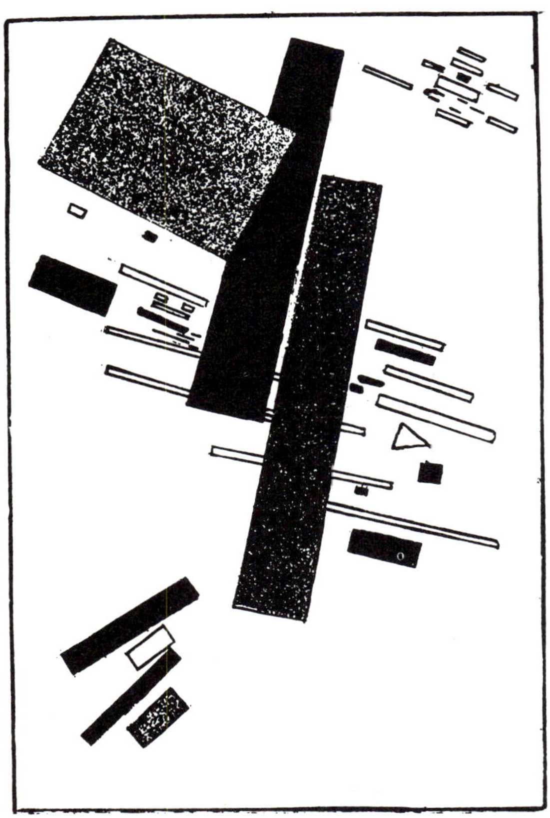

These simple flat shapes have corresponding three-dimensional shapes, which drawing can refer to by some of the techniques we shall discuss later (Sections 20, 30). They can be represented diagrammatically as well. The sphere corresponds to the circle; the cylinder combines the rectangle with a circular section; the cone combines a triangular elevation with a circular section; the pyramid combines a triangular elevation with a square section.

Strict geometric shapes have been used in decorative arts, in architecture, and by many twentieth-century artists. The Russians Malevitch and Rodchenko composed their most famous designs out of virtually nothing else, as they
thought of them as essentially 'democratic'. 8
There is no individuality or idiosyncracy among geometrical shapes of any class.

Machines have to be made in carefully finished geometric shapes; and machines themselves are also the best means of making geometrically simple products. In the early twentieth century many artists and political theorists passionately believed that machines could be used to save mankind from servitude to grinding physical labour. This whole complex of sentiment became attached to simple geometric shapes, diagrammatically drawn and assembled with a cold, precise linear expression. Fernand Léger in France, and Stuart Davis in America, were artists who used geometric shapes in this way. Nowadays we do not share such optimism about mechanical forms.

In practice, we all interpret what we see and draw according to the broad classes of simple
geometric shapes. We think of things as 'round', 1
'rectangular', 'triangular', and so on. And our drawings follow the same principle, referring to the shapes by which we interpret what we see. Art has not usually drawn these standard geometrical shapes for their own sakes, but has used them to contribute a system of order.

Now look at the next image, a printed woodcut book-illustration made in Italy in the fifteenth century. It seems to be nothing more than a simple set of black lines. But the lines are all connected to each other by a very clear and rhythmical system of implied triangular, rectangular and circular relationships of area. It is worth picking out the individual shapes. Notice how they overlap each other; and how some lines act as outlines to several different areas at once. This is actually a very highly developed work of art.

This illustration reinforces another important point: when you are using well-known and accepted geometrical shapes with straight sides, it is not necessary to complete their outlines. The spectator's mind will easily pick up an intended geometric shape even when one or two of its component sides are left out.

One important way you can handle enclosures is to link them in a series by drawing them with a
61 continuous line which crosses over itself. This is related to the grid techniques described in Section 19. It can produce fascinating images, especially if you preserve the rhythmic and feeling quality of the line.

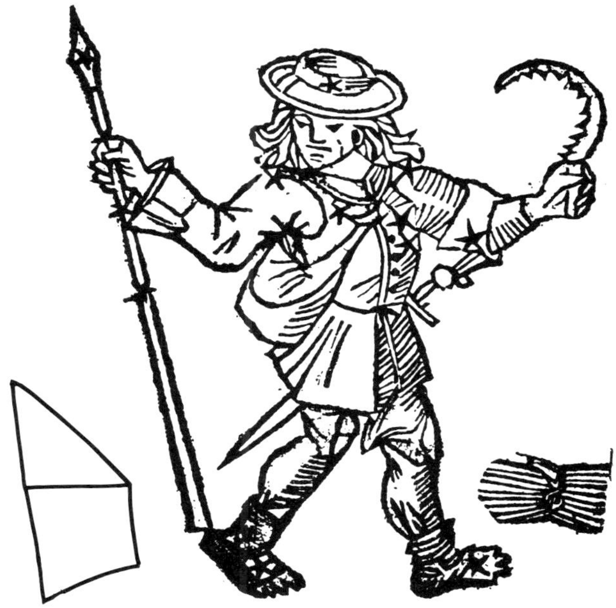

60 Woodcut illustration to a book by Lucianus, representing Hyginus, 1488; and a diagram of enclosures combined into a new shape, which illustrates a process carried out with many combinations of shape in the woodcut.
61 Paul Klee: 'Ships'; pencil drawing.

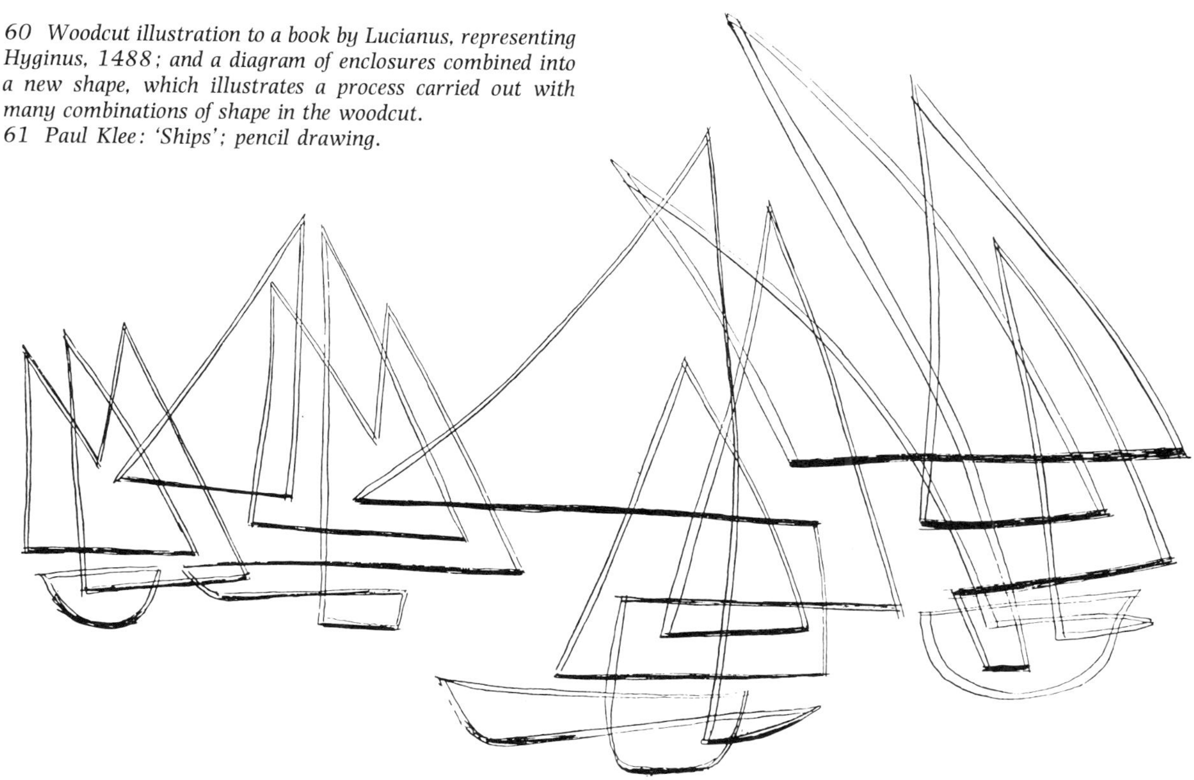

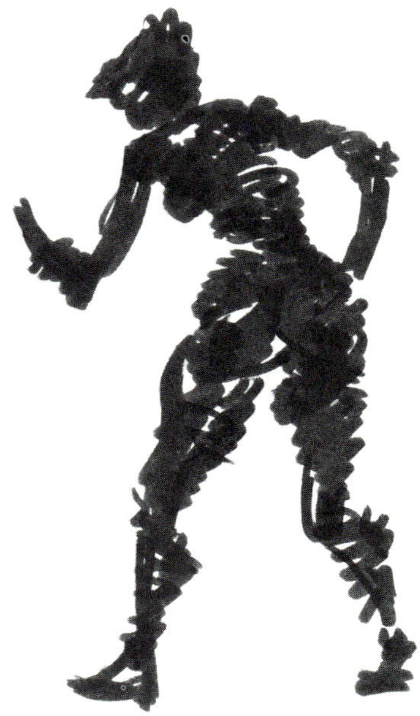

You may remember that in Section 3 we saw how even an apparently simple straight line can be drawn in a number of different ways. It can even be fairly curved, and still have the formal value of a straight line. When you are drawing a series of geometrically defined areas, you can link them by contour lines which have a kinetic value as *lines*, as well as defining the enclosed areas of geometrical shape.

This means that your drawing is dealing with more than one category of form at the same time. Your lines can, in fact, work as purely linear expression; connect with the format; embody rhythmic intervals; and convey a sense of order by shaped areas – all at once. And to carry this richness of suggestion you may find that your
63 outlines need to become quite thick and rough-looking. A thin outline may be far less capable of

62 Female nude, its enclosures drawn from the middles.
63 Eugène Delacroix: 'Moroccan Rider'; pen drawing.

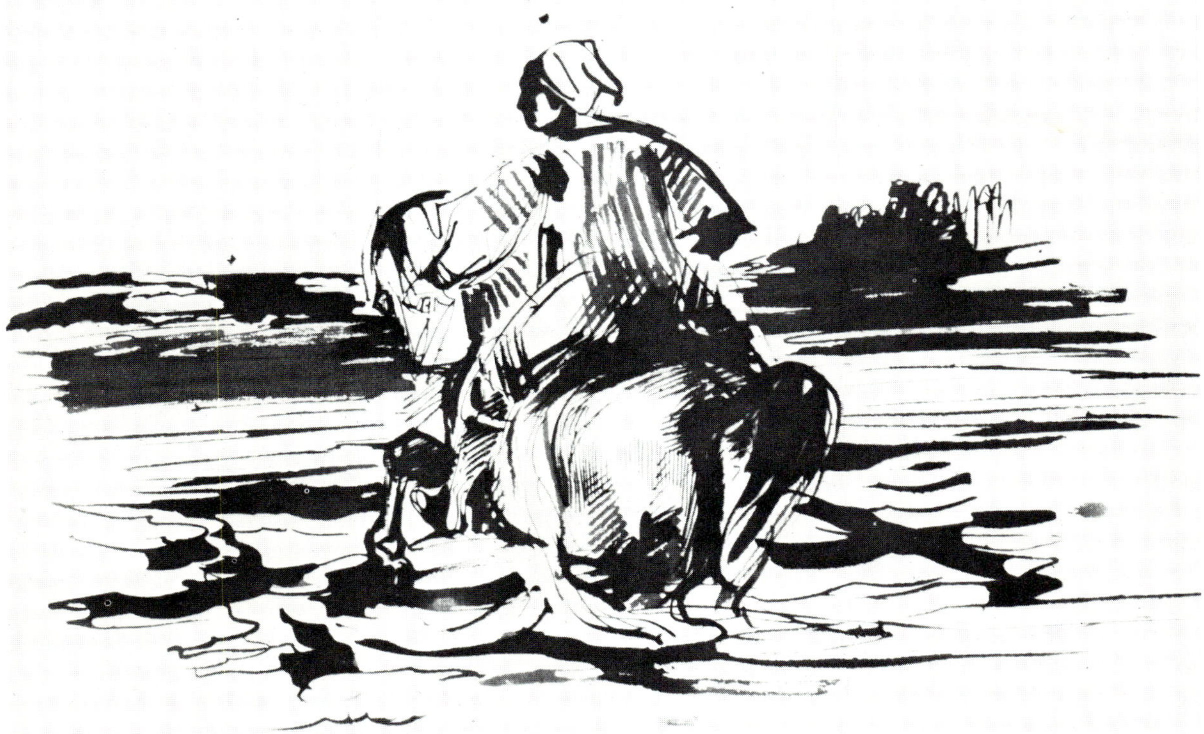

creating such a complex effect. Rough lines can actually be more precise than thin ones. They can gain a new kind of strength and richness from being apparently looser, and thus embodying several readable shapes, directions and rhythms.

There is one further approach to drawing
2 defined enclosures. You start by brushing or scribbling rhythmically in the middle of an area of paper. You work out gradually towards the final shape of the area you mean to define. In fact, the character and quality of the shape you finally reach comes from the same kind of shaping we have been discussing. It is simply arrived at with a different linear technique. You can carry on in this way to develop a linked series of centrally-worked shapes which together compose a single complex unit, such as a body.

Section 14
Negative Spaces

All the enclosures and areas we have been discussing so far have been positive: they associate best with solid volumes. We shall discuss how and why shapes can be seen or used to represent objects in space in Section 22. For the moment, let us take that for granted. Then let us try and turn the idea around, and imagine how one can draw shaped enclosures which stand for the *space* that surrounds solid objects, leaving the objects to be shaped by defined areas of space. We call these 'negative' enclosures or areas. You can see what is meant by comparing these two drawings from Greek pottery. The black shows what was brushed on.

The first vase dates from the sixth century BC and is in a style called 'black figure' because the positive areas of the bodies are defined in solid black. The second is fifth century BC and is called 'red figure', because what appears white in the photograph is in fact the pale red of unpainted clay. The black of the surrounding space is what was actually brushed on. This kind of construction gives as much formal importance to the ground as to the figure.

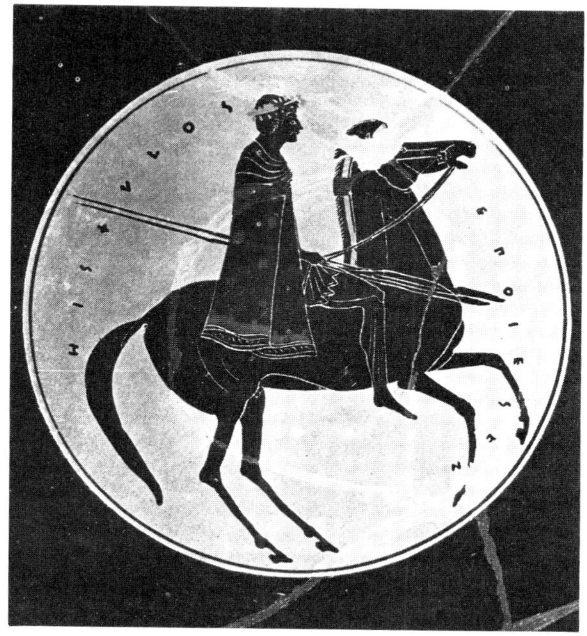

64 Interior of drinking cup, Greek, 520–510 BC: 'Rider', in black-figure style.
65 Drinking cup, Greek, c. 485 BC: 'Girl Washing', in red-figure style.

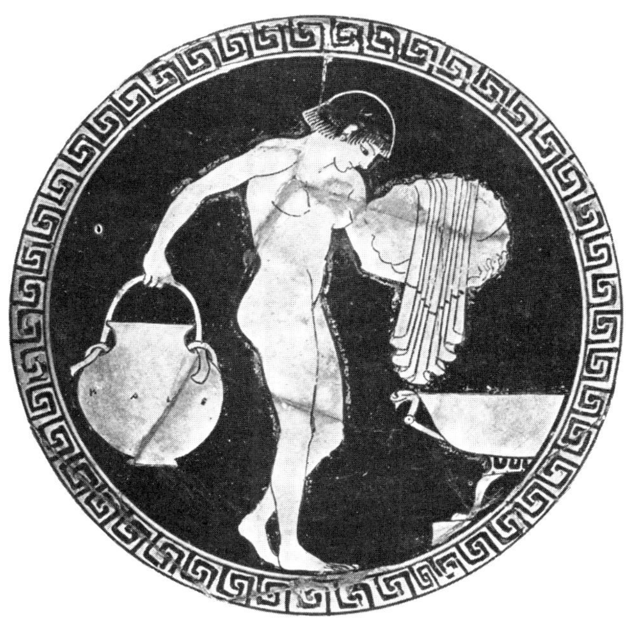

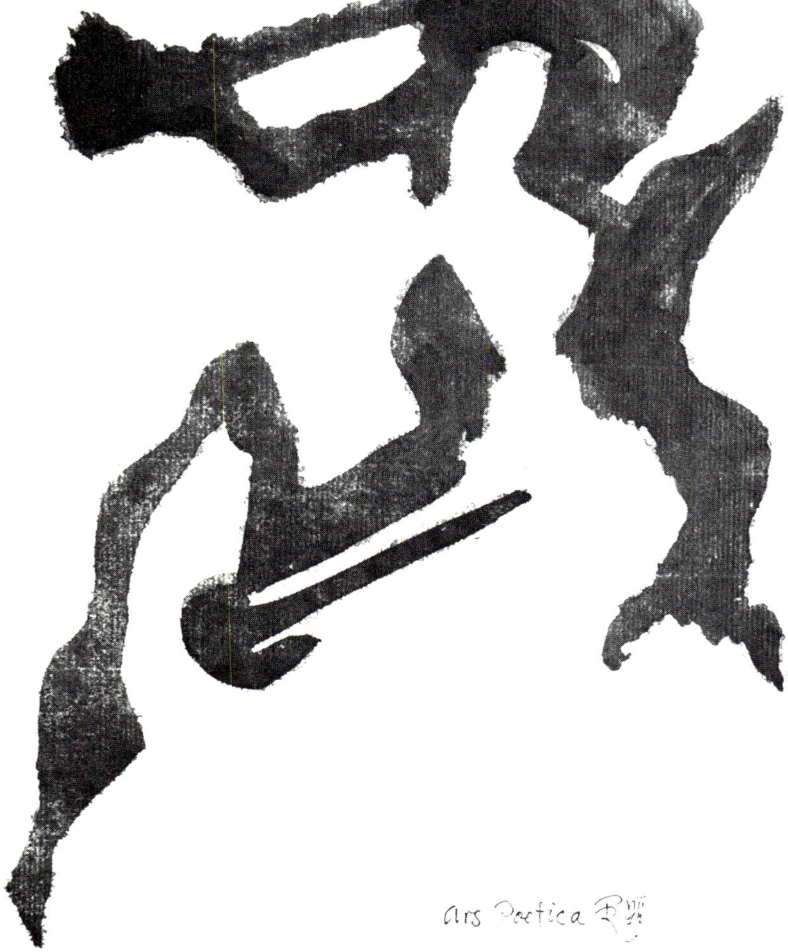

66 Brush drawing combining positive and negative spaces.
67 Shapes drawn as negative spaces.
68 Circular shell gorget, American Indian, 1300–1700 AD: 'Eagle and Puma' incised on the shell.

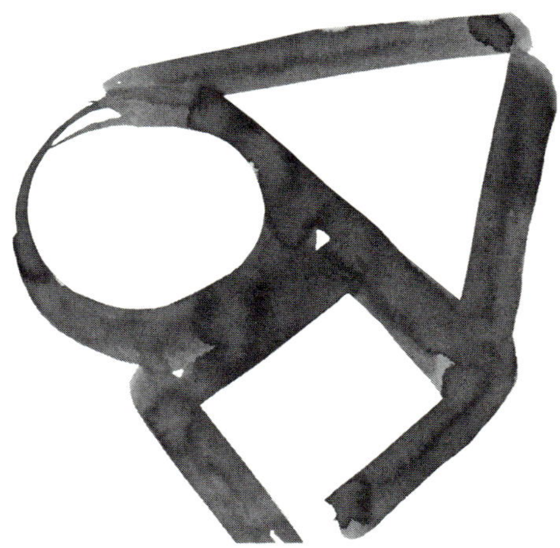

In art such negative areas of space are profoundly important. They can be shaped so as to enhance enormously the active expression of depicted objects. In the marvellous incised drawing on the American Indian shell ornament shown here, the negative shapes are vitally important. They clinch the expression of savagery between the two beasts – look how the shapes *inside* the beak and jaws, the open spaces *between* the claws, express the potential for violent action.

You may find it easiest first to think of a group of positive shapes and then define them by drawing negative shapes. Start with quite simple positives, maybe using some of the geometric and organic enclosures you have already drawn.

It is best to do this by quite free working, *without* first drawing the outline of the shape you are aiming for. This will help you gradually to think of the positive and negative shapes as belonging together and interwoven, as functions of each other. When you then connect up your areas into linear shapes you should be able to think how your outlines are shaping enclosures on both sides of themselves, one set positive, the other negative.

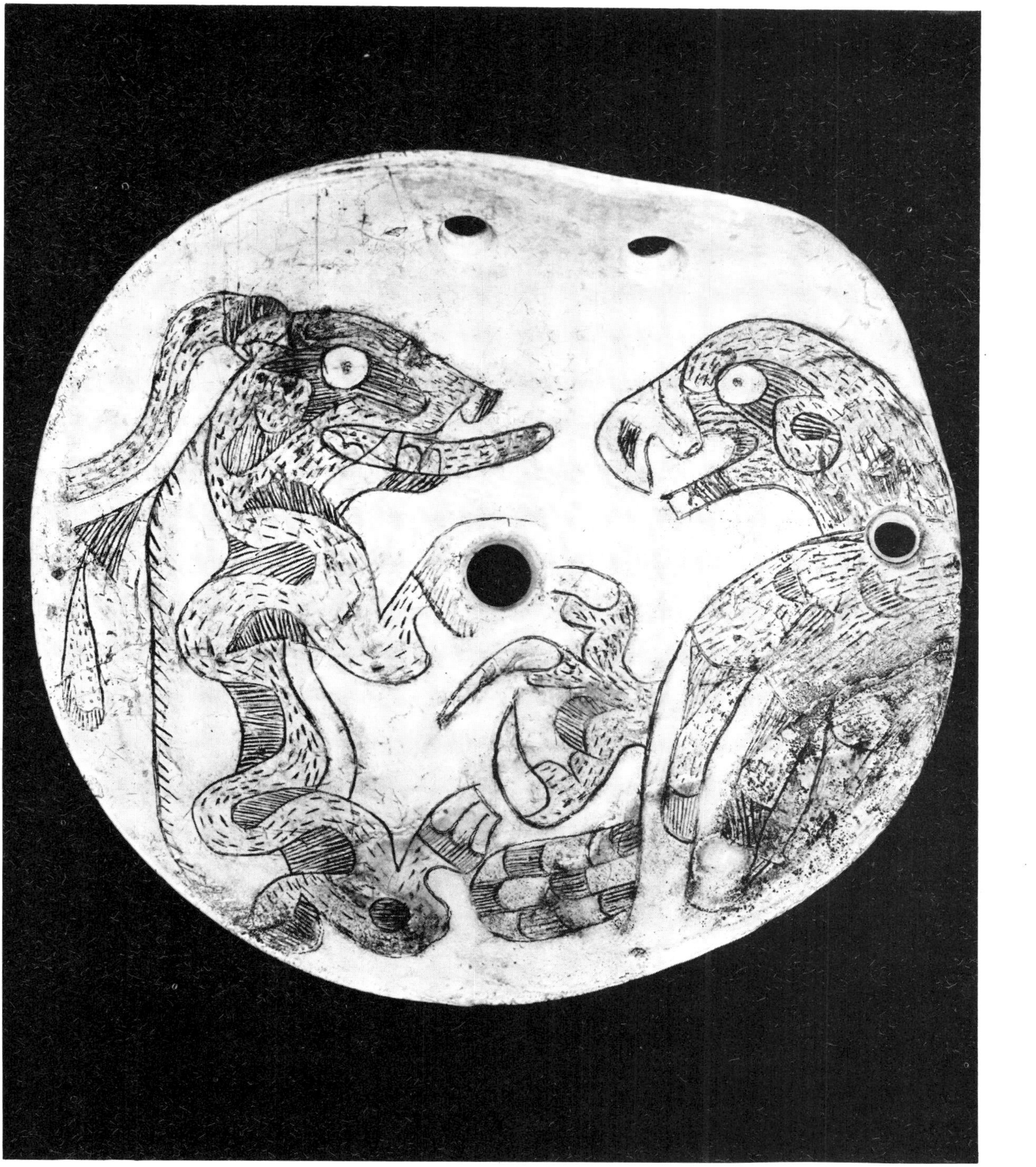

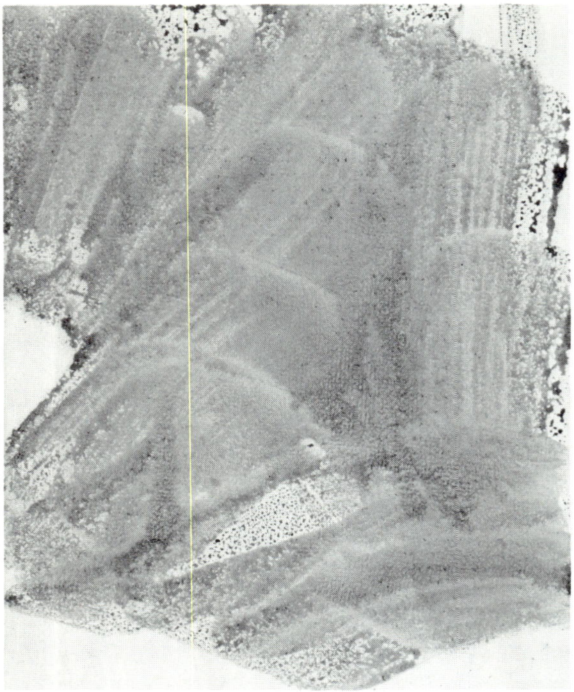

69 *Ink tone brushed dry on to paper.*
70 *Design drawn in wax resist, then brushed over with ink tone.*

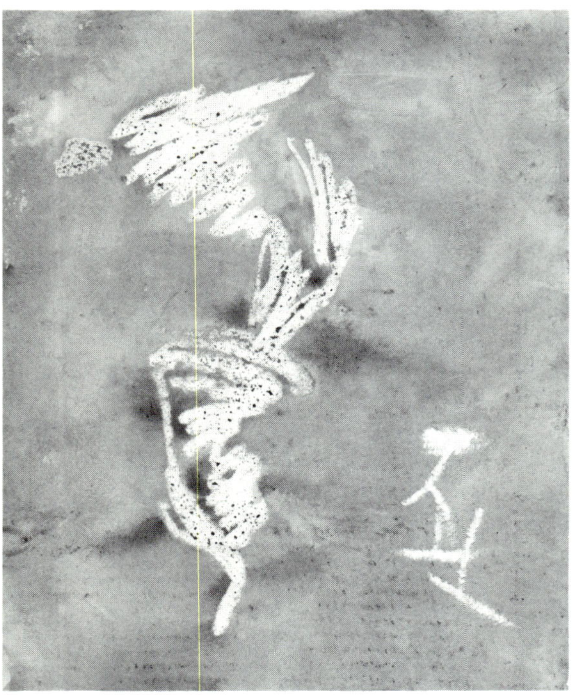

Section 15
Toning

We will now look at different techniques that can be used to emphasize the paper surface. Some of them are based on particular graphic activities; and some, such as frottage and collage, are ways of adding fresh physical elements to the drawing surface.

The first technique may seem very simple and obvious; but it can open up an unexpected number of different possibilities, and connects with some of the representational methods we shall be discussing later (see Sections 30–33). It is to paint the surface with a single continuous palish or darkish tone. You can use diluted ink or an actual colour. In fact, a substantial number of drawings by the great masters were made on a surface toned all over, usually pale blue or brownish red. If you are a figurative artist you can draw tonal images on a toned surface like this with dark and light chalks or pigments together. Here we shall look at the toning process itself.

You can apply the tone to the paper surface when it is dry, sweeping or flooding it on with broad and varied strokes of a brush, a rag or a sponge. If you do not slop on too much liquid, and do not go back over your strokes, you will find that the patterns of your brushing will show up faintly in the tone when it has dried. You can then start to work up a drawn image from the rhythms and spacing of those patterns.

One fascinating version of this technique was often used by Henry Moore. If you first draw on your paper with a wax candle or wax crayon, and then lay on your tone, the waxed parts will not take up the watery tone. If you have drawn with a coloured or metallic crayon, of course, that drawing will show up in its original colour. But if you used a candle, what you drew will be almost invisible until you have laid the tone over it. Then the strokes will show up as a pattern of lights against the dark parts which were not waxed. The textural effects produced by this 'resist drawing', as it is called, are highly individual.

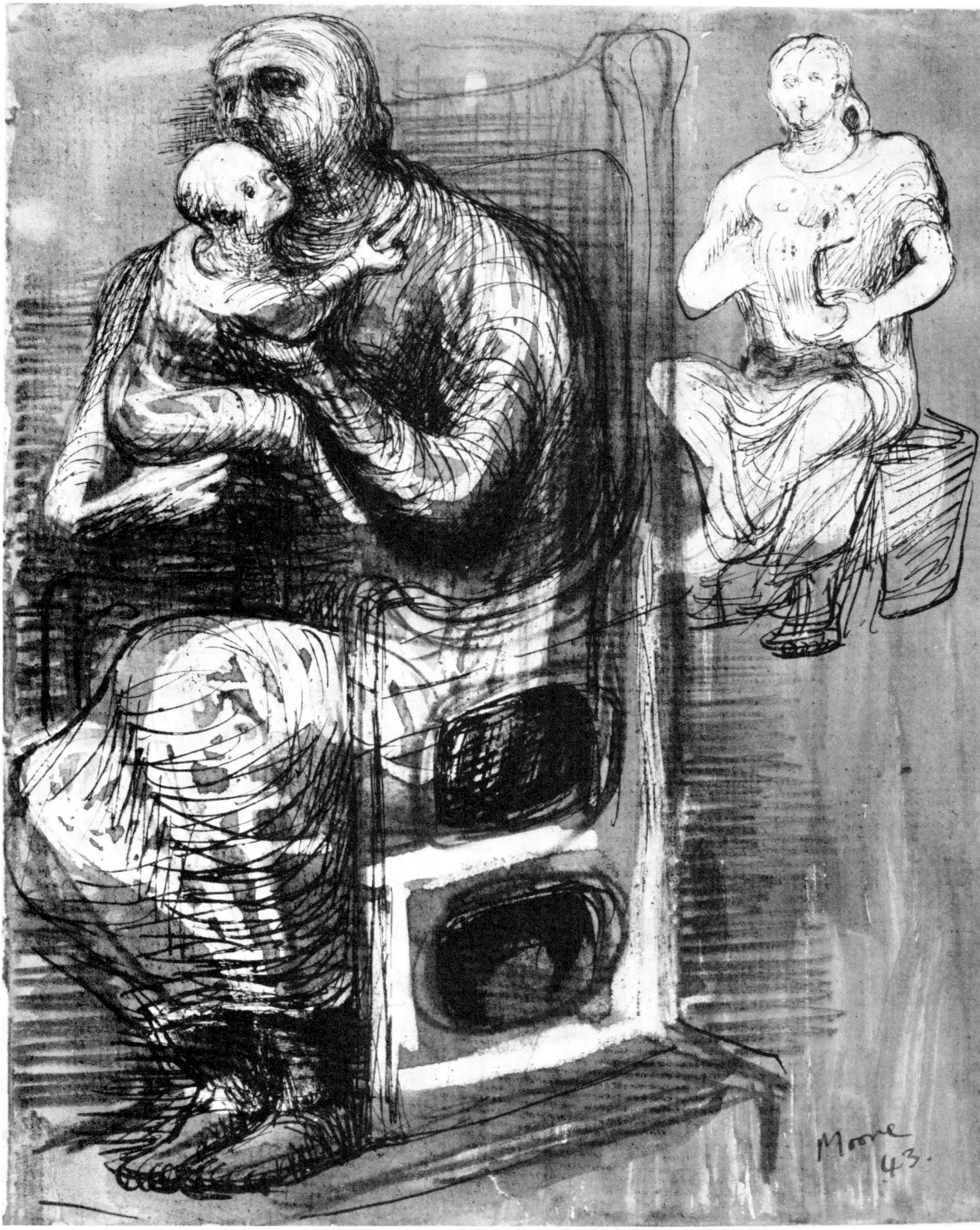

71 Henry Moore: 'Madonna and Child', 1943. Wax crayon, watercolour and ink. The wax gives the highlights to the forms.

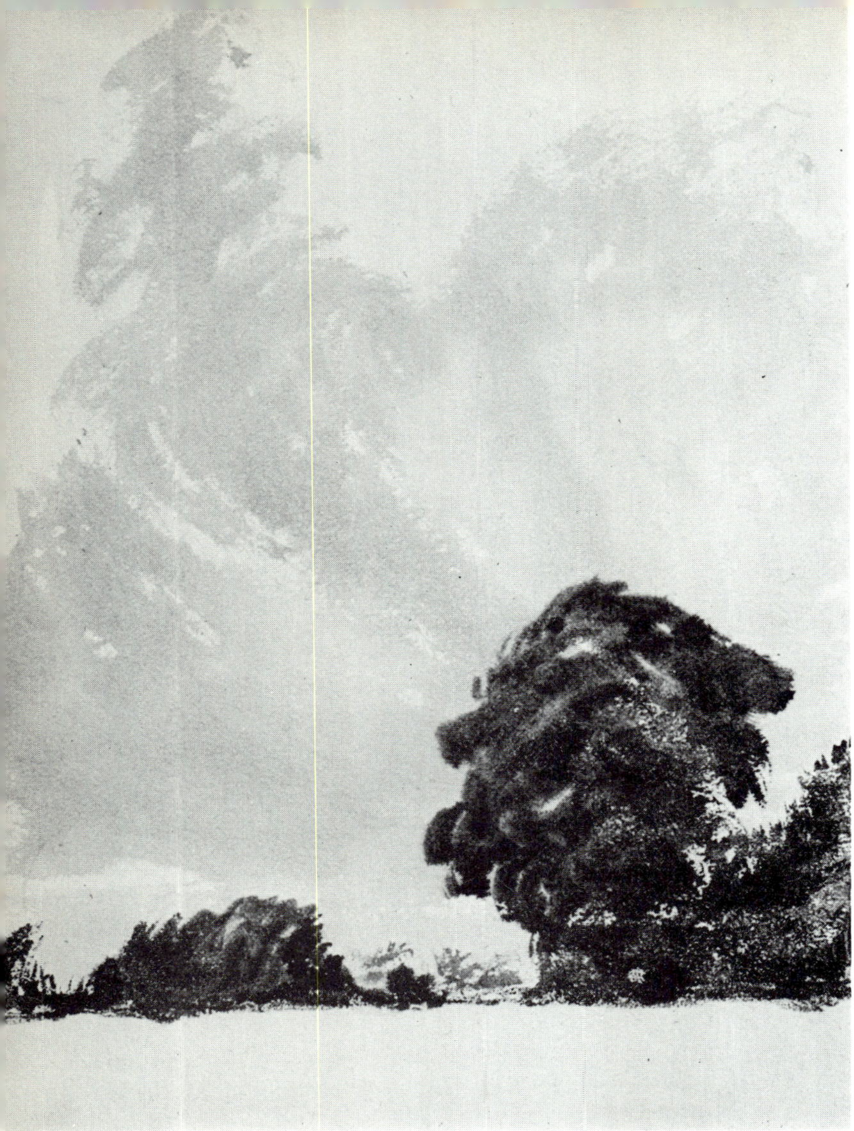

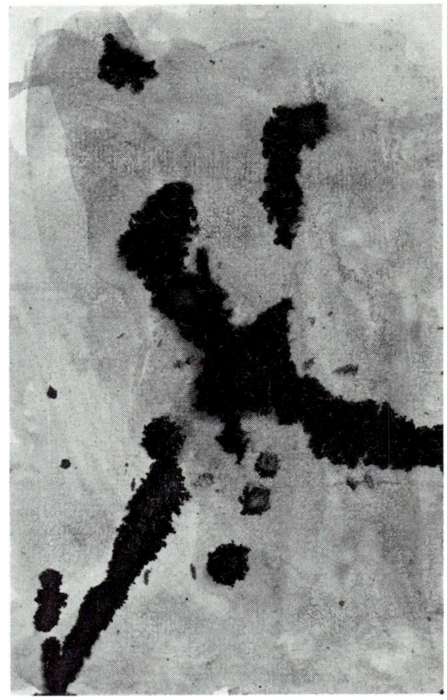

72 'Trees and Cloud'; brushed wet and dry ink tone.
73 Dark ink dripped into wet paler ink.

If you dampen your paper with clear water before you lay your tone – do not soak it – you will find you can brush the whole surface with tone very smoothly and evenly. If too much accumulates in one place, perhaps by running down to the lower edge of the paper, you can take it off with your brush squeezed dry or a tissue.

There are several interesting things you can do to areas of tone after you have laid them on, with the paper either dry or wet. You may like to try out the possibilities in different combinations.

First, you can use a dry brush, a bunch of rag or a tissue, to sweep the tone off in places before it has dried. This will let the lighter paper show through. (You can create a massed foliage of trees particularly well with this technique.)

Then, while the ground is still wet, you can splash or drip clear water on to it. This will produce paler irregular spots. You can also splash or drip on some darker tone, some colour, or even gold or silver paint. Out of these you can create whorls and irregular blobs in the toned surface. These can be very interesting in themselves, and can form the chief substance of your work; or you can use them, like the brushing patterns, as a basis for further development.

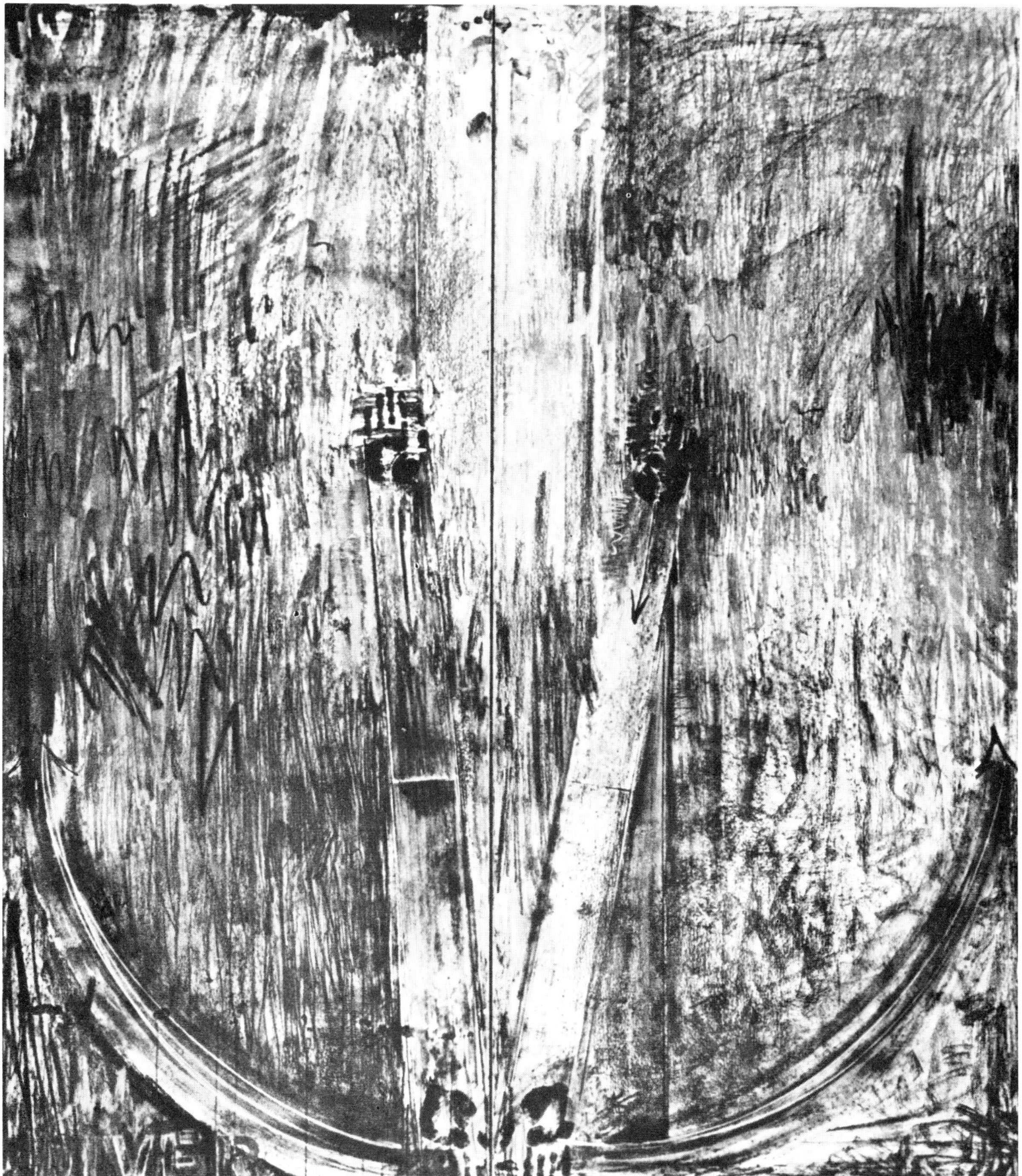

74 Jasper Johns: 'Diver', 1963; mixed media. The imagery refers to the suicide of the poet Hart Crane from a ship.

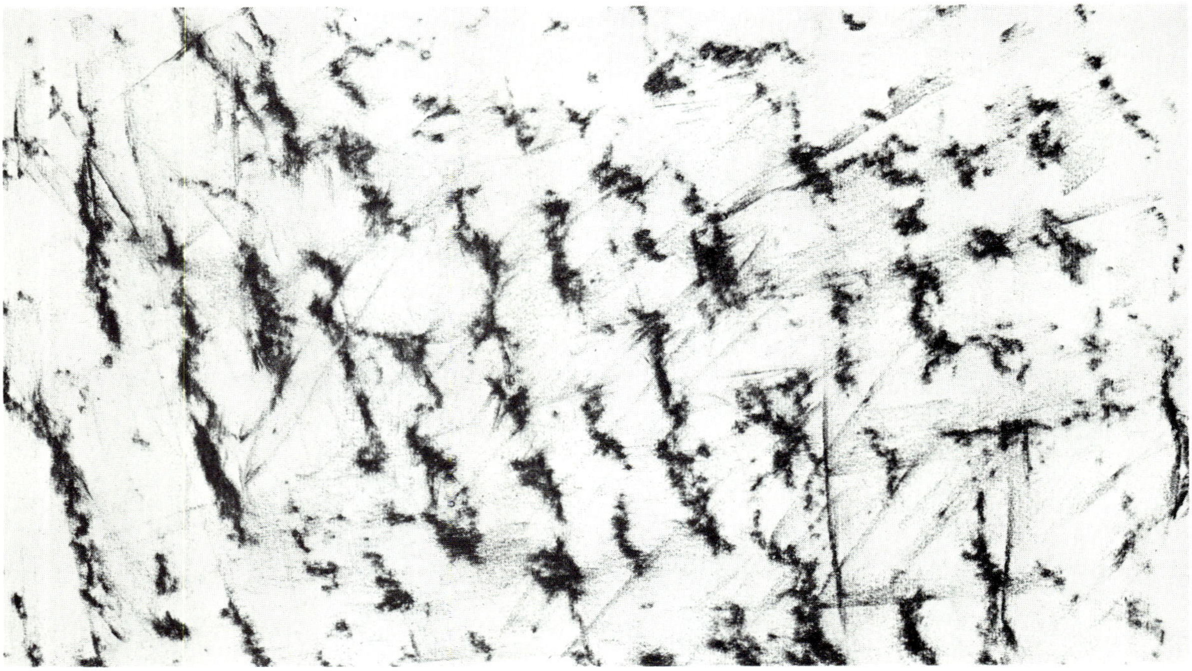

75 Frottage taken from a paving stone, with chalk. The texture is partly created by the rhythmic marks of the chiselling on the face of the stone.

Section 16
Frottage and Collage

Another way of treating the paper surface to give it an objective quality is called 'frottage' (from the French *frotter*, to rub). First, you put a thinnish piece of paper over some strongly textured surface, such as rough stone, tree-bark, leaves, or even a collection of small objects. You then rub the surface of the paper with something soft, such as crayon, chalk, soft pencil, a watercolour block slightly dampened, or even the palm of your hand smeared with colour or charcoal. The texture lying under your paper will then come through and show on the top surface as an interesting toned mottling.

If you make a careful arrangement of objects under your paper, the resulting frottage can be interesting as work in its own right. Some of the objects may pierce the paper as you rub hard, which can add to the effect. But by far the commonest way of using frottage is to tear or cut it up and stick the pieces on to a larger piece of paper as part of a further composition. One of the reasons for doing this is that the best paper for frottage may be slightly too thin to take a full-scale drawing.

This technique of sticking pieces on to a drawing is called 'collage' (from the French *coller*, to stick), a technique developed early in the twentieth century in France by such artists as Picasso and Georges Braque. You can glue on to a drawing anything that will stick – leaves, matches, string, wood, buttons, coins, sand, broken glass, cloth, or anything made of paper or cardboard. But of course, it is vital that each ingredient should be relevant to the image. You can then draw on or around the collaged objects. All these objects have meanings in our lives. You may think of them as

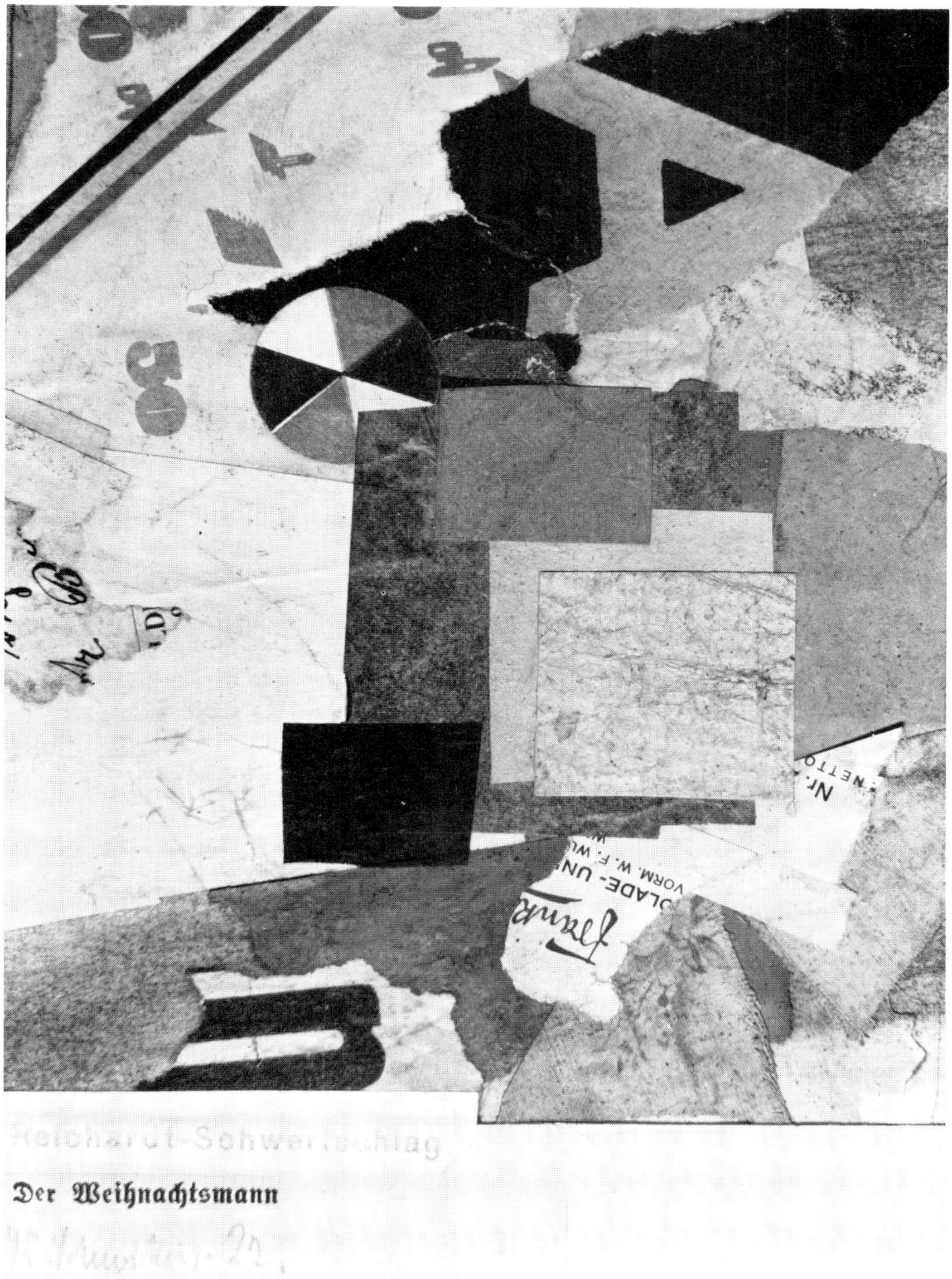

76 Kurt Schwitters: 'Santa Claus', 1922. A collage of paper and cloth. effectively combining positive and negative geometric enclosures.

highly significant elements in your piece of work. Or you may employ them because they are usually discarded or not noticed, and you want people to pay attention to them. Or you may use them purely for the sake of their forms.

One of the ways in which collage has been used especially by Picasso and Braque, is to contribute an objective quality to an image which can also be read as representational. Thus, in an image of a chair, the seat could be a piece of actual wood; or a piece of wallpaper could be cut to serve as the pattern on the dress of a
76 depicted girl. Kurt Schwitters made elegant compositions entirely out of fragments of newspapers, bus tickets and other 'rubbish' (*merz* in German). They were fundamentally 'cubist' in their layout and carried representational references as well; in this way, images of the world could be expressed in terms of its rubbish instead of traditional and 'beautiful' pigments. If some piece of that rubbish is somehow 'framed' or emphasized in a composition, we can be persuaded to look at it with the kind of concentration we would never give it normally.

Another aspect of collage is very important today. This makes special use of the images which pieces of paper or cloth may already carry. Surrealists, such as Max Ernst, took this technique to great heights of expression. Ernst used to cut up nineteenth-century illustrated books, and compose startling images out of pieces of different illustrations.

This technique has its roots in the methods of layout and graphic design commonly used for advertisements. Many American painters who have used the technique, such as James Rosenquist, have worked in advertising studios. You too can collage advertising illustrations or photographs out of magazines and newspapers; you can even include banner headlines or pieces of printed text, cut up and put together again so that they seem to say quite extraordinary things which they did *not* say originally. You can make jokes, by, for example, giving a gorilla some underwear and putting him in a totally unexpected setting with crazy headlines. Or you can be serious, taking, say, contrasting photographic images, cutting them up and mounting them together, drawing on them or around them, perhaps also adding some text. You can suggest meaning obliquely instead of emphatically. The whole effect depends on how you relate the components by size, placing and framing.

Section 17
Tearing and Cutting

Ingredients for collage can be made in two main ways. The first is by tearing shapes out of sheets of paper, and is usually called *papier déchiré*, torn paper. The second is by cutting them out, and is called *papier coupé*, cut paper. We have looked at how shapes get their expressive qualities and how they can be elaborated (Sections 11–13). For the moment we shall just consider a few of the things involved in tearing and cutting out shapes and sticking them on to a base sheet.

Tearing is one of the best ways of overcoming any inhibitions you may have about your sheer skill in using, say, a fine pencil, to draw people and things. If you tear out your basic shapes, you are accepting that you will not be making tight and 'accurate' images. You are bound to be looking for an interesting overall shape. Generally speaking, compositions with *papier déchiré* or *papier coupé* are methods of developing enclosures. But the techniques do introduce their own special effects. With tearing, the roughish edges of torn patches, the way they stand up a little off the surface, the traces of the act of tearing itself, and what that tearing may do, say, to an image printed on the paper that is torn, all contribute to the overall image.

Cutting the shapes to stick on to the base sheet is more precise and more deliberate than tearing. You should use a knife or scissors, so the edges are clean and hard, and it takes some skill to make them varied and interesting. The greatest modern master of cut-paper images was Henri Matisse. His female figures, some combined with leaves or

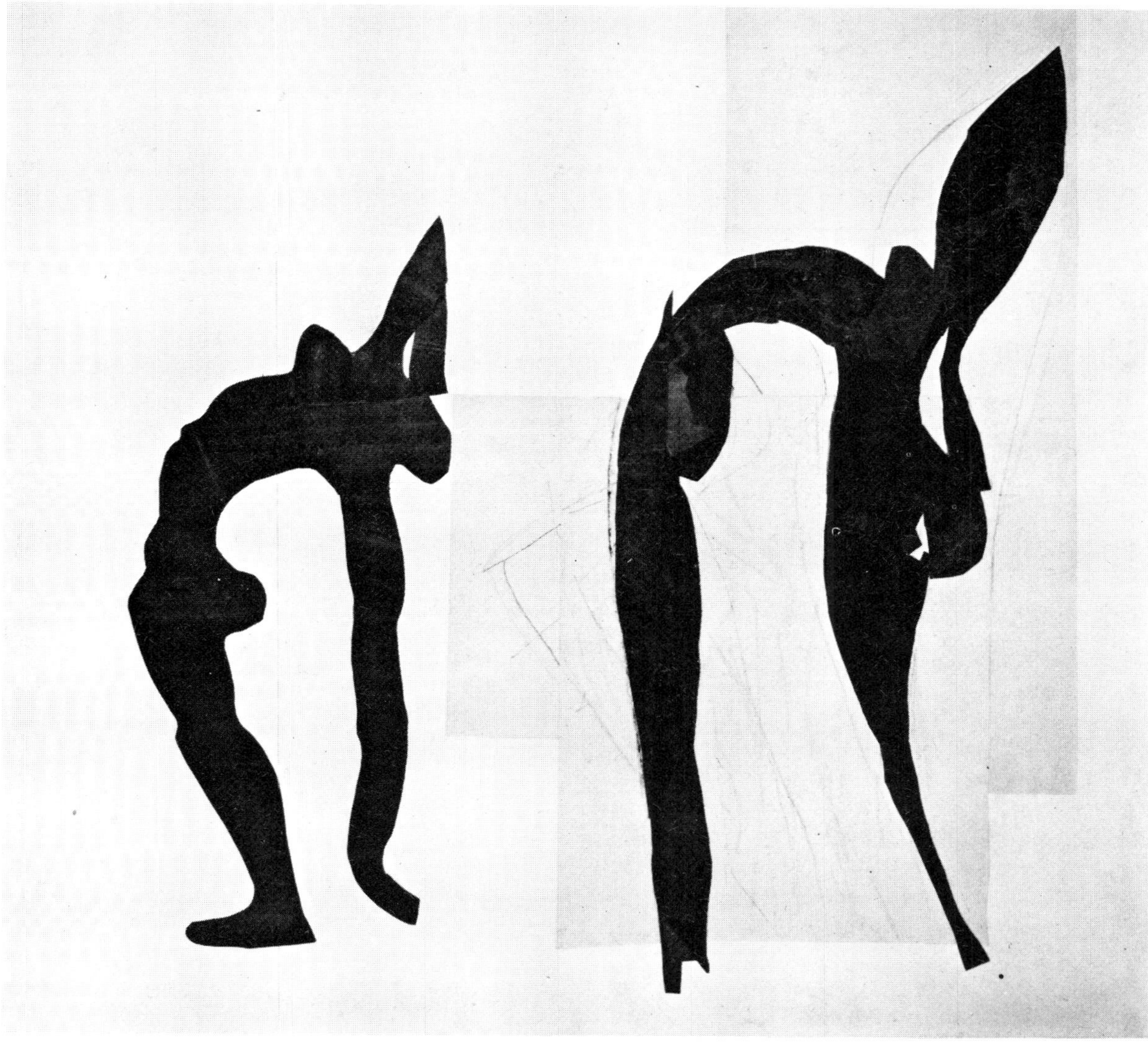

77 Henri Matisse: 'Acrobats'; cut blue-painted paper. Dance-like movements, suggested by complementary positive and negative spaces.

seaweed, are made up of sections cut out with scissors from sheets of paper he had coloured himself.

The paper or cloth or whatever material you tear or cut up should have strong characteristics of its own. You can prepare it by the other activity-techniques – by toning, colouring or frottaging.

One thing that seems to be important in both torn- or cut-paper work is that you should not try to cut out the whole of your more elaborate shapes as single pieces of paper. Leaves and flowers, yes. But components such as human figures seem to work best if they are made up out of groupings of simpler, clearly and individually shaped pieces.

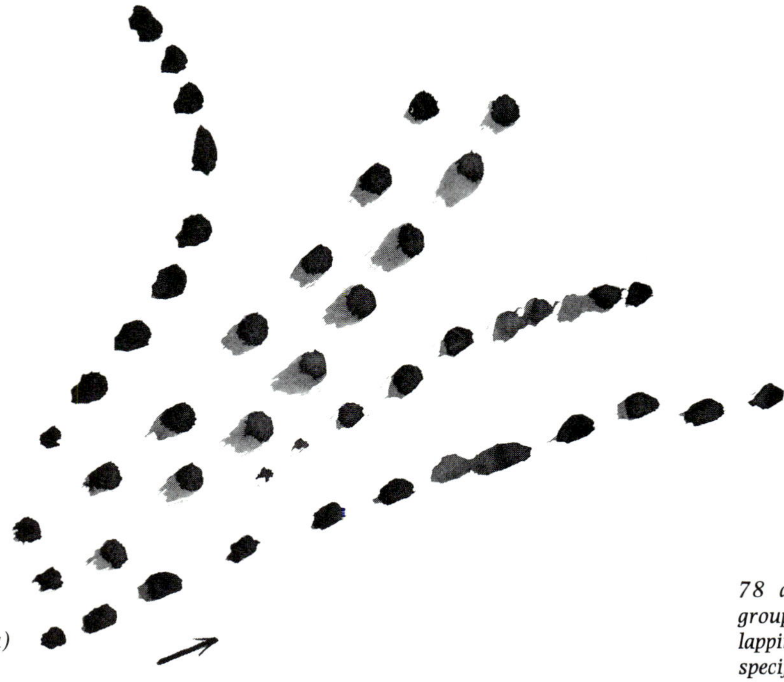

a)

78 *a) Marks constituting a 'flying' group; b) a complex set of overlapping groups, each identified by specific graphic features.*

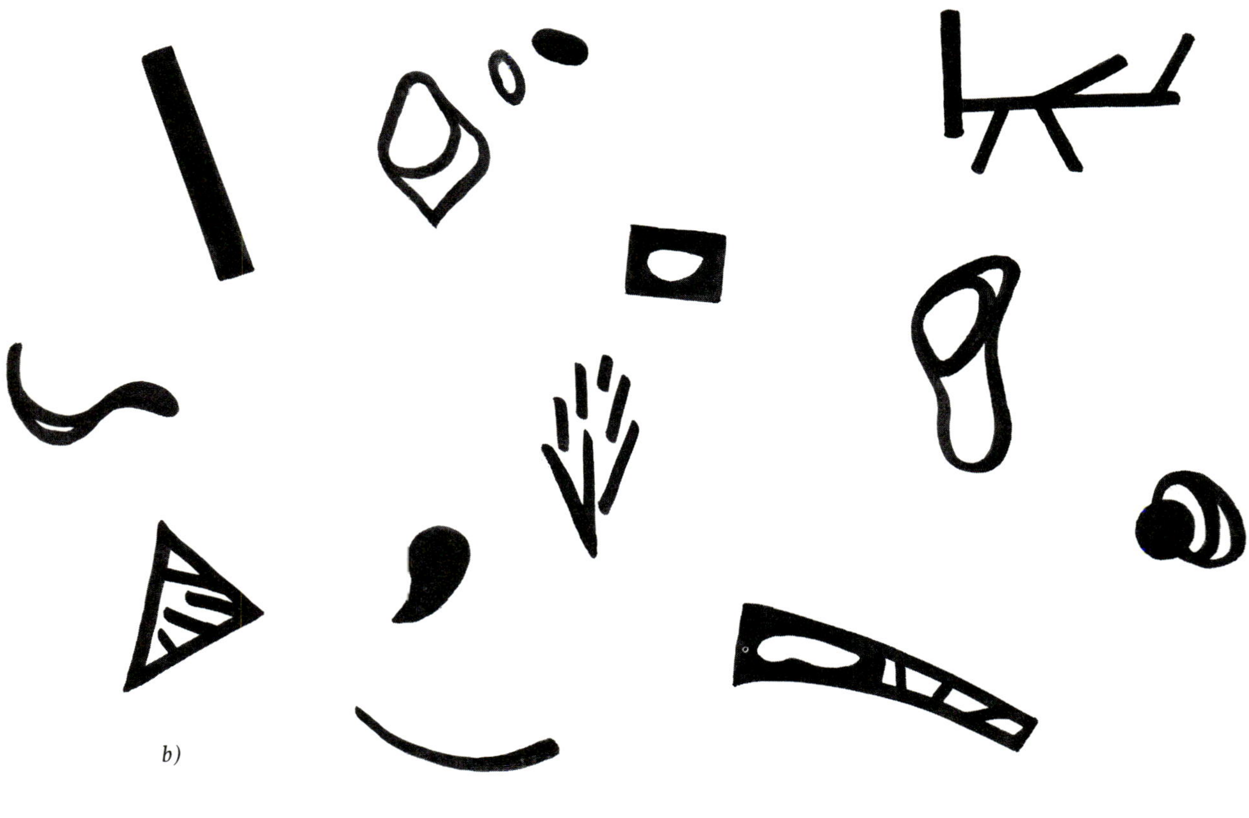

b)

III

Schematic Connections

In this section we shall discuss the 'plan-aspect' of drawing, which we mentioned in Section 1. We shall examine some of the schematic methods by which parts of a composition can be related to each other.

Section 18

Groups

The group is one of the fundamental elements in artistic thought. It can either form a coherent cluster, or give unity to a number of differing components scattered across a design. Groups do not need to have any clear shape; they just make things 'go together'. Generally speaking, we can recognize any collection of things – between three and five in number – which have something special in common as a group. In figurative art those things can be distinct objects, such as heads, feet, hands or trees. But in both figurative and non-figurative art all sorts of graphic components can form interlocking groups of different kinds. In the diagram here, for example, all the shapes incorporating oval-like spaces form a group; so do those incorporating straight lines and those with sets of openings.

The components of a group can form clusters or
3b they can be dispersed across the format. It is especially interesting when groups overlap; a few of the shapes in this diagram seem to have both straight lines and enclosed shapes. Most of the drawing elements we have already met can play a part in group-formation: lines which run in the same direction (Section 4), things which lie on a straight line, or on an obvious wavy line, and things which stand on the points of a basic geometric shape (Section 13). A group can even constitute a kinetic shape, suggesting that it is,
for instance, surging in a certain direction like a 78a
flight of birds.

Try picking up one or two distinctive kinds of graphic shape, and playing around with them to make different kinds of groups, some close, some spread out, some overlapping and some not. You can combine several groups into a single group. You may be surprised at the ideas for compositions you come up with; and you may find quite subtle common factors to define groups.

One important thing you can do with groups is to give them overall kinetic feeling. The great master of this was the Russian Supremist Kasimir
Malevitch. His groups of rectangles often give the 59
most extraordinary sense of interaction. Some look like flights of space-vehicles. Some appear to be sliding sideways, obstructed perhaps by others which either oppose them or set up a quite different sense of direction. Once you have got your mind attuned to this kind of kinetic expression, a great number of artistic possibilities are opened up.

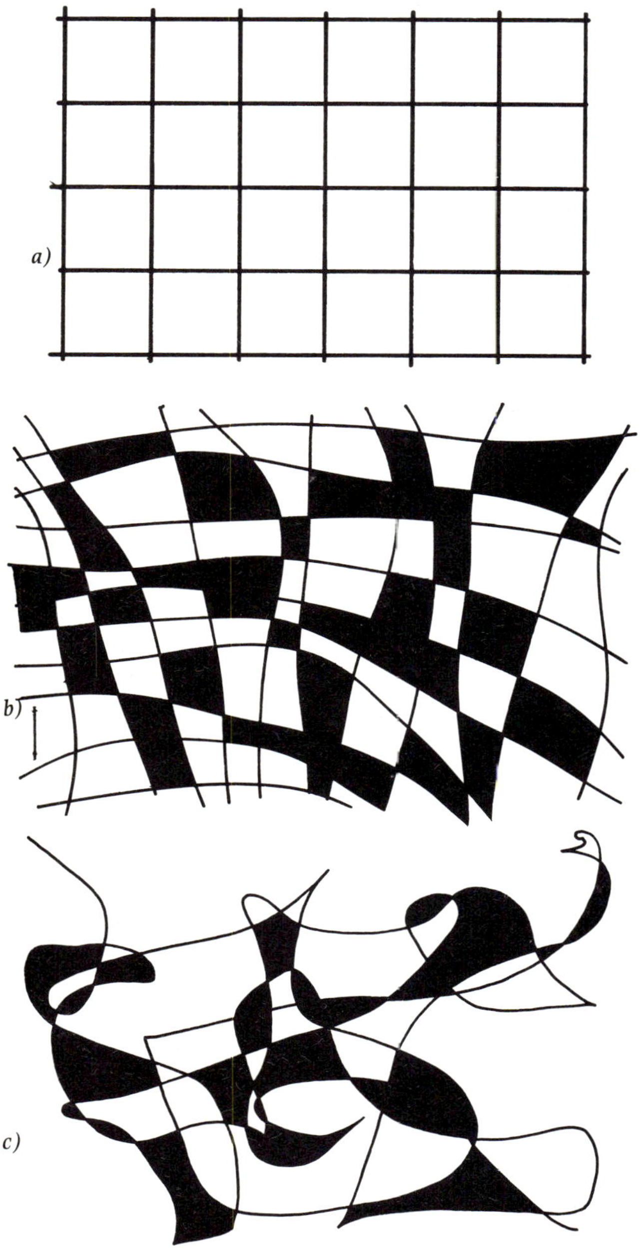

a) *b)* *c)*

79 a) Rectangular grid; b) curvilinear grid with counterchange; c) extravagantly curved grid with sectors filled in.

Section 19

Grids and Counterchange

Enclosures of all kinds, especially geometrical, can be built up into grids. The basic type of grid is made out of lines that are more or less straight, and that cross more or less at right angles. You can also embody in the layout of a grid one of those schemes of proportion we mentioned earlier (Section 6).

However, in practice you can draw a grid with almost any kind of lines which cross over each other at any angle. And varying the quality and rhythm of the crossing lines can produce fascinating results.

Grids can therefore be a major source of ideas. Klee sometimes filled his grids with sequences of colour that could be read up and down, across and also diagonally, as 'colour-melodies'. These he called 'magic squares'. In monochrome drawing artists often use the far simpler but important method of counterchange. This involves giving alternate enclosures similar positive treatments, either along the main lines or diagonally. The areas can be filled in with various grades of tone or hatching, or frottage and collage can play a role (Section 16).

Experimenting with counterchange can help you to develop varied enclosure shapes. You can, for example, include several grid-enclosures in one major treated enclosure; and only a single small one in another.

You can also emphasize only some of the connections between the lines of your grid, perhaps obliterating the rest. The grid need not even be regular. You can weave a long, continuous and interesting line in all directions over your drawing surface, criss-crossing everywhere. Then you can select sets of areas for positive treatment and stress some of the linear shapes by making them perhaps thicker or darker. If you then obliterate the rest of the line (easiest if it was pencilled), its invisible presence will give the image you have picked out a subtle linear unity. And if you draw your original grids with some subtlety, you can

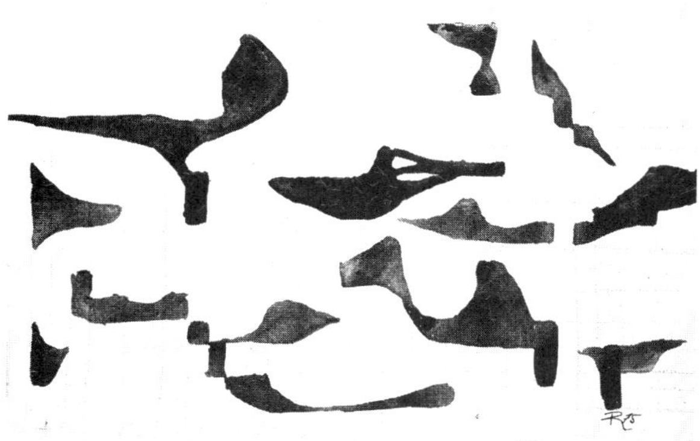

80 Ink design derived from a grid that has been partly erased.

pick organic resemblances out of the treated areas and lines.

Of course, there is nothing to stop you adding stresses by thickening certain pieces of line, or adding a few strokes and marks – eyes, say – to the image, which are not, strictly speaking, derived from the grid. Klee often did it. But it needs care; if you put in too many you lose the feel of the grid.

Section 20
The Diagram

Diagram is a vital element in graphic language. Some parts of it we learn in connection with mathematics; some we learn in everyday life. But as a whole, it belongs to the study of drawing. One reason for this is that many works of art use diagram relationships in their composition; and when we interpret such works of art we need to apply these relationships. Also, drawing diagrams and learning to think in diagrams can develop in an artist a highly important and useful conceptual skill. The ways of thinking which we abstract in diagrams lie behind our techniques of building up graphic images.

Diagrams use graphic stereotypes for mental operations that are usually based on human actions. The essence of the stereotype is that it is conventional and standardized; everyone needs to agree about its meaning. Only for very special purposes do you change the conventions.

A diagram is a way of conveying the relationships at work inside some kind of unity. It is a visual form of logical thinking. So every diagram needs to be supplemented by information on its content. It can be about how the human body works; how to dismantle an automobile axle; how to work out the wind-pattern over terrain; how the ideas in a philosophy or scientific process are connected.

Usually the content of a diagram is expressed in the form of written statements, or a code as in maps (which are themselves a form of diagram). It is very important that your diagram should truly represent the relationships that exist in whatever it deals with. For example, it is obviously no good suggesting in a family diagram that a grandfather is descended from his grandson. Good thinking must go with good diagramming. Sometimes, just laying out a difficult problem in diagram form can clarify your ideas and lead you to a solution.

There are certain important fundamental conventions in diagramming. The first is the line itself. It has one of two meanings: either it represents a connection of some kind, a string or link; or it defines an enclosure that unifies what it contains. The line links one part of the substance to another: precisely how is one of the things we need to agree in advance. In a family tree the lines signify

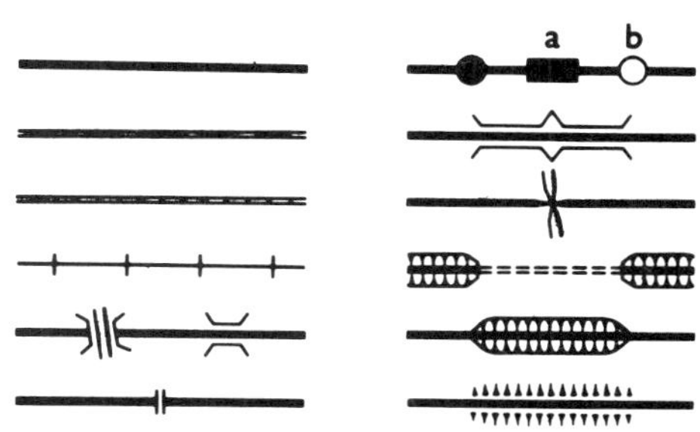

81 Information code from a British Ordinance Survey map.

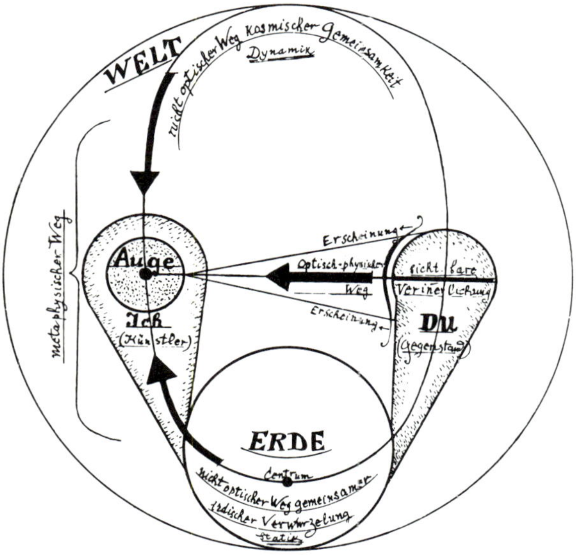

82 *Paul Klee: relationships of Earth and World through Self and Eye.*

connection by heredity. In Klee's diagram they indicate complex metaphysical relationships between the world, the earth and the self.

Two more conventions refer to the vertical and horizontal axes of humans and their horizon: up and down; and left to right. Because of the human experience of gravity, which is that things are moved 'downwards', we usually find in diagrams that processes of development or derivation are depicted from top to bottom. For example, the tree of family relationships, based upon marriages and parenthood, runs from top to bottom, implying succession in time. We normally talk about being 'descended' from grandparents.

Another major convention related to the line is based on our normal direction of writing, whatever that may be. We feel this is a natural direction of succession or evolution. When writing out numbers, for example, we start with 1, and go on to '2, 3, 4, 5, 6, etc.' We do not really think of: 'etc. 6, 5, 4, 3, 2, 1', though we may learn to do this for mathematical purposes. The numbers 2 and 3 etc. are meant mathematically to be related to 1 by a permanent and even timeless logical connection. However, most people feel that the numbers 'come from' 1, by a kind of hidden 'time order', as if they were counting pebbles.

The arrow is a special kind of line which refers to objective movement to indicate direction and/or change. It derives first from the human act of pointing with the finger, then from shooting with a bow. The diagram-arrow is really a version of a line which is 'marked' at one end to show the direction of its movement in time. A genuine artistic line may show its direction simply by the way it was drawn.

Arrows, or skilfully drawn lines, can be used to suggest relationships downward ↓ or across →, two-way relationships ↔, displacement or change of place, reference back, and so on. You can also use them to indicate the direction of a series of evolutionary changes. You can use special forms of arrow to indicate particular processes, such as splitting or convergence, or continuous sequence, or a combination of the two.

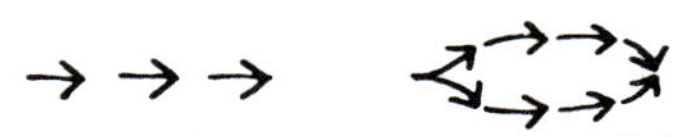

Another major basic convention of the diagram is the enclosure – usually made by drawing a line around an area of the surface, though you can use a patch of tone. It isolates and unites what is enclosed in it. It could derive from the idea of hands actively embracing, collecting or corralling.

It is what you define as being enclosed that is the important thing. You usually use an enclosure to show that groups of things or ideas belong together. On a relief map you use an enclosure to

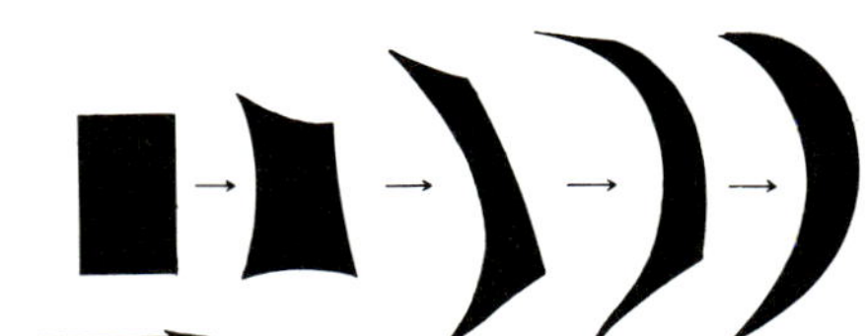

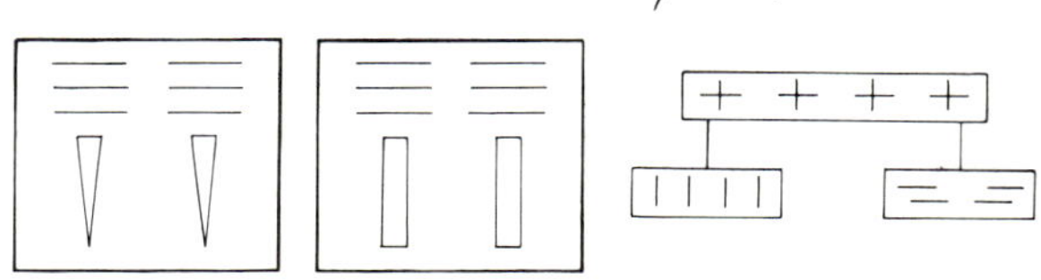

83 *The development of one form into another. This kind of progressive modification is one of the chief resources in drawing for developing new forms from the original shapes.*
84 *Classification and derivation of graphic information.*

define all the terrain, say, above 600 feet (182 metres). You can show how two sets of things are derived from another set. Most interestingly, you can show how two categories of things overlap. You can show how two groups of things split or coalesce.

Other important conventions are those commonly used in mathematics: the long bracket ⏞ which indicates that things belong to the same group; signs indicating 'larger than' > and 'smaller than' < and so on.

One of the practical uses of these diagram conventions is in working out critical flow paths for the processes involved in business and product management: making abstract models for courses of action.

There are also many kinds of logo you can adopt or devise to add to your code. You can make, say, a little figure that on a statistical table can stand for 10,000 people, or a bag that can stand for 1,000 tonnes of grain. These are all quite familiar. But art can use effects that are already halfway to being diagrams in themselves; for example, a figure pointing, or walking. In Ancient Egyptian art this becomes the character meaning 'walking'. Here we reach the verges of the sign and conceptualization, with their implications for our understanding of space (Section 24).

One very important aspect of diagram drawing is three-dimensional representation. It depends on a whole set of geometric conventions, according to which the artist makes, and the viewer reads, abstract images of three-dimensional volumes from sets of two-dimensional lines. Both parties have to agree that what they are looking at are not meant to be purely two-dimensional patterns, though that is just what they are. This ambiguity can give rise to all sort of complications in our reading of them. Some artists, such as M. C. Escher, have played elaborate tricks with the inconsistencies in apparently logical three-dimensional structures, such as buildings, laid out as elaborate two-dimensional diagrams.

The most important convention is that we understand linear enclosures as signifying the edges of surfaces, usually flat regular geometric planes. The lines thus 'become' crests between 86
surfaces; we also have to accept slanting lines as indicating that the planes they enclose run into the third dimension of depth.

If a surface has all its corner angles equal, that plane is supposed to be level with the viewer's eye. If its angles are not all equal it is supposed to run into the depth. Other geometrical solids can be represented in a similar way; but the most important for art are probably the cube, pyramid and cylinder. In fact, any volume can be analysed into outlined facets which will make its inward shape intelligible; it does not have to correspond to one of the regular geometric solids. This is an important factor in representational drawing. Look at the figures in the drawing by Luca Cambiaso. 125

A further ambiguity of reading appears in a diagram showing every edge of a box. It can be read as a concave open box, upside down, as well as a closed, convex box. The lines 'become' exterior or interior corners. It is possible to slip from one reading to another, but not possible to hold both readings of the net of lines in one's mind at the same time. A more complex version of this diagram, called Thiery's figure, offers multiple ambiguities of reading: either flat or three-dimensional, or stacked hollows or solids. It helps to explain the complicated and many-valued spatial effects that Picasso and Braque developed in their cubist art, when they assembled suggestions of profiles and shaded planes of objects into rectangular grids.

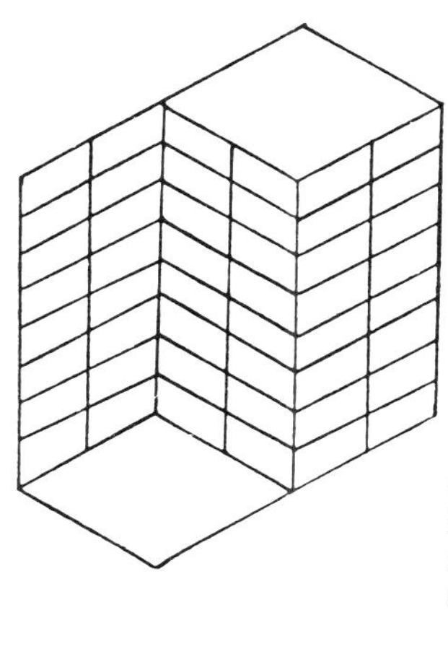

85 Thiery's figure, a box-diagram which can be read as convex or concave, or both.

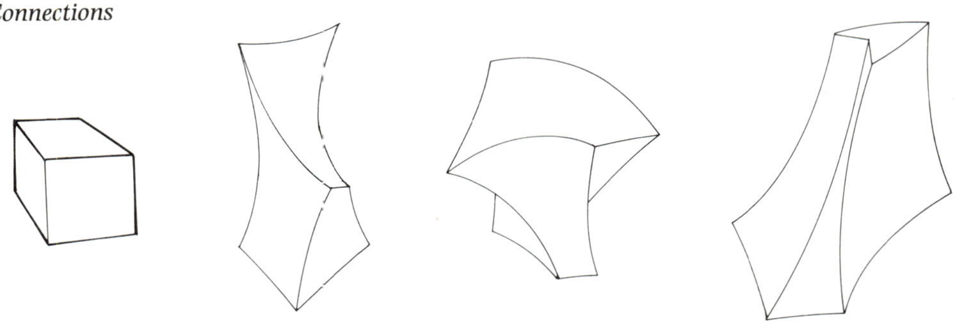

86 Diagram of shapes derived from the box by 'stretching' its substance.

There are specific clues that you can build into such diagrams which can add definition and reduce ambiguity. The most obvious is the use of perspective by shortening the lines that are supposed to be furthest away. You can also explain one volume by adding another to it; and you can use light and shadow from a clearly identified light source.

Perhaps the most interesting development of the three-dimensional linear diagram is when you use it to explore interesting spatial thoughts. You can, for example, take diagrams of the basic forms and extend them in various ways, using the principle of crest-line and enclosure as surface. Such thinking can lead to important sculptural inventions. In the diagrams here, based on the cube, two of the surfaces enclosed within the curved lines have to be understood as twisted as well as curved. It would be quite possible to realize such volumes in three dimensions, and assemble them into sculptures.

Section 21
Constructivism and its Derivatives

Constructivism was a Russian movement which grew out of geometry. It was developed by architects and designers during the Bolshevik Revolution, many of whom, such as Naum Gabo, later emigrated to the West and became leading artists there. Constructivist ideas have had considerable influence on architecture, decoration and drawing techniques and cannot be ignored here.

Constructivists thought of themselves as a new, essentially modern breed of artists, and of their work as setting a totally new direction for art. Their original idea was that a work of art should be a necessary construction, an act of the practical intelligence. It should combine pre-existing or pre-conceived units of form – usually geometric – into a higher unity, without eliminating their own identity. As with the diagram, the thought should be complete before the act of creation. Rigorous Constructivism could only appear in what we might call applied art – housing, workshops, public places, objects for public use and machines. For only these are strictly necessary. Very few genuine Constructivist works were ever actually made or built to full scale. One of Constructivism's particularly successful episodes, in theatre design, a non-utilitarian art form, had to be interpreted as a way of preparing the ground for the public to accept the genuine thing.

Instead, artists began to use Constructivist methods of assembly for non-utilitarian objects. It is this 'intuitionist' version of Constructivism that has spread so widely in Europe and the United States since the 1920s. Theo van Doesberg, the Dutch artist, and the American sculptor, Charles Biederman, played important roles in the diffusion of this version of Constructivism into many different movements. Its fundamental idea is that art is created by putting together a group of recognizable objects, so as to set up a brand new 'higher image'. This activity is now taken for granted in art schools. Assemblages made like this no longer need to display pure constructive intelligence, or obvious usefulness.

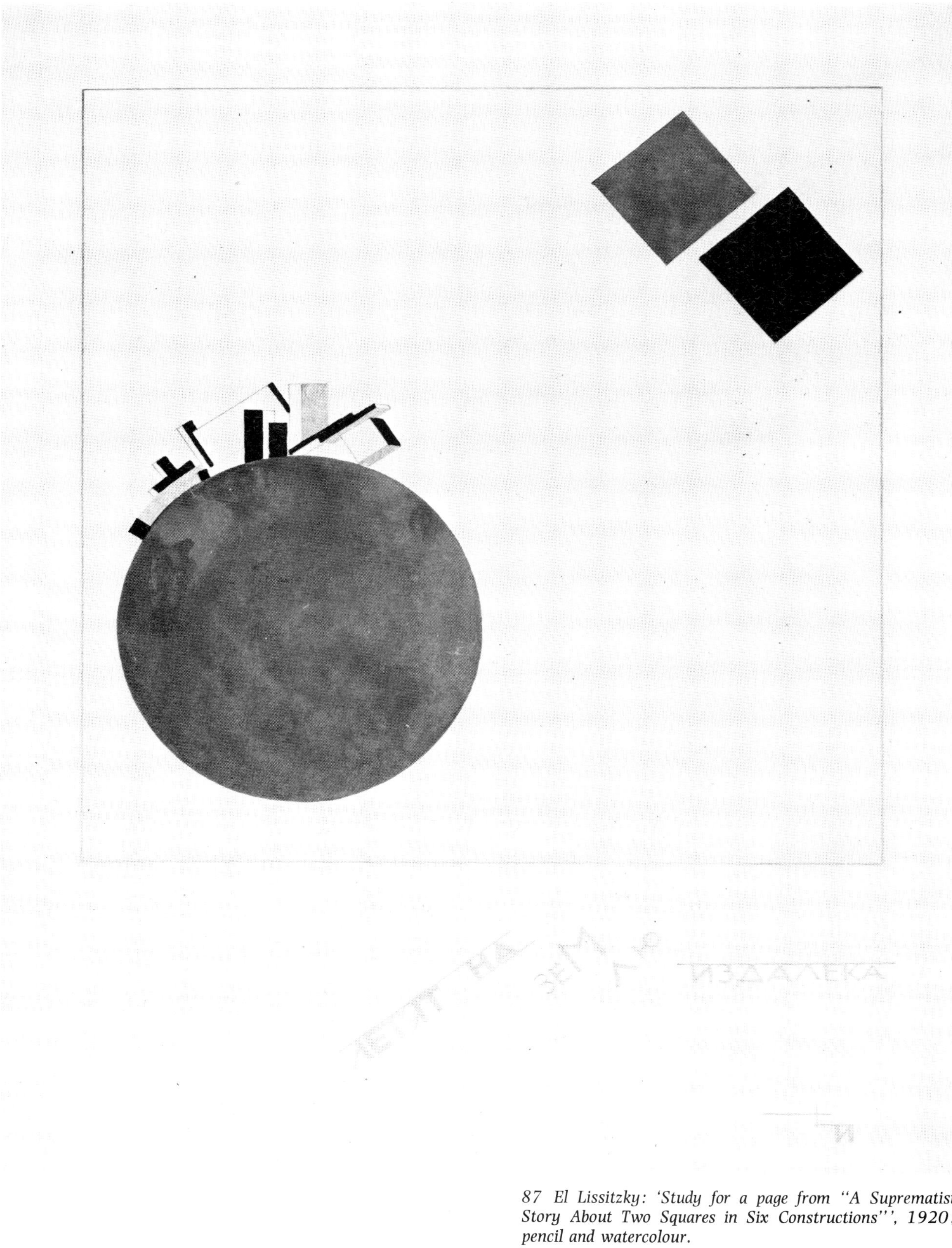

87 El Lissitzky: 'Study for a page from "A Suprematist Story About Two Squares in Six Constructions"', 1920; pencil and watercolour.

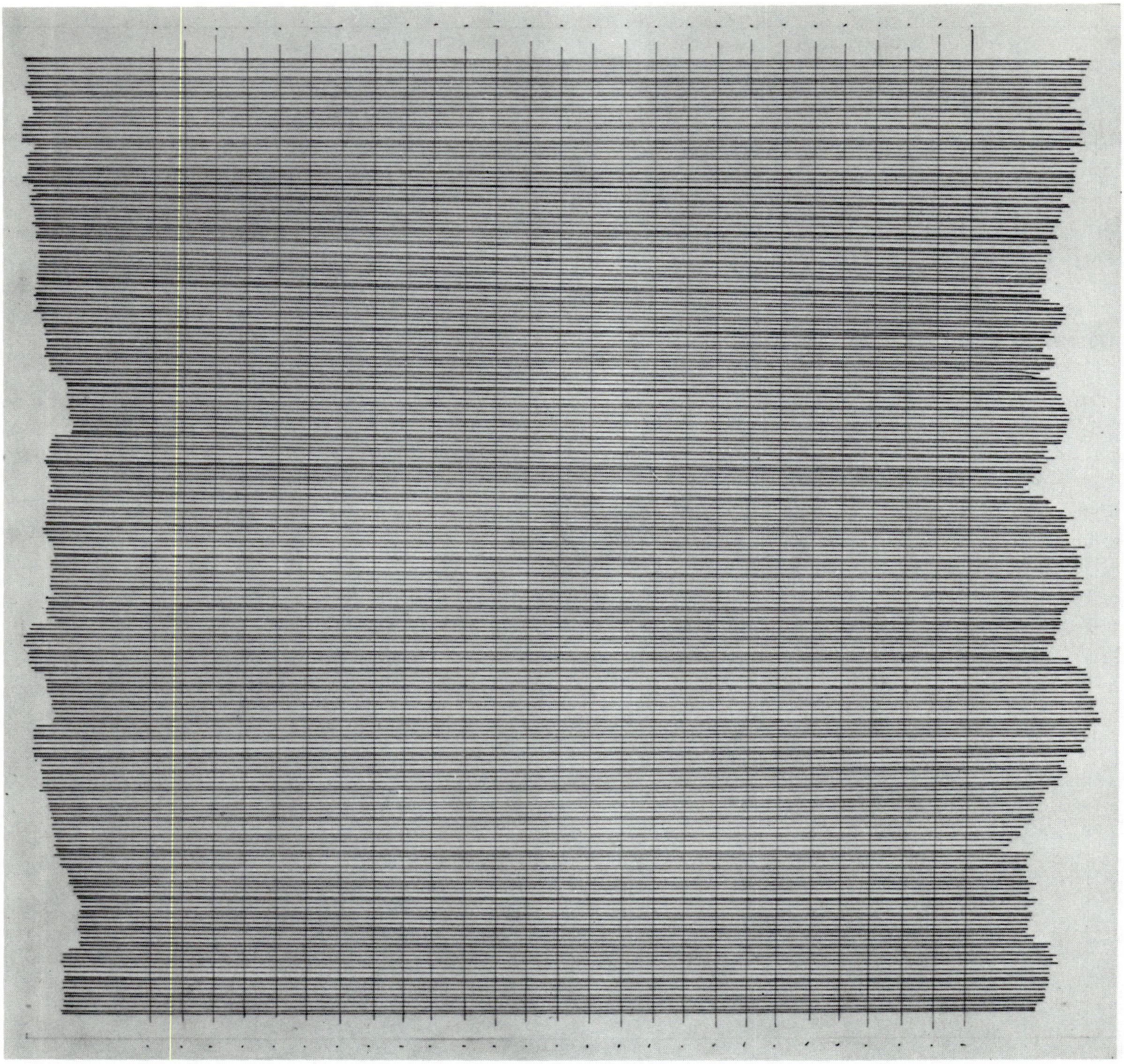

88 Agnes Martin: 'Untitled', 1960. Ruled grid and variations, which generate a field of activity on the surface.

Nowadays you can be purely experimental. You can put together anything at all: wood, nails, cans, plastic, wire, old doors, paint, glue, blowtorch work and so on. You can use standard components according to mathematical formulae as a symbolic substitute for 'constructive intelligence'. You can refer to mathematics as part of the 'higher image' in your art. Assemblages are often made by one or other version of collage; or by locating and relating on the same sheet varied scraps of drawing each of which may refer to other works of art. Bits of text suggesting quite specific books and theoretical ideas may also be included. Or you can assemble separate figurative images of things that you would never normally see together, so that they are visually logical at one level, but 'impossible' at another.

One reason why the method of assemblage has become widely popular is that it can be done by someone who has not learned to draw. Almost anyone can rig up some sort of assemblage of pieces quite quickly and find that it embodies a 'higher unity'. But what you really need to do then is to go on to ask how the *individual meanings* of what you have assembled actually add up to a valid meaning for the whole? What constitutes the unity? Does it matter? And how does it relate to human concerns?

The whole point of putting identifiable things, or their drawn images, into an assemblage is to take away their obvious primary meaning. You can stop your viewer identifying each thing ('Oh yes, that is a so-and-so'), and then not bothering about the wealth of other references and meanings the object and its shape can have. These need not be connected at all obviously with the purpose the object was originally meant to serve. The most famous example of this kind of elimination of primary meaning is Marcel Duchamp's bicycle wheel mounted upside down on a wooden stool. It induces the viewer to look at each component with new eyes. The contexts they give each other give them new meanings. In fact, this kind of operation can take much time and inspiration. You can do something similar not only with objects and images of objects but with all kinds of ready-made shapes.

One of the consequences of the Constructivist movement is that artists are today very much aware of the physical presence of the drawing as an object. You can ensure this by purely graphic means. The marks you make on the surface can emphasize the fact that 'this is a drawing'. You can, for example, copy a photographic image of a face, so that it is very obviously a drawing from a photograph. You can draw harshly defined black stripes, ribbed chevrons or delicately traced lines, either right across the ground, scattered or repeated overall, to bring out the quality of the drawing surface 'as object'. A logical continuation of these procedures over the entire surface opens it into a 'field': as well as being strongly objective, it seems to become active, filled with implied but indefinite and potential movement within its surface.

One way of doing this is by drawing freehand or by ruling a large number of more or less parallel lines right across the surface, vertically, horizontally, diagonally or in patterns, as in *Untitled* by Agnes Martin. You can vary and adjust the widths of the lines or spaces slightly, either so that the eye can scarcely detect them, or progressively enlarge and reduce them according to fairly obvious parameters, across the whole area.

All such sub-constructivist thinking combines shapes which are in some sense ready-made. They have the quality of objects. You do not actually invent the lines ruled in grids, the stripes, chevrons and so on. You may make your own versions of them; but what you contribute is the arrangement. In it you may discover forms of diagrammatic order, which go far beyond the usual conventionality of the diagram. Different kinds of grouping can play a part. So, too, can arrangements that may not seem schematic, but draw out proportional possibilities in the elements you are putting together. You may also set up sets of rhythmic relationships amongst the edges, widths, lengths and spacing of elements that you can repeat either strictly or according to progressive patterns. You may set up sequences of angular progression, or increasing and decreasing widths and densities of tone. You may even develop sets of concentric or interlocking diagrams which produce quite a strong sense of movement among the components, as in this image by Viktor Vasarely.

89 Viktor Vasarely: grid design (1959) incorporating progressive variations.

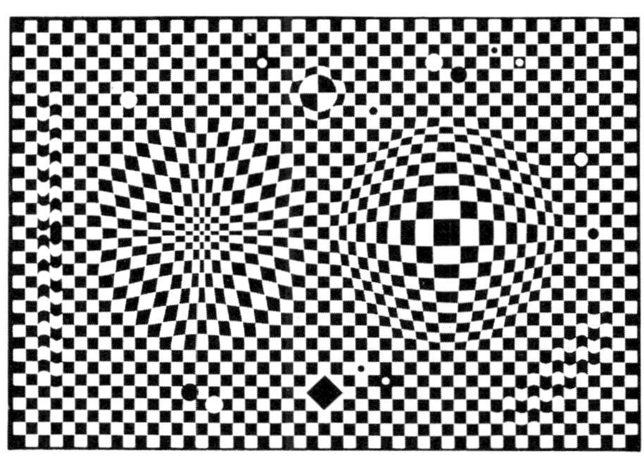

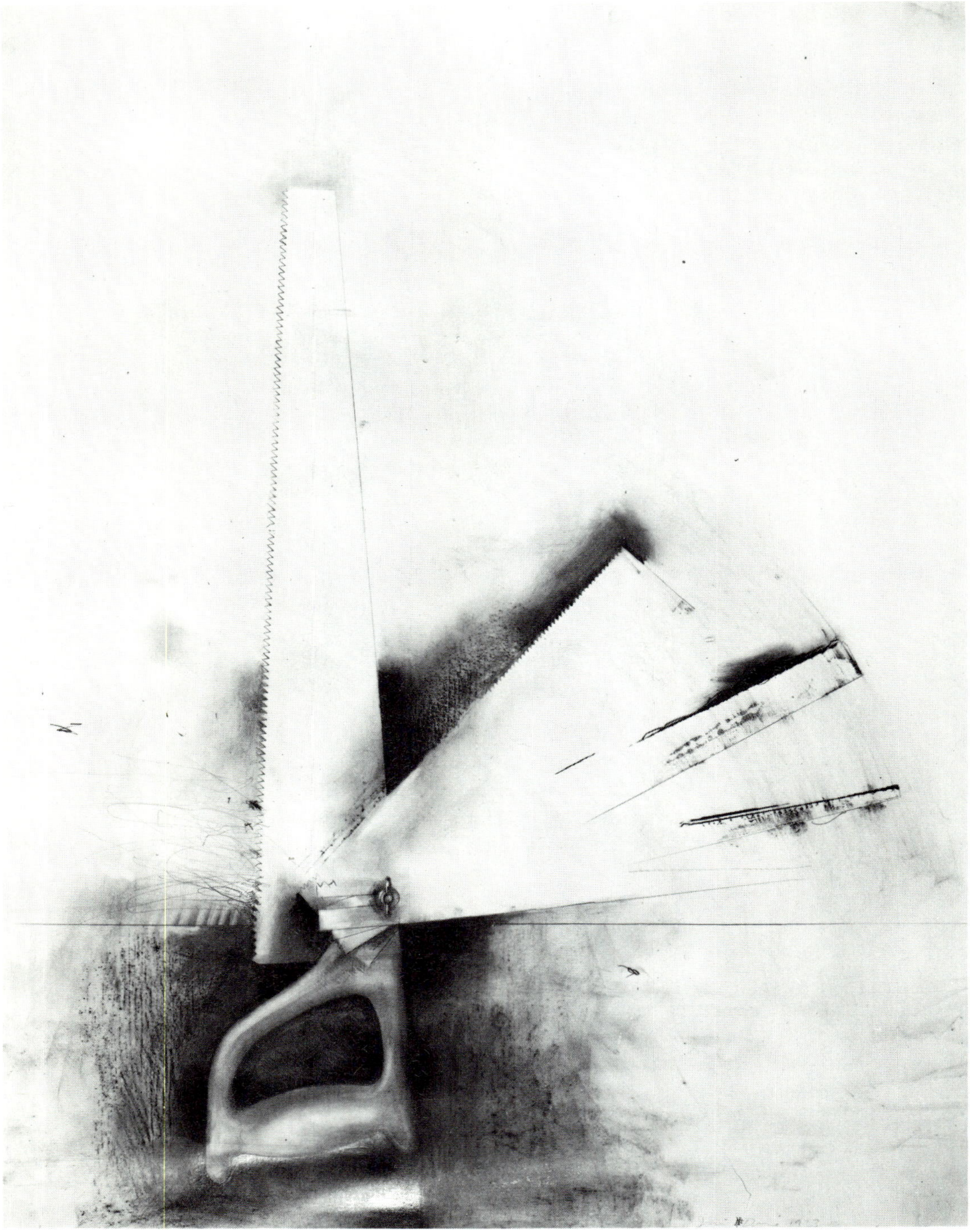

90 Jim Dine: 'Five-Bladed Saw', 1973; large charcoal and graphite drawing. For all its apparent realism, this drawing is not meant to tell you simple facts about an object. No representational art does that. Nor should you respond to it as to a functional object. It is as much a pure image as is Maillol's nude (pl. 133).

IV

Representation and the Third Dimension

We shall now discuss and put into practice the elements of convention and recognition, exploring how different shapes have meanings and contain references to the visible world. We shall discuss the process of scanning the world of objects and begin drawing from the object. We shall practise the various graphic methods for introducing a sense of the third dimension and volume into individual figures and objects, and into groupings of objects.

Section 22
Recognition and Figuration

When you look around yourself in everyday life, you automatically try to identify people and things. This involves making *sense* out of them. Is this smiling person friendly? Is that motorbike stationary or approaching, perhaps at a dangerous speed? Such recognitions are guides to action. According to what the clues suggest, you respond by saying 'Hi!' or jumping for the sidewalk. Your memory is full of the recognitions that have helped you all your life to understand what was going on: all those twitches of the hands, body-postures, sprays of kicked-up dust, and shapes of movement. You have scanned flaking paint and moving water, assessed bulk and distance. Your mind probably also files the feeling-qualities of those experiences. It is the visual material in this bank of memory-traces that art seems to activate. We studied earlier how drawn shapes connect with feeling and memory in a general way. Now we need to look into why and how those shapes can be figurative.

Even 'abstract' art has to refer to *something*, if it is to have any meaning at all. But true figuration has another function and can give your work a special kind of conviction. It connects the different levels of your experience, the conscious world of everyday life and sensuous experience of solid things, with the traces of those other kinds of real experience submerged in your memory.

We must never forget that drawing cannot actually copy the world of things. By far the greatest proportion of the world's figurative drawings are done from the artist's imagination. Drawing states relationships between parts of its paper and its marks and only from these can a viewer infer any 'presence' of things. When you draw figuratively you are illustrating your thoughts about things. To do that you need to keep your creative imagination alive, which can be quite difficult in the presence of the almost infinite wealth of reality. Delacroix said that nature was the artist's dictionary. Nobody creates by just copying out a dictionary. The artist uses nature to stock his mind and imagination ready for the positive work of creating.

You do this by setting down a series of basic units of graphic sense, and linking them together. Each unit gets its meaning in the same way as lines do, from the memory traces it awakens in the viewer of similar shapes met before

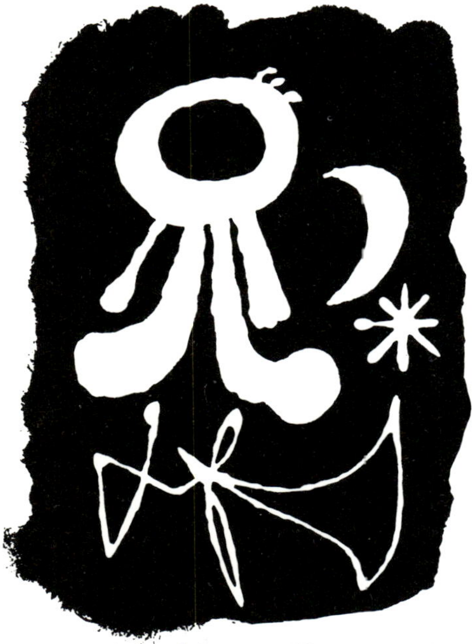

91 Joan Miró: brush drawing. We recognize signs for figure, moon and star, and a sign indicating some kind of movement.
92 Rembrandt van Rijn: 'Woman and Child'.

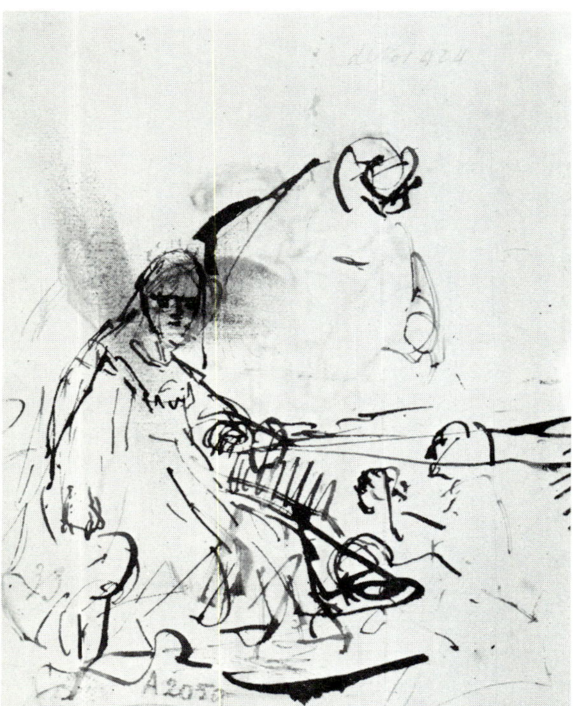

either in life or art. The collection of those memory traces adds up to a 'field of reference' for each of the component forms.

This kind of unified and meaningful shape we call a 'glyph' (part of the term 'hieroglyph', which means 'sacred sign'). Glyphs are fundamental units of expression in all graphic and pictorial art; they are emphatically *not* standardized units. Lines can amount to glyphs; but so can areas of tone or scribble. Artists can go on inventing fresh glyphs all their lives; and a good artist is able to shape strong and varied ones. Illustrated here is a good example by Rembrandt, which really challenges recognition.

Making a drawing means putting together glyphs that you and other people recognize as referring symbolically to some kind of objects in some kind of space. As people read the glyphs their minds fill with echoes of their own experiences. You do not need to compare a drawn image with any actual things it depicts to understand what it means. You simply recognize what it is saying.

One of the best keys to understanding how recognition works in figurative art is the Chinese game of Tangrams. You take a square piece of paper or card and cut it up into a set of varied standard shapes. You can arrange these shapes into all sorts of different images but you never add extra bits. Thus in each image the component pieces retain a natural coherence, however they may be arranged. None of the separate pieces actually looks very like the object or the part of an object it is supposed to represent. It does not describe detail. But you recognize what it is intended to 'be' the moment you latch on to the whole image. This tells you, for example, that the little curved piece must stand for the moon; so you accept it as a valid representation. The same with all the other shapes, and you accept empty paper as a stretch of water. Try making a set of shapes for yourself and see what familiar images you can build up with them.

There is one important difference between real art and Tangrams. As an artist you *can* modify your shapes as you arrange them, working variations on them for the sake of both expression

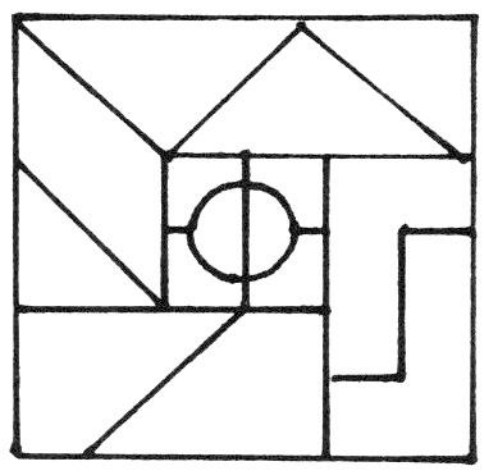

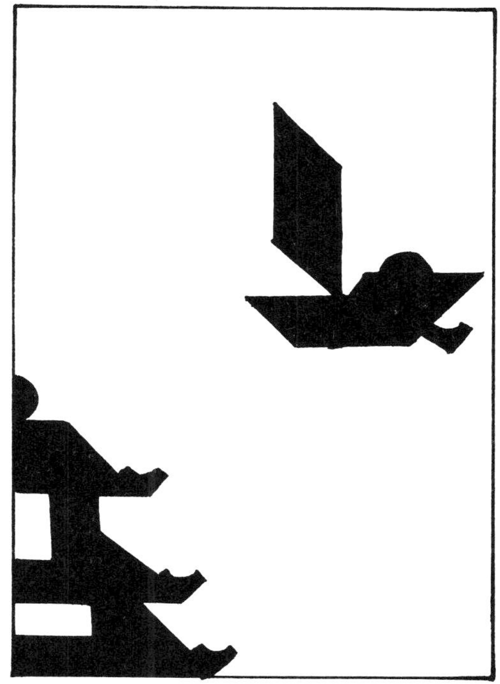

93 Chinese Tangrams, made up of pieces cut from a square sheet as shown top left. The same pieces stand for different objects at different distances in space, according to the context in each design. From a Chinese nineteenth-century woodcut Tangram book.

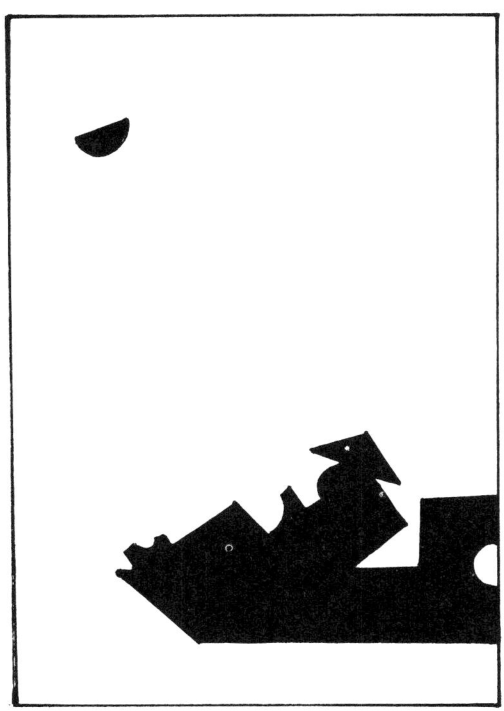

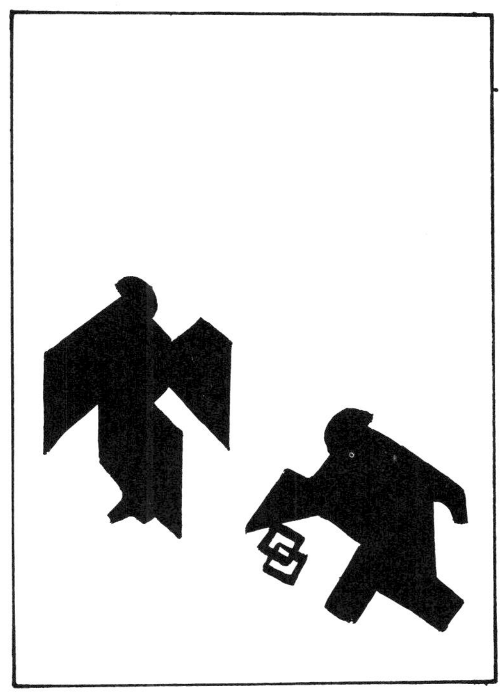

and coherence. You also use glyphs which may be far more complicated than the Tangram pieces.

Every artist uses his own repertoire of distinctive glyphs. Your drawing will develop its own set which will include lines, rhythms, positive and negative enclosures, groups and tone-patches, all connected and related. Generally speaking, the stronger and more clearly distinct the glyphs, the better the art. When drawing becomes sophisticated and imitative, it can lose its clarity and coherence.

When you put your glyphs together properly you give to each one a context of other glyphs. You know how easy it is to see faces in the patches on a stained and flaking wall, animals in clouds and pictures in a fire. You recognize images in these circumstances because some overall pattern appears. One patch like a nose, say, runs down towards another like a mouth; which means that the blob beside the nose must be an eye.

When you look at drawings your mind looks for such analogical connections. But it goes beyond mere recognition of the overall image to pick up all the references it can out of the handling and the inner coherence of the drawing marks. You can even collage areas of frottage into a figurative image which the context will tell you should read as cloud, rocks, sky or clusters of houses. Max Ernst often did this.

Look again at the Rembrandt drawing of
2 *Cottages Beneath High Trees* in the Introduction. You will see that the individual ink-squiggles on the paper do not look at all like real objects in a real landscape. The whole thing is just marks on paper. When you read the marks the scratchy loops may not make you think only of trees. Other analogies may well appear: waves, for example, froth and fountains. These visual references work like poetic metaphors. But they are integrated firmly by the overall image. And they collaborate with the rhythmic spacings and the luminosity to give a strong atmosphere to the drawing. Only Rembrandt could have made us feel like that about a commonplace scene in the Dutch countryside.

For the whole point of figurative drawing is to produce marvellous forms and relationships out of
everyday materials. All lines convey expression 20
and so every drawing is bound to have its own 21
atmosphere. It can be warm, vigorous, harsh, violent, cold or neutral; or even a combination of feelings for which we have no words.

Look now at the Persian drawing that depicts 111
the legendary beauty, Queen Balq'is, the beloved 113
of King Solomon. Purely as a human type the lady follows the ideal conventional at that time. But the lines themselves, in their musical flow, convey an experience of beauty of a different order. That beauty attaches itself to the image of the woman.

The Japanese printmaster Utamaro creates expression in his drawings by elaborating nothing
but the lines, as in his *Lovers with Fan*. He relates 112
lines to edges – of faces, the folds of clothing and so on. These lines are open-ended. They do not close down into silhouettes; and they have no obligations at all to enclose volumes that connect together. They are rhythmically independent, and follow a careful and well-practised pacing of their own. They are what was expected of him in his society, which was interested in elegant gestures. He lays down different lines with different expressions in each part of the composition. As we connect a line with a part of the object, we call up memories from our own sensuous experiences of similar objects: of cloth folds drooping at the neck, say; or of the smoothness of a cheek or leg.

These are some of the ways in which figurative art uses contexts to bring into focus the possible meanings of the glyphs. The figurative image gives them unity and relevance to each other. Its qualities arise from one's own experiences that it summons up.

However, nowadays artists accept that there are different kinds and degrees of recognizable images. Your graphic components do not need to fit together so as to copy a scene observed at a single moment from a single point of view. Our true experience of the world includes different views of the same things seen at different times or in quick succession. We move around objects. They move around us. Their different aspects may suggest to us normally unconnected graphic shapes. We then need to find new ways of

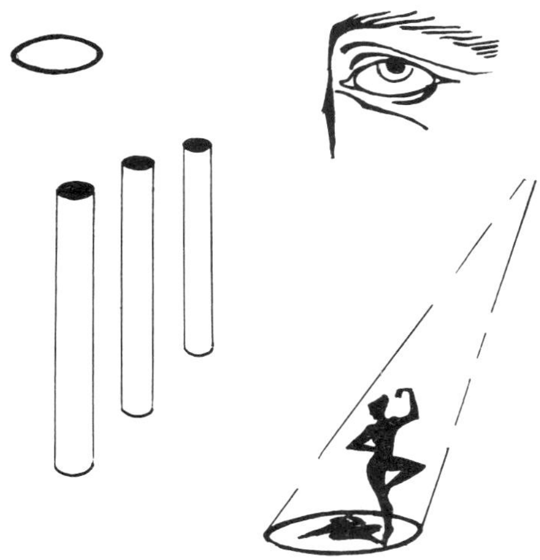

94 *The ellipse is interpreted as meaning different things in different contexts.*

integrating such graphic shapes, whilst still creating recognizable images. We can synthesize aspects of reality no one has ever seen before, or ever could see all together at once. Picasso is one artist who has explored intensively the possibilities of this kind of synthesis.

All this illustrates how the individual basic forms you draw with can change their meaning radically according to the way you combine them with other forms. Within obvious limits, almost any kind of shape can stand for all sorts of things. What matters is the context. The actual glyph 'disappears' into the whole image while you are reading it, but its clarity contributes to the strength of the image. No single glyph carries meaning by itself, except by pure convention.

Section 23
Chance

You can approach drawing and the image from two directions. You can either start by making disorganized but suggestive marks amongst which you try to discover some sort of coherent image, or you can start with conventional imagery which you then seek to give life to. Your choice of direction may be a matter of temperament, education and cultural pressure. Let us discuss the first approach.

It seems likely that during Palaeolithic times the human race began to produce recognizable images by making quite small alterations to natural objects. In big cave-complexes such as Pech-merle, for example, you can see where early hunters added a few scrapings of charcoal or coloured earth to a lump on the rock-face, turning it, say, into a mammoth. Nowadays artists quite often interpret natural objects in a similar way.

It has also long been a common artistic practice for artists to provide for themselves something to interpret, some patch or blob to stimulate their imagination and help them escape from routine thinking. They may do this by enlisting hazard in various ways.

Chinese artists were using *p'o mo*, 'splashed ink', in landscape painting by the eighth century AD. And for centuries afterwards Chinese painters used sometimes to blot in the first ideas for their landscapes or figures, either with ragged bunches of cloth or by blowing ink out of their mouths. Leonardo da Vinci recommended that an artist wanting to paint a landscape should gaze at the weathered irregularities of an old wall to stimulate his imagination to produce shapes. John Robert Cozens recommended his pupils to start imaginary landscapes by scattering random blots of ink on the paper, and then tease them out with a brush into images of hills and trees. All of these artists were aiming to make chance give variety and a sense of life to their overall recognition image.

During the last thirty years many artists have tried trailing and dripping blots and splashes, intending to find an image which does not suggest objects. They have devoted themselves to devising methods for producing chance results to give life and variety to their glyphs, and to help make each piece a reflection of a unique moment in time and space.

Jean Arp, for example, would let pieces of torn or cut paper float down on to his drawing surface,

and fix them where they fell. Other people have strewn things on to sticky surfaces; yet others have ridden bicycles or dragged nude girls smeared with pigment over their drawing sheets.

Any marks made by chance can be read as glyphs. The viewer will always tend to look for experiences with which to identify the glyphs. Some artists of course try very hard to prevent too obvious recognition. You can choose to develop your glyphs so that they evoke things with strange unexpected qualities – hauntingly ravaged human beings, for example, or tangled skeins of organic growth. Such an image may arise from the technique itself. Each new mark you add may contribute some suggestion to the whole.

Section 24

Sign and Conceptual Drawing

Another approach to the image takes the solid, tangible object for granted. The image starts as a minimal sign for a separate object.

Here we stand at the meeting place between drawing and writing. Three great cultures evolved written scripts around 3,000 BC: Egypt, Mesopotamia and the Indus Valley in India; and China maybe a bit later. All of these scripts appeared alongside, perhaps even as functions of, an art of ceramic decoration based on schematic drawing of animals, people, water, mountains and weather. The drawings may, of course, have been done on other materials as well; but pots and incised stones have survived best.

In writing, the signs gradually became fixed into an alphabet, and their original references to objects grew slighter. Few people bother now about what our letter forms once meant. However, you could do some research on this to inspire your work. Start by checking where our own capital letters came from. Then try and explore the

95 Jean Arp: 'Arrangement According to the Laws of Chance'. Collage with squares, stuck down where they fell.

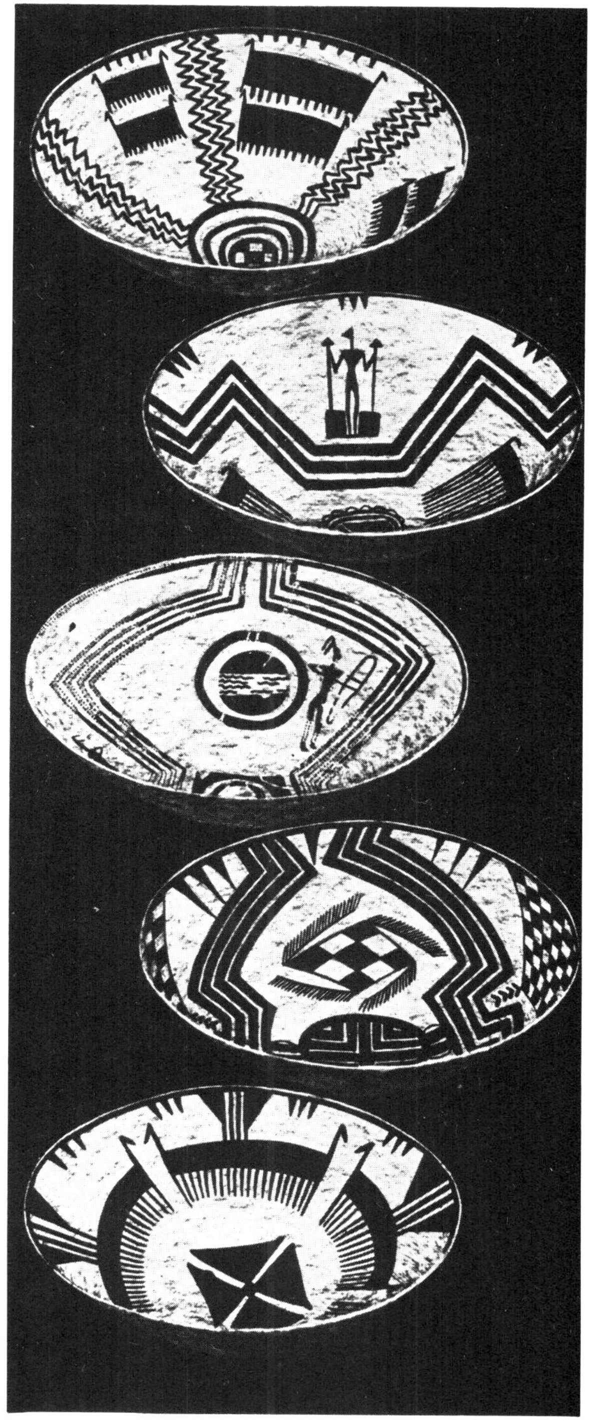

96 Pottery from Susa, c. 4000 BC, painted with signs for flocks, rivers, men and pool.

possibilities of developing and combining elements from writing for the sake of the significances hidden in them. For example:

A comes from the face of a bull
B from a house
N from water

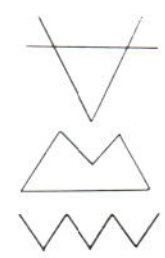

A very interesting way of exploring sign imagery is to take letters of the alphabet and turn them around, lie them on their backs, stretch one part or another, distort their shapes or break them up, to discover what ideas they suggest. Then combine 'stretched' forms of the letters into coherent designs over a whole sheet. You can apply all those different rhythmic and proportional methods we have discussed. Needless to say, you can also hide a verbal message of some kind in the letters you use. Letters and message together can increase each other's expressive power.

Another thing you can do is to employ basic elements of letters – straight strokes, loops, curves and angles – to make up your own signs: signs that do not only point at things, but say something extra about those things by their shapes. In *Lady Apart*, Klee makes his sign for a woman convey to us very subtle impressions of her character. Of course, such a sign can only get its meaning from the same sort of recognitions by analogy as any other drawing.

Another artist who used signs profusely was Picasso. In the course of his artistic life he developed a whole set of signs by which he could refer to human experience: signs for the profile of a suffering woman, the curve of a female flank, the spray of folds of cloth. These are by no means abstract. They are meant expressly to refer you to a wealth of real experience. Designs composed by putting them together are meant to put together not only the signs, but the meanings of the signs.

You can turn a large number of your own experiences into sign-language. To be understood you will always have to refer somehow to recognizable objects, even if the resemblance is minimal. Picasso's signs point both to specific objects – part of one of his girl-friends maybe – and to all *you* can imagine that thing can stand for in human experience. And all the characteristics of each sign, and the way it is assembled, mean something.

This little Egyptian drawing on a mummy bandage is composed of signs. One 'person' has a jackal's head; that means he stands for a god called Anubis. He is holding the hand of another 'person', making a particular gesture. This other 'person' stands for someone's soul. Because both pairs of feet point in one direction we naturally read that these 'people' are 'going' somewhere, one 'leading' the other. The place is the 'kingdom of the dead', indicated by a 'gateway'.

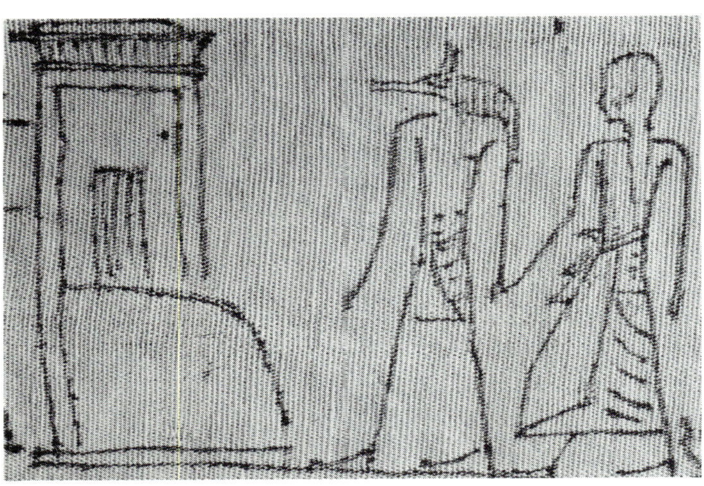

97 Mummy bandage, Egypt, 21st dynasty. Pen drawing of scenes in the after-life.

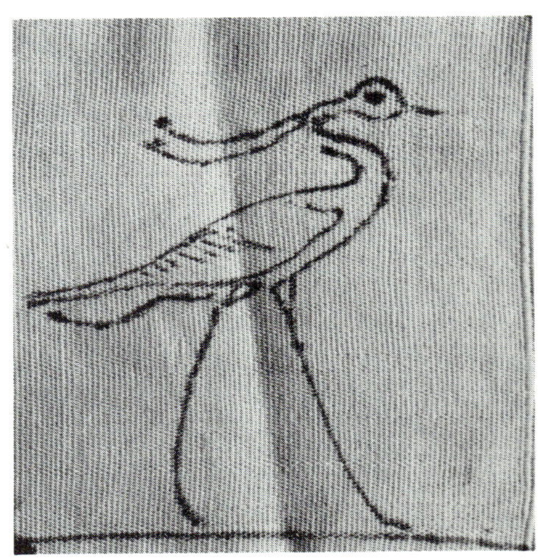

98 Paul Klee: 'Lady Apart', 1940; brush and ink. The thick paint has crinkled the fine paper.

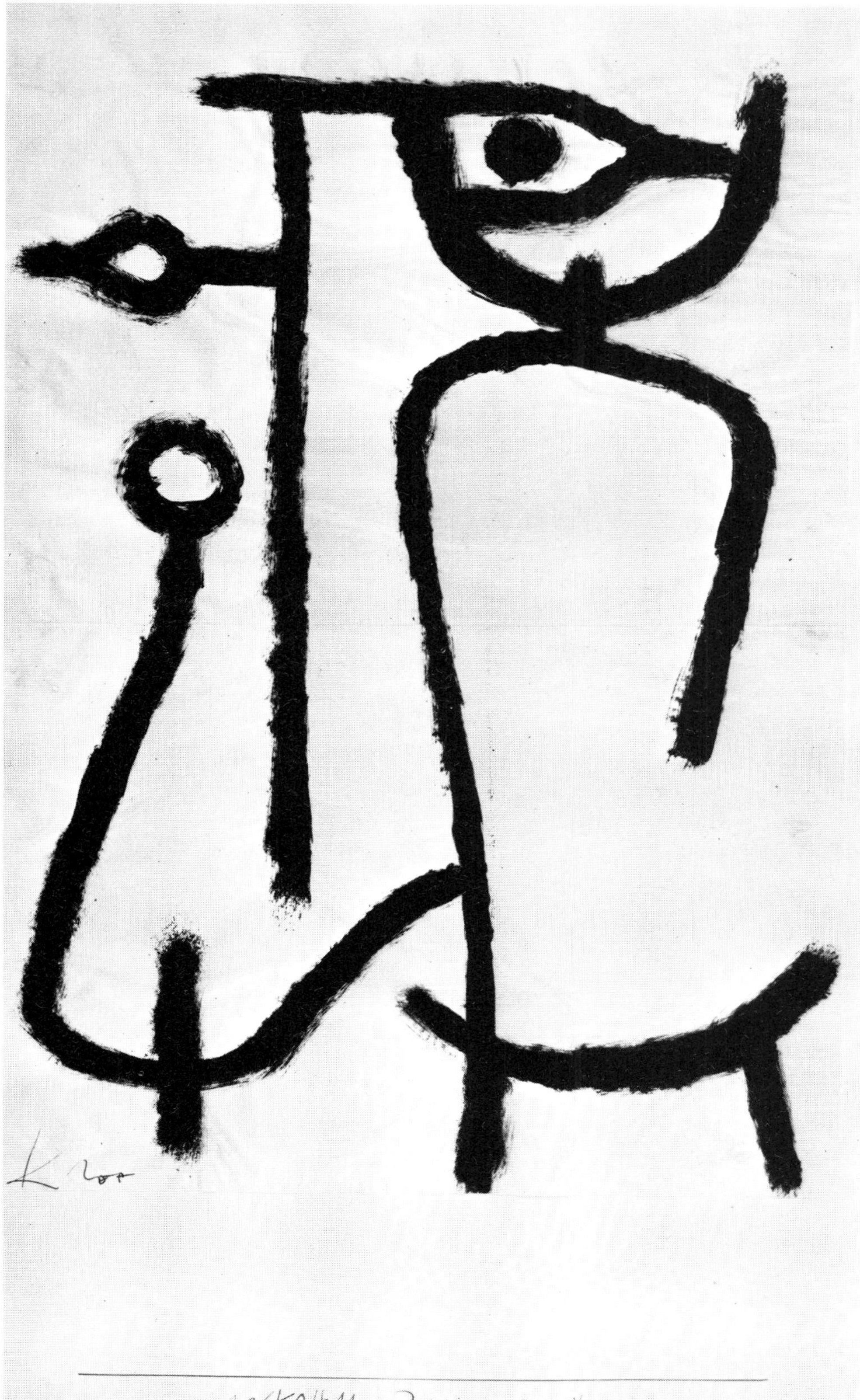
Klee
Dame abseits

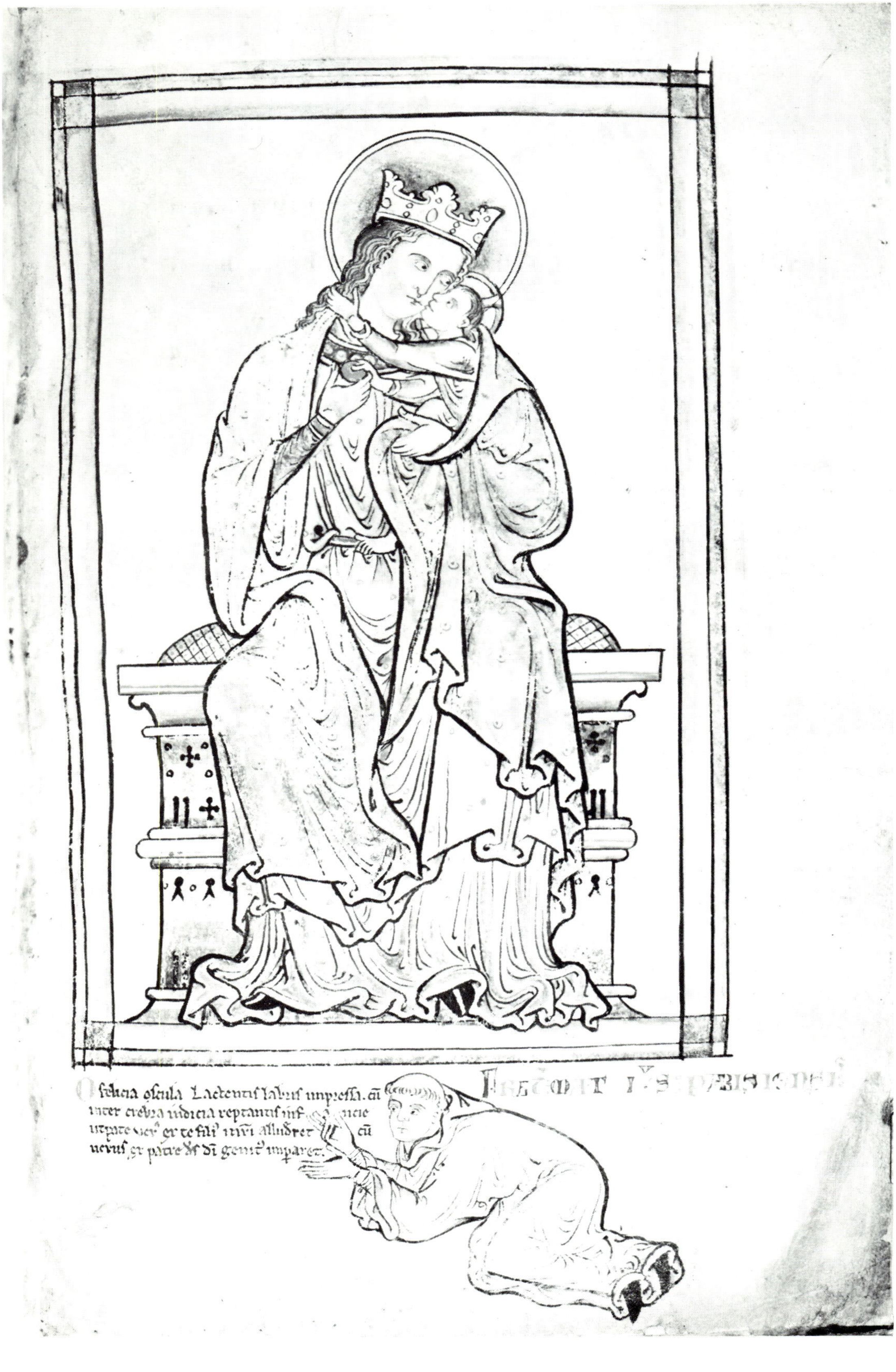
O felicia oscula lactentis labiis impressa. cū
inter crebra indicia reptantis inf
ut patre ver⁹ et te fili⁹ mihi alluderet cū
verus et patre dē di genit⁹ imparet.

There is not a very big gap between this kind of artistic sign and the glyphs we have discussed already. The difference is mostly a matter of convention. Standard sign languages usually depend upon the reader already having some familiarity with how the signs work. If you invent your own artistic sign language your viewers may need help to get the message.

There are, however, some twentieth-century artists who have taken great pleasure in actually obscuring the meanings of their invented signs under layers of allusion – to slang, jokes and philosophy. Marchel Duchamp is one. He assembled shapes abstracted from his own drawings along with scraps of text, or even with accumulations of fluff. Such signs can only work if you know how to track down the meanings of the allusion.

The gap between the sign and the true glyph is filled by what is often called 'conceptual drawing'. In this you extend the components of the sign towards glyphs. You bring the relationships between the components of recognizable objects into a closer correspondence with visible fact. But the relationships between the objects depicted remain at the level of sign-reading, and close to the diagram (Section 20). Large means important; small means less important. You represent what you know, rather than what you see. If you want to show people inside a building, say, you may show them literally surrounded by the walls, maybe with no roof, or with the front wall missing. If you want to show someone on a journey you can draw a sign for the pathway of the journey, then draw a figure of the person in three places on it, perhaps doing three of the things he did on the journey. Comics use conceptual conventions a lot.

In the medieval drawing by Matthew Paris shown here, the Virgin and Child are drawn large. The artist, a monk, has shown himself small, placed crouching humbly at the feet of the Virgin as he offers her a manuscript he has written out. This expresses very clearly a relationship the artist asserts to be true. You read the meaning in a similar way to how you read the Egyptian image. But here the artist tells us far more about the appearance and feel of clothing and humanity than we learn from the schematic people in the Egyptian piece.

99 Matthew Paris: pen drawing of a monk dedicating his work to the Virgin and Christ child.

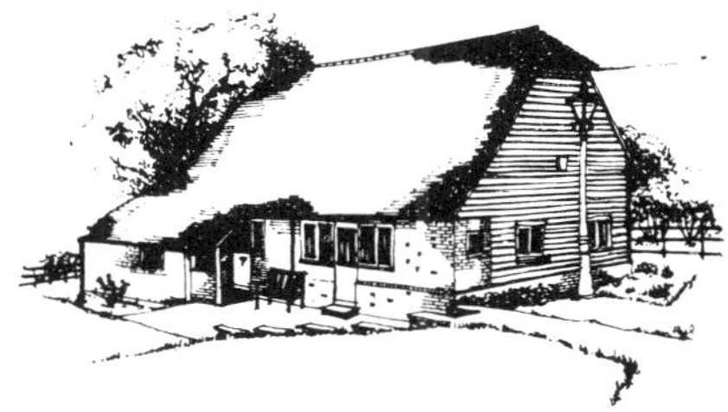

100 Drawing to advertise a house for sale, 1981.

Most of us draw conceptually when we are young. As we grow up we gradually learn to reconcile conceptual fact with appearance. But conceptual fact stated in the language of signs is the basis of even the most sophisticated drawing. Figurative drawing is always the art of illustrating relationships between thoughts by stating relationships between things.

There is a number of important uses for conceptual drawing in modern life. Some also incorporate drawing-systems developed for scientific and technical purposes. Generally speaking, they convey factual knowledge by means of simplified outlines. All you need to be able to recognize in such drawings are certain specific facts about what they depict. For example, the drawings in workshop maintenance manuals may show the order in which to reassemble the components on some shaft in an automobile, or which way round to fit the drive belt on a vacuum cleaner. Most architectural and design drawings are meant to show how a structure is to be assembled. If the structure itself is to be beautiful, the drawing may convey that recognition to someone who knows how to read a technical drawing. Some drawings are also meant to present buildings as attractive in graphic terms – for instance, drawings of new homes for sale in advertisements.

Some drawings by great masters focus on factual information. Poussin made drawings to note details of Roman clothing for use in his paintings. Ingres felt it was particularly important that likenesses in his portrait drawings should be correct. And in sixteenth- and seventeenth-century Europe members of royal families, who had never met, married each other partly on the strength of drawings done by their court artists.

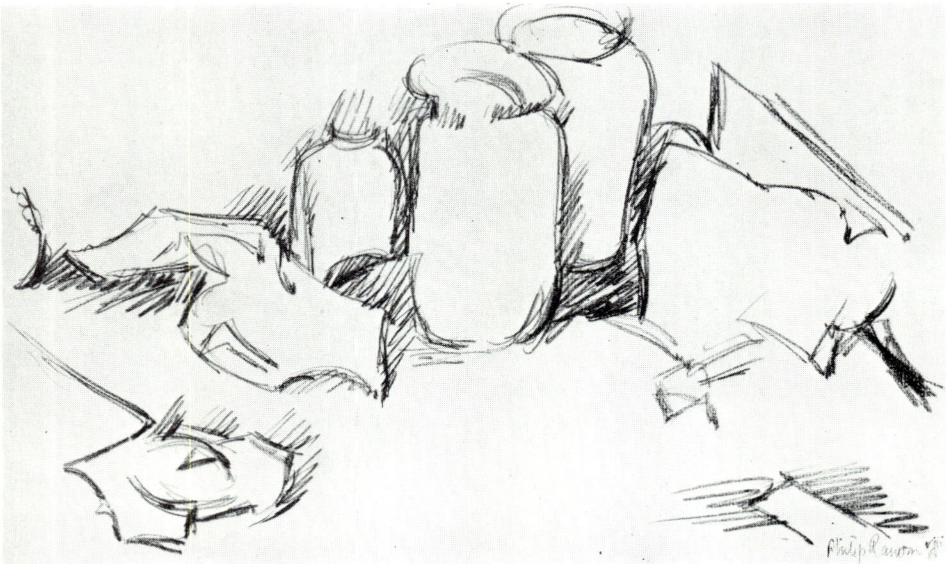

101 Still-life in chalk. This illustrates how the casual litter on a table top can provide material for drawing.

Section 25

Scanning and Basic Figuration

When we examine the external world we do not do it with a blank and motionless stare. Watch anyone who is interested in what is going on. Their eyes move constantly as they scan the events before them. Behind that scanning activity is a brain which is constantly at work matching up those scans with each other, and with previous scan patterns tucked away in its memory.

Recent physiological research suggests that the human eye has been adapted through evolution from an organ only sensitive to differences of tone. Where a sharp shift from one tone to another appears – which usually corresponds with a shift from one object to another – the brain identifies that tonal gradient as marking a major shift in the world. We also distinguish objects from each other because we experience each of them as a unit with a constant border that seems to move when we move. The associated alignments of tonal shift registered by our eyes may be what we illustrate artistically as black outlines.

As you read the rest of the book, you may like to have by you something to draw from, say a still-life with fruit, food and crocks on a table top, and try out the techniques. It is worth remembering that the way you arrange such subject matter can contribute to your image.

To get your drawing hand moving easily you can adapt basic scanning to do one of the simplest kinds of drawing: just lead a line along the edges of things in front of you, without considering any other factors. First, make sure that the size of your paper corresponds with the optical size of your subject image at your distance from it. You can check how they correspond by holding up your sheet of paper at arm's length in front of the subject, and then assessing how big you should draw it to fit the paper. It is easiest if they correspond pretty closely. Now lay your paper on a board on your lap; set your pencil to one side of the paper; then, starting at the equivalent point on your subject, run your eye along the edges and match the movements of your eye exactly with the movements of the tip of your pencil or pen over your paper: *without looking down!*

102 Edgar Degas: 'Ballet Dancer'; pencil on tinted paper. The figure gives a strong sense of surrounding space and of the floor.

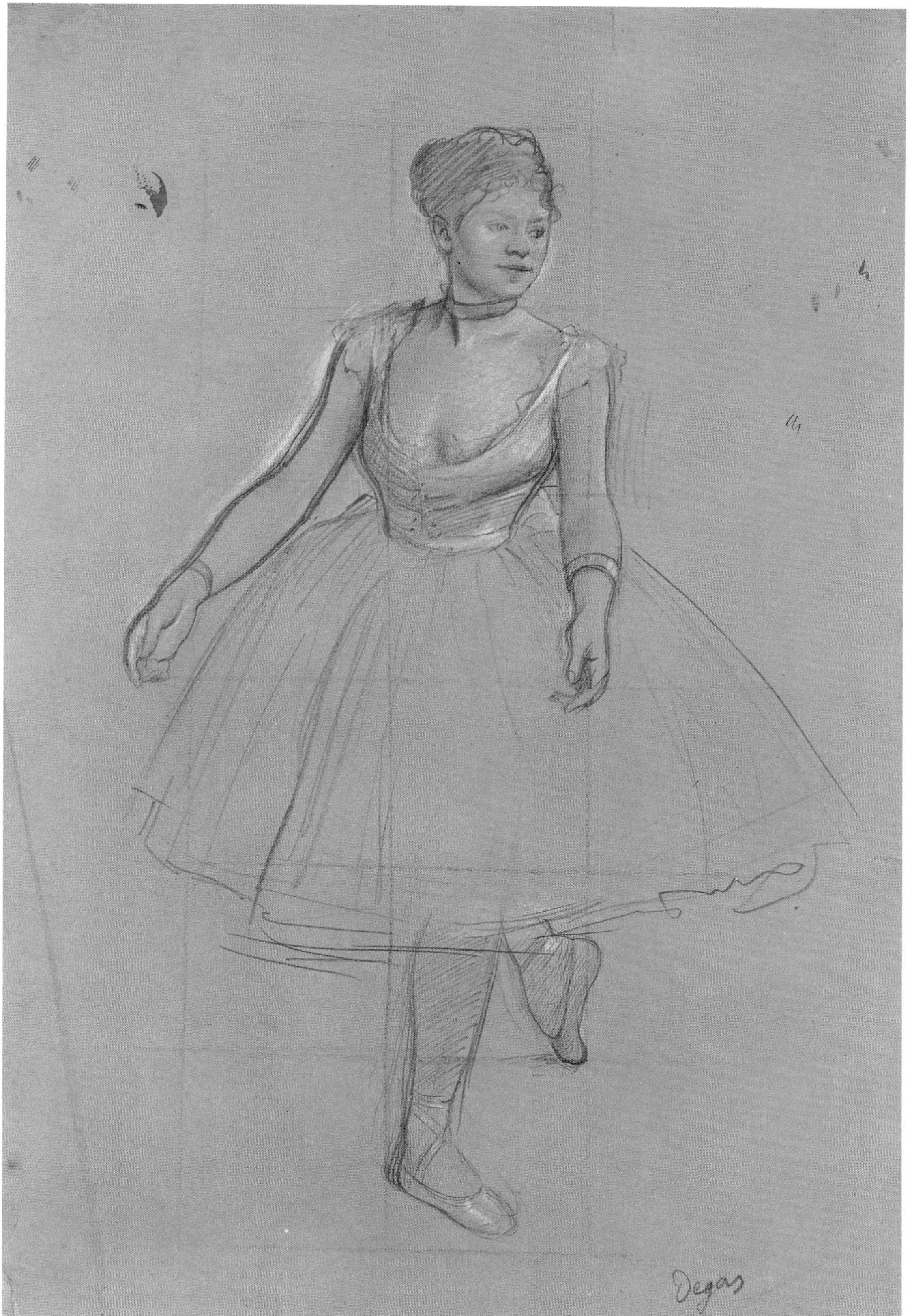
Degas

Be careful to keep your drawing point and your eye working together and not to let one run ahead of the other. This is most easily achieved if you keep your point on the paper the whole time. If you need to go back up an outline to start off in a new direction along a fresh sector, make your point travel back along with your eye. If you can, do all this without looking down at your paper. You may be able to get the feeling that you are actually stroking the surfaces of your object rather than the paper.

This is a particularly good way to introduce yourself to life drawing. It is, however, pretty basic figuration. You can get reasonable results very quickly but it is far from being the whole story: apart from anything else, it ties your image firmly into two dimensions.

The next stage is to allow your point to run not just along the edges of the objects, but all over them, wherever you can see any distinction of tone which can be linked up into continuous, unbroken movements. In this way you can begin linking shadow shapes into the whole. You can do this basic exercise in front of any object. It can be quite a good way of starting each drawing session.

Now study the drawings you have made, and check to see how well they incorporate the techniques we have studied in earlier sections. You may find that shaping and forming in terms of rhythm, lengths, directions, linkages and relationship to the format have been very difficult to preserve. If so, start tracking those edges again; but try now to introduce into your drawing those other methods.

When you feel confident about this, start breaking up the stretches of line you use. You can come to a stop where a line seems to end naturally. Then you can look down and start again by picking up from a line you have laid down already, rather as though your new line was a small branch taking off from a larger branch of a tree. This will help you to preserve a sense of organic unity in your drawing. Think quite hard about where to stop your lines and where to pick them up again. You may, for example, find it helpful to compose your main continuous lines from edges belonging to two or three things where they cross over each other. Then you can avoid just tracing vaguely undulating lines all the way around single objects; instead you can make your contour lines work as genuine shapes and vivid glyphs, which give qualities and character to the things we recognize that they enclose. 1

Section 26
Complex Scanning

The human mind, however, does not remain content with scanning at the basic level. Its complex image of three-dimensional reality derives from how we scan and understand a multitude of relations between objects and their setting. Our eyes hop, jump, measure and compare, from one side of the field to the other, and from near to far. We judge close projection against flatter distances, continuous against broken surfaces. We put together the evidence of senses other than visual: of reaching and touching, of walking into or around things, of hearing the resonance of spaces, of expecting and anticipating.

When you draw a figurative image, your marks work best if they arise naturally out of all your scanning procedures. To draw teaches you to connect up what you see far more intensely; and when you produce any drawn image you are inviting your spectators to follow your scanning patterns. You will want to make these as vivid and varied as possible; so it is best if you work from objects that genuinely stimulate your imagination. When you have a well-developed armoury of methods, even the humblest set of objects can offer you strong glyphs.

Here we come to a central problem in figurative drawing. We have seen how all drawings are composed out of units of sense – glyphs – which the artist combines to form images (Section 22). This means that figurative drawings need to be composed out of units that make graphic sense.

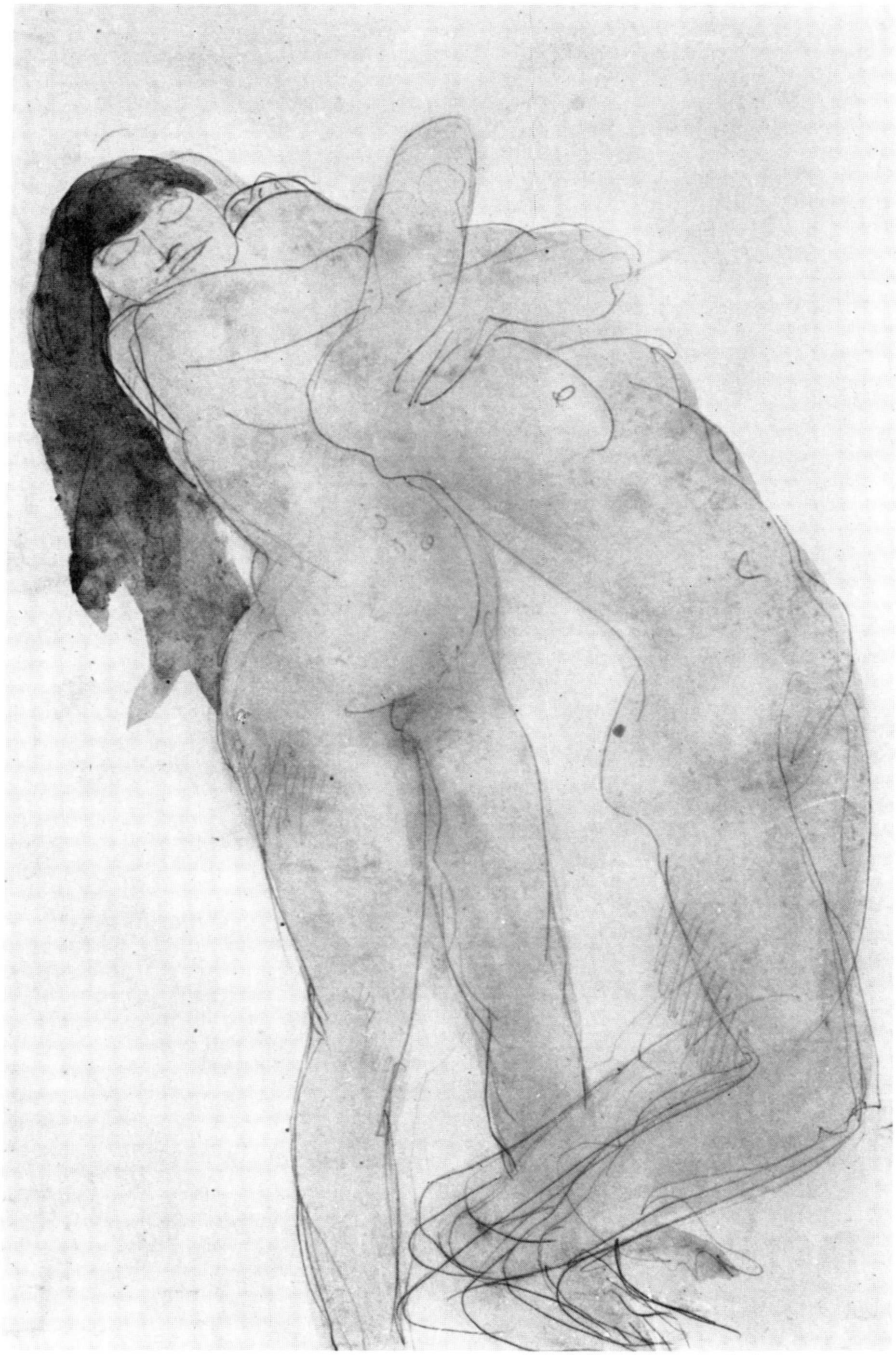

103 Auguste Rodin: 'Two Nudes', in pencil and wash, done swiftly from moving models in the studio.

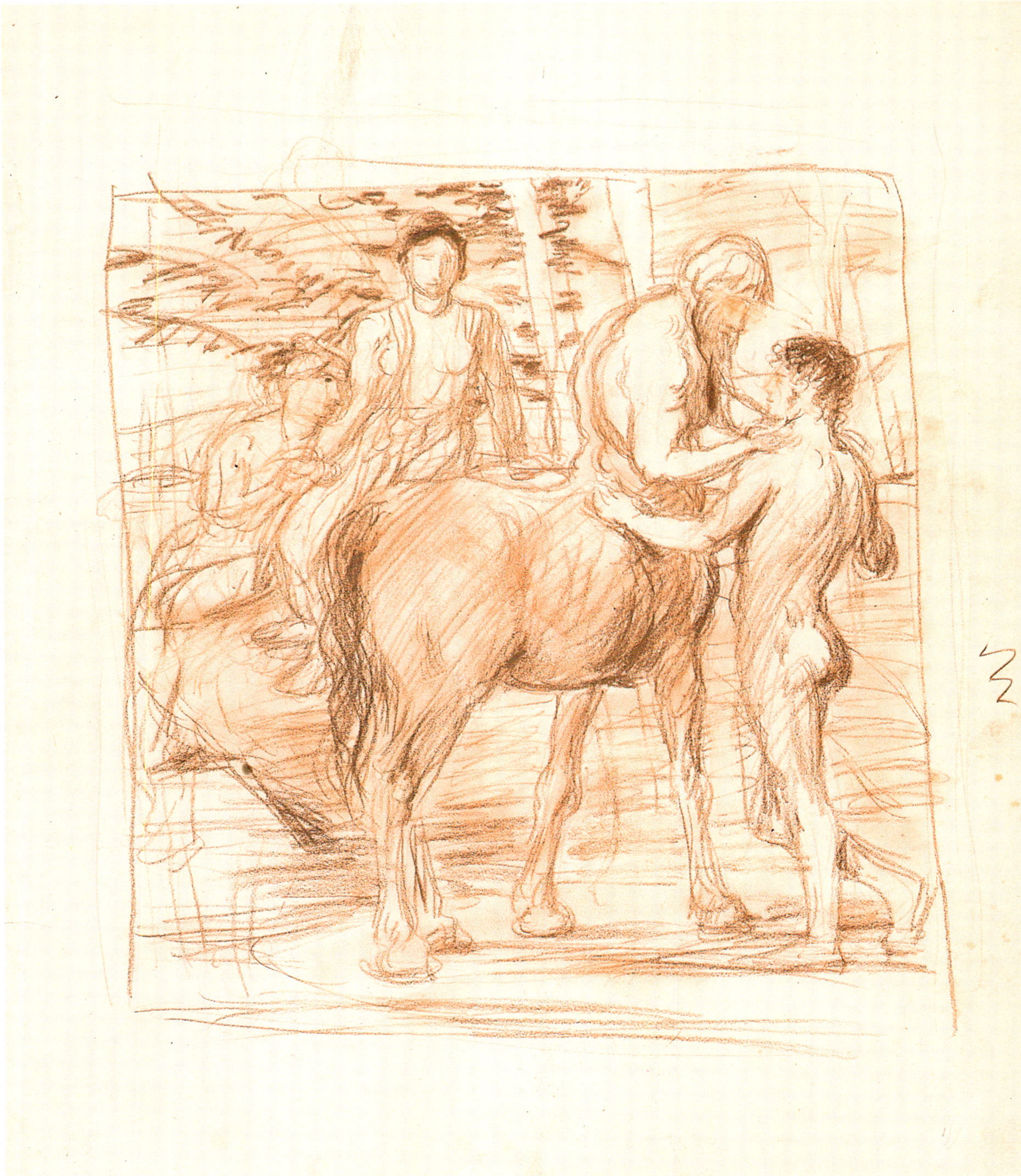

104 Hans von Marées: 'Cheiron and Achilles'; red chalk. A late drawing embodying a close encounter in the dialogue of its marks, tones and volumes. It illustrates beautifully how networks of glyphs can accumulate to produce an image whose emotional content reaches far beyond the significance of the sum of the individual marks.

105 Antoine Watteau: 'Head of a Man in a Turban'; red chalk. The shading which models the volumes of the face is laid on with a soft touch. The drawing shows how the imagination of a great artist can work with gentleness without sacrificing strength, and with elegance without sacrificing vigour.

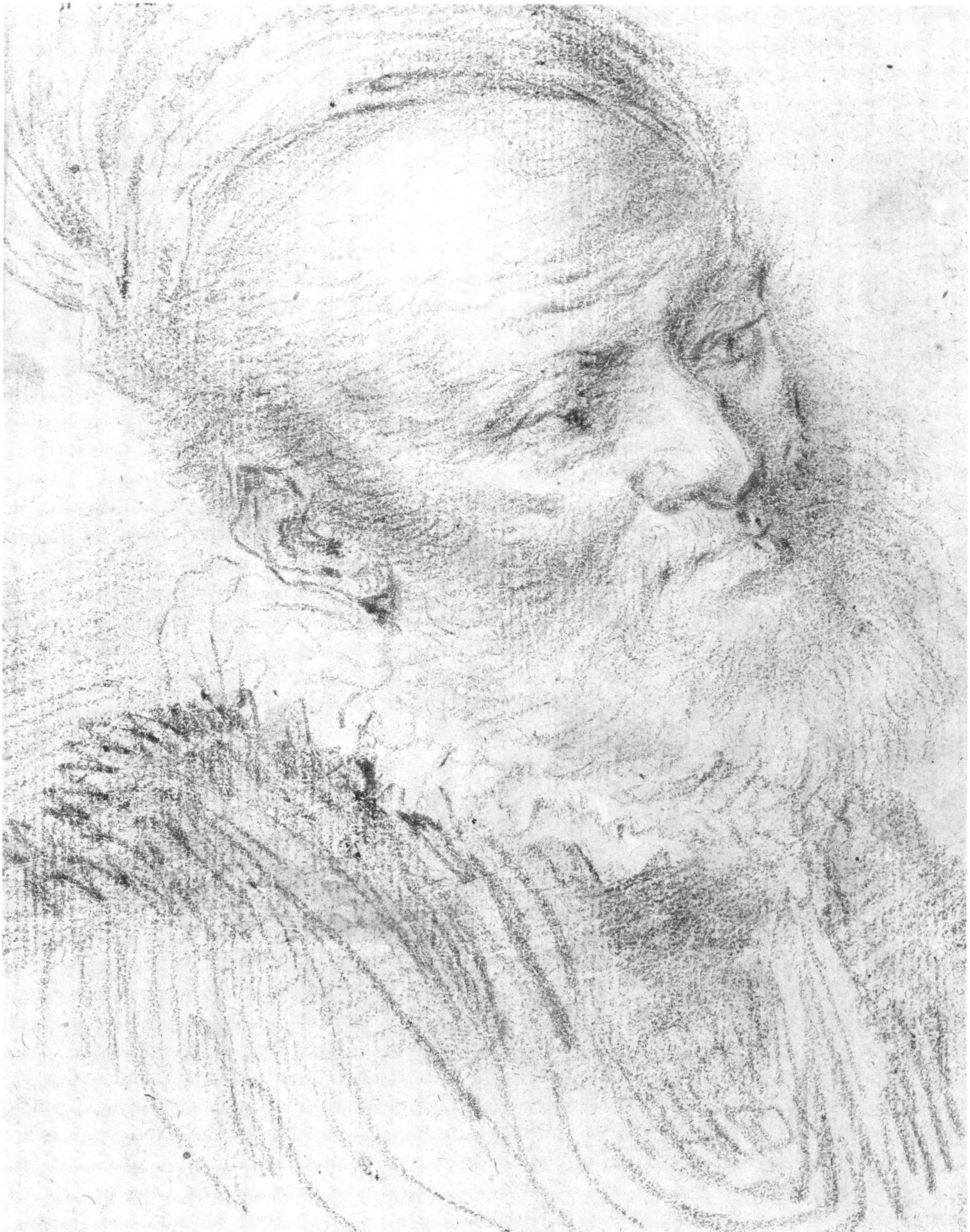

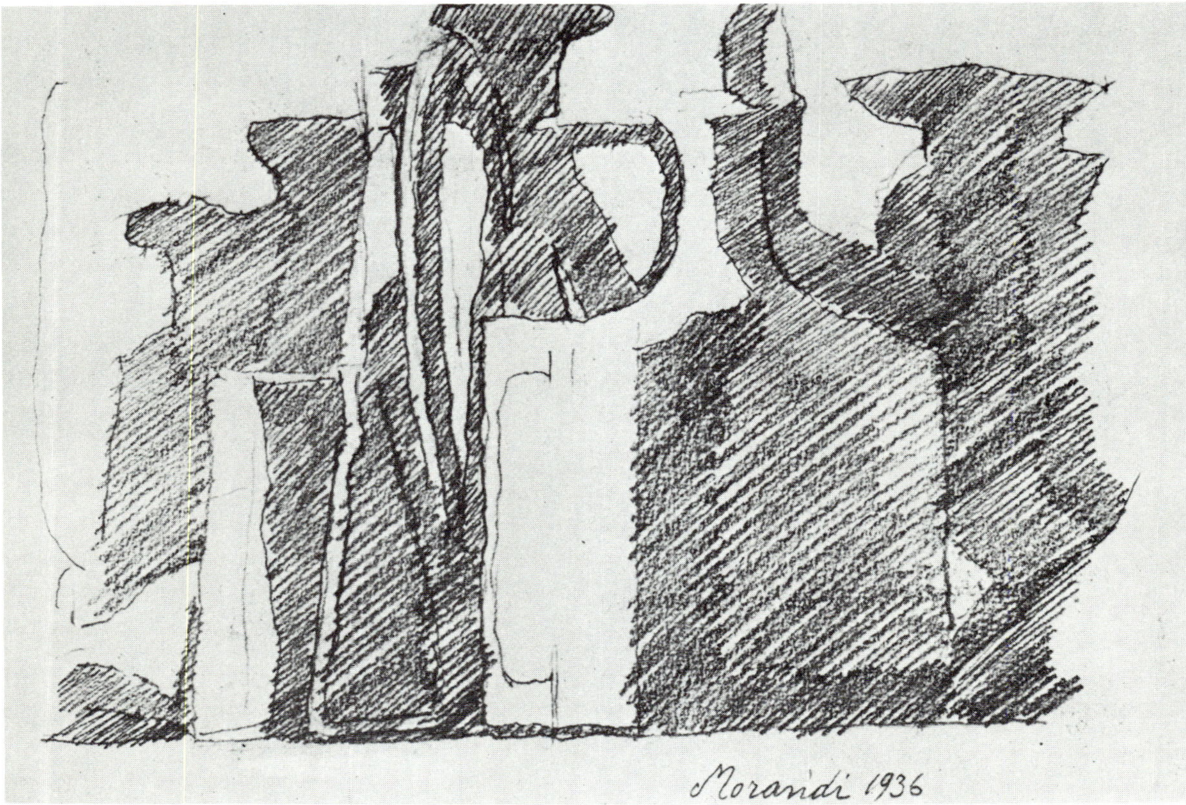

106 Giorgio Morandi: 'Still-Life' of bottles, here reduced to a few essential rhythms, negative spaces and hatched shadow-areas.

It is not enough that they refer merely to the separated things you can identify in words – 'bottle', 'mug', 'apple', and so on. Your task as an
101 artist is to find graphic units of shape – glyphs – which will evoke the presence and togetherness of things, which is reality. So a figurative drawing needs two aspects: the units of sense, clearly grasped; and the articulation of these units into an image by rhythmic placing. Look at this drawing by Lipchitz. You can easily pick out its units.

One of the simplest ways of getting your drawing to work this way is as follows. Think back to our discussion of the spaces between things (Section 14). Say you have three differently shaped bottles in front of you. If you concentrate only on outlining the shapes of the bottles, you will not be telling the viewer anything very interesting. The bottles are mass-produced; their shapes are standard. Even if you change your angle, you will just be repeating the same dull story. But if you draw the shapes *between* the bottles, between their edges, the edges of the table and the pattern on your tablecloth, and the rhythmic intervals between their 'feet' where they stand spaced off from each other, you will be beginning to say something interesting. There is no need whatsoever to 'complete' outlines in a drawing of this kind. It is better to stop if you cannot find a new glyph.

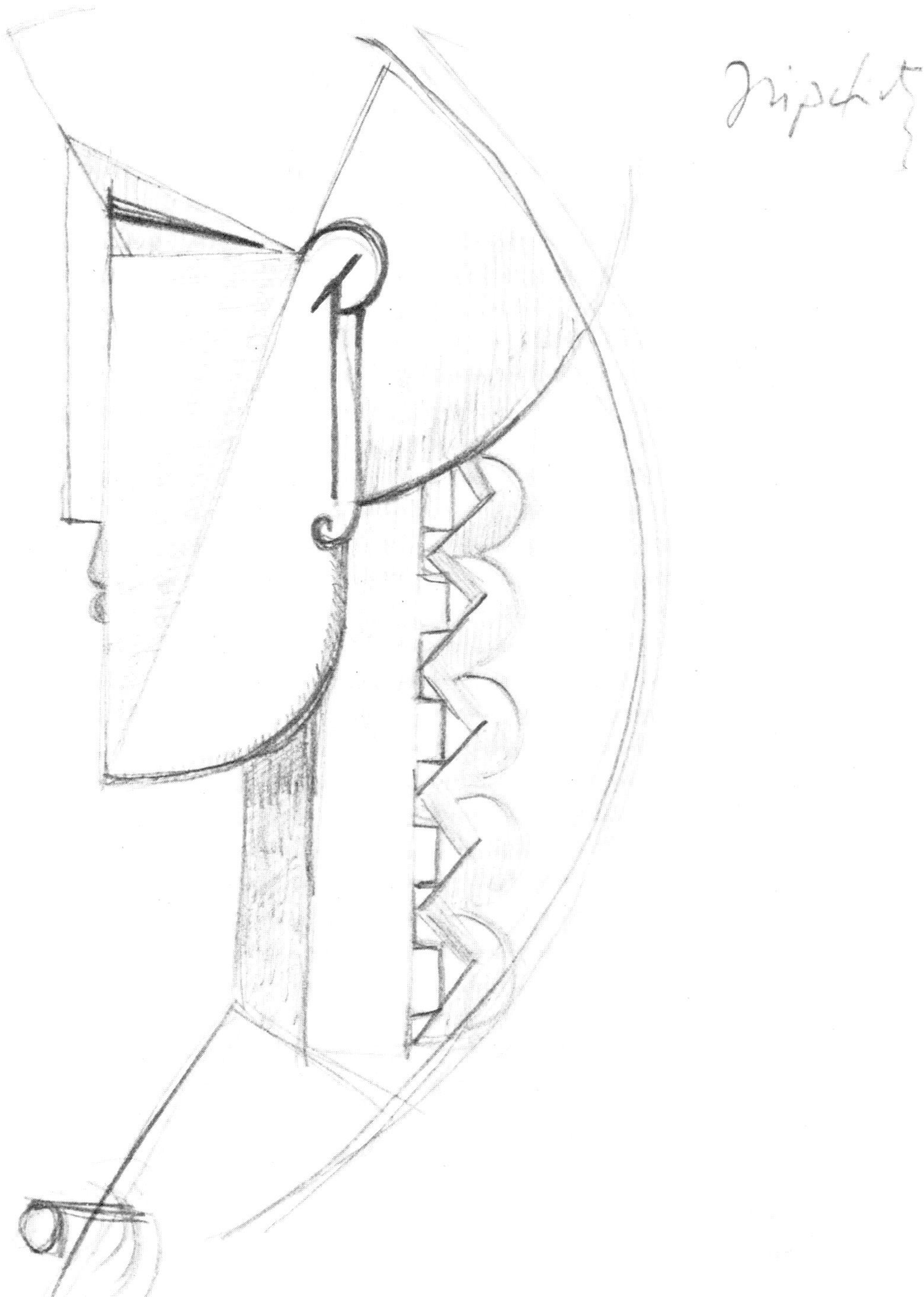

107 Jacques Lipchitz: 'Girl with Braided Hair', 1914; pencil. A sculptor's drawing, emphasizing geometrical relationships.

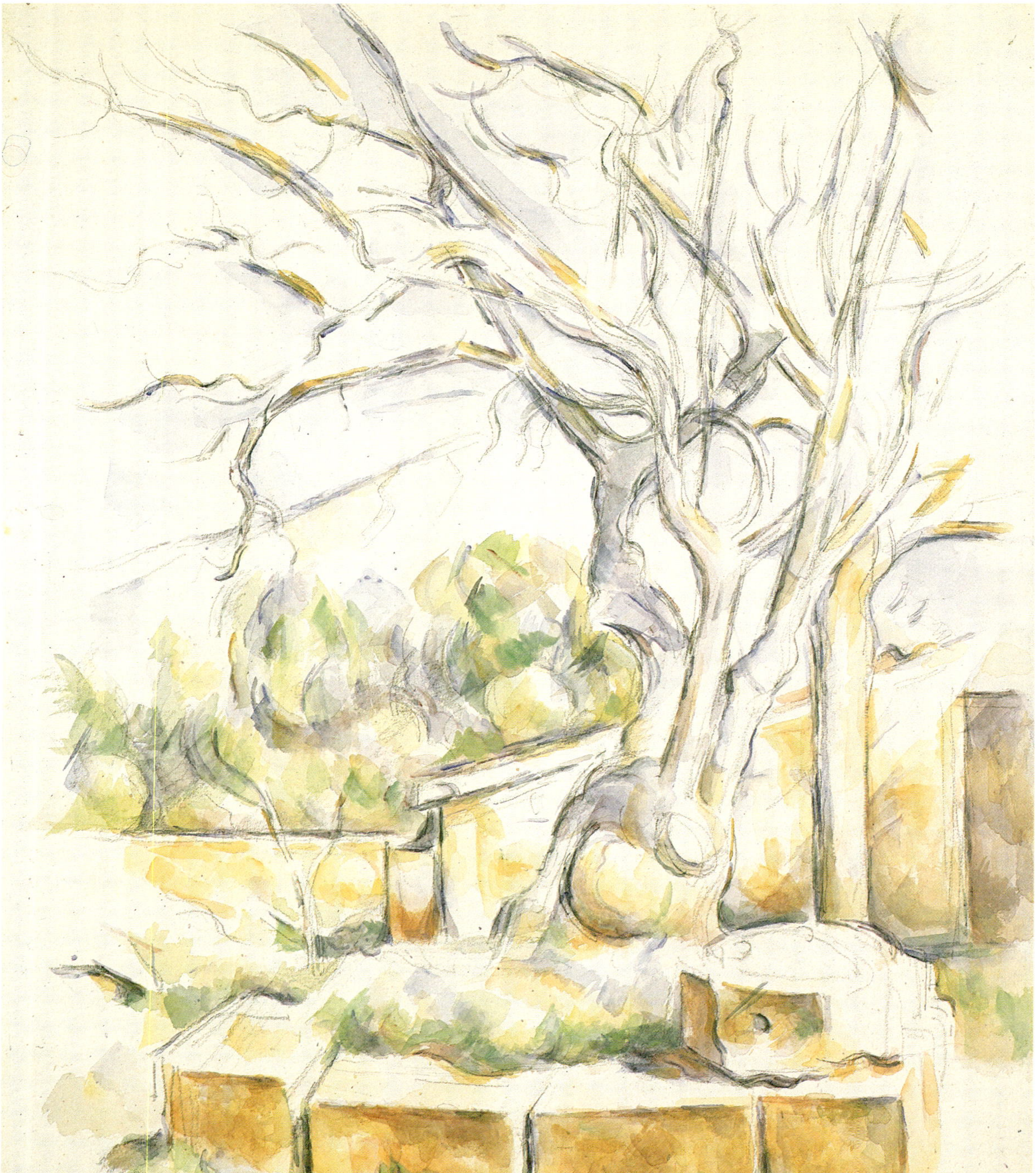

108 Paul Cézanne: 'Pistachio Tree in the Courtyard of Château Noir', c. 1900. The structure is based on sets of marks, rhythmically related to each other transversely, which are incorporated into paths of shadow. The units of mark are a constant size.

109 Claude Lorrain: 'Campagna Landscape'; pen and wash. The tower is the key element in reading the depths of the image and the quality of light. We can easily understand the bands of space through which we pass to reach the tower, and the dark silhouette emphasizes the brightness of the sky.

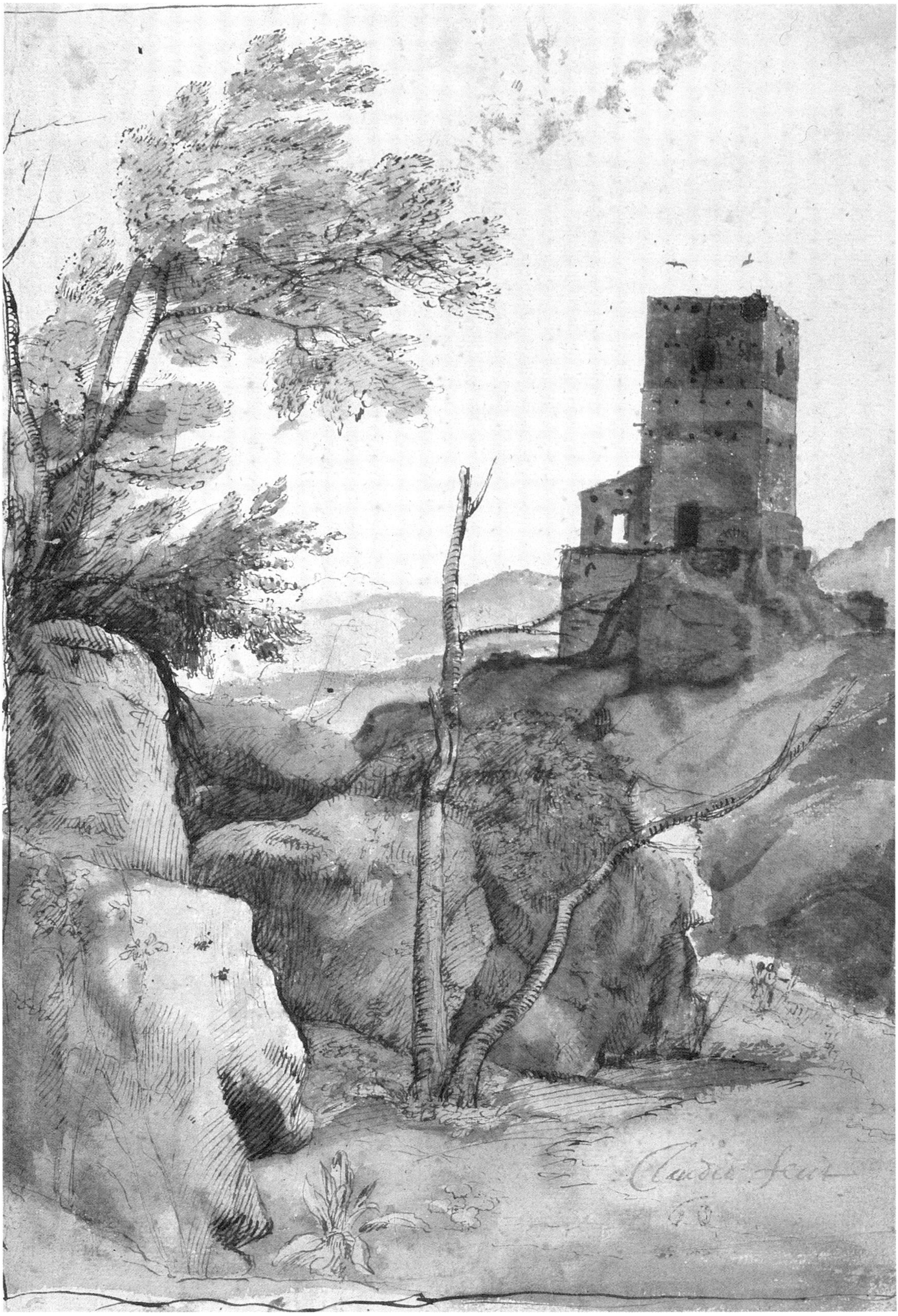
Claudio fecit

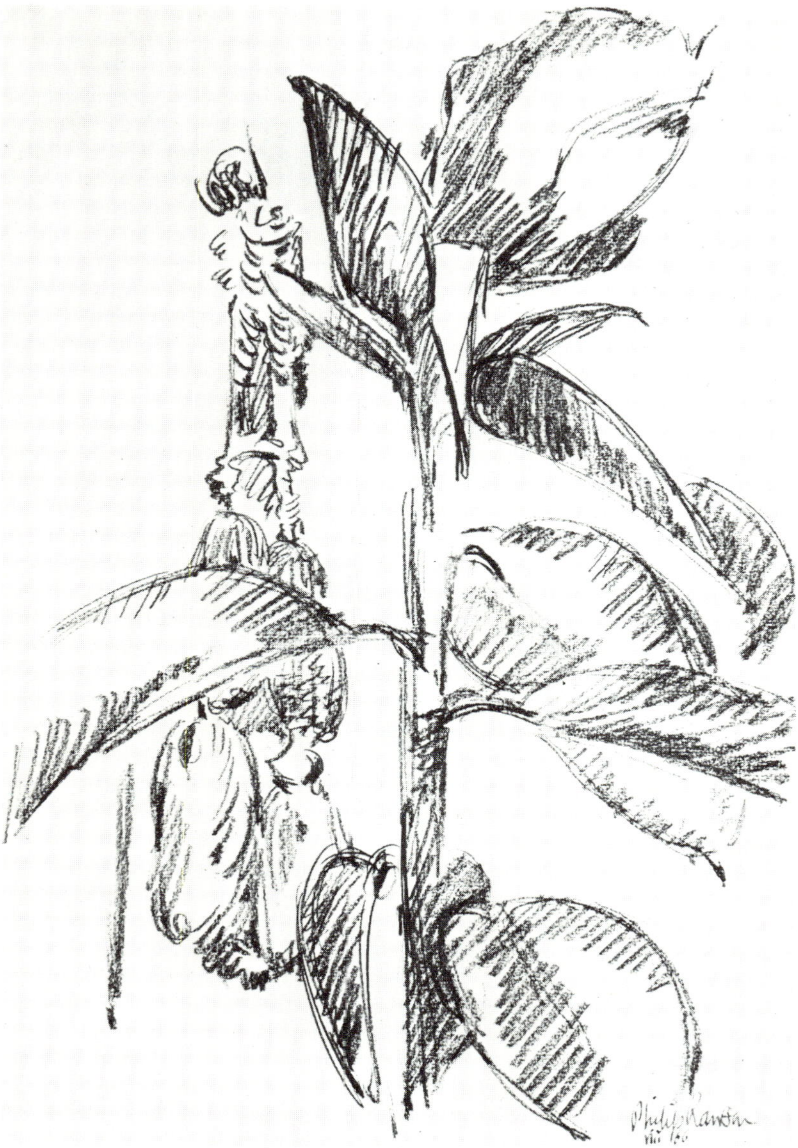

110 Rubber plant and hanging necklace, drawn in chalk. This combines the use of glyphs as tone, as components of rhythmic sequences and as definers of negative space. The same subject could show quite different forms when seen from a different viewpoint.

Every time you change your angle of drawing, you will find the subject offers you different shapes.

You can evolve your units using all the methods we have discussed so far. You must look for ways of deriving clear glyphs – lines, enclosures and so on – from the objects in front of you. Then you can pick out, condense and state genuine and interesting unit-shapes. They may be found in a mixture of shadow and edge; at the place where a pair of bulges meet; in a set of overlapping edges belonging to folds of cloth; in triangular enclosures around a knee in trousers. It does not matter in the least whether you are able to draw complete and lifelike things. When you can pick out your first clear, graphic shape, set it down, with all its individual character. Exaggerate it even. Then pick out and set down another one which connects up rhythmically with the first. Then the next; and the next. Arrange them on the paper so that they are all clearly related to each other *in purely graphic terms*. Do not worry at all about roughness, or drawing several alternative versions of the same line on top of each other.

Collage can help here too. You can draw each of your derived graphic shapes on a small piece of paper; then trim the paper down so that it is not much bigger than the drawn shape. When you have got a good set of shapes you can try out various arrangements for them on a base sheet. When you think you have got the image you want, stick the pieces down, and add maybe a few strokes. Check back to Section 22 at this point, to remind yourself about context. If you use charcoal you can rub out a whole section and redraw it in a better place. But, provided you draw only light strokes at first, it is best if you can actually leave these visible – because they were part of the act of drawing. If other strokes supersede them, this can show how your thoughts developed.

There are many ways in which lines and unit-glyphs can correspond with the three-dimensional aspect of the 'outside world'. They can:

1) stand for open-ended edges between things, as we have seen;
2) accumulate to define positive and/or negative enclosures which we identify as parts of the world;
3) state tone or shading;
4) define the shape and character of surfaces which mark out the picture space;
5) define the ridges or shed-lines between the facets of a crystal-like volume;
6) define the shapes of the places where surfaces intersect.

Some lines can do two of these things at once. Different artists use different combinations of these correspondences between lines and the world we know.

11 Many Oriental drawings tell your eye to follow
12 out sets of open-ended lines which are connected
only with the edges of things. You are meant to
make longish sweeping scans along the lines
before you start matching the lines up. Goya's
77 drawings lead you along brushstrokes into great
pools of shadow which you can only understand by halting now and then, and trying to understand what they are the shadows of. In both it is the rhythm and spacing between the elements listed above that make the paper surface 'become' the objects and their setting.

Now look at Rembrandt's *Cottages Beneath High Trees* in the Introduction. It is interesting because of the different kinds of scan-patterns it offers – looping outlines, rows of partial edges, transverse rhythmic jumps, measured smears implying both shadow and surface. None of us can possibly be expected to do drawings as good as Rembrandt's, but he can show us that the marks and lines in really good figurative work do not claim your attention and admiration for themselves. They move your attention away from the distant edges and somehow present you with the surfaces of objects that face towards you.

Section 27
The Third Dimension

Look at somebody close to you. Run your eye over their surfaces crosswise, from edge to edge. See how those surfaces undulate towards you from one edge, up towards the nearest point to you, then undulate back again until they disappear round towards the back. You know perfectly well that the surfaces continue behind the person even though you cannot see them.

As an exercise, try to draw a cross-section of one of those undulating surfaces. You could try looking down on the person to get a better idea of the cross-section at a given place. But you should end up able to draw such cross-sections by imagining them.

Draw these section outlines just as carefully and rhythmically as you would your non-figurative lines, shaping them by straights and curves, by a scale of directions, enclosure form, and so on (Sections 4, 8, 11–14). It is worth making a few section outlines in front of every object you draw. They will make you very aware of its three-dimensional quality.

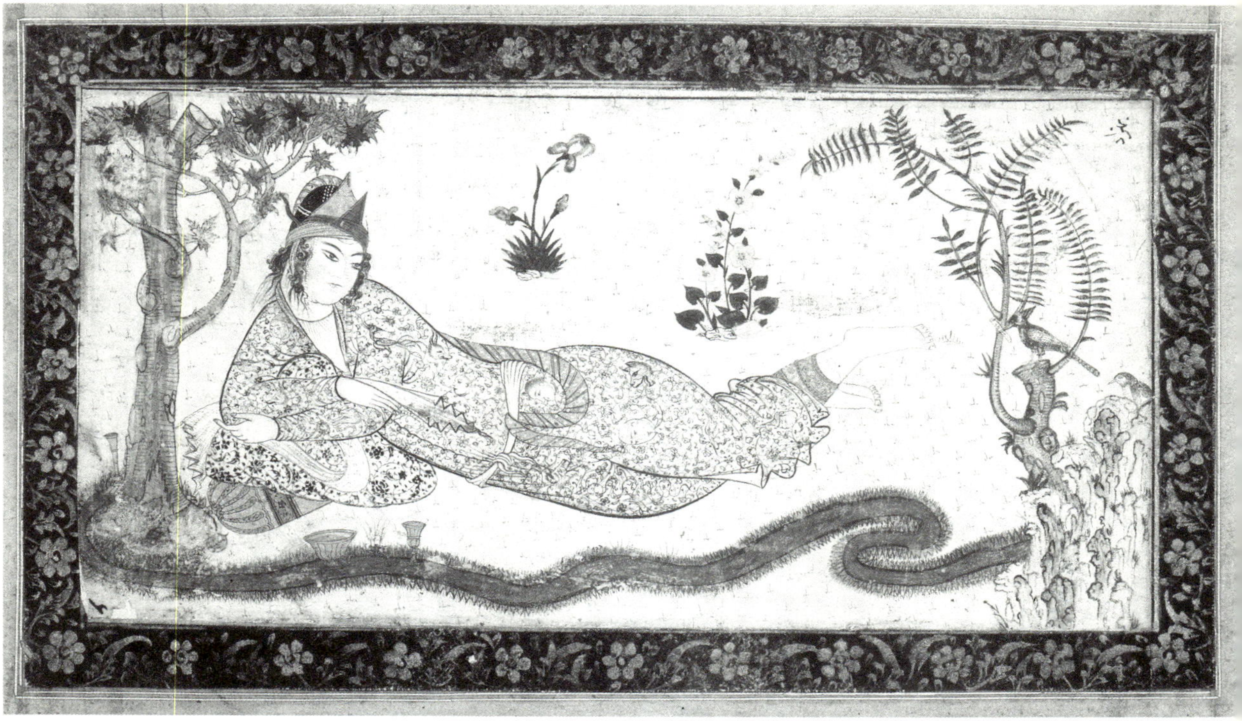

111, 113 Unknown Persian artist: 'Balq'is, Queen of Sheba', c. 1590; pen and brush. She is receiving messages of love from King Solomon. The formal and fluid calligraphic beauty of the lines express the beauty of the legendary queen.

112 Utamaro: 'Reclining Lovers with Fan'; woodblock colour print. The lines running along edges link up into a web of implied movements. The drawings show how styles based on linear calligraphy can produce different effects.

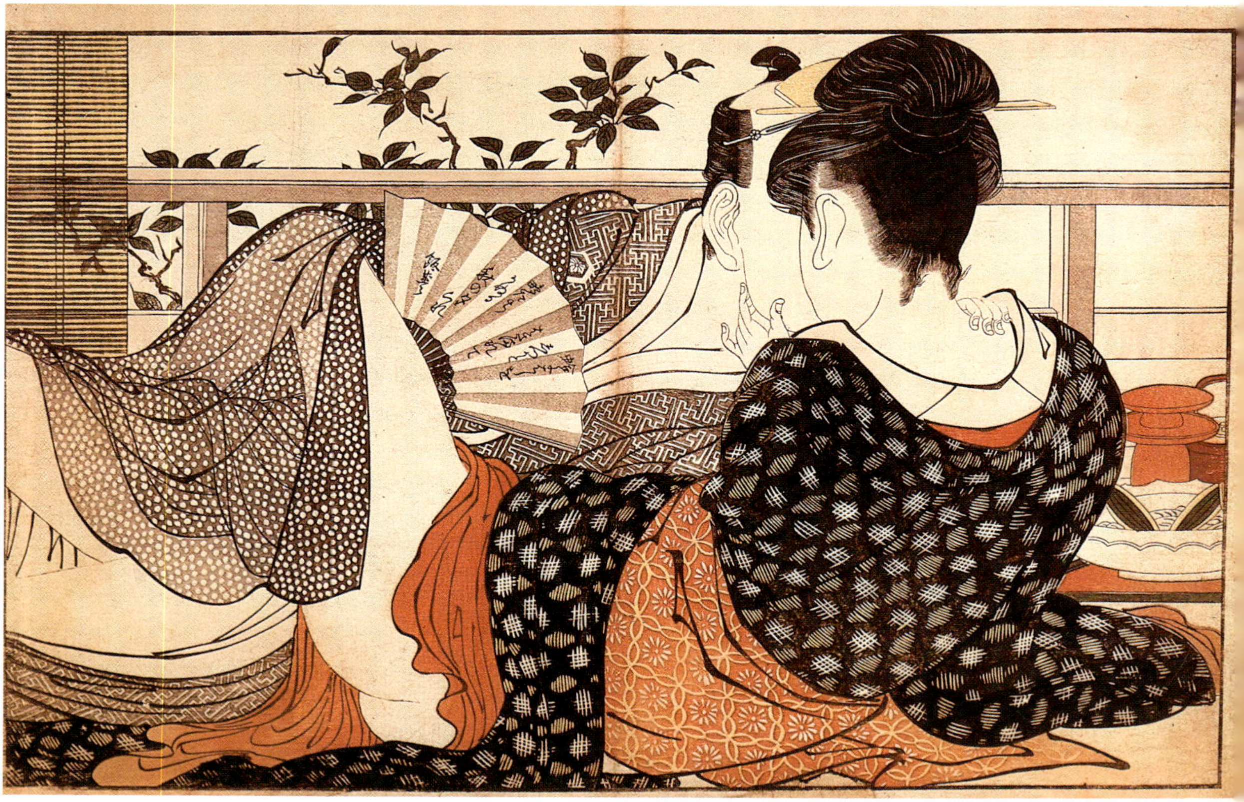

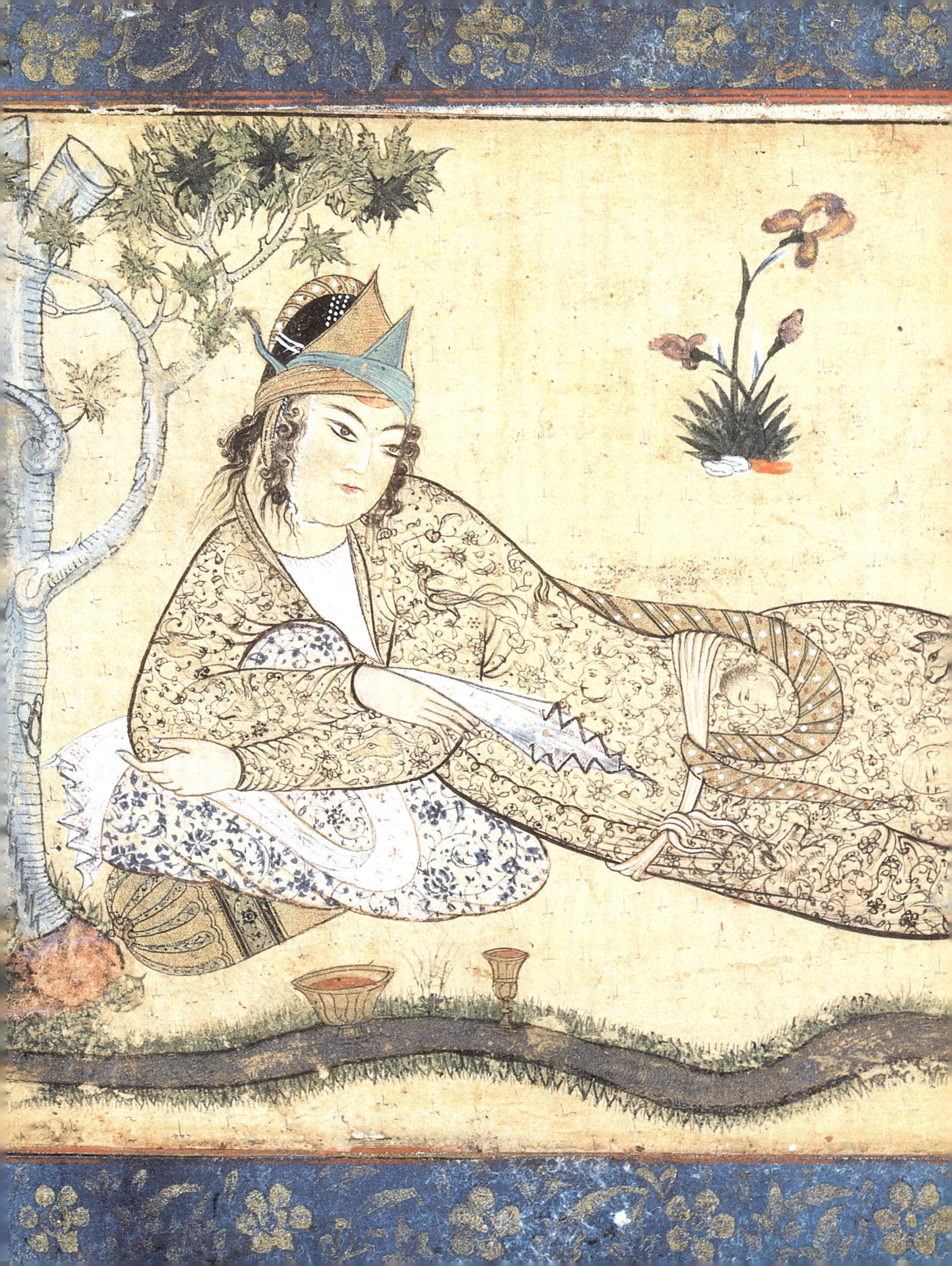

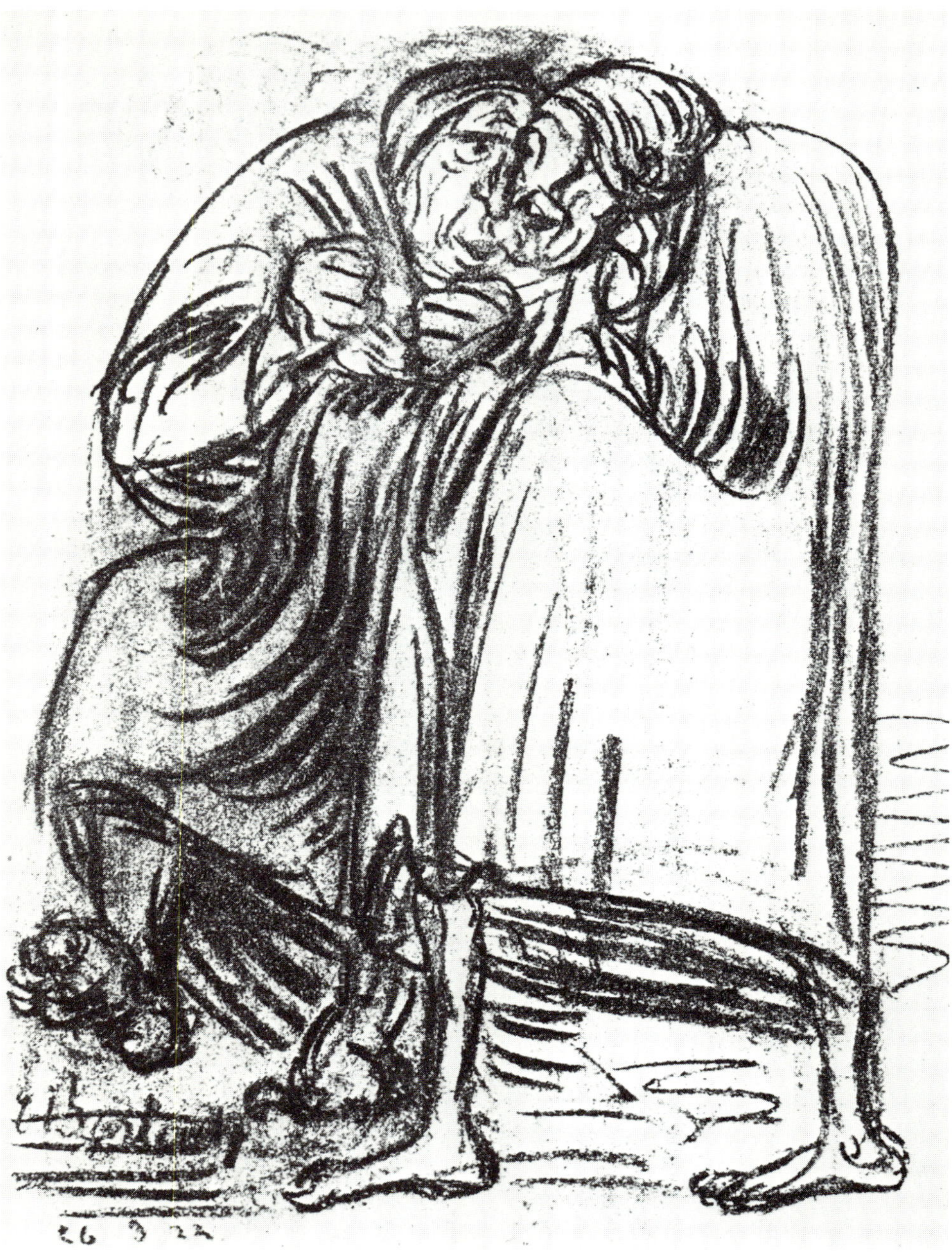

114 Ernst Barlach: 'Pair of Furies', 1922. The charcoal strokes define the three-dimensional surfaces of the garments, as well as the expression of the faces and the gestures of the bodies.

The only way you can handle total three-dimensionality successfully is by breaking down the image into units of volume which stand in space. It is not often you can include complete outlines of sections in any of your figure drawing; except maybe where you are thinking of something pointing out of the surface towards you, foreshortened, as in Tintoretto's *Figure Study*.

If you try, however, you may be able to pick out one or two places where you can introduce clear section-lines. The bottom edge of a skirt or the rims of dishes and cups are examples. Always exaggerate the width and curve of section-lines of this sort – as if you are tilting the plane of the section up towards the viewer to show to him the third dimension in two-dimensional form.

115 Jacopo Tintoretto, 'Figure Study'. The swift chalk drawing, which suggests volumes and a vivid posture, has been squared-up for enlargement.

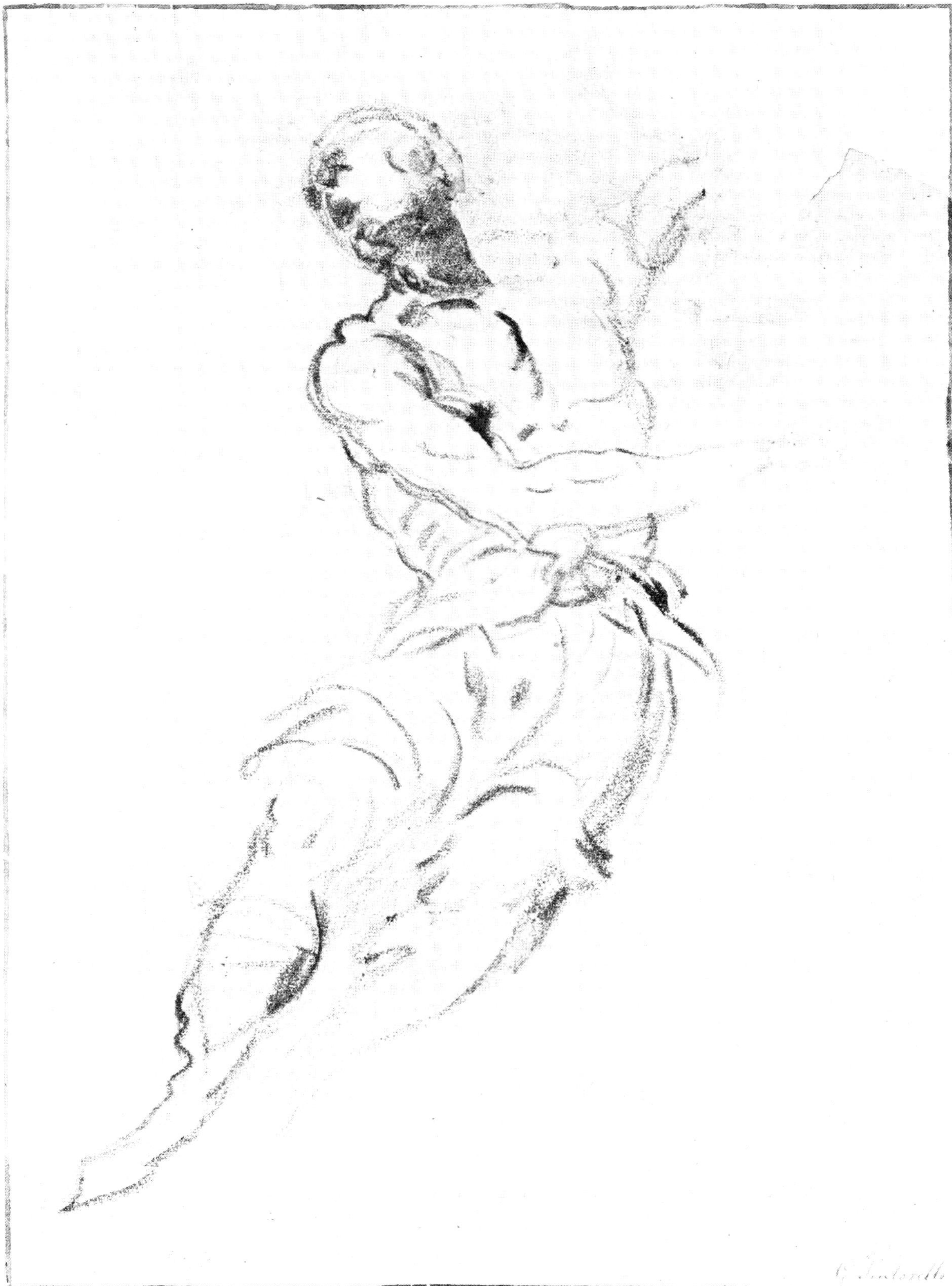

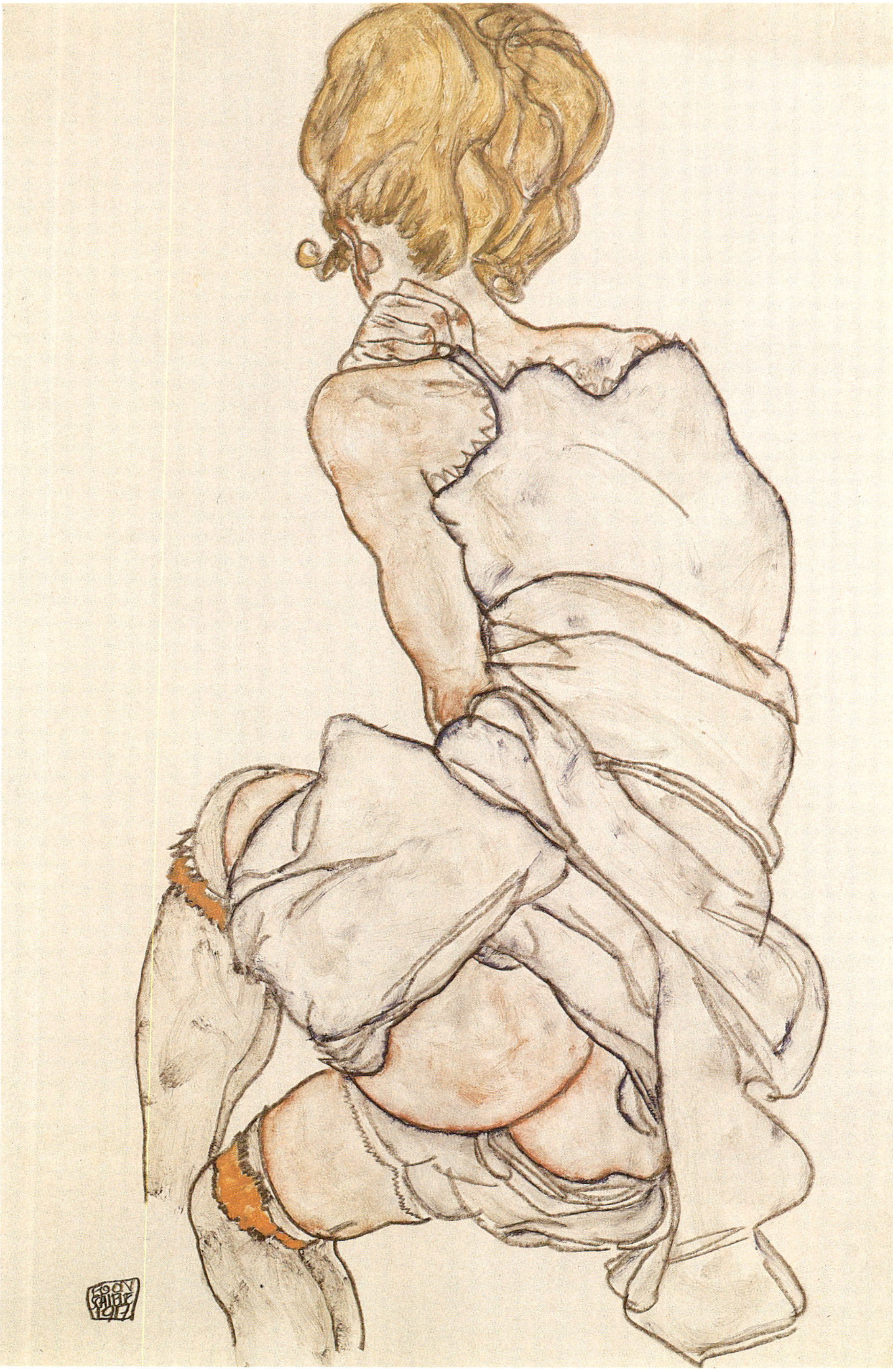
EGON
SCHIELE
1917

When you are dealing with three-dimensional volume you should separate in your mind one complete shape from another; and then join them to make a continuous contained volume. With a face, say, think of a nose in one shape, and set it on a volume made by the cheeks, then articulate it with the volume of brows and forehead. We shall look at the way you can shape these volumes in a moment. Remember: in drawing, clarity is the key to vigour. Most good figurative drawing combines a strong two-dimensional structure on the surface with strong three-dimensional parts which challenge that structure without breaking it. The three-dimensional parts are usually worked up at a few particular sites within the overall and unifying flat composition.

This brings us to one very interesting aspect of drawing. Within any given image you may be able to divide up the responsibilities of different parts. Some, as we have said, may be specifically used to express volume and the third dimension. Other parts – say, faces and hands – may be devoted to the linear expression of human feelings, and need not be fully three-dimensional. Yet other parts, say clothing creases, may be devoted to clear two-dimensional patterning. If you try to make every part say everything at once, you can easily end up with a weak overall effect.

Section 28
Contained Volume

One vital aspect of the presence of objects is the way they seem solid, to have a content of inner space shaped by their outer surface. If you only draw things by running lines along their silhouettes they will seem like cardboard cut-outs. When our eyes look together at an object up to about 13 feet (*c.* 3 metres) away each eye sees it from a slightly
6 different angle. Each eye sees part of one *side* of the object, as well as its front. So when the brain co-ordinates the data into a single image, it recognizes that the object has side surfaces as well as a front face. Many of the world's great figurative artists have spent a great deal of effort on evolving methods for signifying bulk or volume on the flat drawing surface. We often describe the artistic qualities that result as 'plastic', derived from the German word *plastik*. Sometimes we call these qualities 'tactile', because one feels able to touch or clasp the volumes. You produce this effect primarily by drawing bulky objects with clearly shaped side-planes.

116 Egon Schiele, 'Seated Girl', 1917. The contours define overlapping edges, and imply a languid sexual expression in the body.

One major technique for suggesting the plastic solidity of single volumes is to draw pairs of lines curved so that each pair seems to contain between it an oval volume whose surface curves away from its nearest point to us back to its outline. In this kind of volume both front and side planes are not yet distinct from each other.

If you close the ends of the curves to make a complete circle or oval, the area tends to turn into a flat enclosure. If you leave the ends of the ovals open, it seems that the volume between them has some kind of axis running along its centre; and hence that it has a rounded cross-section in the third dimension.

You will find that these oval volumes can correspond easily with the convex volumes – arms, legs and torsos – of human and other organic bodies. The oval has an obvious organic quality, suggesting that it is swollen and lightly bulging with life like a fruit. Try assembling 28
human bodies out of ovals for yourself.

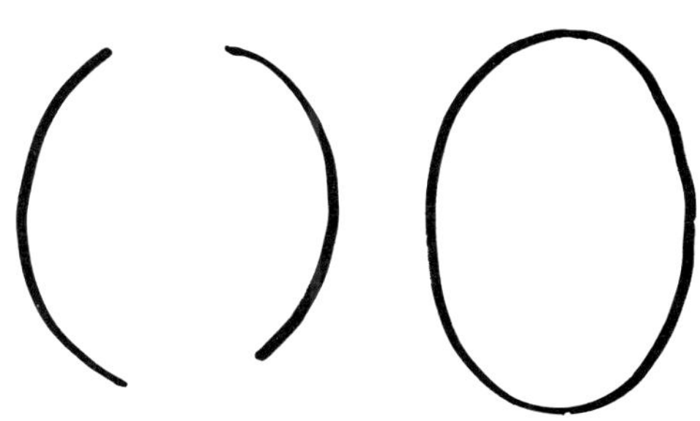

117 The oval as an indicator of contained volume, open and closed.

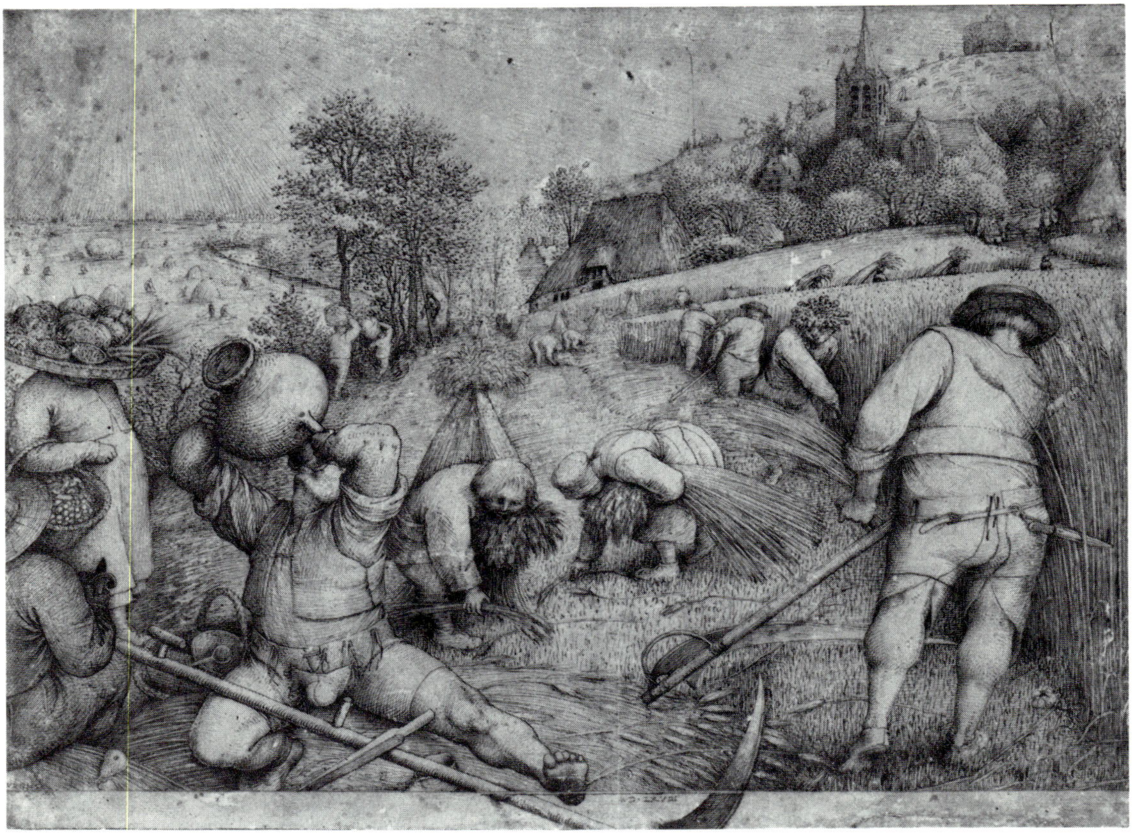

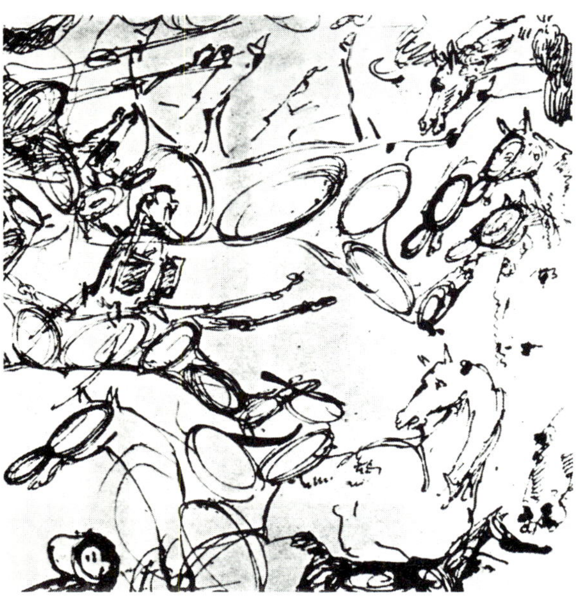

This has always been a very important technique in all artistic cultures that have been influenced by the Greco-Roman tradition, including the European Renaissance, India, China and even Japan. Most of the great masters of post-Renaissance Italian and French art used these oval volumes to symbolize strong physical presence and organic vitality. They drew each volume to 'correspond with' some part of the reality they were depicting. Precisely which part each oval was meant to signify is defined by its obvious context. Remember the Tangrams (Section 22). You do not need to make each single oval read as a single nameable part of the body, such as a forearm. It can just correspond with a volume which is 'in the right place'.

To make any drawing out of identical mathematical ovals would not correspond at all with nature's variety. Look back to Section 4 where we

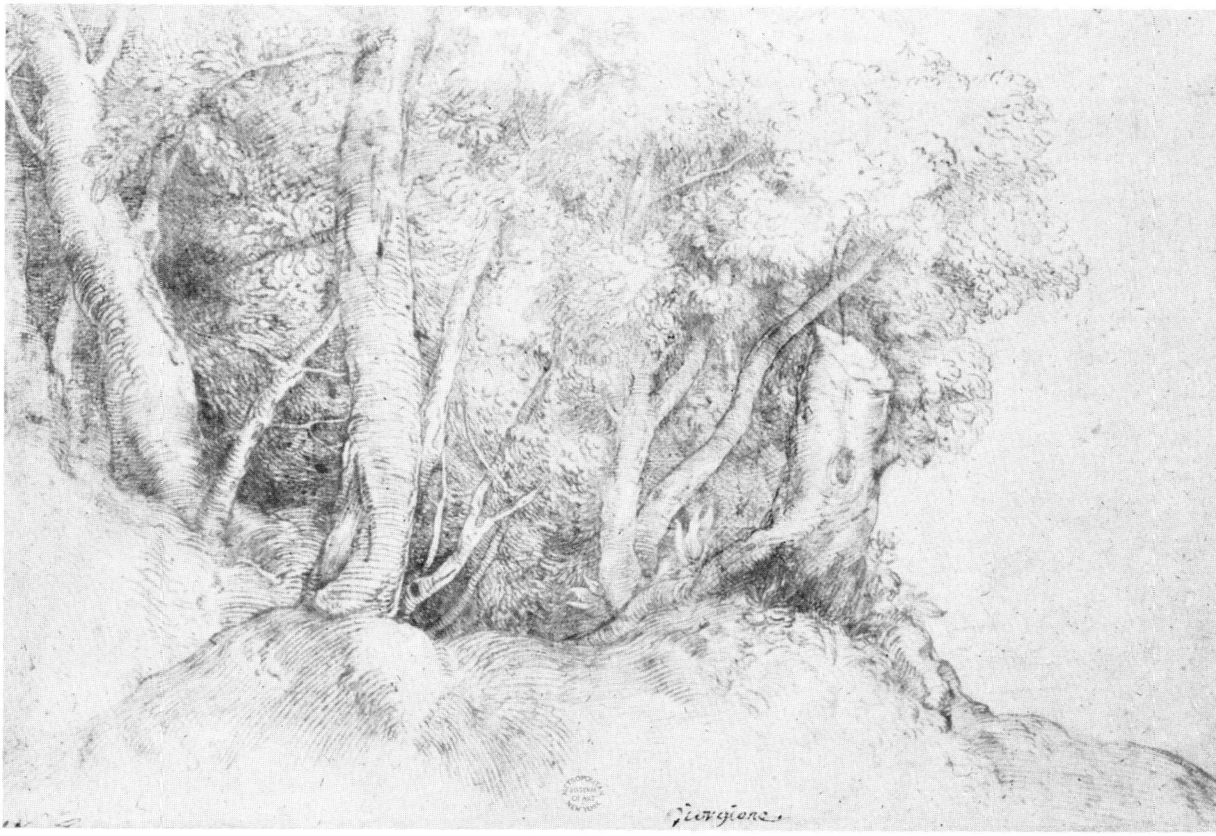

discussed how you can make curves differ from each other by varying the quanta of direction or straightness implied in each one. This applies just as much to the inflection of the curves that make up our ovals as it does to two-dimensional
18 curves. In this way you can produce the appearance of volumes that are very different from each other.

When you make these differing volumes convey different parts of the human body – or even
20 different parts of a tree trunk – it is important that they should run into each other to give the feeling that the solid object they are suggesting itself contains a continuous and modulated volume to which they contribute. And if you can combine the technique with depth slices piled one on top of another (Section 35) so much the better.

I mentioned that these volumes seem to have a rounded cross-section, related to an axis. There is

118 Pieter Breughel: 'Summer', 1568; pen drawing. Rounded volumes, bodily postures and gestures, and spatial depths, are all beautifully conveyed through a basically linear technique.
119 Eugène Delacroix: 'Horses'; a sheet of pen sketches illustrating the use of ovals to define basic volumes.
120 Titian: 'Study of Trees'; pen and bistre. Volume and depth are interpreted by bracelets and shadow, and the image is shown from below.
121 Ovals with implied axes and varied contours.

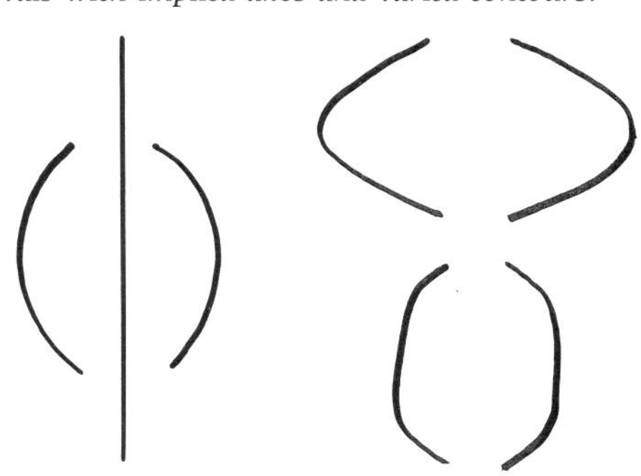

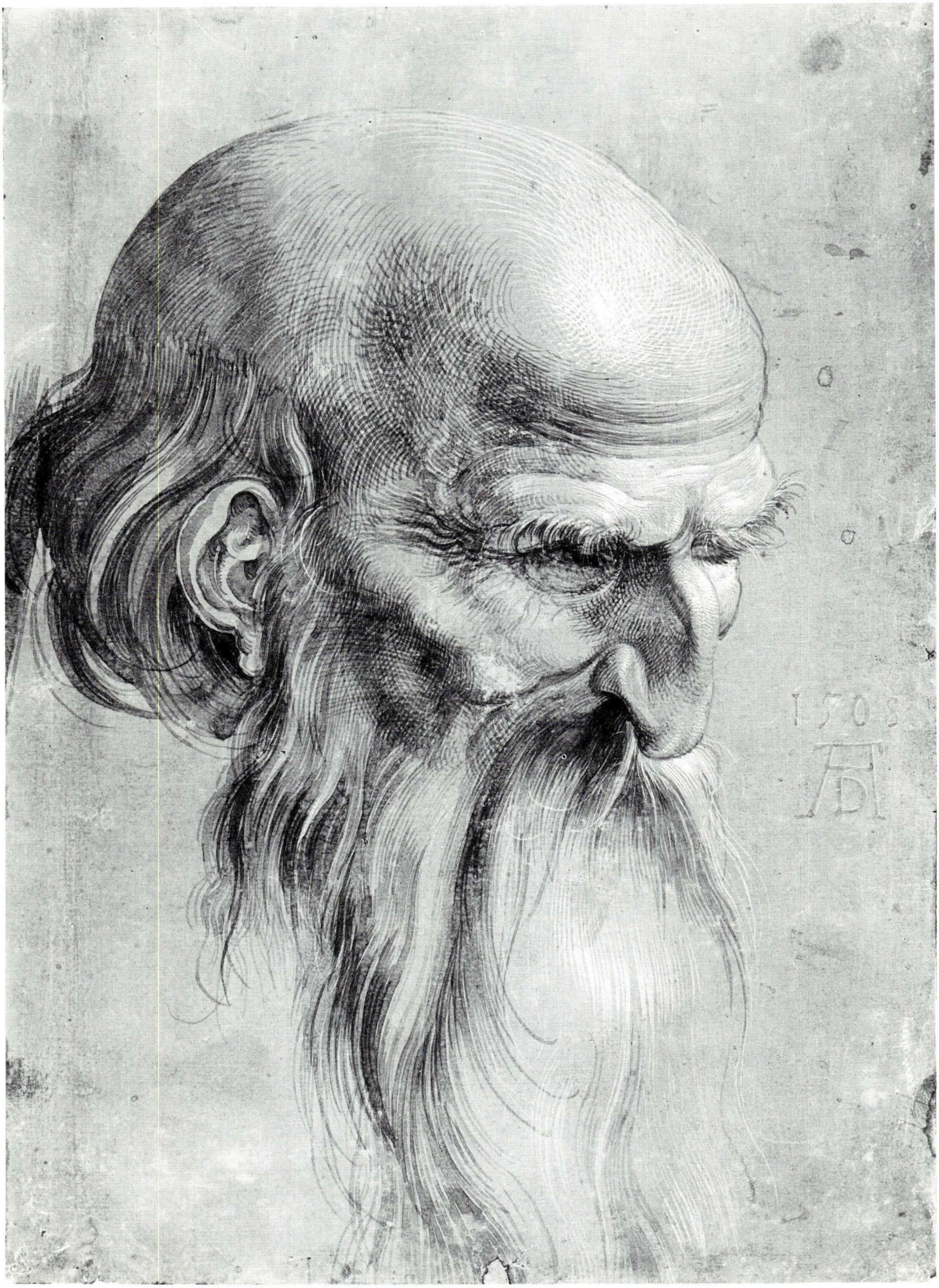
1508

22 a technique, known as 'bracelet shading', that makes the rounded surfaces of such ovals imply a volume completed in space by a back. The technique was probably invented in Germany in the later fifteenth century – perhaps even by Dürer. It was picked up in Italy by Leonardo da Vinci, and then adopted by engravers, who spread it widely around the world.

You apply bracelet shading where you would shadow; but you compose it from small curved lines which look as if they loop right around every volume like miniature cross-sections. Bracelet shading thus fortifies the sense of axis in such volumes by encouraging one to imagine an invisible 'other side'.

So when you set out a composition in terms of oval volumes, you generate whole sets of these axes which all contribute to the feeling of space in the image. They may seem to recede or project project out of the surface. A good draughtsman can make a great deal out of this feeling of axes. He will make the axes correspond with his two-dimensional scale of directions (Section 4).

You can practise this first at a very simple level. Then, once you have grown accustomed to pairing your lines, you can make your designs more complex. You will always find the technique very useful when drawing figures from your imagination as it enables you to locate quite quickly on the paper general volumes which can stand for people or parts of people. You can then adjust their proportions and relationships before you need to commit yourself to final decisions about their specific outlines and individual shapes.

Section 29
Facets and Volume

You will recall that in the previous Section and in Section 3 we considered how to make curves interesting by varying them. The cross-section of a volume can be varied in the same way; but in practice it is usually not drawn completely as a line but only implied, especially by shading (Section 32). Now refer back to Section 13, where

122 Albrecht Dürer: 'Head of an Apostle', 1508. A late pen drawing that develops bracelet shading to its maximum.

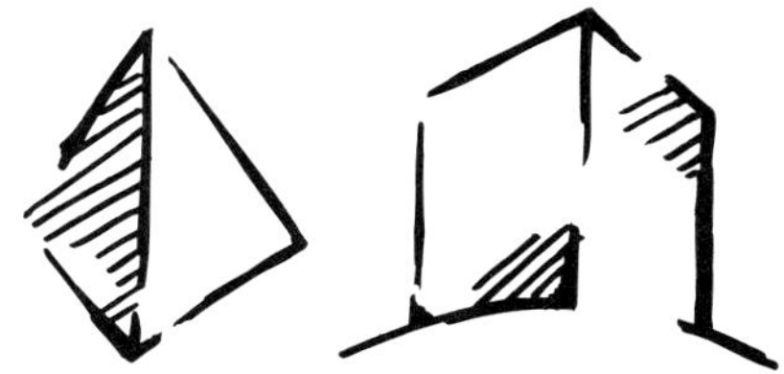

123 Conventional faceted volumes drawn with unconventional glyphs.

I mentioned that three-dimensional volumes could be derived from geometrical enclosures. Here we shall bring this idea together with the ideas of drawn volume and variation of curve.

Our earlier diagrams of the common geometrical solids were drawn with hard and clear outlines. Three of them, the sphere, cone and 58
cylinder, are those which Cézanne referred to as the patterns which guided him in interpreting the volumes of reality. Their crucial characteristic is that they are all three-dimensional shapes with rounded sections; their surfaces thus have nearest points, from which they are rounded away from the eye towards their distant edges. You can give to ovals spherical, conical or cylindrical qualities by inflecting their curves. Try doing versions of these shapes yourself. Remember that you cannot create an actual solid, only an image of one. So try to draw them in varied ways. 123

You can think of these rounded volumes as organic – resembling fruit, for instance; and of the faceted three-dimensional volumes as crystals – because they have planes which meet at angles, defined by 'shed-lines'.

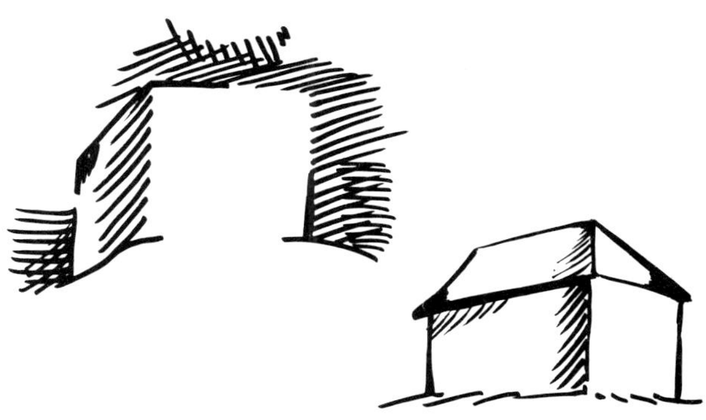

124 Different ways of shading simple faceted volumes.

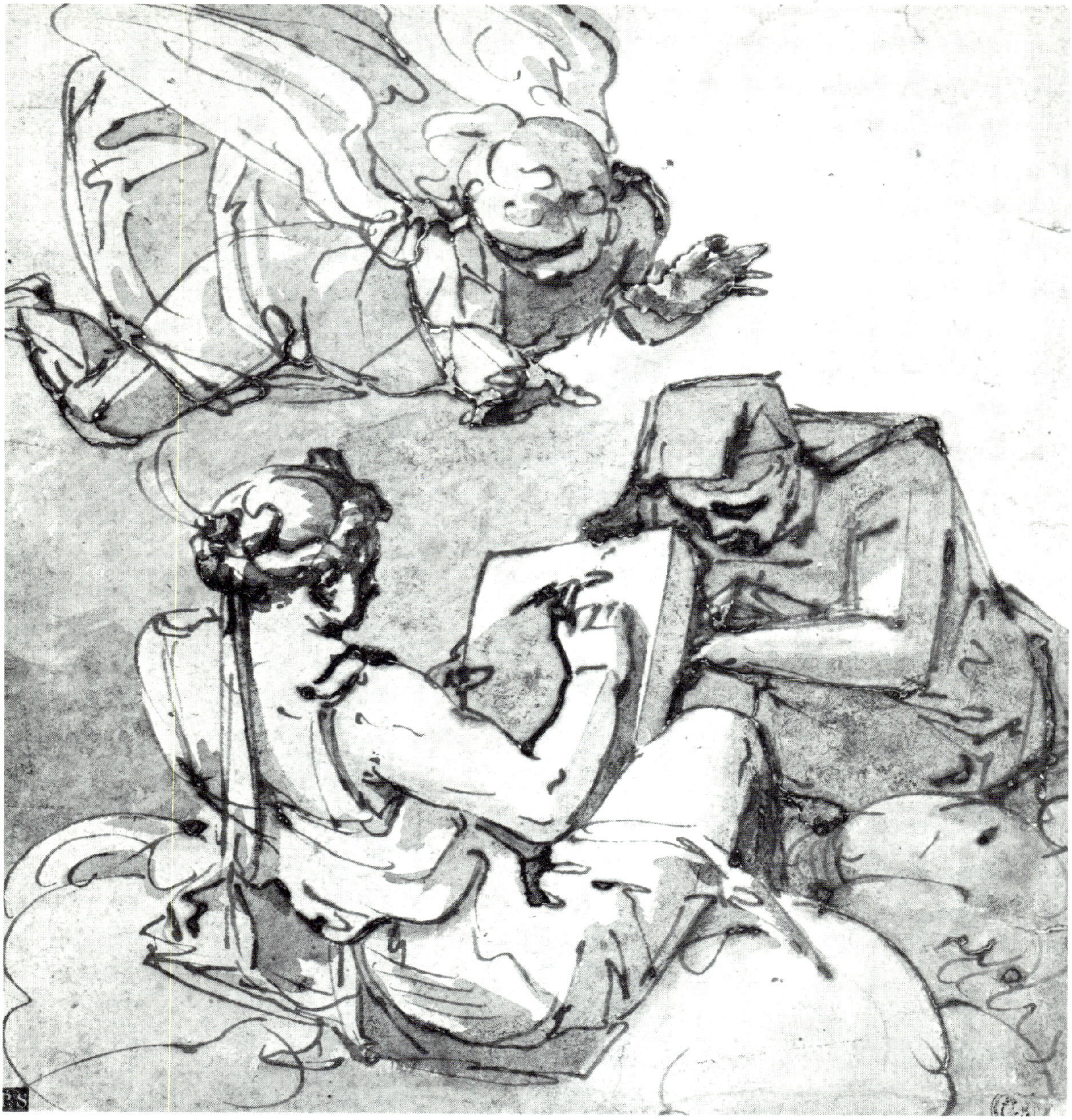

125 Luca Cambiaso: 'Allegory' of artist, model and genius. Pen and wash drawing which emphasizes the facets of the volumes.

Faceted volumes can be thought of as following two basic types – cube and pyramid. But you can obviously work all kinds of variations with them, as you can see in these diagrams. Obviously the cube, or cuboid, is implied in almost everybody's image of a house; if the house has a pitched roof it has a version of the pyramid added on top. You can interpret the ground on which it stands as itself part of a faceted or geometrically faceted volume.

Something organic can also have its own underlying structure of facets or planes. The important point is that these should make the

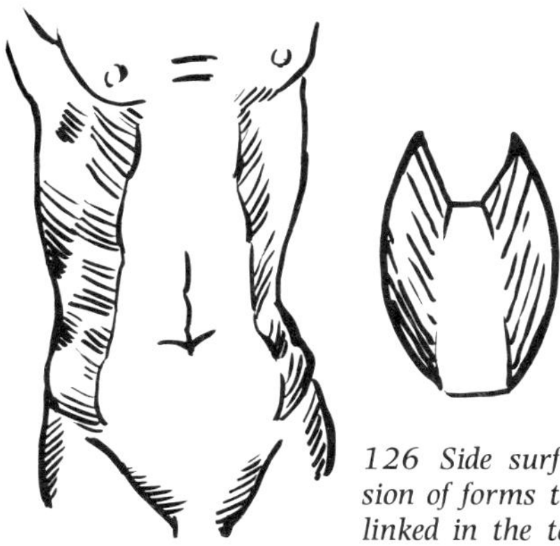

126 Side surfaces showing recession of forms towards the contour, linked in the torso, isolated in the oval.

contained shapes of their volumes intelligible, and the key to this is the way you handle the shed lines which break the surfaces of objects. I am not suggesting that you have to assert them emphatically; but you do have to state their presence somehow, or they will easily get lost. Connected up, they can also unify a continuous series of shaped volumes that make up solid organic bodies
26 such as, for example, the human torso.

When you define faceted volumes you will find that you actually have to define their side surfaces as shaped planes running away from you at an angle into the space of the picture surface. We have already considered how our two eyes see *both* sides of an object (Section 28). If you are going to suggest that any volume has genuine bulk, you need to show not just *one* of its receding sides, but both. If you simply 'draw what you see', even a real cube can look quite flat.

The surfaces themselves do not all have to be flat. You can think of them as curved. The important thing is to make the viewer understand how the side surfaces run away into space, and then turn round behind the volume to close it. You can do this by representing the object wider at the back than the front, by showing the shapes of those depth-defining sides, and by reducing the emphasis on the distant edge-lines.

1 To draw things with a strong sense of volume, you can invent lines to show their sections in the
15 third dimension whenever you can. In figurative work, you will find there are particular places where some surface in nature 'cuts' the surface of your three-dimensional forms. If you look down slightly on someone in still water, you will see how the surface of the water makes a shaped ring round their leg or arm. Such a ring gives you a marvellous chance to draw the third dimension.

In life-drawing you may find a crease which runs partway round a stomach; or the line the model's rump makes where it spreads on to the horizontal surface of a chair (Section 36). Anything which obviously goes right round something also gives you a marvellous chance to draw a section: a collar round a neck; a bracelet round 118
an arm; or the hip-band of briefs or swimming trunks. Shape these loop lines carefully without flattening them, and you will go a long way towards giving your forms a sense of volume.

In the work of the great masters you will often find lots of two-dimensional lines used to illustrate sections. They may appear simply as exaggerations of an outline. For example, the human eye, seen 122
from the front, is really quite flat. But to make you feel how the eye 'looks' at you by bulging forward, many artists give the contour of the upper eyelid quite a deep curve. In many drawings of the male nude you will find the line under the chest muscles or around the stomach exaggerated into a far deeper curve than you would really see in a frontal view. You should take every chance any subject offers you to include in your drawing such two-dimensional signs for the third dimension.

One very simple approach to figurative drawing which helps a lot with problems of foreshortening, is this: draw the plastic parts nearest to you first, and hang all the other parts from them. This gives your objects a strong sense of physical presence. It is truly surprising how many people go on drawing the outside edges first, and then try to work inwards from them.

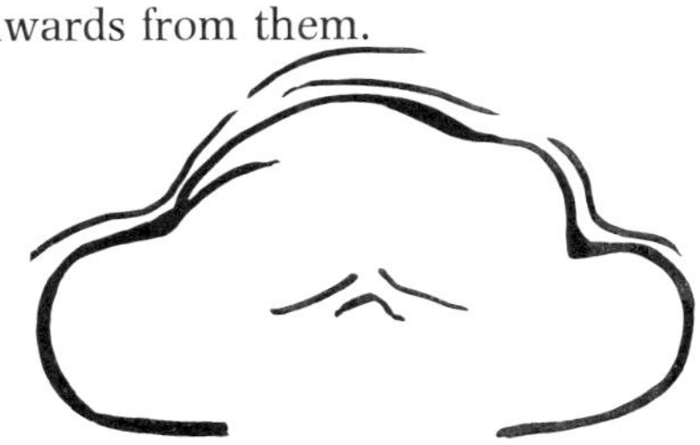

127 How water illustrates the three-dimensional section of a body.

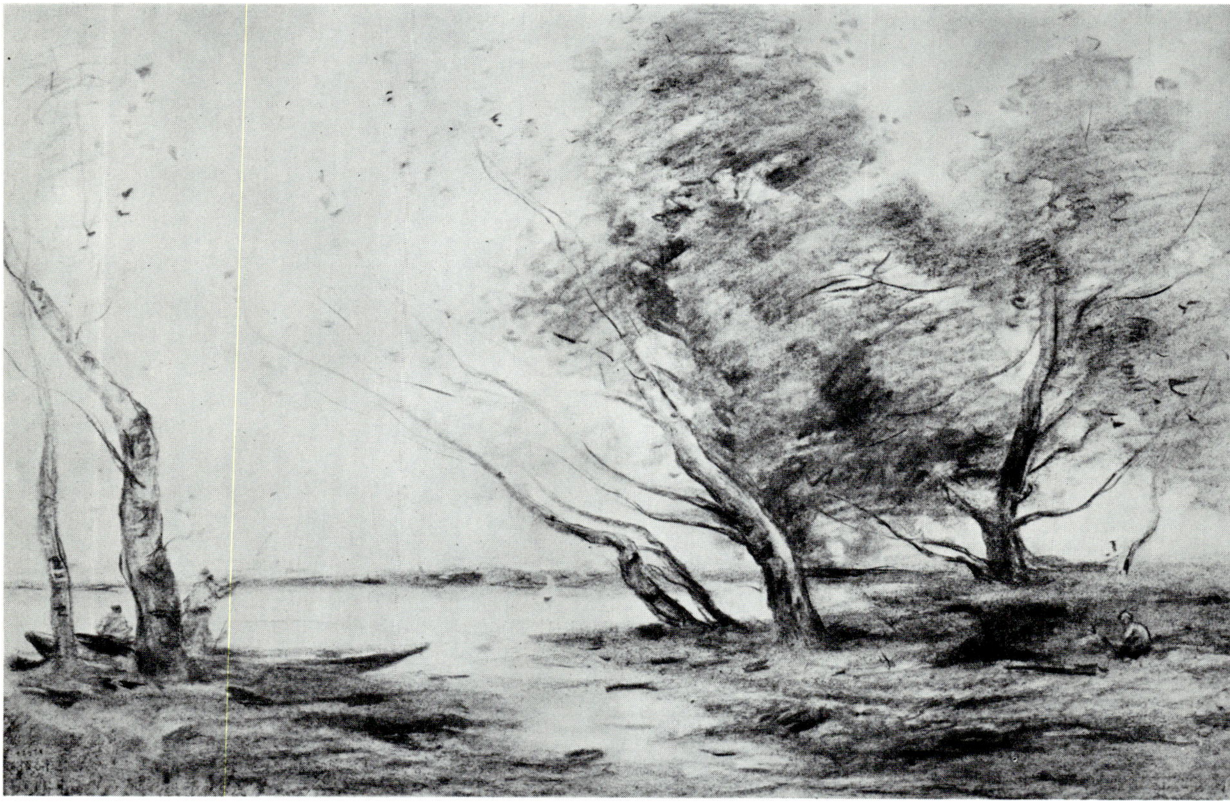

128 Jean Baptiste Camille Corot: 'Landscape with Trees'; charcoal. This is an example of Corot's late and gentle style, when he used virtually no other resource than tone. He has abandoned the formal rigour of his early landscapes, but the depth of form has not been lost. His lines may seem free, but they are also accurate.

V
Tone

We shall now look into the techniques and resources of tone and chiaroscuro *as ways of defining, distinguishing and unifying objects in the visual image.*

Section 30
Figuration and Tone

There are no black outlines in nature. As a result of our convention of tracing the edges between things with a drawing point we 'see' black lines where none exist. In reality the edges are not the most emphatic parts of any object. They are the places where the positive surface stops. When you look at natural objects you see them as wholes without continually running your eye around their edges. Look at somebody face to face. There are no black outlines. You take in the person as a whole; and you are probably aware most strongly of the parts closest to you, well away from the outlines. You see mobile surfaces unifying a solid physical presence inside them.

Now look at your two-dimensional drawing sheet. To translate that physical presence on to it just by black outlines may seem impossible, even using the three-dimensional techniques we have already discussed. But we have another resource.

The blackness of your medium can be used to convey other facts about reality than sheer separations between things; it can be used to integrate them. You can turn it into tone and so convey that sense of touchable volume, of varied undulation in the surfaces, which makes you feel you are in the presence of a solid reality. Tone is one of the draughtsman's greatest resources.

Nearly all drawing is done with dark media on a light ground. The media are usually black, grey, reddish or brown, occasionally greenish or blue. You can use any colour or group of colours that contrasts with your drawing surface. Tonal techniques are ways of extending the natural darkness of the drawing medium out into the open areas of the image.

You should expect your tonal medium to contribute some scale of graded tone-values to your drawing. This can serve as a stimulus to your imagination as well as establishing a sense of order. Many artists have used a single dark drawing-line accompanied by a single paler area-tone – the simplest tone-scale. Others have used three or four tones. The important thing is to keep the scale distinct and consistent.

There are two main types of medium for tonal drawing: the wet and fluid, applied with a pen and brush; and the dry, that you rub on. They produce tone in different ways.

a)

The commonest fluid medium is a wash made by diluting with water your drawing ink or water colour, usually applied with a brush. Claude Lorrain was one of the greatest masters of wash drawing. Before setting off to go landscape drawing he would mix three or four grades of ink with water in a set of little bottles. He applied them in turn, the palest first, the darkest last; then put in the final accents with pure ink.

Two things make a big difference to how your wash-tones work. First, whether the surface is damp or dry: if you wait for each tone to dry before applying the next you will find it much easier to control the final colour of each tone than if you apply each to a damp surface. Second, the quality of your paper: thick absorbent paper will take up a second tone readily, whereas non-absorbent paper will stay wet and refuse it, leaving you with a confused mixture. Of course, when you have become expert you can take all your tones straight off a single cake of watercolour, diluting each dab correctly with your brush loaded with water. A master may seem to work by instinct, but he still differentiates his tones carefully.

As with the linear scales (Section 4) you can vary your tone-scale from drawing to drawing. Suppose you have decided to use four tones, you can have, say, two pale, one mid-tone, and the ink as the darkest. Or you can have only one pale tone, one medium dark, and the ink.

Another important technique for laying down
129b tone is 'hatching', which you can do with any
medium, wet or dry. You do this by making a
carpet of strokes. Close together they produce a
dark effect; where they are wider apart the effect
106 is paler. Traditional hatching uses parallel diagonal
strokes which give a feeling of unity to all the

b)

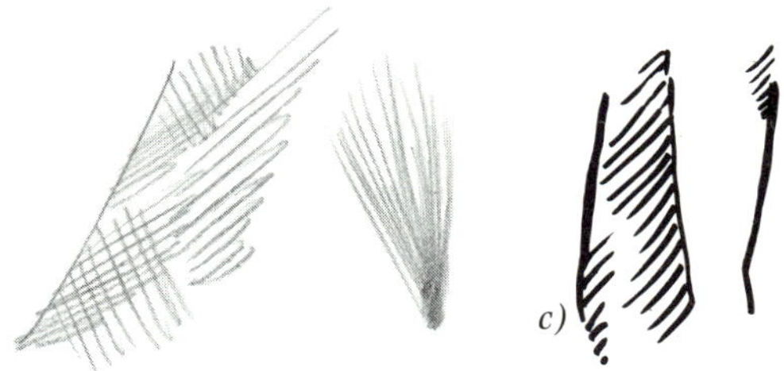

c)

129 a) graded set of wash tones; b) pencil hatching; c) hatching used to define a shed-line.

shadows in a composition. But you can develop many varieties of hatching, each with a strong linear expression of its own. For example, you can do it with nervous marks, slightly stabbed, in several directions, or with faintly wavering horizontal lines. Areas of hatching can be vague in shape, or they can be sharply defined as shaped enclosures. You can even use quite a wide variety of different hatching strokes to fill a solid area in order to build up darks with a very lively feel.
This is what Seurat often did. 1

One important special use of hatching is to define the shed-lines in faceted volumes (Section
29). A single row of hatching along one side of a 1
shed-line can give a strong sense of three-dimensionality. And you can apply hatching slanted at a different angle to define each of the receding surfaces of any set of volumes that has a front and two side faces, so giving it an almost sculptural effect.

In using dry media it is easy to lose track of your scale of darks. It is particularly hard to keep
control of more than two grades. Charcoal is 1
perhaps the oldest and commonest of the dry media. It is dark grey and powdery. An ordinary charcoal stroke adheres quite loosely; so you can easily erase mistakes. You can use it to rough-in

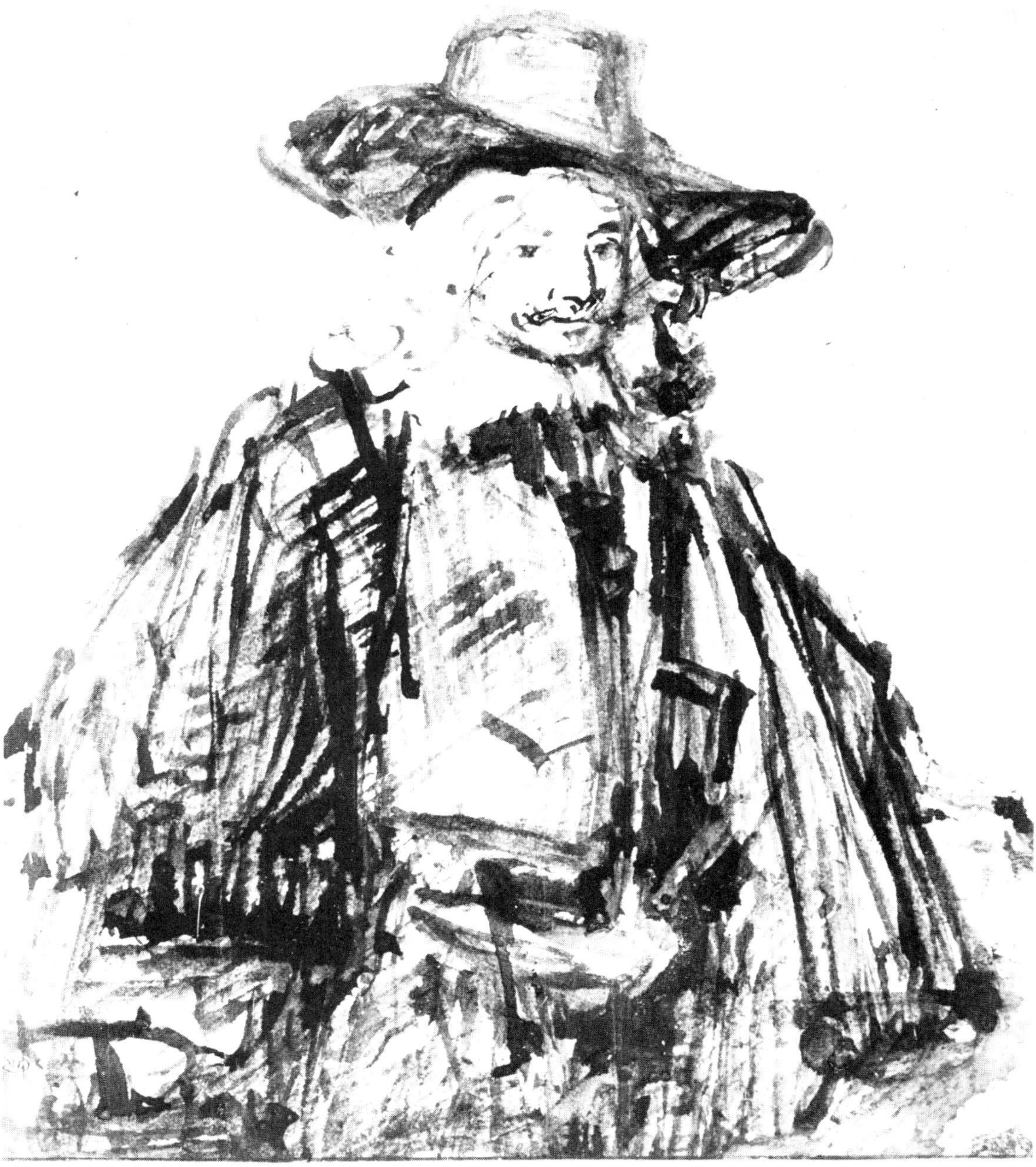

*130 Rembrandt van Rijn: 'Portrait of a Syndic', c. 1662–5.
Elaborate pen-hatching defines different kinds of darkness.*

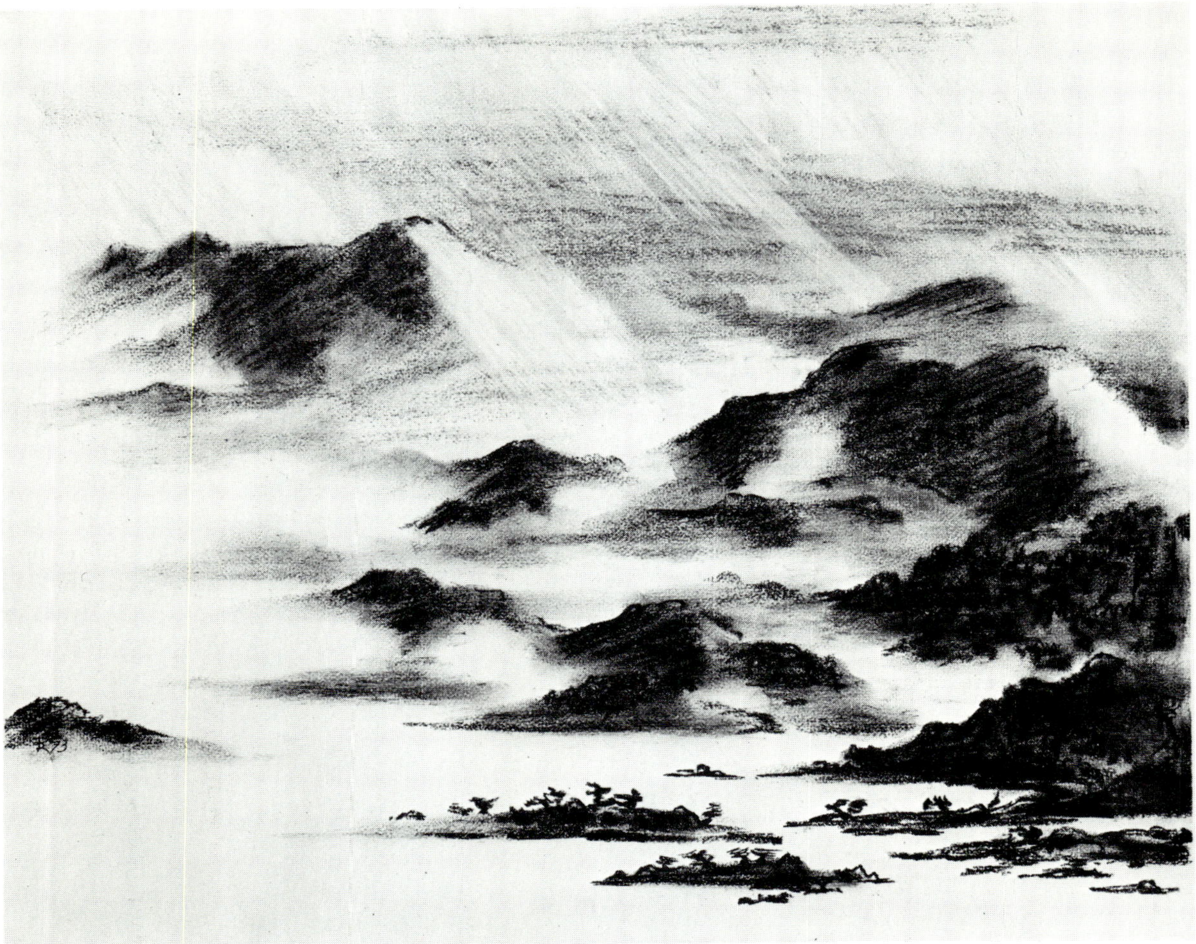

131 Stormy landscape drawn in compressed charcoal, with erasing.

the plan of a design you mean to finish later in some other medium. You can also develop pale and mid-tones by making a series of charcoal marks, and then rubbing them out on to the paper surface with your thumb. It is quite difficult with ordinary charcoal to get very dark tones. Compressed charcoal is a darker and more flexible medium; you can make it adopt any tone of a scale that you want by a combination of rubbing and hatching and you can use an eraser to take out lights. Since no charcoal adheres very strongly to the surface, and needs in the end to be fixed by some kind of lacquer spray, some artists fix parts of the drawing as they go along, and then add more dark tone on top of the first to achieve stronger degrees of dark.

Chalk and carbon-pencil behave rather like compressed charcoal, though they adhere more strongly and are therefore slightly less easy to spread by rubbing. Chalk of any colour can make very attractive areas of mid-tone if you use it on a paper with a rough or 'toothed' surface, and do not press very hard. The paper is then only marked by the chalk on the tops of its roughnesses, leaving the crevices white. If you press harder you will fill the crevices and produce a stronger, solid dark.

You can also use two or three chalks of different colours which naturally have different tones, say a red and a brown or black. One of the classic ways the great masters used chalk tone was on tinted paper with white added for the lit areas. This is one way of arriving at a ready-made scale of three tonal values. It can give you extra tonal refinements depending how you apply each chalk.

Pencil is a more delicate medium. Unless you are using one of the blackest leads – say 5B or 6B – the hardest stroke you can lay on is relatively pale. An HB, or any of the harder H numbers, can be very pale. So to develop any scale of dark at all you need to use quite elaborate hatching.

Finally, it is worth mentioning a very effective technique whereby you can modify or even apply an additional graphic image to an area of paper already toned. You can scratch off the tone, either with your finger-nail or a knife point, so that the natural light tone of the paper is uncovered. You can do this either to make a simple highlight, or to add a complex light glyph.

Section 31
Varieties of Graphic Tone

You can employ the tone-value of your medium figuratively in three principal ways. First, you can use it to 'colour' areas of your drawing which correspond with parts of your subject that are more darkly coloured than others. Secondly, you can make the tone of your outlines correspond with the way surfaces of rounded volumes turn away from your eye towards their furthest edges. This is called modelling tone. Thirdly, you can relate the darkness of your tone to shadows: to modelling shadows and cast shadows. To do this consistently you need to make sure that the dark of any outline you draw belongs either to the outlined object or to its background, whichever is the more shadowed.

It is a good idea to use each of these techniques separately first of all, so as to get to know what each involves. Students often become confused about what they are really using tone for in their drawings; and you can miss out on opportunities for development if you do not know what the possibilities are.

The first way of handling tone, as colour, is the
2 simplest. To fill in areas of your drawing which correspond to darker coloured objects, each with a single tone, gives you the opportunity to develop the shapes of those areas as enclosure glyphs. You can compose an entire design out of areas of different tone. You can also draw linear shapes into the areas of tone with your darkest medium. The tones then become almost tints for the different objects referred to in your composition. To combine tone used as colour with tone used as shadow in the same composition can be a real challenge. Rembrandt often did it in his ink and wash drawings.

The second way of handling tone isolates individual objects, defining them and distinguishing them strongly from any background. It accepts the intrinsic darkness of the outline; the tone then extends inwards from the outline, lightening as the form turns towards you. Conversely, as the tone darkens it suggests that the form turns away from you until it disappears 'round the corner' at the maximum dark of the outline. This is not the same as shadow. It symbolizes recession.

132 Kuo Hsü: 'Boy on a Buffalo's Back', (?) 17th c. The brushed-on tone emphasizes darkness and bulk.

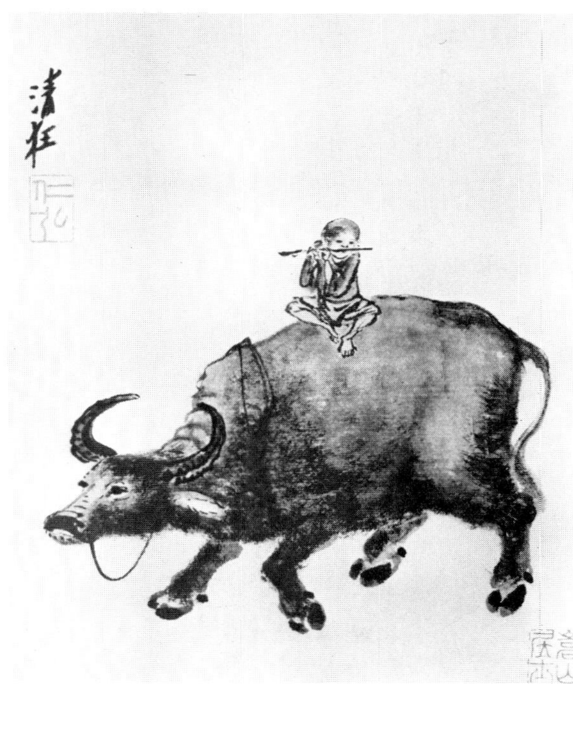

Most artists who use this technique develop it as a way of defining their bodies in terms of those oval volumes we discussed in Section 28. It can illustrate the projection and recession of an undulating sequence of surfaces very clearly. Sculptors – for instance, the French sculptor Maillol – have made good use of this technique. It matches their way of isolating single bodies from the confusion of commonplace reality. Some painters have also used it, notably Renoir, and the wall-painters of fourteenth-century Italy and fifth-century India. When you use it you need to feel that the objects you are isolating absorb your interest completely.

This is one of the methods for which you can use two chalks of different colours and tones – say, lighter red ochre and darker brown. The red gives the slighter recession, the brown the strongest. The effect of the technique is similar to the way fine nylon stockings emphasize a girl's legs, enhancing their plastic presence. The weave of stockings also appears to darken as it turns round away from the lighter middle.

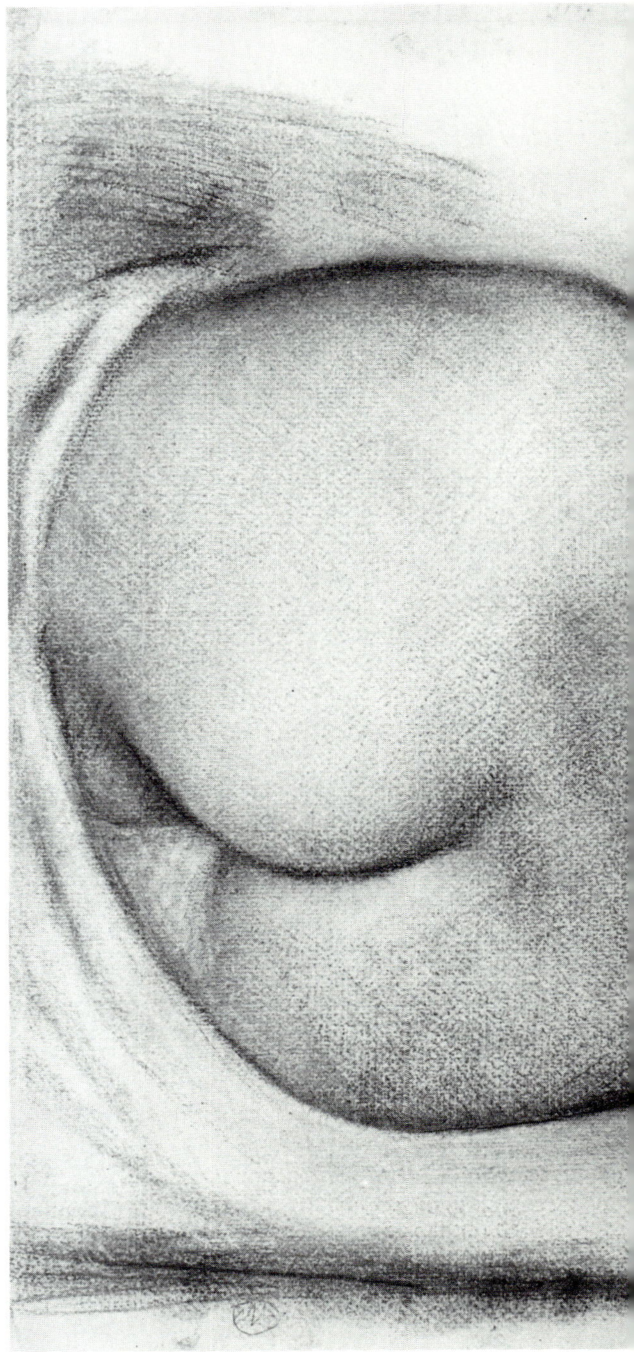

Section 32
Tone as Shadow

The third way of handling tone is to treat it as standing for shadow. In the fifteenth century the Italians applied to it the term *chiaroscuro*, meaning 'light-dark'. In fact, both Greek painting of the third century BC and Roman painting used *chiaroscuro*. But we have no drawings from those periods. Our earliest evidence for the technique comes from fourteenth-century Europe.

Tone used as shadow illustrates the fact that in the real world shadows appear in parts of the visible world which are deprived of light, which is a positive presence. Drawing normally reverses this natural relationship. You start with the light paper, and then cut down its luminosity by applying shadow to it, which is a positive action.

You have to train your eye to read tone as shadow, rather than as colour. Chinese connoisseurs who saw European paintings for the first

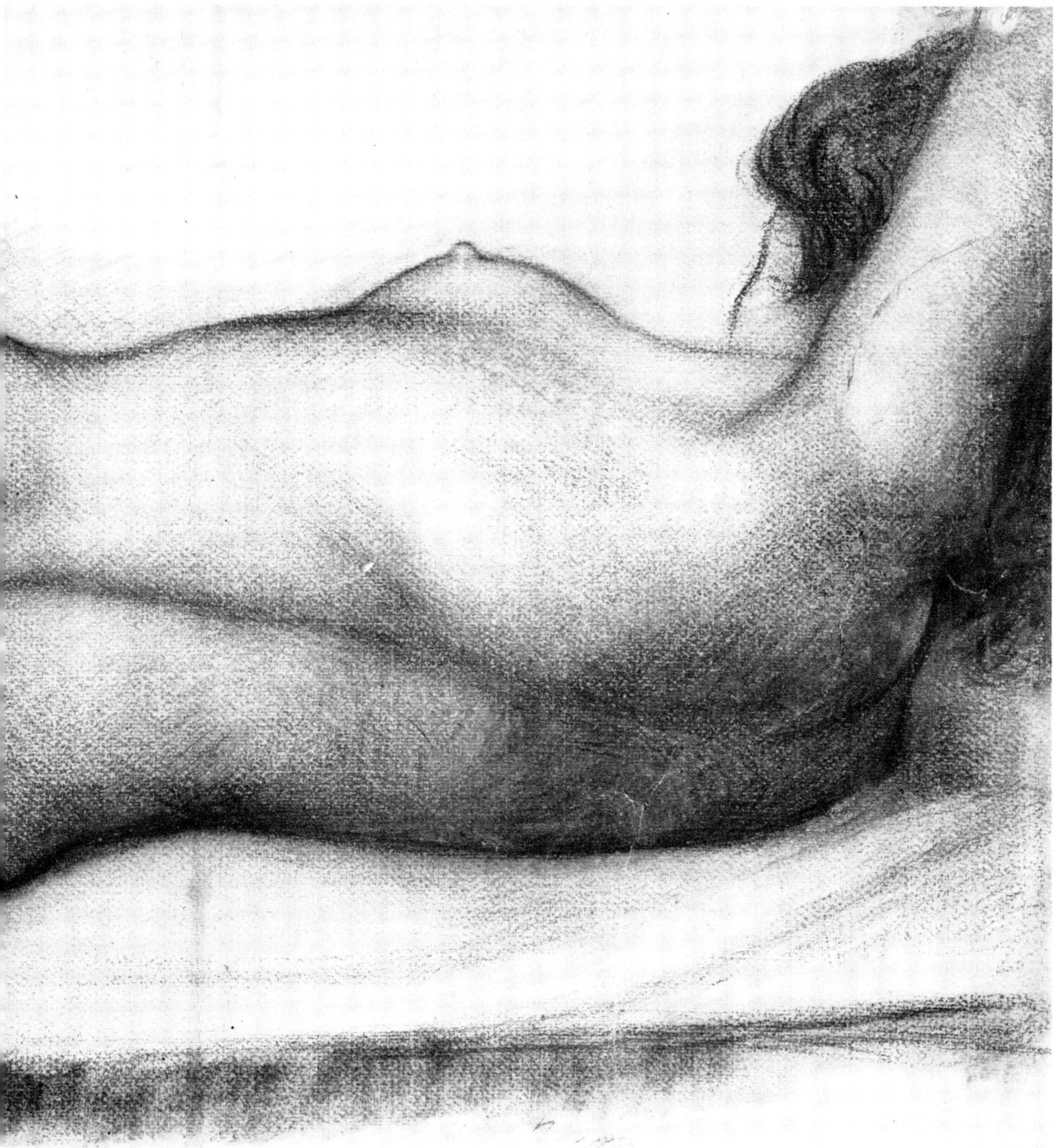

133 Aristide Maillol: 'Reclining Nude', c. 1932. A sculptor's chalk drawing that defines distance towards the contour by darkness of tone.

time in the eighteenth century were perplexed that the European ladies in *chiaroscuro* paintings appeared to have a dirty snuff-mark under their nose, and one filthy cheek. The Chinese tradition was to read tone as colour.

We can distinguish two fundamental types of shadow to which tone refers: modelling shadow and cast shadow. They are both the result of the same facts about light. The first was used earlier than the second.

Modelling tone was developed in medieval art to supplement dark linear drawing, not to replace it. It defines the three-dimensional shapes of things by illustrating how they appear darker as they turn away from the light. But medieval draughtsmen did not suggest precisely where the light source was in relation to their figures. They were satisfied with a general effect of shadowed volume. Then, about 1420, in what is now Belgium, the Van Eycks discovered shadow as such, and took possession of it for art. Ever since it has been one of the basic resources of drawing.

In his drawing of Cardinal Albergati you can see very clearly how Jan van Eyck assimilates the dark strokes of his chalk into the shadow image. He leaves no dark marks unaccounted for; they all read as shadow. And that shadow is intimately related to the undulations of the surfaces of his objects. Van Eyck was working very close to a live tradition of sculpture; and a sculptural feeling for three-dimensional form underlies his tonal imagery.

This is one kind of definition you can aim for in your own work. As you reach towards it make sure that your shadow-glyphs remain interesting, and do not lose their clarity and variation.

134 The shaping functions of modelling and cast shadow.

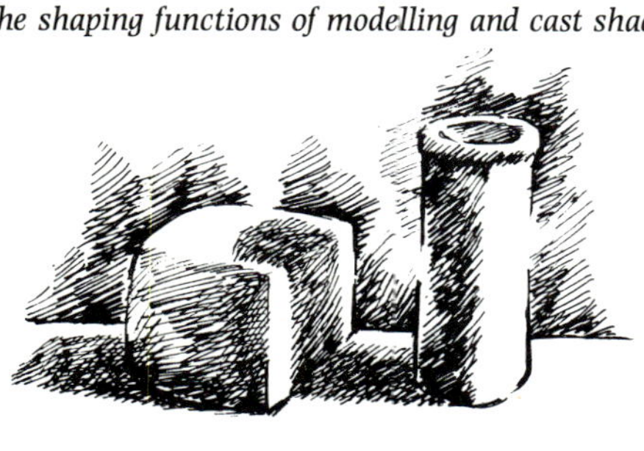

Modelling shadow lies on the surface of a body, defining its volumes. Cast shadow results from a solid body interrupting the light that falls on the surface of something else. It defines the spaces between volumes. It can also clarify the three-dimensional shape of the surface it falls on. The shadow of an arm, for example, falling across a leg, may show up the three-dimensional curve of the leg's surface.

Although cast shadow was indeed understood in the sixteenth century, it was used surprisingly little until the seventeenth, and then only as a kind of extension of modelling shadow to define the volumes of figures and clothing. A token
patch of dark was often put on the ground beneath 1
figures. But its commonest usage was to provide deep pools of dark in a composition – in the hollows of robes or in the cavernous depths of a background – against which the illuminated volumes of the principal figures could stand out.

When you use shadow in this way, you will find you need to invent it as thoroughly as you need to invent lines and volumes. You can also give your dark outlines a new function: they can help to spring apart different components of your design, suggesting clear three-dimensional space between your lit surfaces and the dark surfaces against which you silhouette them. Following the example of Van Eyck, make sure that the tone of your contours is fully assimilated into the shadow
on one side or other of the edge. Take a series of 1
clear-cut decisions as to which side of the contour is darker than the other. In some places this may be the background; in other cases the object outlined. Note your decision with patches of tone at intervals along each of your outlines and this will give you the basis from which you can build up a complete tonal image.

The world is full of cast shadows. You use them 1
to understand the spaces and distances between things. Most important of all, the directions in which they fall show you where the light is coming from. By drawing cast shadows that are consistent with each other you can give a strong feeling of light to your composition, since shadows imply the presence of light.

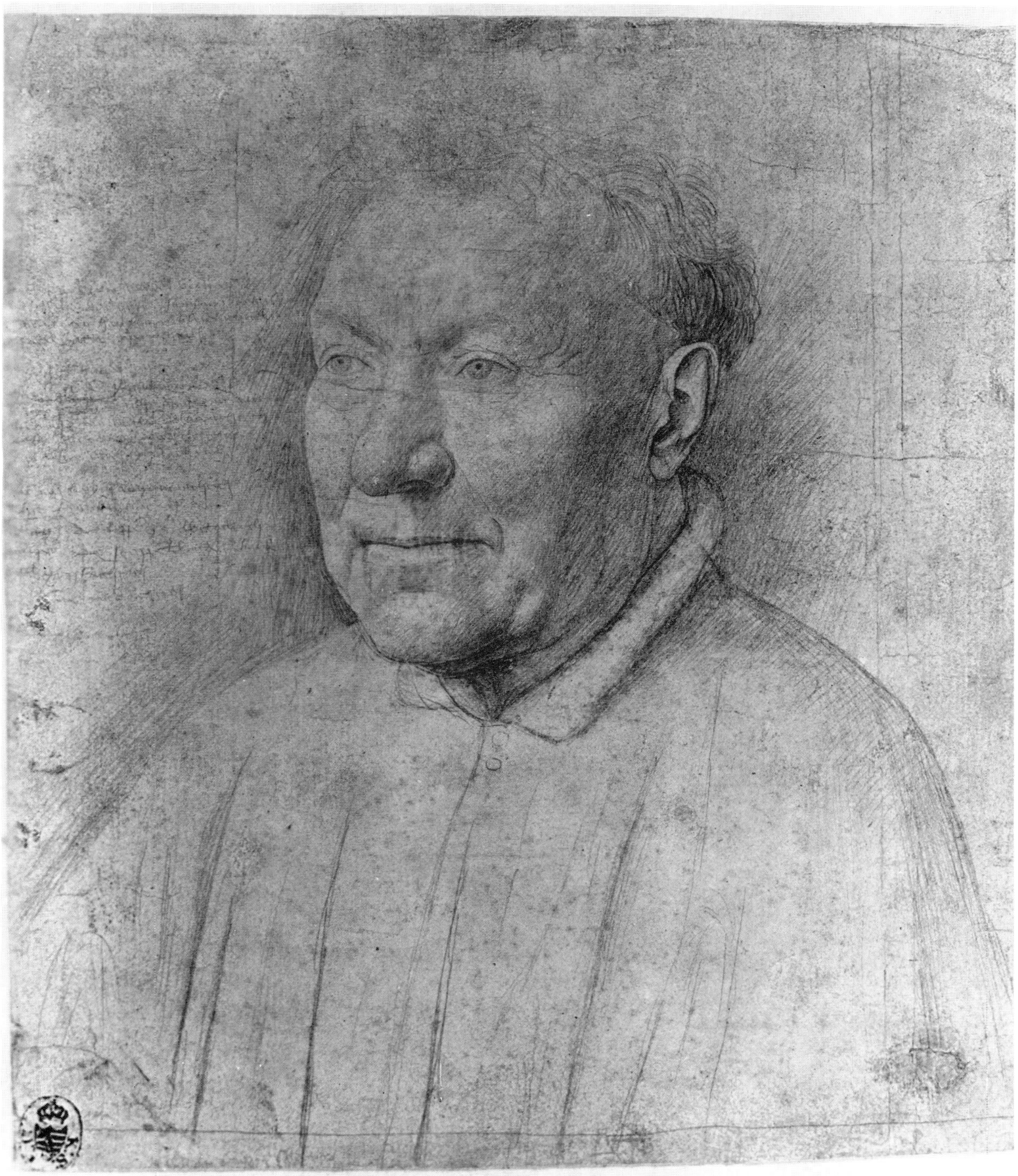

135 Jan van Eyck: 'Portrait of Cardinal Albergati'. The dark drawing lines are all incorporated into the shadow-image.

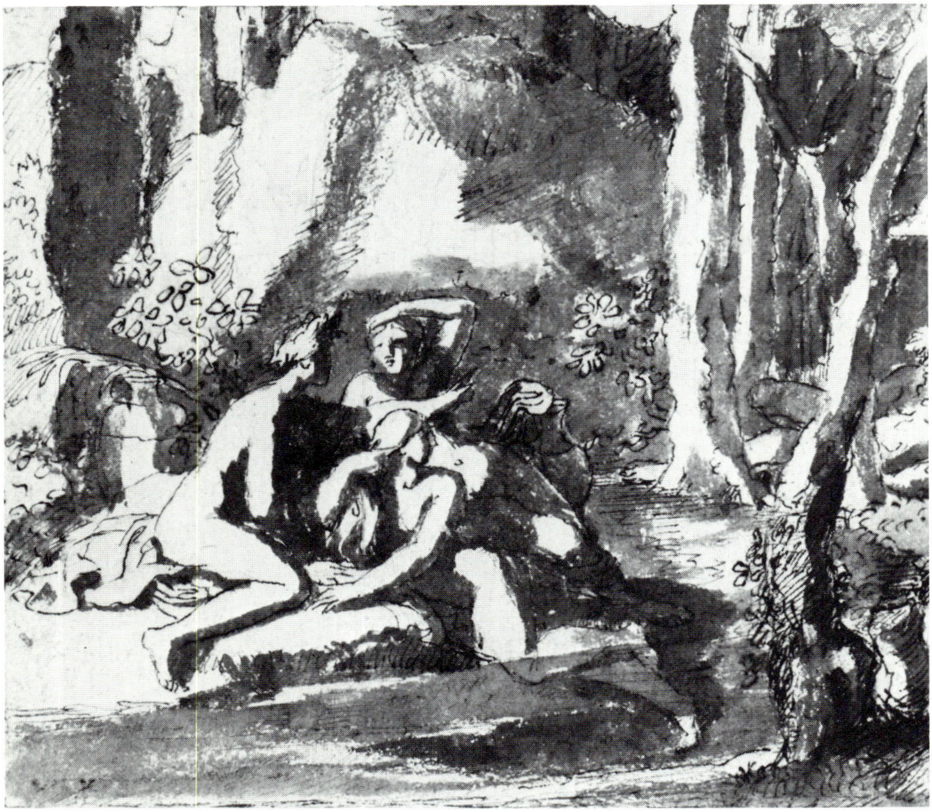

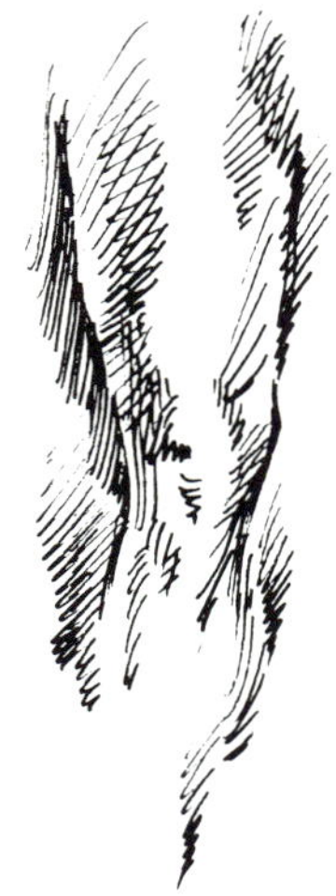

136 Nicholas Poussin: 'Three Nymphs', c. 1633–5. The modelling and cast shadow image unifies the figures and their landscape setting.
137 Drawing with tonal hatching only, uniting leg with ground.

Cast shadows naturally blend with modelling shadows, for shadows usually run off from the dark side of the object that casts it. When you are
138 actually drawing your shadow-glyphs you do need to be clear in your own mind which is which, but you will also find that the two kinds of shadows used together can join one object to another, connecting volume with volume or defining the space that lies between volumes.

In his *Nymphs*, Poussin uses his shadow wash very convincingly at the same time to define the volumes of his bodies and to connect them one to another. This drawing makes the point that when you are inventing shadows, you are also inventing the shapes of the objects that cast them.

When you set out to draw from nature using *chiaroscuro*, make sure you have a good single light-source. In direct sunlight there is no problem. But if you are working indoors it is best to set up your subject – still-life or model – so that the light falls on it from one side to produce interesting shadow shapes. This is something you should experiment with. You may find that a smallish fairly low window to one side of the subject gives particularly beautiful shadows. Rembrandt seems to have developed his style inside Dutch houses lit by such windows. Lamplight can do the same.

As you study your subject you will see that as well as the light that falls on objects from the main source, the objects themselves reflect that light back on each other from their own lit surfaces. A shadow on the dark side of one object can contain quite bright patches of light reflected back into it from an object whose own lit side faces into that shadow. The brighter the reflecting objects, the brighter the lights in the shadows.

138 Oskar Schlemmer: 'Study for the "Triadic Ballet"', 1922; a tonal image compounded of gouache, ink and collage of photographs.

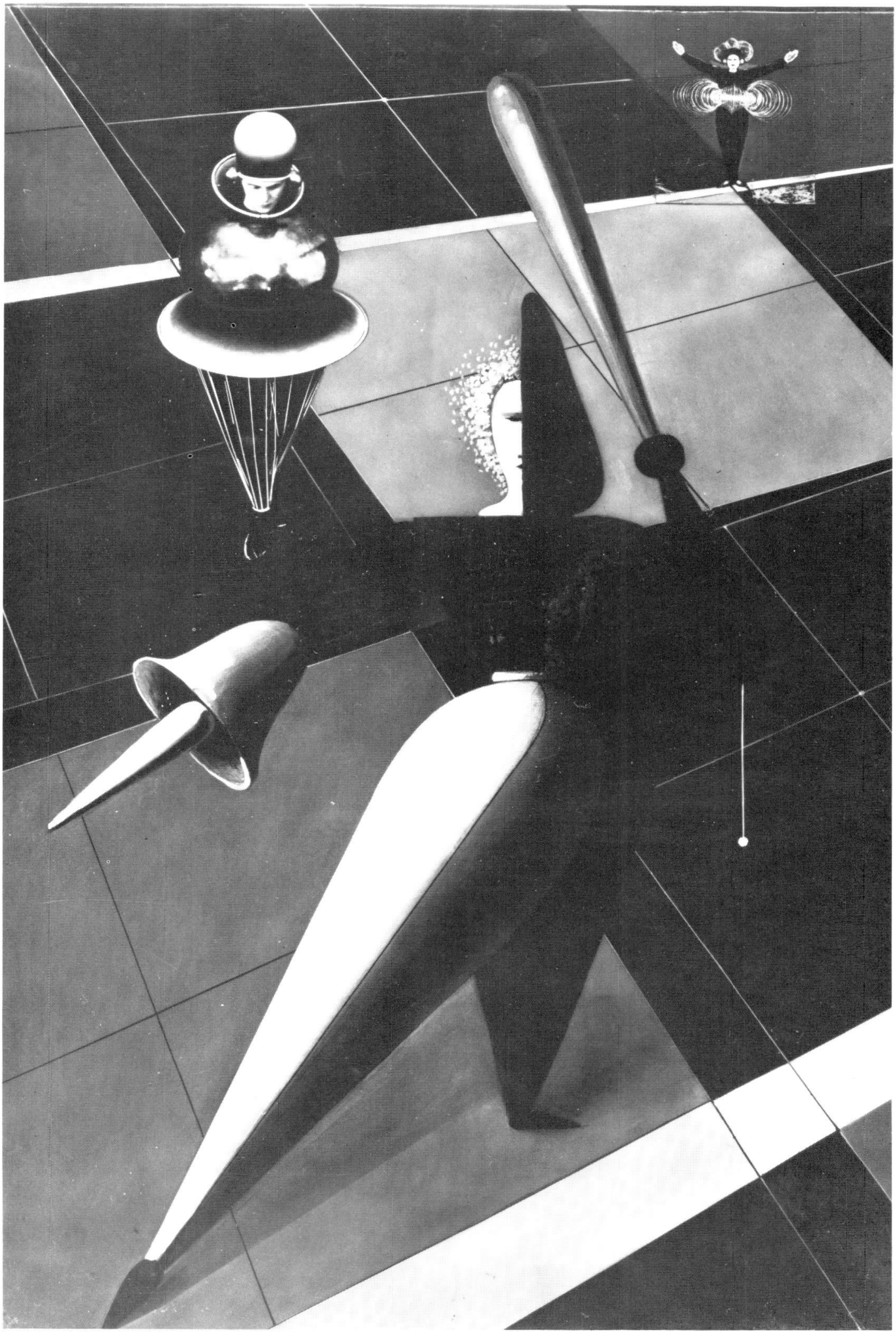

139 To draw in reflected lights is one of the ways of giving life to your shadow-drawing. To begin with you may find it quite difficult to recognize them in reality. Once you have become aware of them their importance is obvious. Without them shadow-drawing can feel slightly dead.

You should therefore try always to make sure your subject has lighting that suits your drawing style and stimulates your invention. Artists can use tone in their own personal ways to produce distinctive luminous images.

Students are sometimes expected to draw from subjects in bright, evenly lit studios that offer them almost nothing in the way of interesting dark shapes. In life-classes this may be a hangover from old-style teaching, which used models to teach students anatomical fact rather than artistic shadow-structure. In landscape drawing, out under a grey sky which diffuses the light of the sun, clear patterns of shadow can also become difficult to find. You may have to think of tone under these circumstances much more as colour-tone rather than as true shadow. But there are usually some places where deep shadow lies. And a few good dark shadow-holes, carefully placed in the format, can do wonders for a landscape design.

Section 33
Special Techniques

It is possible to draw on a toned surface rather than a white one – grey, blue, brown, reddish or green. Until the middle of the nineteenth century many artists used toned paper. If you use it you will find you can add to your dark shadow-drawing a complementary drawing in light glyphs. Instead of stating only those parts of the image where light does *not* fall, you can also state those places where it falls most brightly. The mid-tone of the untouched paper can serve to unite these two images. If you lay transparent tints of colour over this kind of drawing you will have a surprisingly complete picture, with real graphic depth.

Nowadays the idea of producing such images on toned grounds is becoming popular again – partly because it is now thought that design and colour are understood in separate sectors of the human brain. It is important to consider this point because we are still rather under the influence of Impressionism. The Impressionist artists expressly set out to combine drawing tone and colour into a single luminous medium. This involved surrendering many of the traditional resources of drawing.

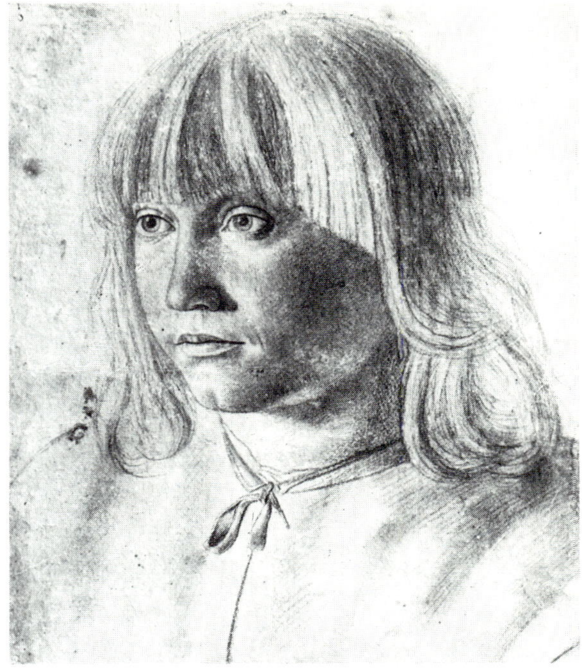

139 Antonello da Messina: 'Portrait of a Young Man'; based on a contour drawing which is amplified by modelling shadow with reflected lights.

Two major Post-Impressionist artists, Seurat and Cézanne, whose influence is still very strong, worked to regain graphic ground without losing Impressionist colour. Their drawings constitute such an important part of their work, and are so important in the recent history of drawing, that we should consider them individually.

In his fully developed style, Seurat worked his paper into a continuum of modulated tone, from deepest black to full light. According to a system of mathematical proportions and directions he placed a few edges marked by the steepest contrasts of tone. He was not interested in volumes or lines as such, but in the expressiveness of the silhouettes of figures conveyed entirely by tonal gradation. Those figures are usually solid blocks of dark tone, laid on with a live touch.

140 Georges-Pierre Seurat: 'Seated Woman', 1884–5; a study in crayon for one of the figures in his painting 'Sunday at the Grande Jatte'.

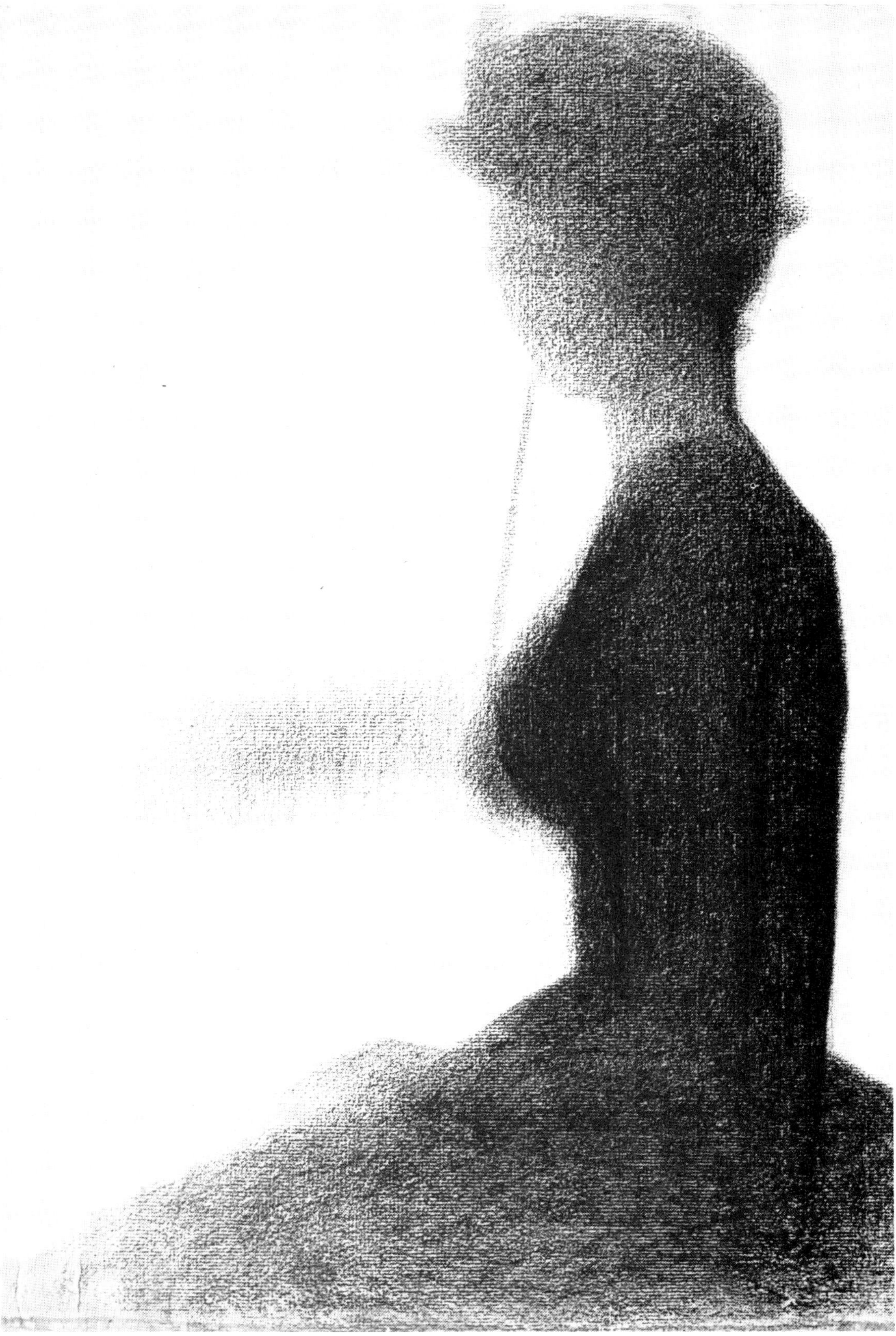

Cézanne also drew primarily with tone. But he conceived of tone as a function of volume and space. His art was devoted to presenting an image of the visible world as a continuity of rounded volumes, without any conceptual separations between one object and another. He did this by eliminating the kinetic quality of his drawn lines, and assimilating them entirely into the tonal image, just as Van Eyck had done. He laid on his tone in small, carefully graded patches, which he built up slowly and progressively into patches of shadow. The patches themselves he related to
108 each other by a strict mesh of transverse and radiating rhythms, running from one side of the format to the other. No mark went on to the paper that was not part of some interlocking set of rhythms, and did not play a part in defining and relating volumes. As a result of the demanding compositional standards he set himself, his drawings are always sparse.

Twentieth-century figurative artists have not developed the graphic possibilities of tone. By far the greatest number use tone primarily as colour. But recently, partly under the influence of photography, artists have once again begun to explore the resources of tonal gradients and structure.

One general consideration in all shadow-drawing is this: avoid putting on more tone than you need; and avoid especially putting too much of your darkest tone everywhere. Keep the blackest darks, the shadow-holes, for a few well-planned places. There are plenty of artists who use lots of black; but you may weaken your composition if you overdo it.

141 Paul Cézanne: 'Still-life', 1881–4. This pencil study shows the structure underlying this artist's use of modelling shadow.

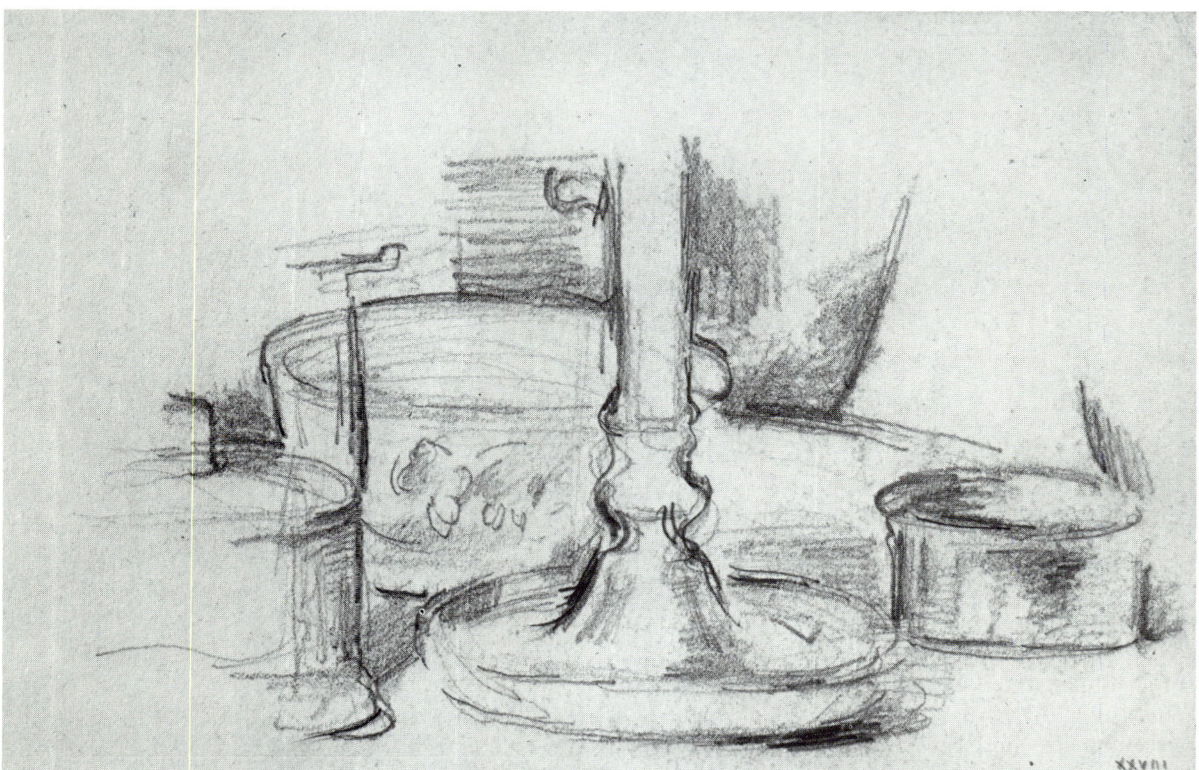

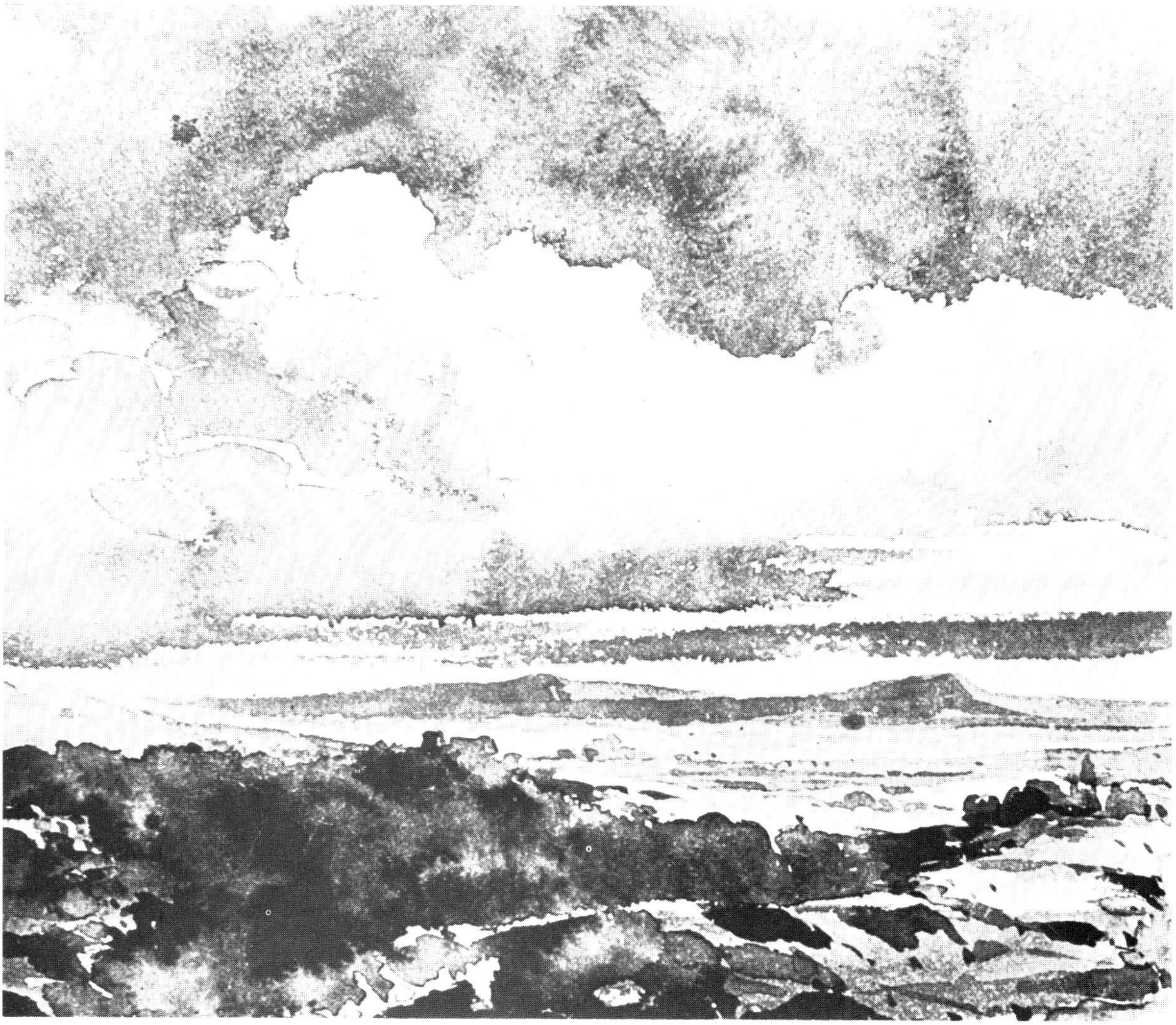

142 Eugène Delacroix: 'Landscape' in sepia wash. It reveals a sense of atmospheric vitality uniting earth and sky, expressed purely by tone.

There is one special way in which tonal drawing can represent deep space. It is often called 'atmospheric perspective', and is used mainly in landscape drawing. We know that water vapour in the atmosphere can veil the distance in a kind of luminous haze. As a result distant objects tend to seem paler, and have fewer distinct tones in them, than nearer objects. So to draw with atmospheric perspective you need to use only your palest tones for the distance. And what you draw as distant may also seem fuzzier. However, in, say, a desert, clear dry air can reduce or even eliminate the atmospheric effect; and far distant things, such as scrub on mountainsides, can be clearly defined. So you may be able to use your full range of tones even for the remotest objects.

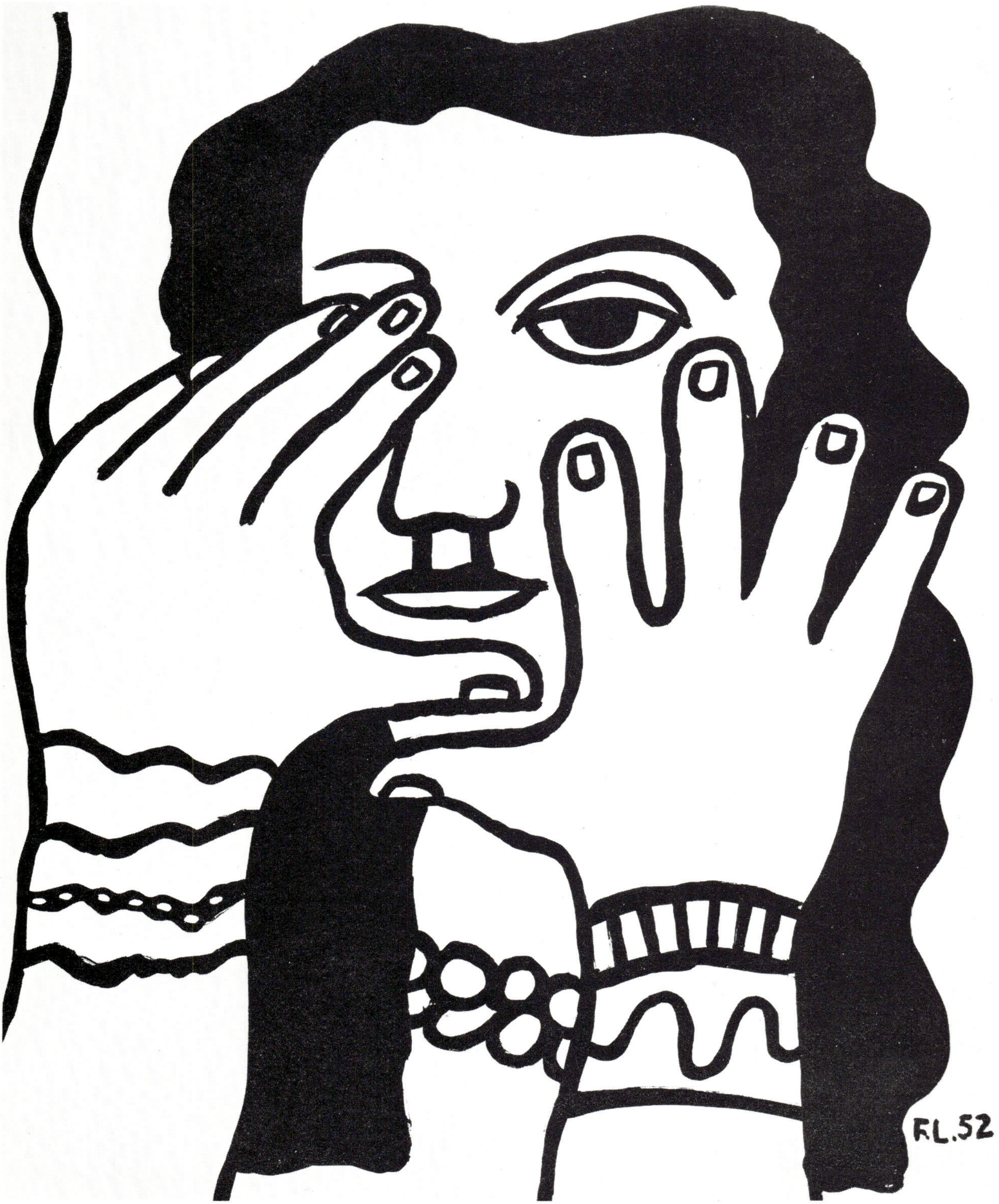

143 Fernand Léger: 'Face and Hands'. 1952; brushed in ink over pencil.

VI
Space and Figuration

We shall look into the problems of space and perspective, and discover ways of turning the drawing surface into a field of space, and of making figures inhabit that space. We shall look at drawing machines and the peephole perspective they produce.

Then we shall look more closely at the human body, the natural focus for human interest. It is through insight into our own bodies that we understand much of what goes on in the world. We have seen some of the ways in which this insight can be expressed in glyphs. We have also studied a variety of ways in which we can express our sense of the reality of the body. But art deals above all with human relationships and attitudes; and many of these can be expressed only by implication.

We shall investigate the expressive possibilities of bodies. We look first at ways of capturing the life of the individual body, and drawing from the model. Then we shall study the possibilities of developing graphic images of dramatic interaction between a variety of figures.

Section 34
Space as Relationship

Let us take up that question raised in Section 6, about the way the drawn image turns the drawing surface into a special kind of reality. The moment you recognize any group of marks as relating to familiar objects of the real world, you are accepting that they refer to three-dimensional things in space. Your sense of rhythmic interval and shape are vital to your grasp of any field of space.

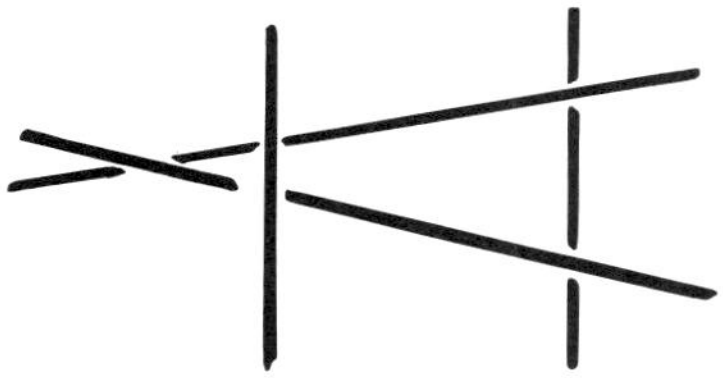

144 Diagrams of lines converting each other into objects in space.

The important thing to remember is that you cannot actually *draw* space or volume. The nearest you can get is to fill in the negative areas (Section 14). You can only give bodies a sense of presence and suggest a sense of space through suggesting relationships. Take a simple example. Let a single line stand for an 'object'. It is only when you add other lines that you can suggest the first line occupies space as if it were a body. There are four possible ways in which you can think of the space.

First, you can think of the paper as the support for an image which is meant to project into the space *above* the drawing surface. This is a way sculptors quite often draw. An artist will draw
like this to emphasize the final silhouettes of 133
bodies, to cut them free, so to speak, from the surface. Byzantine painters used to draw like this. In those tiny churches built in Greece and

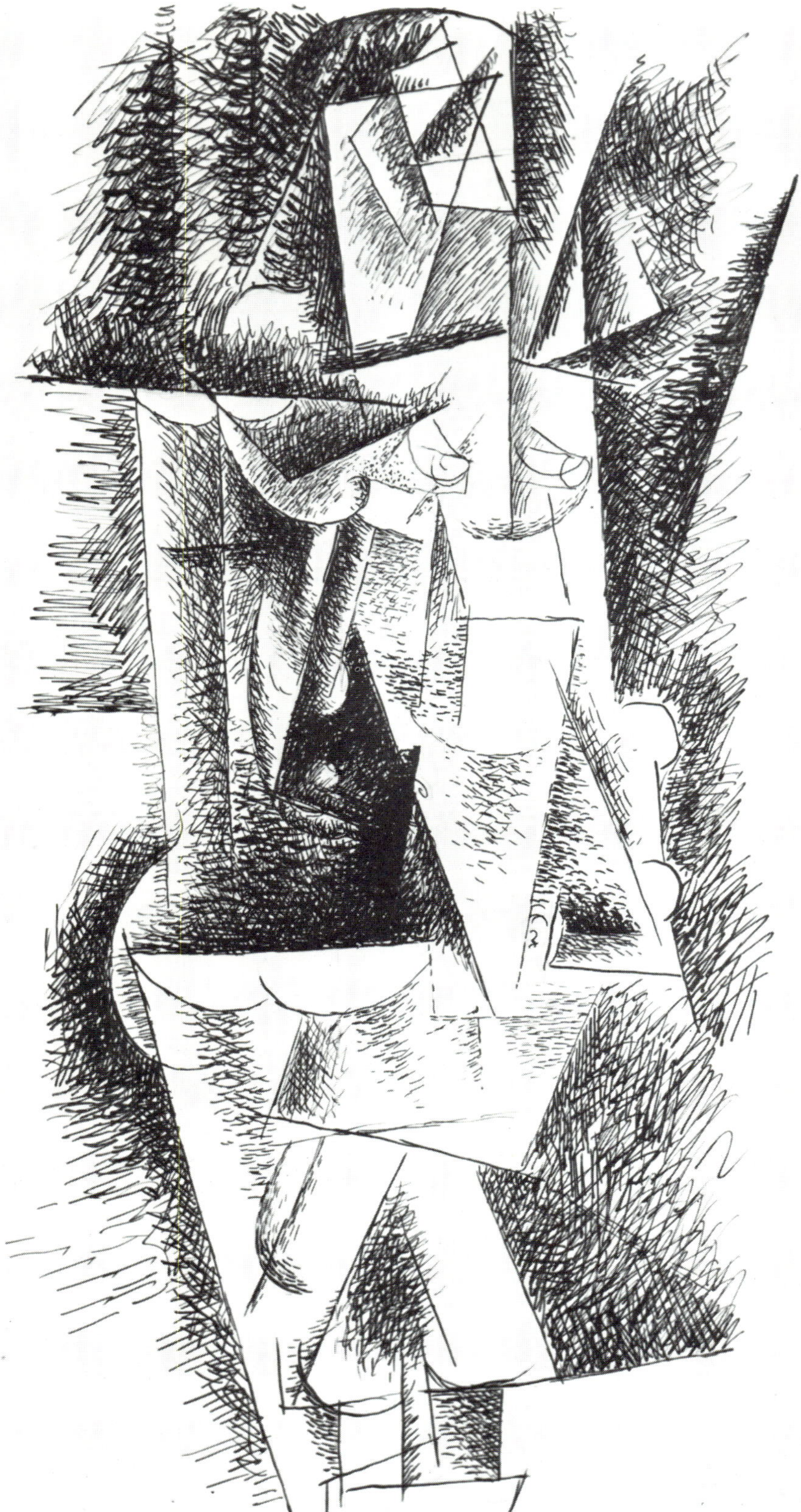

Yugoslavia between the eleventh and fifteenth centuries, which have interior wall-paintings of the life of Christ and saints, you often feel that the people depicted are inside the small enclosed space with you. Some painters of Palaeolithic caves in France and Spain seem to have thought of their images in this way, too. The bulk of the bodies of their animals often seems to 'blister up' from the bulges of the rock on which they are drawn.

Secondly, you can think of the paper surface as having a thickness of some kind which the image only implies. The most obvious example is the 'playing-card' image. Drawn enclosures divide up virtually the whole area and read as defined parts of a solid body – though not usually the whole of it. So the format of the sheet may cut off the space inhabited by the body, like a frame; but at the same time, only the positive volumes in the image are defined. A number of twentieth-century French artists, such as André Derain and Fernand
43 Léger, have used this way of treating space, imitating seventeenth- and eighteenth-century French playing-cards very closely. Picasso, too, often treated space this way. You can even bring sections of landscape and background into the system, provided they are not too large or dominant. You may also find that you can use the frame of the format to cut off the figures in different ways. And you can draw different thicknesses of lines to show up different qualities of the bodies.

The third way of treating the paper surface is the most familiar to us – so familiar, in fact, that many people assume it is the only possible one. The format becomes a kind of window-frame, behind which depth extends away, back towards the sky and the stars. Chinese Tangrams use this kind of space.

One reason for its familiarity is that it is the kind of space naturally generated by the drawing-machine, especially the camera. These machines (which we will discuss in Section 38) are all based upon the general laws of the science of optics. However, the laws of optics are not the same as real human experience. They only apply if you look at the world in the same way as the camera does – through a peephole. In fact, we perceive through two eyes, set apart in a head that is continually moving and attached to a body with legs, arms and hands, which all play a part in building up our image of the world. In addition, memories of moving and touching can be as important as pure optical recording in building a drawn image.

A fourth way of registering space only appeared in art during the twentieth century. Between about
1910 and 1916, Picasso and Braque in Paris 145
developed a kind of picture space usually called either 'flat pattern cubism' or 'synthetic cubism'. Both terms can be misleading. But this way of
working can still offer very interesting artistic 85
possibilities.

You start by recording the strongest profiles of the objects you are drawing, from different points of view, with strictly geometric lines. You then assemble them on to a grid or skeleton of horizontal and vertical lines. You relate these to the edges of your format by transverse rhythms and proportions (Section 5).

You then identify among your objects the chief planes that run, slanting diagonally, into the depth. You then emphasize these planes, and incorporate them diagrammatically on to the same grid or skeleton, defining them with straight edges. You may co-ordinate the edges of these planes as sets of parallel diagonals, spaced again by transverse rhythmic intervals.

The different elements will intersect in different ways, creating enclosures. As with grids (Section 19), you may stress some of these enclosures and abolish others. Some lines will remain, some will go. Some lines and enclosures may dominate others.

You can then introduce a further suggestion of space by springing apart edges or corners of the enclosures that remain, which you do by using hatching or shading on one side of the lines. Your space then becomes a combination of concepts, diagram, visual image, light and dark, composed by aesthetic choice. Your architecture of the horizontals and verticals tie all these different elements together. A powerful sense of the actual and even commonplace can result.

145 Pablo Picasso: 'Mlle Léonie', 1922–12; pen and ink. It exemplifies the cubist reorganization of abstracted profiles and planes.

Section 35
Overlaps

Japanese drawings are often thought of as flat. Certainly their lines are firmly attached to the surface of the paper. But they create a strong sense of space and movement in space by using lines to
112 indicate a multitude of overlapping edges belonging
to the folds of garments. These advance before and disappear behind each other. As we know that bodies and garments are joined to each other, we read the overlaps as clues to an order in space among the various components. The nearest edge overlaps all the others. The middle distant edges overlap the far distant. The same line may do both things, at opposite ends.

This is perhaps the best way of showing that your picture space has depth. It may be obvious, but it is by no means simple. You still have to suggest that your 'things' are solid bodies of some kind, or the overlapping will not work. The edges will just remain lines. You can show this solidity in several ways.

First, you can draw your shapes as continuous enclosures which overlap each other. You can then reinforce this impression by filling in your positive enclosures with tones or textures, as
59 Malevitch does. Alternatively, you can use frottage
or colour. If you use two or more kinds of filling-in, or give your outlines different qualities, one area may seem to advance in front of the others. Generally speaking, a hard, strong outline will make its enclosure stand out in front of an enclosure which is softer-edged, or drawn with a paler outline. And clear-cut shapes, especially geometric ones, may tend to stand up nearer than fuzzy or organic ones. Try working with a variety of overlapping shapes, treating them in different ways.

147 Any set of overlapping shapes can suggest a
natural arrangement leading into space which the shapes seem to occupy as bodies; because, of course, in our normal experience things nearer to us block out our view of other things behind them.

You can state your clues to the 'advancing' and
178 'receding' qualities of the areas of any body by
means of overlaps. Making the clues conflict can often produce interesting effects – although you have to be careful not to let them cancel each other out. Only experiment can prove what will work for you.

Overlaps can be perhaps the most important 116
technique in all figurative drawing, especially when you start to use them in a sophisticated way.
Look back at the tangram (Section 22) which 93
illustrates a man in a boat by means of an overall silhouette of the man and boat together. The pieces of which that silhouette is composed have no obvious connection with the pieces of reality. The image could be redrawn and divided up according to the overlaps that would be there in reality. The gunwale would cut across the body; the arm across the body; the hat across the face; and so on. At once this gives us a series of overlaps to read, producing a sense of depth. The lines mark the edges of parts of the object, preserving its unity, but implying three-dimensional presence.

You can use clear overlaps to give a sense of presence to the foliage of a group of trees, for example. In the diagram of the arm shown here the overlaps of the folds of the clothing enable you to read a sense of the bulk in the bodies. This is not a simple technique. It combines enclosures (Sections 11–13) and transverse rhythms (Section 5) as well as overlaps.

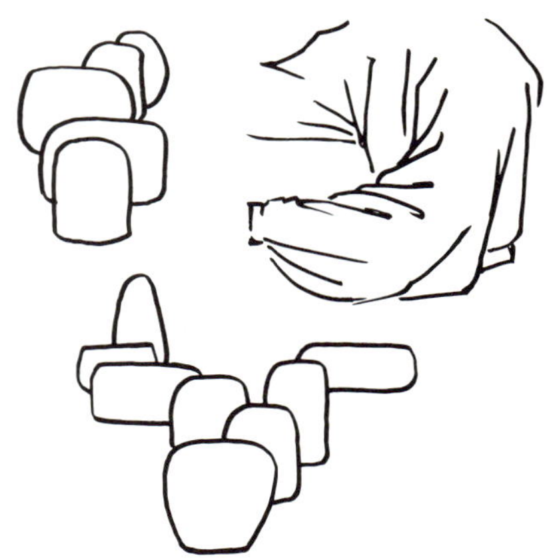

146 Sequences of overlaps generate the sense of depth in space.

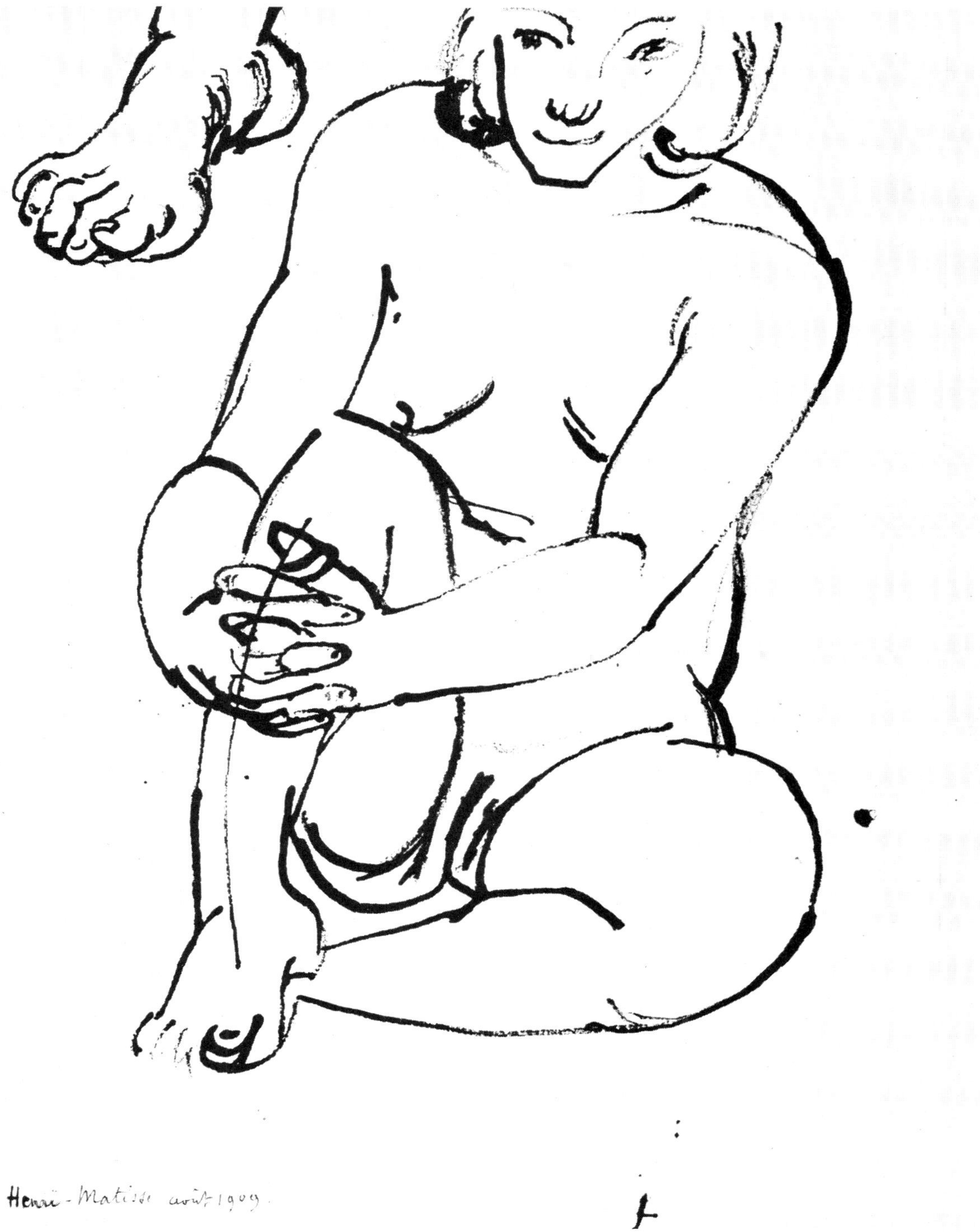

147 Henri Matisse: 'Woman Nursing her Knee', c. 1909. This pen drawing creates its sense of depth by contour overlaps.

109 You can use overlaps, especially in landscape drawing, to lead the eye far into the depth of the image. You can make your overlaps in such a way that they suggest specific pathways of steps into the picture-space. Each overlap thus gives the viewer the sense that it is a slice of depth.

You can even draw the slices of depth as general shapes before particularizing them. This allows you first to make sure that the overall contours uniting them in the flat, two-dimensional sense are rhythmically lively. You can, of course, start with the lines, and then find the depth-slices to
148 link them. In some traditional Chinese landscape painting, sets of these depth-slices were fantastically elaborated into broken and jagged mountain peaks. The slices do not have to be completely outlined. You can combine two or more opposed
155 slice-contours which do not close together, but give a series of step-backs on alternate sides of a continuous object. This is what many Chinese and European artists have done in landscape drawings.

148 Tung Ch'i-Ch'ang: landscape, 16th–17th c. The accumulated brushed ink dots define overlapping depth slices.

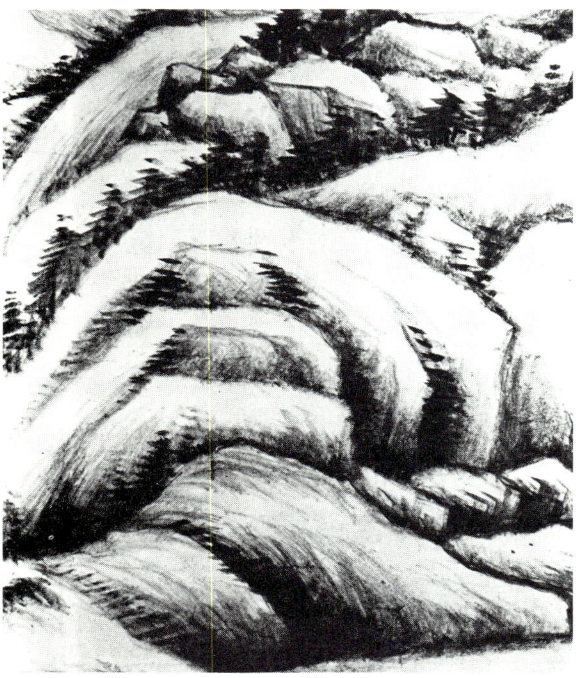

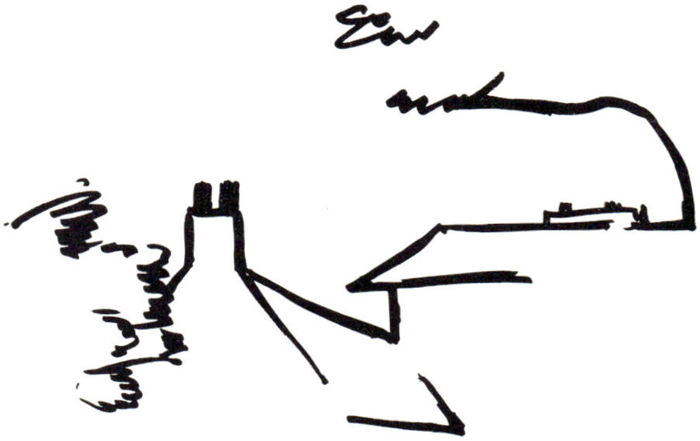

149 Live contour may unify essentially separate depth slices.

With a landscape of buildings, you may find that the first thing that strikes you is the interesting skyline. You will want to be able to state this, provisionally but clearly. From it you can then work away, by adding new transversely-measured edges marking new overlaps, shed-lines, continuities derived from it, until you are able to establish a fully three-dimensional image.

When you draw any overlaps of this kind you will find it best to exaggerate the effect in two ways. (Exaggeration to begin with often helps, because as you work on with any drawing it tends naturally to 'soften' slightly.) First, exaggerate the *angles* at which edges cross each other. Secondly, exaggerate the way the edge behind the overlapping edge is broken.

Michelangelo's sketches of the well-muscled human body allow us to see these techniques very clearly. They also show you how to break up outlines which actually look continuous in nature into overlapping sections. Each segment of outline suggests that it encloses a slice of the object in depth. If you arrange the overlaps of your segments so that the outline of the slice projecting nearest to the eye overlaps the next and so on, you can give the feeling that you are not drawing just edges, but presenting the front surfaces of the object. Some of these slices may have clear-cut edges; but some, especially the nearest bulges, may not, in which case you may have to draw outlines which are not edges. You can draw them faintly, or use a row of dots or a bit of hatching. Each of these slices may correspond with one or more oval volume (Section 28).

150 Michelangelo: 'Studies of a Crucified Man', c. 1504. The pen strokes that define volumes give a powerful sense of sculptural projection.

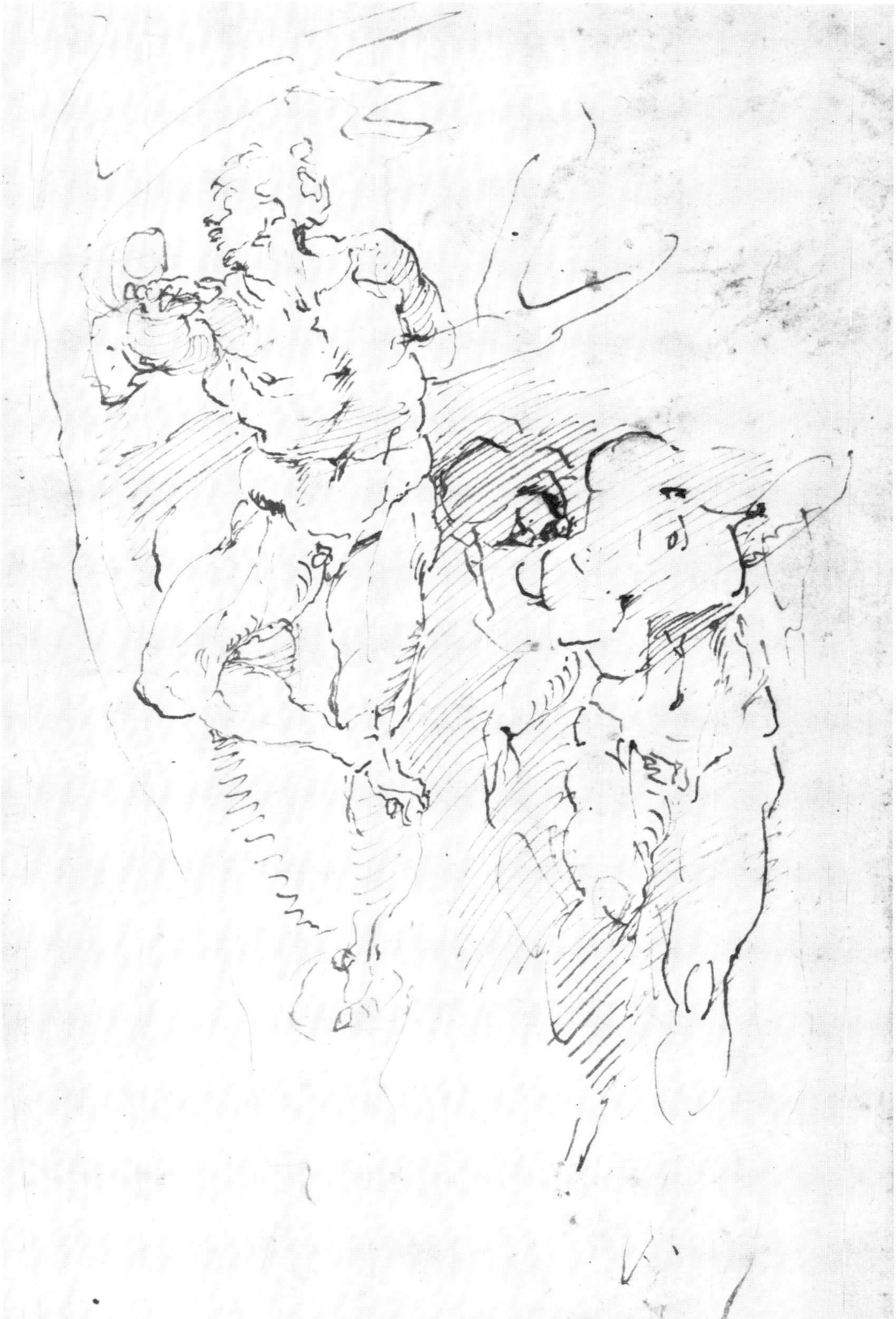

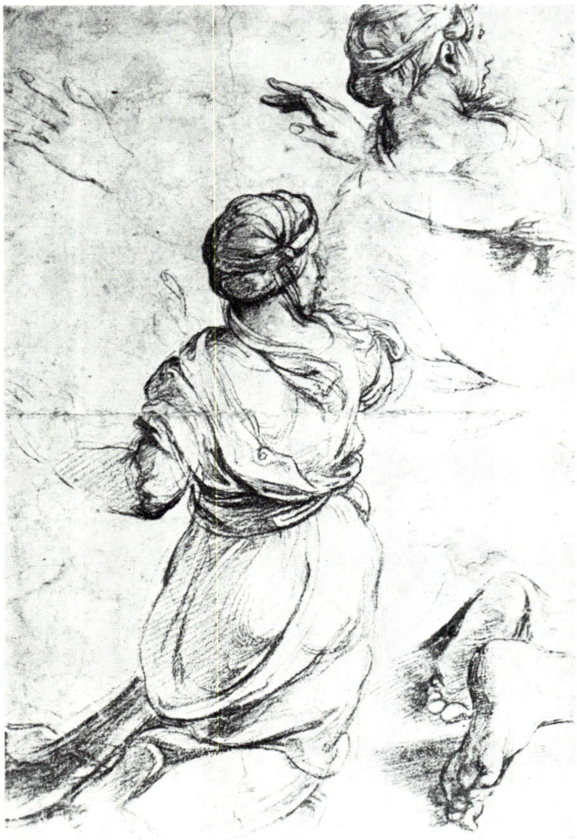

151 Raphael: chalk study of a figure for a fresco; spiral overlaps give a vigorous sense of movement in space.

Towards the end of the fifteenth century, a number of European artists developed their series of overlaps to suggest three-dimensional spirals running round the underlying volumes of bodies.
3 Leonardo da Vinci and Raphael did this particularly successfully.

Section 36
The Floor

By far the most important surface which runs into the three dimensions of space is the floor or ground. It ends at the level of the horizon. All the objects in our world stand on a floor of some kind, simply because of gravity; and so unless you suggest a floor, any set of overlapping objects will seem to float. That indeed, is how you show such things as clouds, bodies in outer space and flying angels.

Since we normally stand on the same floor as the things we are looking at, the floor links us to the world which figurative art presents to us. We feel it runs up into the image from under our feet,
and ends at a horizon whose placing on the sheet 15
helps to show our *own* position as spectators in relation to the objects depicted.

With different kinds of subject matter you will need to treat the floor in different ways. If you are supposed to be standing in the same room as a dancer, say, you can simply draw the dancer's feet standing in correct and intelligible relationship on a floor which you seem to be seeing from eye level but which you do not actually draw.
The dancer by Degas shows exactly what I mean. 10
The horizon line seems to be about halfway up the figure. However, if you want to suggest to the viewer that he is supposed to be lying down or

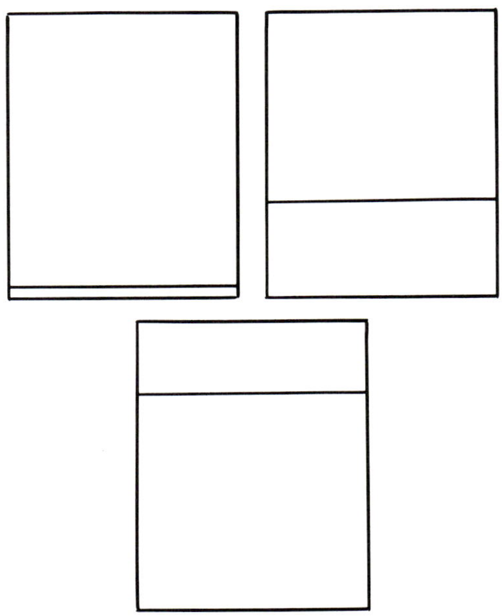

152 A differing sense of space is created by different horizon lines.

sitting, you make your horizon line low down and the ground plane narrow. If you are supposed to be high up, say at the top of a tower or a mountain, then you can make your ground plane long,
2c extending right up to a very high horizon line. This also enables you to draw section rings (Section 28) for the nearer objects. As objects get further away their sections become narrower.

You will also see very clearly from my drawing of islands how useful and important a rhythmic series of standing places on a floor can be. In this case the floor is water. The shores of the islands give you sets of rhythmic transverse intervals across which you can read on into the remote distance.

You can use any floor, as I suggested above, to lay out a kind of ground-plan for the objects in your image: the feet of chairs and the bases of other furniture in a room; the bases of haystacks and barns and the routes of tracks in a landscape; the tyres of automobiles and the feet of people in a street scene. However, at the other extreme you can do as Cézanne did. By deliberately abolishing any sense of connection between viewer and image, he created the sense of loneliness and impersonal distance that characterizes his work.

You can play all sorts of tricks with your floor. Draughtsmen like the Persians developed it into a fantastic carpet by lifting the horizon almost to the top of the picture. This allowed them to add all kinds of events, people and things in profile which you would never normally be able to see together in one scene. You too can tilt the floor steeper than it should be, and you can suggest a
2a steep slope up. If you flatten it into little more than a line your viewpoint will seem low in relation to the 'feet' of anything standing. This *should* imply that the viewer is looking 'up and under' at anything which stands at all near to him. If you set
0 your horizon below the bottom edge of the format you can make objects tower above you.

There is no rule that every part of a drawn composition should be entirely consistent spatially. You can think of the format of your drawing sheet as divided into separate cells, in each of which a different kind of space may operate.

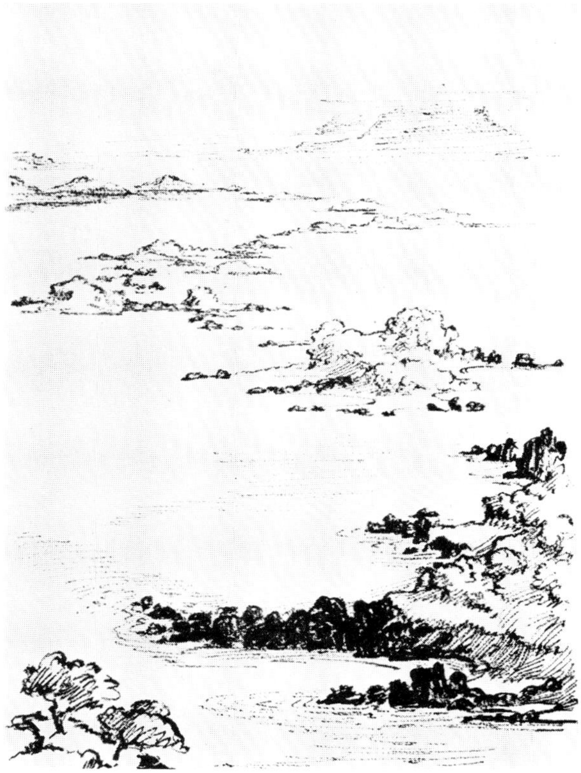

153 'Islands', in pen and ink, illustrates the 'floor'.

This is basically an extension of conceptual space (Section 34). The extreme example is the page of the illustrated comic book, where you have to know how each frame connects with the ones each side of it in order to understand the conceptual space-time of the story. Movie conventions help us here.

You can keep the cells but abolish their frames, so that they seem to make a continuous tissue of space. This works particularly well in illustrating stories. Successive episodes can be shown in different space cells of a single composition. This was often done in large wall-paintings, such as those in the Campo Santo at Pisa, in Italy (fourteenth century) and in the cave monasteries at Ajanta, in India (second century BC to AD 600). Modern artists such as R. B. Kitaj use the same technique.

Section 37
Visual Perspective

In late fifteenth-century Europe, the idea developed that the format of every single picture *had* to be a single visual unity, which *had* to reflect an instantaneous view of 'the world'. This idea encouraged artists to apply theories derived from the science of optics to art. The science of optics considers the functions of light, lens and eye as working within an independent static system and ignores any active contribution from or involvement of the viewer. The artist was supposed to plot or diagram a second version of nature which would show you as viewer a scene as if you had actually been there watching it, but were motionless. We call this 'peephole' perspective, because it is only through a peephole that you ever see reality in strict perspective. The fixed peephole or aperture is the essential element in the drawing machines we shall discuss in the next section.

Of course, nowadays we know that our perception of the structure of our world cannot be explained by the theory of optics alone. Many different kinds of experience play a part in our visual understanding of reality. Indeed, the older, pre-optical methods of depicting space can be truer to reality in many ways than the purely optical.

Perspective as a valid artistic theory consists of a logical binding together of several simpler things, including some of those we have just been discussing:

1) Things meant to be close are shown larger than distant things.
2) The edges of nearer things overlap and blot out things which are supposed to lie behind them (unless the nearer things are meant to be transparent).
3) Nearer things stand lower down on the 'floor'; more distant things stand higher up, closer to the imagined horizon. Nothing stands above the horizon line unless it is floating or flying.

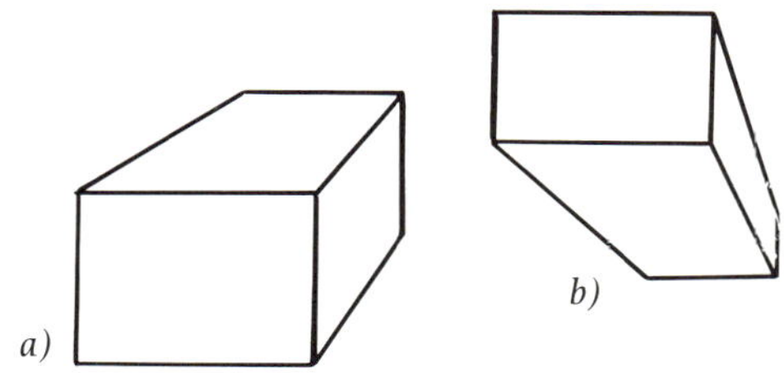

154 Diagram of ways of illustrating objects a) below and b) above the viewer.

4) Flat surfaces, for example walls or floors, diminish in height and width as they run off into the depth of space.
5) When you mean the viewer to feel as if he is above something, you show its top. When he is meant to be below something you show its underneath. You draw flat tops and bottoms according to (4) above.

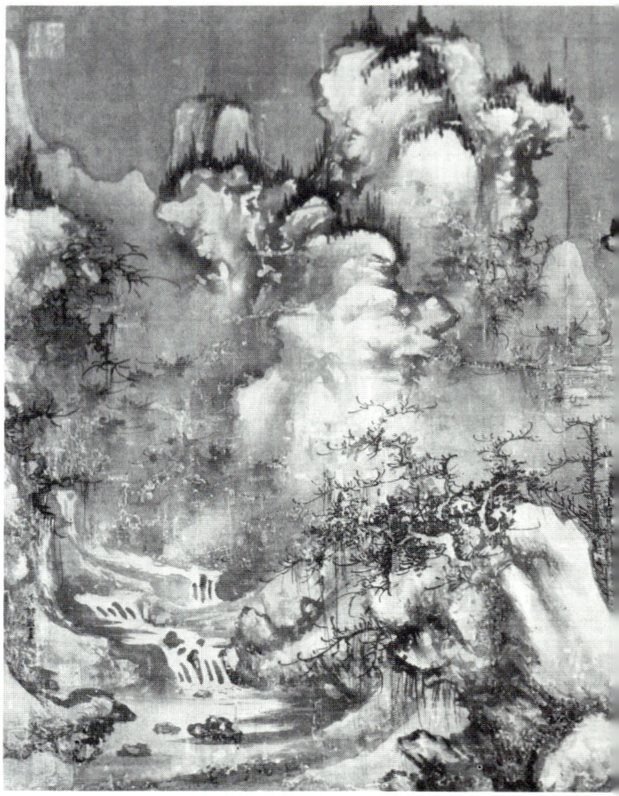

Most of the world's great art has made do with these simple rules of perspective. However, it has not always observed them very strictly. Here are some of the rules that have been broken: most non-European and early European art often made the most important people or things in a scene much bigger than the others and also tended to avoid unnecessary overlapping of one figure by another, save among the less important people and things; sixteenth-century Persian art tended to show both near and far distant figures as the same size; in Chinese landscape-drawing of the twelfth to eighteenth centuries, the relations of scale amongst the mountains, rocks, trees and rivers were more or less 'normal', but startling dislocations of space were sometimes created by illogical overlaps.

Provided you make reasonable calculations of the relationship between size and distance, you can produce perfectly satisfactory perspective drawings by following the basic rules, without knowing about optical theory at all. The calculations depend upon you as artist agreeing with the viewer about what the separate objects that you are representing are supposed to be, and how big those objects usually are. A person 'near' you in a room usually seems a good deal bigger than a person at the far end. The head of someone near to you usually seems larger from scalp to chin than the height, say, of a substantial mountain ten miles away. Hold your own hand out in front of you and you will see how such a small thing can cover the largest of distant objects.

If you are dealing with a subject that is spatially complicated, such as a landscape, you may like to follow one method used by the great masters of the past, in both the West and the Far East. To

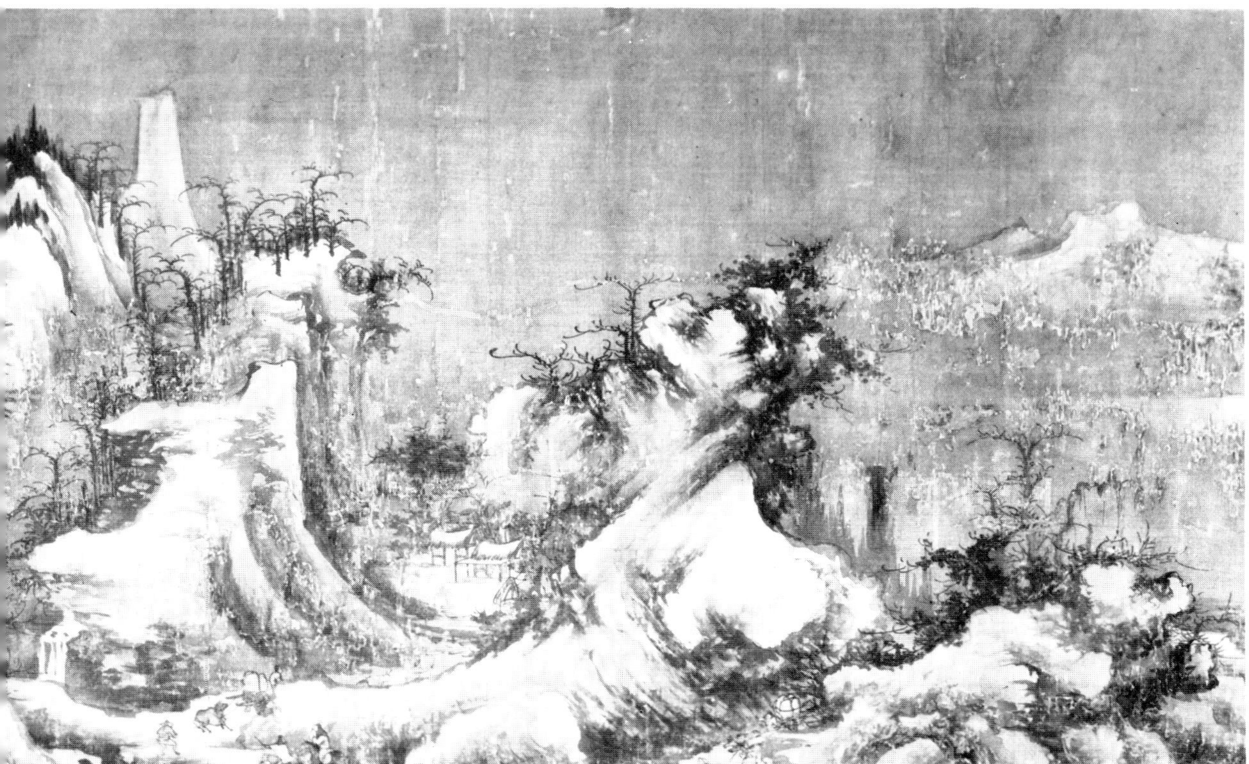

155 Kuo Hsi: Chinese winter landscape, 11th c., part of a horizontal landscape scroll; brush and ink. This illustrates the creation of space by bands of depth, overlaps, spaces opening between masses, and by atmospheric perspective.

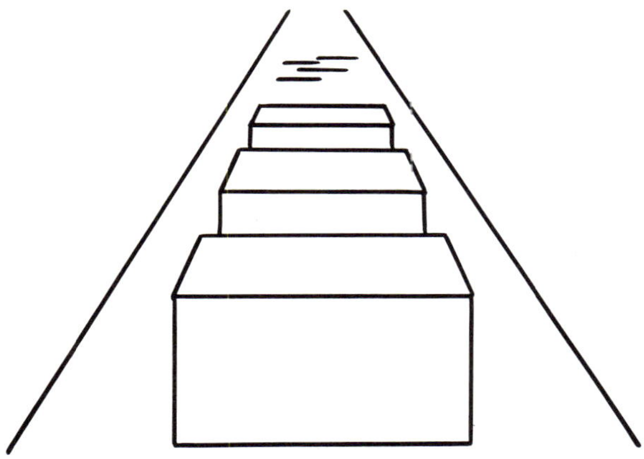

156 *Diagram of depth bands.*

make it manageable they divided up the whole vast space between the foreground and the distant sky into bands of depth – usually three. These bands correspond more or less with the shifts of focus needed as you concentrate on the near ground, the middle distance and the far distance. Within each of your depth-bands you can set up your groups of overlaps; and you can link one depth-band to another by overlaps. You just need to be careful not to spoil the clarity of your separate banding.

Once you agree with the viewer about the depth-bands, it becomes much easier to develop your ideas. You can use conflicts of reading, for example. If you do an ordinary drawing of a person, but set it fairly high up on your drawing sheet, you can make that person seem like a giant by putting in shapes suggesting smaller figures lower down. This then becomes a foreground if you connect them up according to the logic of the 'floor' and rules (2) to (5). Goya does just this in his painting of *The Colossus*, adding clouds floating across the figure's hips for further effect.

The Chinese tangram images (Section 22) are actually made up of same-sized pieces, yet each image as a whole suggests different contexts of space-depth. In one image you accept a piece as a foot, say; in another you see the same piece as a distant mountain-promontory. Experiment with these techniques in your own drawings, and you will quickly find your way into deep-space imagery.

Section 38

Drawing Machines and Cameras

The discovery and study of the science of optics in the fifteenth century led to the development of the drawing machine. All drawing machines work according to optical principles; so they naturally cut out a whole level of expressive possibility. However, they do enable artists to portray correctly and easily all sorts of difficult visual effects, including proportion, perspective, foreshortening, likenesses and the massing of drapery folds. They therefore became standard aids for the professional painter who, from about 1420 on, was expected to paint portraits and elaborate scenes combining far distance with close portrait figures for patrons who knew about optical phenomena. Drawing machines are still on the market, some very modestly priced. But you can make a good one for yourself quite easily. You could work from Dürer's illustration of his drawing machine. Leonardo da Vinci also left drawings of an artist using a similar machine. Dürer also devised some more complicated ones to illustrate the theory as well as the practice. The modern camera is a descendant of this original drawing machine.

The machine is based on a board about three feet (*c.* 91cm) long. At one end you mount crossways a frame measuring about 24 by 28 inches (*c.* 61×71cm), standing at right angles to the board, and containing a sheet of glass or transparent paper. At the other end you fix a stake; on top of it is either a point, to which you put your eye, or better, a peephole through which you look with one eye. It is best if you make the distance between frame and stake adjustable, and thus adaptable to very close and very distant subjects (as with the adjustable focal length of the camera). Correspondingly you may need to make the height of the stake adjustable to place your image where you want it in the frame. The 'rising front' of the old-fashioned plate camera reflected this need. The whole thing needs some kind of stand.

You then look at your subject through the peephole and the glass in the frame. Keeping your eye at the peephole, with a grease crayon you follow along the outlines of your subject where they appear to lie on the glass. You will then have a crayon outline on glass giving optically correct proportions and perspective. You transfer this to a sheet of paper either by tracing or by squaring off. You square off the drawing by applying a grid of squares to the glass; then rule a corresponding grid with the same number of larger squares on to your copy-sheet; finally you copy the original, piecemeal but larger, from square to corresponding square. Squaring off, incidentally, is a standard way of enlarging or reducing an original drawing – often used by wall-painters.

The next stage of the evolution of the machine took place about 1540. If you take a totally 'dark room' (in Italian a *camera oscura* from which comes our word camera) and poke a pinhole in one wall, an image of the lit scene outside will appear, upside down, on the wall opposite the pinhole. You can trace around this image. If you make your 'room' the size of a large box, you will get an image on the wall of the box – again upside down. The problem is then how to record it.

During the sixteenth century techniques were developed for grinding optical lenses and making mirrors from good-quality glass. The back wall of the box could then be made out of a sheet of ground glass. If the artist got under a black cloth behind his box he was able to trace the faint upside-down image on the glass. The pinhole was also replaced by a lens of definite focal curvature, which gave a good clear image on the back wall. Later, sets of mirrors were put behind the lens, so that the image from it could actually be projected on to a sheet of drawing paper the right way up; the artist, under his black cloth, could trace it quite easily and directly. The modern camera technique, invented by Daguerre around 1836, is to put a sheet coated with light-sensitive emulsion at the back of the box, and to fix the image chemically.

Vast numbers of artists used different versions of the early machines, from Dürer and Holbein to

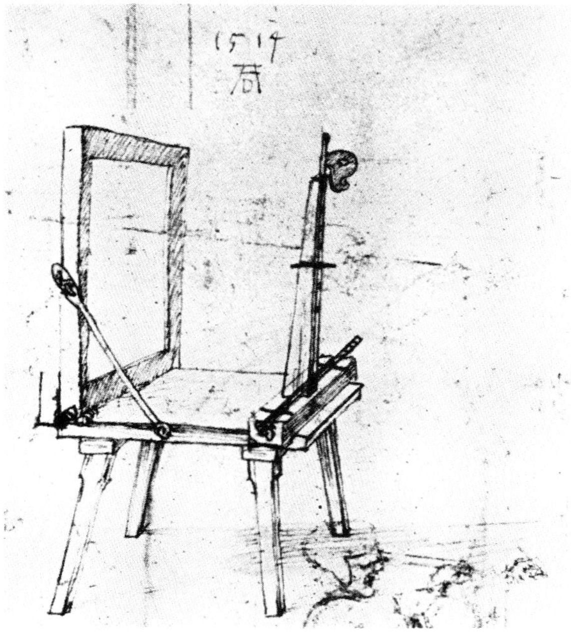

157 Albrecht Dürer: 'Drawing Machine'; pen and ink.
158 Diagrams of the drawing machine (top), and the principle of the camera obscura (bottom).

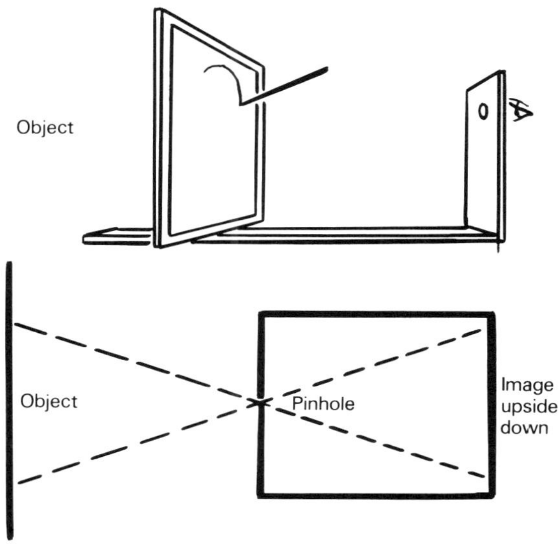

Vermeer, Canaletto and Constable, and virtually every eighteenth- and nineteenth-century portrait and landscape painter. So it is not in the least surprising that artists eagerly took up working from photographic ('light-drawn') prints when they became available. One of the first was Delacroix, and after him Manet, Degas and all the great Impressionists, as well as hundreds of academic painters. All commercial illustrators and professional portraitists and landscapists, as well as Andy Warhol and the California Hyper-realists, nowadays use machines, most commonly cameras, to give themselves a ready-made and accurate base, often projecting transparencies on to their drawing surface.

The question is: a base for what? It is possible to use the series of methods described in this book to produce coherent and expressive drawn compositions which are based on mechanically accurate images. Nowadays our eyes have been so conditioned by the huge numbers of photographs we have seen that we tend naturally to admire artists whose art and vision were based on 'mechanical-seeing'. When we say 'naturalistic' we probably mean 'mechanical'. We love, for example, the work of Vermeer and Degas.

No one now doubts that the photograph can be a work of art, but there is still intense argument in the art world – as there has been for over a century – about its status as such. Collectors certainly pay very high prices for prints by, say, Ansell Adams. If photographs can be works of art, perhaps drawings based on photographs can be too. Nowadays artists even imitate effects that were originally photographic, such as lens distortions which exaggerate parts of the object, the graining of emulsion on blown-up prints, or the effects of the telephoto lens.

However, the photograph has one big limitation. It usually produces an optically standardized layout of the world. It can usually only correspond to the static image seen by one motionless eye. It has none of those implications of time, movement and kinetic metaphor in which drawing – and real experience – are rooted. Some artists like the feeling this gives, and may incorporate it into their own drawings. However, many of the really great masters of European or Oriental tradition carefully avoided submitting their graphic thoughts to the viewpoint of the machine. They built their imagery up stroke by stroke from nothing. The foundations of their designs rest in linear concepts, using their own invented emphasis, layout and rhythms. Michelangelo, Titian, Rubens, Caravaggio, Goya and Klee, for instance, all lived in the era of the drawing machine without using it; Delacroix and Cézanne drew from photographs for information. None of these artists incorporated ready-made, mechanically produced design as a component in their final work. Figurative drawing can do far more fascinating things than layout machines or cameras will usually let it do.

Let us look now at the history of box-perspective and at certain procedures you will need to follow if you are to use this method of drawing.

You are almost certain to have heard of strict box-perspective and to have seen diagrams which illustrate how parallel lines laid on the ground or defining the faces of buildings run away together into space; and how the angles at which they run away are determined by a vanishing point on the horizon at which they all meet. These are based upon applying peephole perspective strictly and consistently to a scene, and arranging it to show as many surfaces as possible which can offer converging lines.

Following the examples of Leonardo da Vinci and Dürer during the later fifteenth century many artists explored the possibilities of using vanishing points on the horizon to create images of open city squares as a setting for their figures. During the sixteenth and nineteenth centuries Dutch artists in particular adopted elements of this technique. This may well have had something to do with the fact that Holland was a country where many optical scientists and lens-makers lived. Following their example, artists everywhere came to adopt the vanishing point as a useful means of integrating their scenes.

These artists thought of many different ways of introducing into their compositions the image of lines running together to converge into the distance. A common one is to include a floor that is chequer-boarded with square tiles, or a building façade or interior carefully laid out to show its architectural outlines converging. Indoors, tables and cupboards were carefully drawn according to the same rules. To lay out all these designs to comply with the optical rules, draughtsmen needed to draw schematic diagrams before they began the drawing proper. So they took to using the drawing machines, which produced correct optical perspective automatically. Many artists came to find strict perspective an unnecessary tyranny, which inhibited their expressive invention. So it was gradually abandoned.

Nowadays, however, the imagery of strict perspective has been revived. You may find it useful yourself. Science-fiction illustrators employ it continually as a way of demonstrating the vast size of fantasy space-machines, and of integrating them into enormous landscape vistas. Since such illustration is anyway based upon scientific imagination it is highly appropriate that its drawing style should itself favour the abstract optical diagram.

Another area where strict perspective drawing can be very important today is in designing and executing sets for film and television productions. A person skilled in perspective can design, say, a medieval street set which looks as if it is a hundred yards long, when it is only thirty feet long. Artists who work on film sets also paint, for example, perspectives on glass which work as distant backgrounds to scenes actually shot in the studio.

One way of using elements of abstract perspective diagram has been important in modern art. Klee, for example, used it a great deal at one time. This can be called 'free-plane' invention, and is very interesting to experiment with. You draw out images of rectangular planes in perspective, such as you would find being used to define, say, a table top or front of a building. But you treat them as free from reference to specific solid objects. You then combine them in any way you like to produce an image. They can intersect quite freely. Although many artists prefer to keep them more or less horizontal and vertical, you do not have to. Most interesting of all, you can use such complexes of planes as a way of analysing an actual figurative scene without ever stating the outlines of bodies. You look for the principal directions of the surfaces in any group of objects or people; and then draw perspective diagrams to define those directions. The planes alone can produce an extraordinarily subtle image of space.

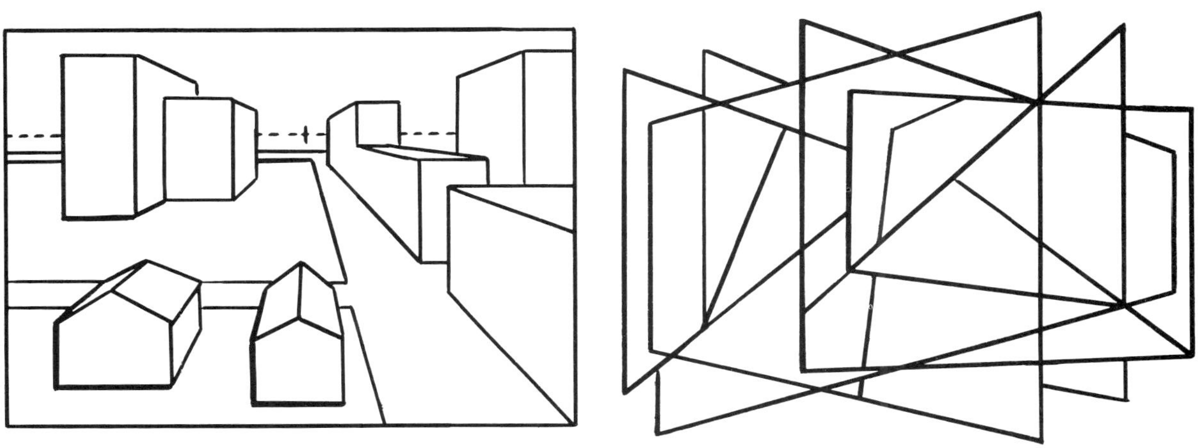

159 a) standard vanishing point perspective; b) free combination of planes in perspective.

Section 39
The Body

Most people naturally feel that the human body has a 'normal' shape, and can only execute certain particular bends and twists. We also feel that a certain scale of sizes is 'right' for different parts of the body. Even the smallest alterations to the human body appear to us as distortions. This is true for animals too; it may not, however, be the case with trees, for example. You can draw trees without bothering too much about how they conform to standard shapes and proportions.

Body-images in drawing make implicit reference to the norm. Every figuration of a body asks the viewer to interpret the image of the body as a version of the intimately known object that their own body is.

There are two ways that one can deal with this
160 implicit image. The first is to think of the human body as a sort of puppet, composed of standard shapes which you arrange in different positions to build up attitudes. Artists with a classical turn of
45 mind, including Michelangelo and Raphael, have always done this, using 'ideally beautiful' bodily parts, following the venerable theory that art should only concern itself with beautiful beings. Even advertising art does something similar with its currently fashionable human types. Most straightforward representational artists do actually stay well within convention.

The alternative is to use what may seem to be quite radical and impossible distortions which may not contain much direct reference to the norm, but nevertheless get their effect from the way we compare them to our image of the norm. Cartoonists, for example, often exaggerate the size and shape of some bodily feature of a famous politician: his bat-like ears, his tombstone teeth. If we did not recognize the reasons for the enlargements we would miss the point.

Picasso often shows hands or feet vastly enlarged, challenging us to think what it means. He may show us the flank of a female figure executed only in terms of a sinuous stroking movement; and this may be connected to a few other such strokes indicating breast, nose plus forehead and hair. The rest of the body-norm is left out. What he *does* give us can never be fitted into a complete body-norm mapped on the drawing surface. Yet we have to identify parts of the whole – 'flank', 'breast' and so on – to understand the image. This is one of the most important ways context works (Section 22). The unrepresented body-norm provides contexts for the meaning of its component shapes.

Between these two extreme uses of the norm there lies a range of possibilities. Some artists feel that it is possible to have a graphic norm as simple as a child's, but most have worked very hard to develop their own versions of the norm before they felt free to take it entirely for granted. You should do this too; it will contribute to your individual style. You should continually try to work out body-images for yourself on your paper, away from the object, experimenting with different kinds of glyphs to compose it – lines, enclosures, volumes, tones – and consulting drawings in this book.

Many books on drawing and drawing courses used to lay great stress on teaching the anatomy of the human body and face. It is probable that Leonardo da Vinci began this tradition, by learning from dissecting corpses. Michelangelo is supposed to have studied anatomy in a similar way. Through the eighteenth and nineteenth
centuries academic art in the West continued to 16
require that the artist had accurate knowledge of all the bones, muscles and fat layers on the human body. A great deal of the work that used to be done in the traditional life-class consisted of getting the outlines of the posed nude model both optically and anatomically exact.

Exact anatomy could thus be thought of as setting a kind of factual norm for artists, setting up conventions about the elements of the body that every artist had to follow. But the more you are required to demonstrate your knowledge of anatomy the less aesthetic freedom you have. Great masters, such as Michelangelo, Titian and Rembrandt, although they may have had

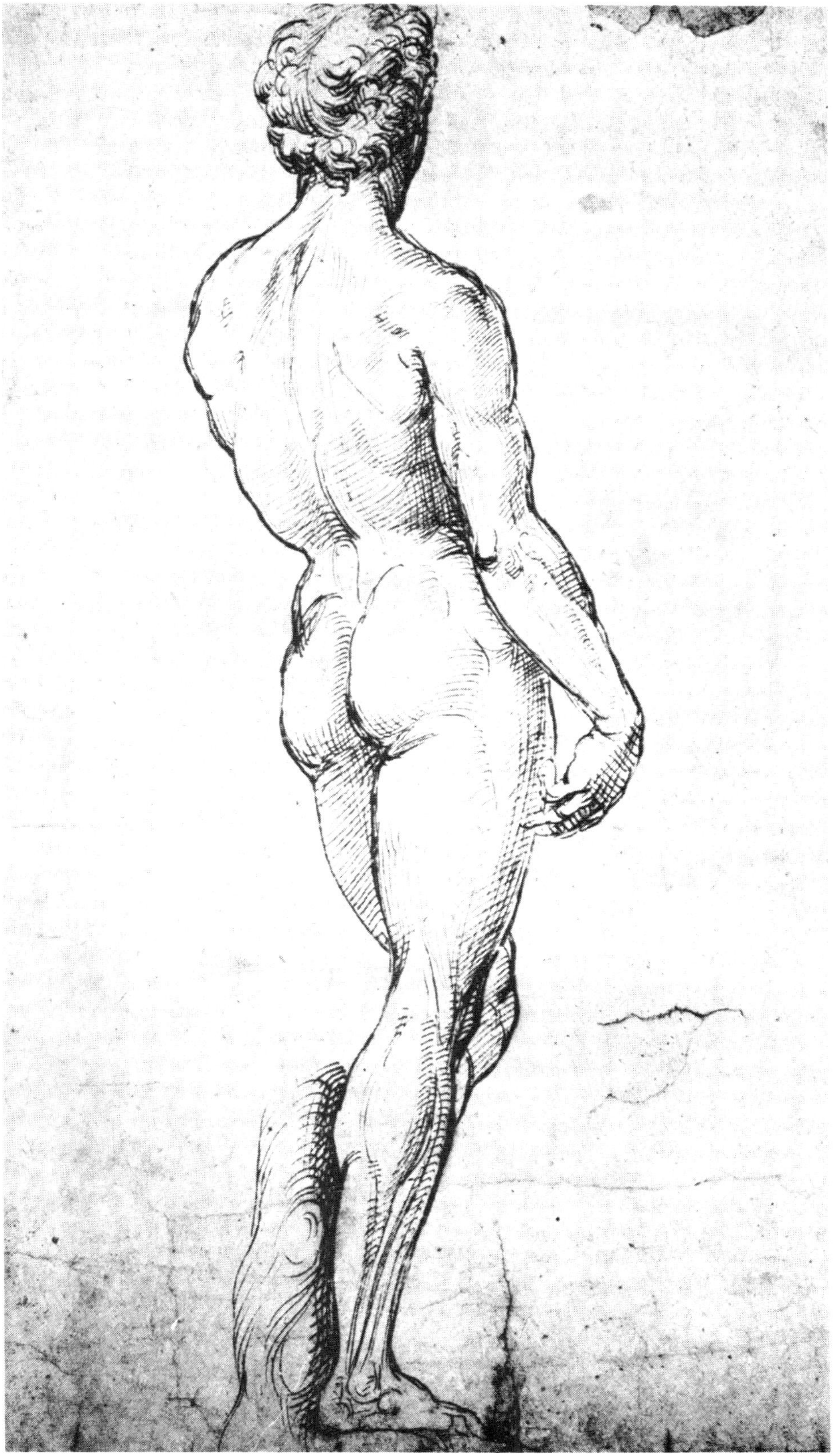

160 Raphael: the ideal body of Michelangelo's David, its volumes reinterpreted in Raphael's linear style; pen drawing.

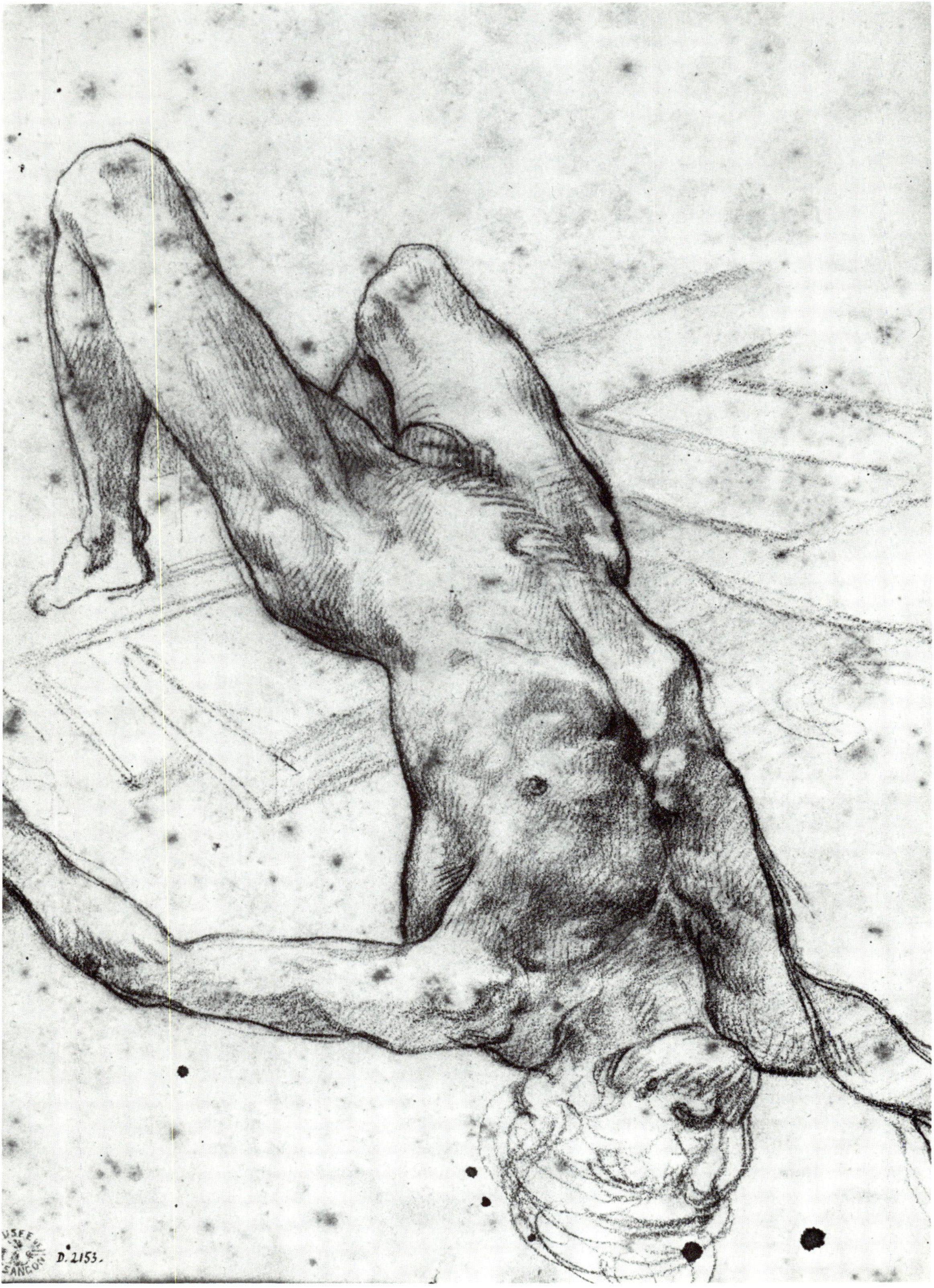
D. 2153.

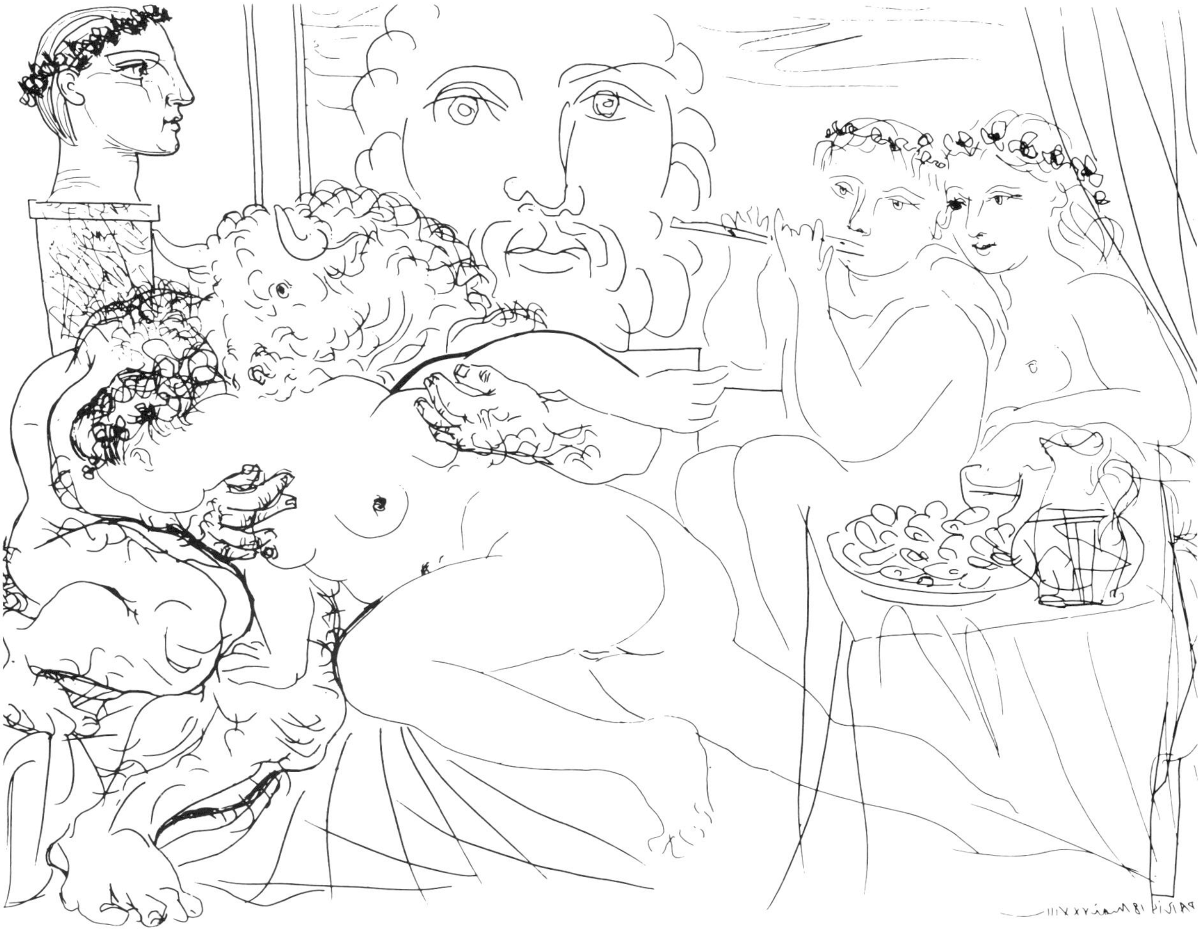

162 Pablo Picasso: engraving from the Vollard Suite. Free assembly of fragments of contour, referring to Classical prototypes.

substantial anatomical knowledge, treated the scientific side of anatomy with great freedom.

In reality you make convincing body-images out of convincing glyphs. Broadly speaking, you need to respect the relationships of the main rigid long bones, the main bulks of head, chest, belly and hips. Draw them in faintly first. Then begin to develop your own body-images around them.

There is one interesting extra factor. When
62 you think of a body-norm in terms of component units, you will emphasize units you are especially interested in. The way you shape each of them will show how you feel about them. Analogy comes in again here. You will find you may draw a chest like a box, a belly like a bag, legs like pillars or a skull like a dome. This is actually one of the great resources of art – metaphor, linking parts of the body with other elements of experience. It is also one of the reasons why too much anatomy can spoil art.

African sculpture shows very clearly how evocative such parallels between units of the body-norm and natural forms such as shells, horns, gourds, even mountain shapes, can be. Through Picasso, Braque and the German Expressionists, this African usage has been assimilated into European art. When it was first introduced some people felt that the artists were aiming to illustrate deformed people. They could not accept the challenge to their conventional body-norms.

161 Theodore Géricault: chalk study from the model for a dying figure in 'The Raft of the Medusa'. Contours and shadow lines together create enclosures signifying volumes.

Section 40
The Face

143 The human face is one of the main carriers of social and emotive signals. It is thus a part of the body we focus on very intently and naturally think of as having an expressive identity of its own. But we also have a strong sense of its norm.

In the Far East until recently social convention barred strong emotional expression in faces, save for demonic types. In the Japanese head of a deity

163 Face of a Buddhist deity, Japanese, 8th c.; brush on cloth. The ideal of supernatural beauty in China and Japan.

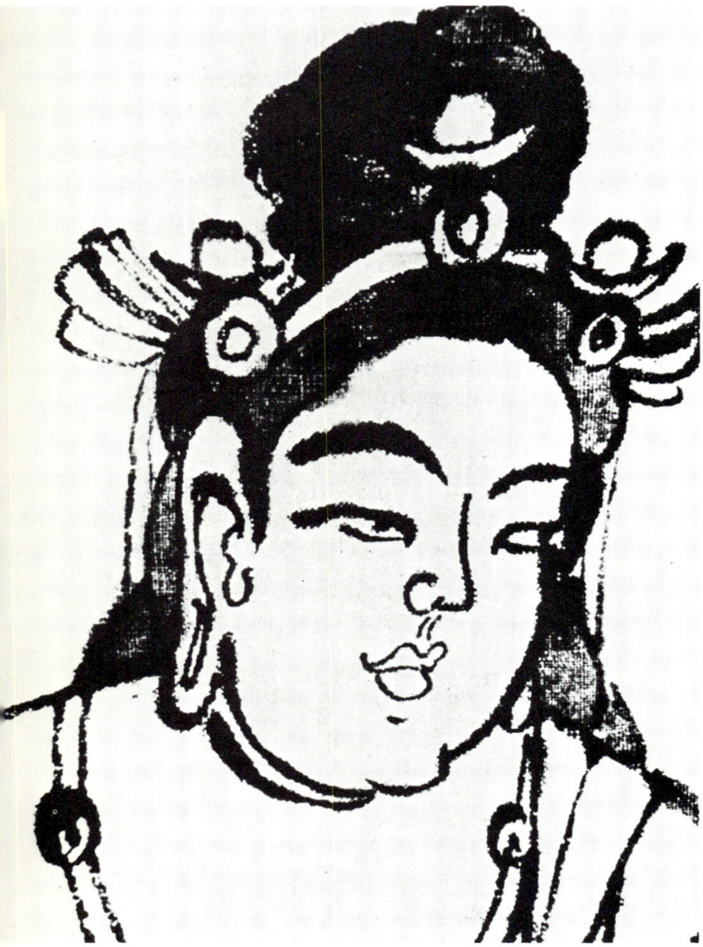

shown here we can see a standard norm for the face: a set of glyphs for eyes and eyebrows, nose, mouth, chin, cheeks and hairline, ears off to the sides, all beautifully executed as lines. Western comic strips or cartoons have less beautiful versions of very similar basic formulae. Virtually every artist starts off thinking like this. You yourself are bound to. 1

In the West, however, we are very interested in facial expression. One of the skills we value in a portrait draughtsman is his ability to read and record the traces of his sitter's habitual expressions. What show on the sitter's face as lines, or as proportional relationships between different areas, the portrait artist can capture by means of glyphs, tone and spacing. The artist can exaggerate them too – as Otto Dix does – to express some kind of moral judgment. 1.

The glyphs do not even have to correspond one to one with the basic units. You can invent a set of glyphs based, say, on a blend of shadow-shapes and volumes across the whole face, without settling down to describe the named features at all. A single pen line can join an eye-socket, its brow, the ear root, the corner of a nose and a mouth, into one very vital glyph, while a single patch of shadow defines the whole of the opposite cheek. 1

You may think that only very experienced artists can ever do this. But once you pick up the technique of catching a characteristic image of each face in your mind, giving your unconscious recognitions a chance to work through your hand, you may be surprised at how vivid you can make your own images of personalities.

When you read the expression and character in a face you focus on details which are very small in relation to the whole figure. You would not normally focus on things so small if they were not features of a face. But we are accustomed to grasping what people are thinking and feeling from tiny shifts in the relations between their eyes and eyebrows, nostrils and mouth. 1 1

However, when you focus on the face in this way you cannot focus on the whole posture and gesture of the figure; and when you draw a face you will find that the signs you make for its

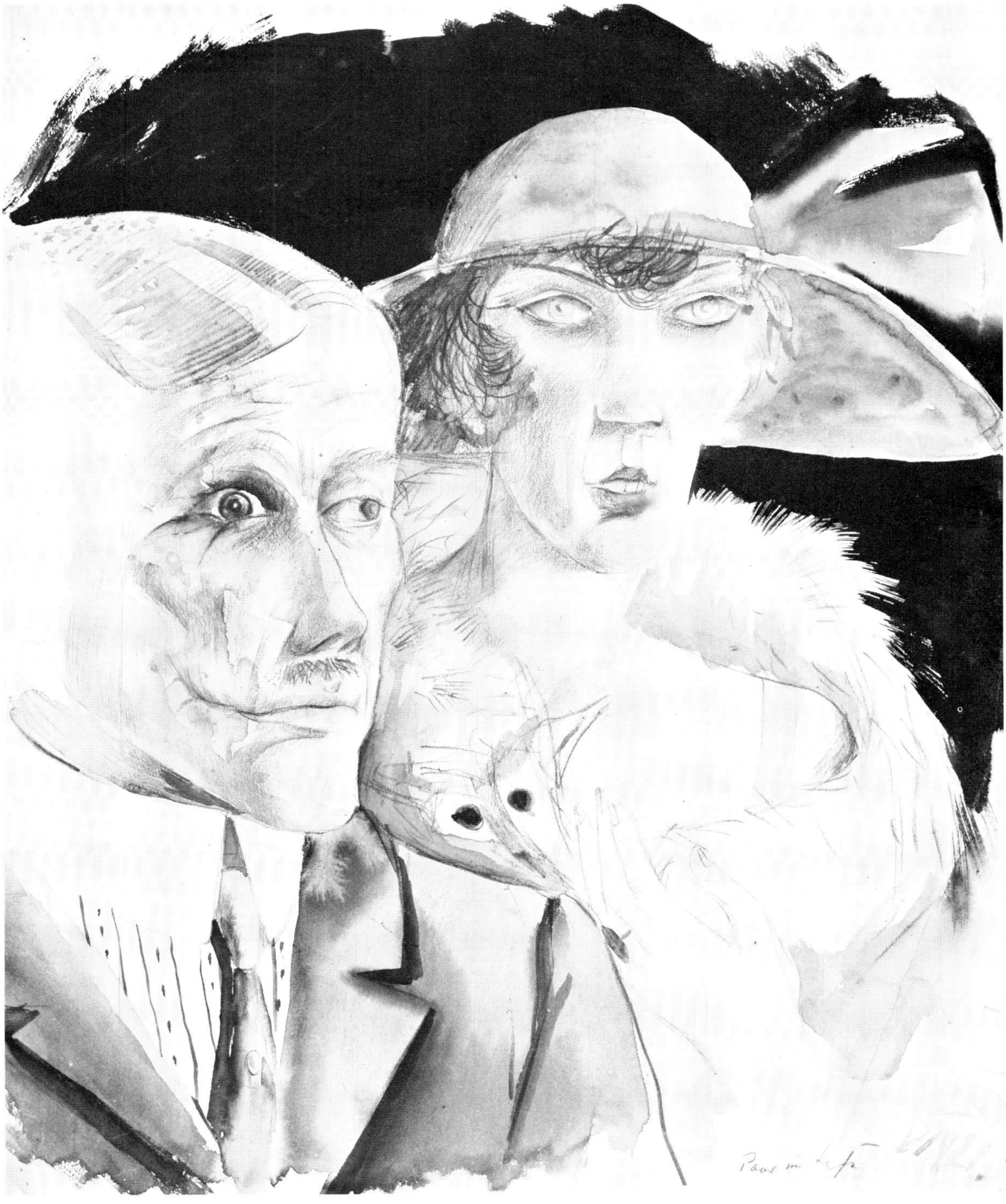

164 Otto Dix: 'Café Couple', 1921; pencil and watercolour. All the expression comes from the placing of glyphs.

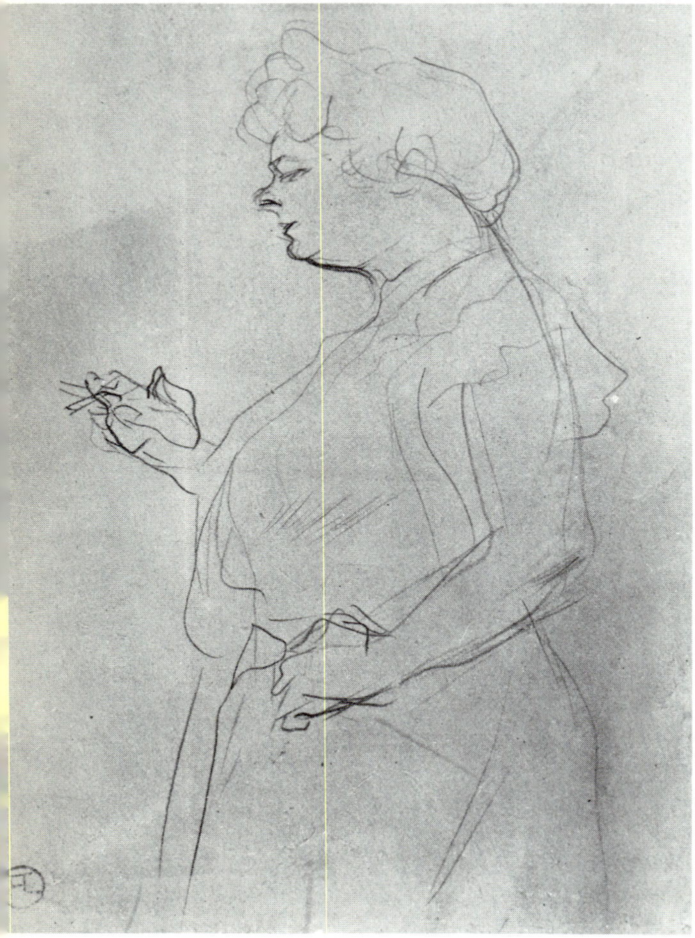

165 Henri de Toulouse-Lautrec: 'Aux Ambassadeurs'; pencil drawing of a character seen in a brothel. In very few lines the artist has captured the posture and gesture and facial expression of a person of very pronounced character.

103 features are also very small in relation to the size of a whole body. To finish the face in portrait detail can seem to demand that you finish the rest of the body in the same sort of detail, and that can be a terrible task. Some great artists, such as Velasquez and Munch, did achieve full-length figures that were also good portraits. But the ambiguity of focus can be very difficult to handle. It is best to accept that portrait and full figure drawing cannot really be done in the same drawing. When you do drawings in which complete figures appear you will find it best to treat the face in a different, much more abbreviated way. 11
You may simply note the major divisions with small token marks or broad shadows, for nose, mouth and brow. If well placed, even these can be 15
very informative.

There is one aspect of drawing faces which some African artists, for example, have felt that most Western art conspicuously lacks. It is the same kind of invention that can go into the body-units: metaphor. Once again it is Picasso and the Expressionists who have used it most powerfully.

It involves treating the face as a kind of mask, 10
developing each feature very carefully as an individually-shaped plastic unit. You then give each of these units a strong metaphorical likeness to things in the natural world. The mouth and its lips can actually be shaped like the petals of a flower, the nose like a formal block or even a big fungus. If you draw them as emphatic volumes they may have quite a strong sculptural effect. Picasso's mourning woman has one eye drawn as a dagger to illustrate the feeling of grief. Her face is composed of 'stripes' which have overtones of reference to certain Congo Baga masks, and perhaps even to whip-marks on Christ's body.

Section 41
The Body and Expression

Some artists seem to have a natural ability for 4
capturing the life of faces, figures and animals by vivid line drawing. It seems to go with a gift for mimicry. This is not by any means the same as a gift for art; but you as a draughtsman must be able to imagine yourself doing what your invented bodies and faces are meant to be doing. Then your mind will be able to produce glyphs which are graphically full of life. The image of a body does not have to have a face to be expressive. When you see dance in the theatre, you cannot usually make out much in the way of facial expression.

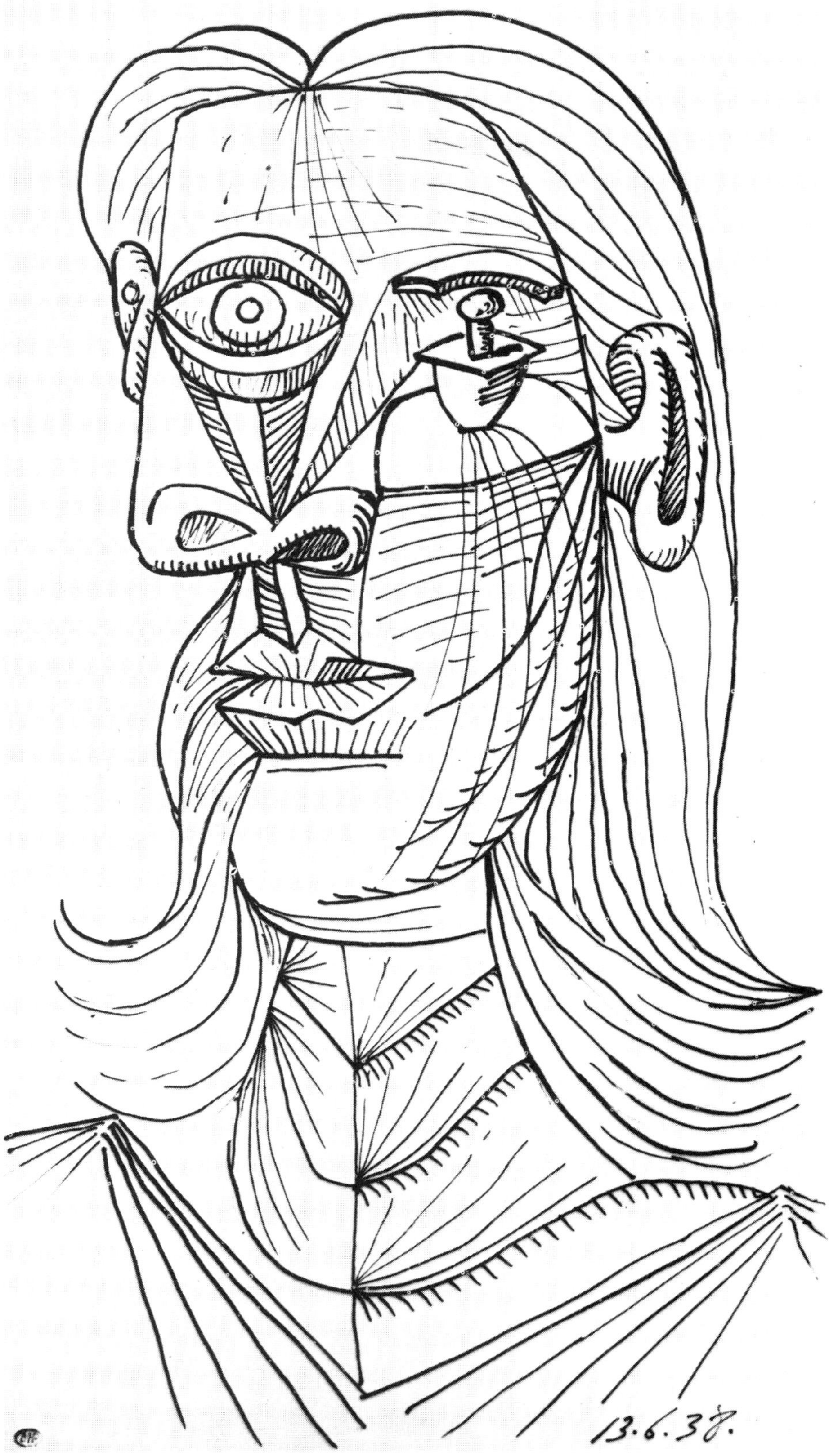

166 Pablo Picasso: 'Head of a Woman', 1938; pen and ink.

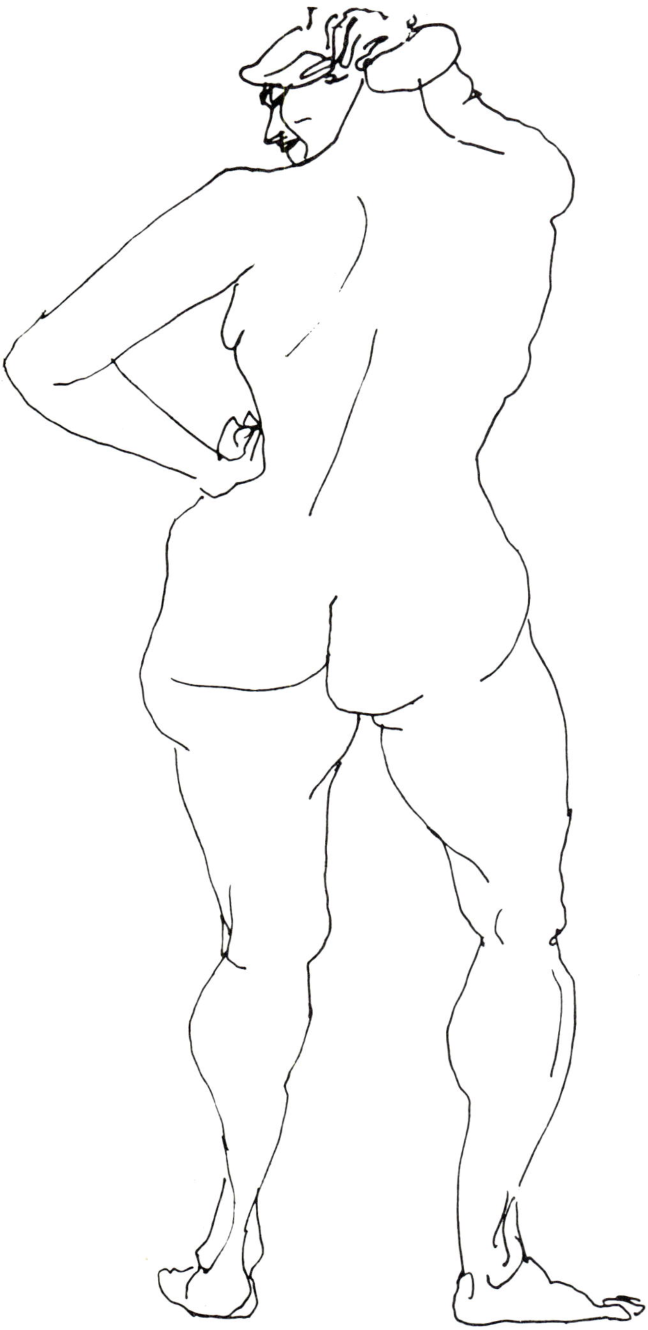

167 Henri Gaudier-Brzeska: 'Standing Nude'. This pen drawing was obviously done very fast with the eye keeping pace with the drawing point. Individuality and sculptural emphasis were the artist's aims.

Whenever you draw the figure from posed models it can be very difficult indeed to take an imaginative grasp of their 'life'. Their boredom can show in their bodily expressions. Short poses are a particularly good thing: they prevent your model from slumping and sagging; and they also compel you to take a clear grasp of the image in the pose and set it down quickly. This ensures that you act boldly and do not resort to creeping round the edges of the figure, feeling lost in the 10
white desert of your paper.

Another good idea is to ask your model to go through a short series of movements twice, then stop and rest. During the movements you can pick out a body image, finalizing it in your mind when you have seen it for the second time. Then you can set it down clearly and fairly quickly on paper. Ask your model to go through the same movements once or twice more, to refresh your memory while you are drawing.

You may very well find that it helps your imagination if you include in your image of the model parts of the surroundings. Because, of course, your image of the body involves the body's relationships to the background, the floor, and to objects in the same space. Tone can contribute vitally to this image. Also, do remember that sheer outlines are no more the essence of life drawing than they are of any other kind of drawing. You can set down any kind of glyphs anywhere. 1

You may find it particularly helpful to lay out quickly a preliminary schematic basis for your figure and its environment, to make sure your image fits into the format. There is one trick to help you do this. Check the format of your paper in relation to what you are drawing by holding it up at the normal drawing distance as if it were a frame. Then draw only what fits into the frame. If you want the whole figure in, move away until you get to where the format again frames exactly what you want to draw.

Long poses are important chiefly because they 16
allow you to study thoughtfully how the forms of the body work together in detail. It is very rare indeed for a long pose drawing to come out as a vital piece of art; and it is virtually impossible to

'complete' one with equal intensity all over. So use long poses as a means of consulting what Delacroix called the dictionary of nature, to consolidate images of, say, how a leg and foot look at a certain angle, of how a belly creases, or how a set of folds radiates from a knee in trousers, how a neck emerges from a collar, and so on. You can ask the model to take positions you wish to study, perhaps to prepare for future work in some other medium.

5 Any figure drawing is more likely to be lively if the model is reacting to you, the artist, in some way, or seems to be participating in the life of which you are also a part. That is one reason why sketches can seem much more interesting than studies executed in the cold neutrality of a studio. Art is always, in some sense, about life.

There is one important way of handling this aspect of all figure drawing, which is also used by film-makers and photographers. You place the viewer in some kind of personal relationship with
76 the figures you represent. This results partly from the way you place yourself to draw them. You can represent them looming close up, filling the format, seen either from below or above. You can show them towering over the viewer; you can suggest that the viewer is looking down on them, or standing beside them to give a sense of intimacy. You can make them meet the viewer's eyes, or look away. Or you can show them in profile from a distance, which gives a sense of remoteness. If you think about your relationship to the figures, and the meaning of their presence to you, you can even give your viewer a vivid sense of involvement with figures seen from quite a normal viewpoint.

Section 42
Posture and Gesture

The living body conveys its expression in two ways: through posture and gesture.

67 Posture is stationary. It appears as a stance, a bracing of the parts of the body to balance its weights and take its strains. You understand a posture by a kind of athletic sympathy, by imagining your own body adopting it. This will help to awaken those inner responses that contribute so much to vital drawing. You can then record the posture first of all as if it were a kind of capital letter, a geometry of signs laid out on the paper. Leave out superficial details, and concentrate on exploring the essential character of the image as a diagram of forces, using any kinds of mark that will convey the idea. Draw bold straight

168 Coal miners in the pit; pen sketch.

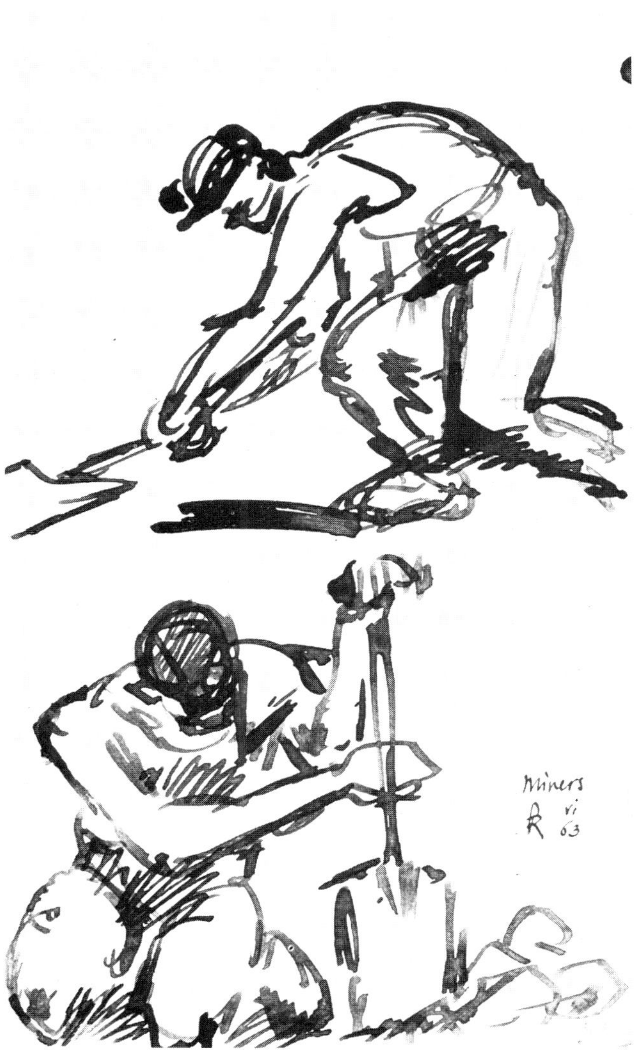

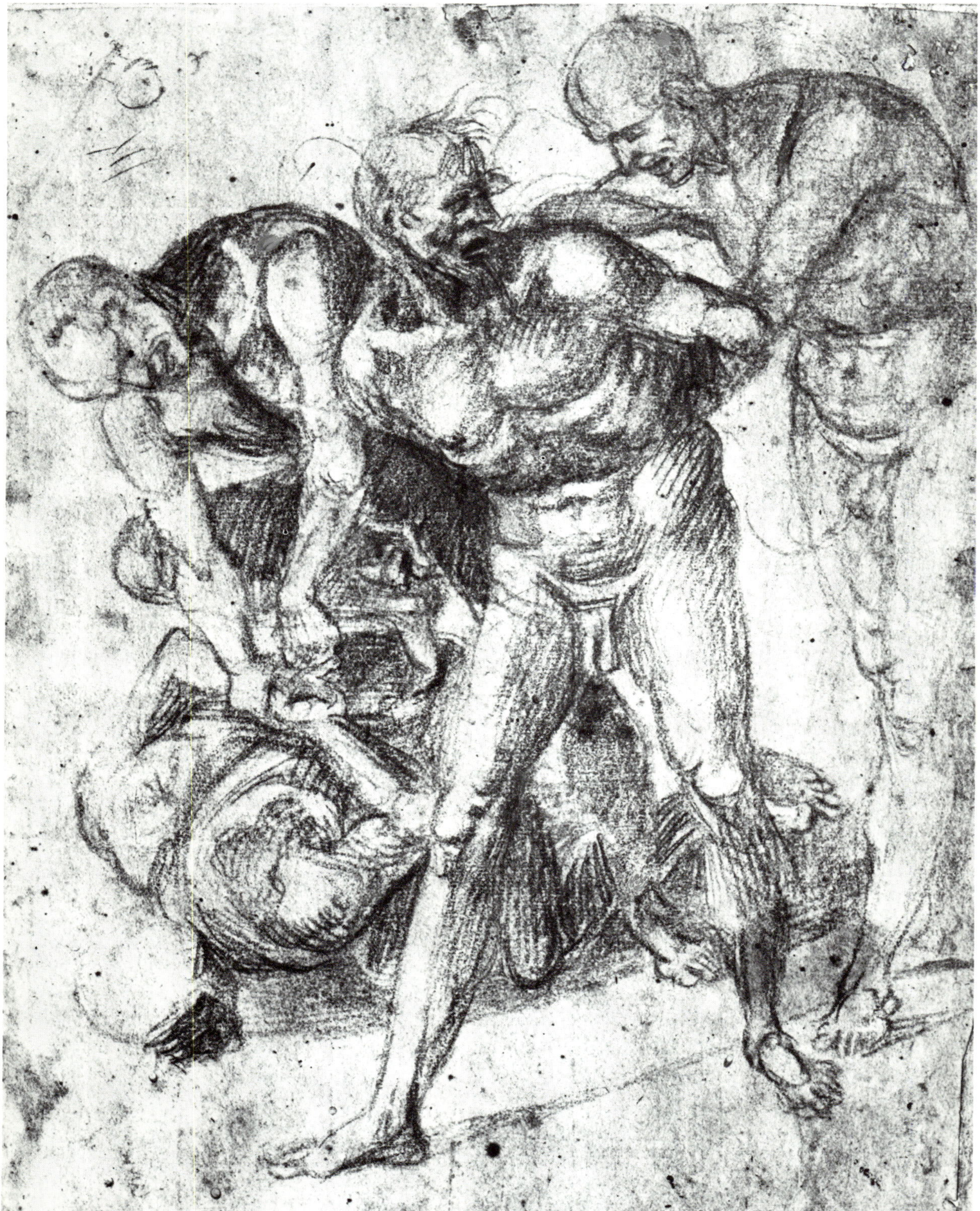

lines down the middle of the legs or arms to illustrate the straddles and bracings. Signorelli probably drew the figures in *Nudes Being Bound* entirely as expressions of his inner imagination of the postures.

There is no need to try at first for anything more than the sheer posture. As you begin to catch it, you can go on modifying it if necessary, and then flesh it out with positive and negative enclosures, volumes and tone, and all the other methods we have discussed. With practice the two stages will blend; and eventually you will find yourself beginning to make the first statement of the posture in terms of the group of graphic glyphs which will eventually constitute your personal style. Without *some* basic posture-statement, however, you will find it very hard to give your image vitality.

It is particularly important to avoid 'filling in' a drawing for the sake of completeness. Leave out anything you cannot formulate clearly into glyphs. Mere filling-in can deaden what you put down when you took your first grasp on your image.

It is interesting how seldom most major draughtsmen have used foreshortening as anything more than a modest component in figure composition. A few, such as Mantegna, occasionally attempted to draw totally foreshortened bodies. Michelangelo often took chances to incorporate heads, thighs or arms into his figures, tilted into the picture space to add depth to the body imagery. But even he drew most of his figures laid out substantially across two dimensions. In this book you will not find any diagrams analysing 'how to draw' heads and torsos in steep foreshortening. If you do look at, say, a reclining model end on, you will find it relatively easy to deal with the image by means of depth-slices, each defined by the cross-sections of the body that appear as contour loops overlapping each other into depth (Section 28).

118 Gesture is not quite the same as posture. It is the dynamic aspect of posture, and results from the body expressing something inward by an outer movement. To capture a sense of gesture you need to take your image of a posture a good deal further.

169 Luca Signorelli: 'Male Nudes Being Bound'. Chalk study, conveying vivid gesture and group interaction with slender means.

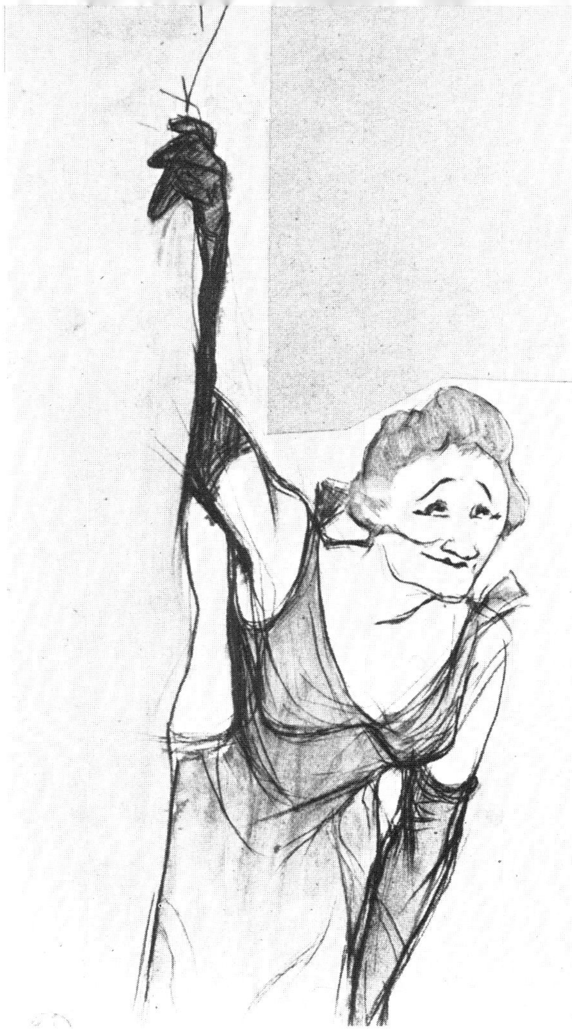

170 Henri de Toulouse-Lautrec: 'Actress'. Sets of original glyphs compose the lively face, and crossing lines capture the posture of the body.

When you read somebody's gesture in real life you are actually following out the implications of several movements: of body, arm, hand, fingers, head and eyes together. You can make the gestures of your drawing supplement the pure posture of the figure by implying the pattern of movement it was following and how it would need naturally to act out its implied movements.

Gesture is therefore one aspect of figurative art that you can never study properly in the studio. You can only study it by sketching living, moving
figures. So carry a sketchbook with you all the 151
time, and use it to note people's gestures, questioning their meaning as they actually happen.
Clothing and its forms can contribute powerfully 40
to expressive gestures and your reading of them.

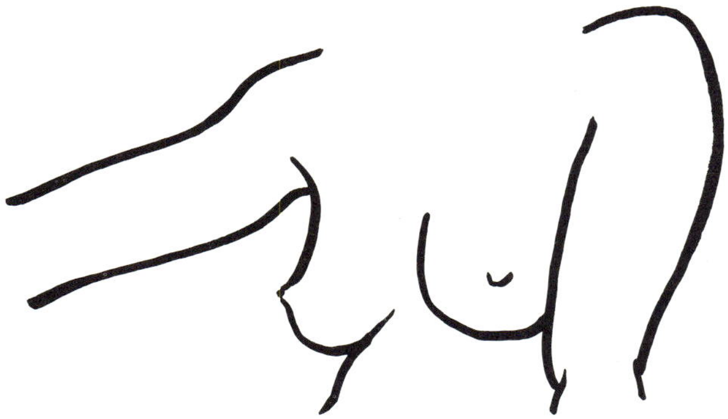

171 Contrasting outlines of two arms.
172 'Group of Trees': Chinese woodblock print, 17th c. These trees constitute a strongly marked group that gives a sense of how they all grew up together, influencing each other.

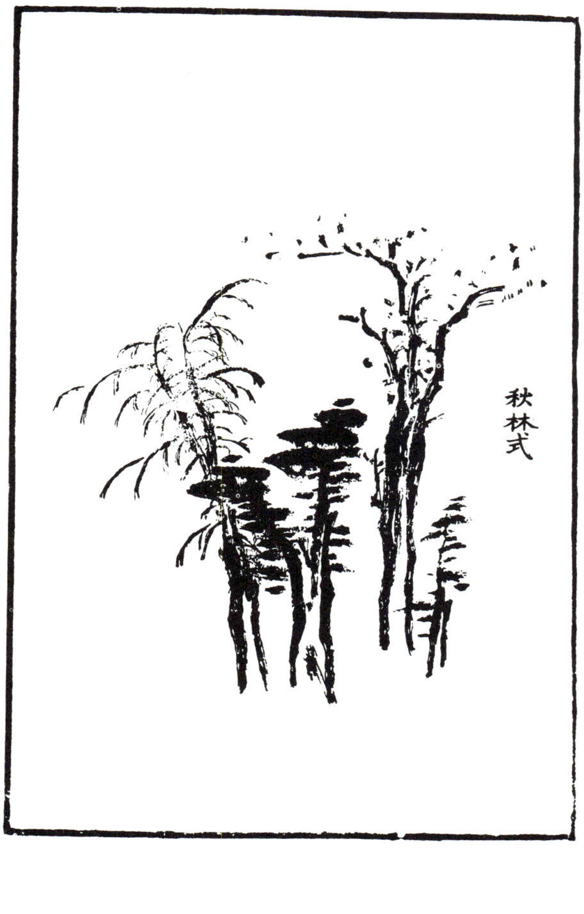

As you develop your drawing style you may concentrate in more detail on how the different parts of the human body and its clothing themselves 'gesture' in different ways, even when they are quite motionless. The flesh on one arm which is relaxed may droop with an expressive shape which may be quite different from the shape taken by the same part of the other arm. Clothes crease in clear patterns of pulls. Find and note quickly and immediately these different qualities of shape in your glyphs.

One very interesting area to explore is the 4
characteristic gestures made by moving animals and birds. To do this you need to spend a lot of time with them. Nowadays we may no longer be so sheerly amazed at the variety of their forms, as Dürer was when he first saw a rhinoceros. But as artists we can attempt to capture the extraordinary variety of the ways their anatomies and life-style express themselves as posture and gesture.

You can choose to study animals you are familiar and therefore sympathetic with, say, horses, cats or dogs. You may well even experience quite violent action and response between these animals. You will probably never get the chance
to see in real life what Delacroix so often drew – 174
savage battles between lion and tiger, violent hunts of ferocious beasts. However, to try and visualize and work out such drawings can quite often help to set your imagination going.

If your style is very emphatic you can elaborate the character of any gesture by exaggerating the relative size of the body components. This can introduce new and strange readings for body
posture and stance. If you draw a reaching arm 49
that terminates in a colossal, block-like fist, you are obviously presenting a very strong gesture-image. The work of Picasso and Orozco is full of this kind of expression. Here too the relationship of figure to environment can strengthen the expression.

You can also read qualities of animate gesture into inanimate objects by a kind of inner mimicry. This is something that all great artists were capable of, as their drawings illustrate. And you can also interpret many things in the natural world in terms of their apparent gestures. You can draw trees and plants with strokes which seem to follow out the evolution or lively expression of their shapes. The Chinese and Japanese used to draw trees as histories of their own growth, from root to tips. Leonardo da Vinci was fascinated by the spiralling movements of plants – and even of the weather – and seems to have felt these very strongly as patterns of inner gesture. The branches of shrubs, the way plants hold their flowers, the way we say that rocks 'crouch' or 'rear', that an automobile 'squats' or a distant headland 'thrusts' or even 'takes off' into the sea – all help to show how we can feel our way into expressing the work of forces in nature.

It is worth your exploring this aspect of reality in drawing. A homely example can illustrate the point very clearly. Imagine a plastic bag filled with water, its neck fastened, standing on the top of a small, rigid table. The bag has totally different implicit gestures from the table on which it stands. The lines by which you would draw the meeting of the two objects would need to express the differences of 'feel' between the bulging and sagging soft and the rectangular thrusting hard. You can convey your sense that the bag presses down and spreads on the table-top, and that the table-top also resists its weight, flattening the bottom of the bag.

You can read a great deal of our apparently stationary world of objects as full of interactions, visible to the artist's eye; and use your graphic medium to explore them. There are forces of pressure and resistance among rocks and trees and light and dark objects, of opening and closing between objects in a landscape, of scouring and
42 eroding by wind and weather. Cloud and light work together upon vistas of countryside; and every city shows the effects of human habitation and action both in its patterns of growth and in details of its appearance. You can think of all these broadly in terms of gesture – as extensions and readable traces of change, certainly imbued with feeling, which you can express in the character of your glyphs.

Section 43
Dramatic Interaction

People usually gesture when something is happening between two or more of them. But it is quite rare nowadays for any artist to deal directly with dramatic gestural interaction. Think of the number of works you have seen which show figures sitting or standing still, usually facing out of the picture-frame, or stationary objects. Maybe we do not nowadays have so clear-cut a language of gesture as, say, the Italians did in the sixteenth century. But we have our own. It is there to be explored by artists in all its subtlety.

For when we read the meaning of the gestures of 114
a group of people, we are reading something which is, strictly speaking, invisible. From what we see we can only infer the feelings, intentions, responses, which are internal to the individuals making and recognizing the gestures. But perhaps because we ourselves have made similar gestures and experienced them many other times in various situations, we are able to identify inner facts and responses that each gesture by somebody else is externalizing.

Your job as a draughtsman can be to recognize these phenomena and then find graphic equivalents for them. To begin working along these lines it really is best to study a few major drawings that show dramatic interaction at its most intense. You can find it in the work of practically every major master of the Western tradition before the middle of the nineteenth century. Then the interest seems to have died away in visual art, and gone into time-based work such as films.
Picasso and Beckmann are the two twentieth- 162
century masters who have used interaction as a vital ingredient in their work. This distinguishes them very sharply from formalist artists.

It is as well to read very carefully a number of dramatic drawings, such as those in this book, to understand how this can work. It is all too easy to miss the implications an artist intended you to pick up. And you may need to respond with feelings that you may not have felt before in the presence of

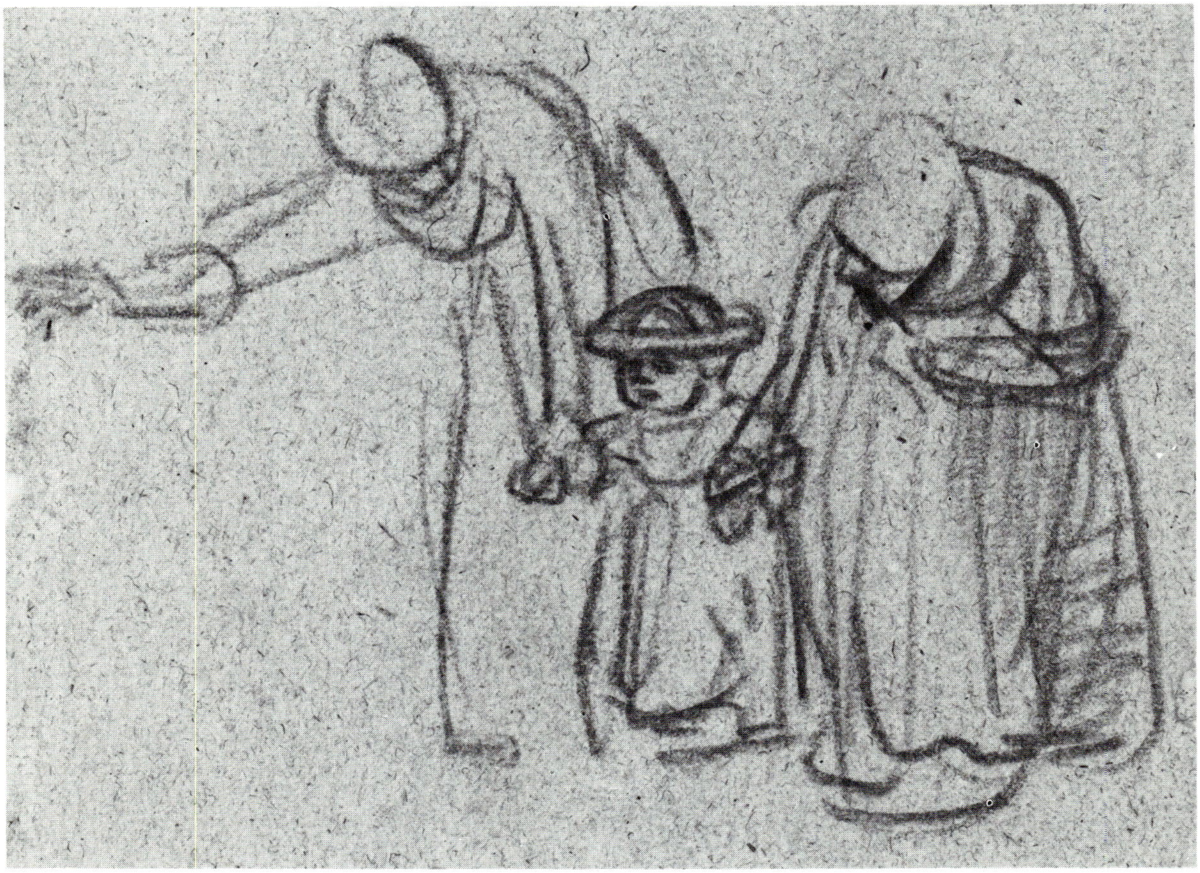

173 Rembrandt van Rijn: 'Child Learning to Walk' (seen from the front). A few chalk strokes convey dramatic interaction between the figures.

104 works of art – feeling of pride, tenderness, companionship or compassion, which twentieth-century art theory may seem to have banished from non-figurative art.

Traditional art of the fourteenth to eighteenth centuries may seem to concentrate very much on retelling a very limited number of stories from the Bible or about lives of the saints. But once you realize that the story is only a vehicle for much more profound kinds of dramatic expression you will see that the similarities between works are only superficial. Each good drawing presents a fresh dramatic image. The artist brings out interwoven patterns of gesture and response among
his figures. He amplifies these by rhythmic spacing, 17
by implied rhythmic connections between the folding and movement of garments, by his handling of tone. Elements of landscape may set a
mood, and share in carrying gestures over from 23
one figure to another. Architecture can frame a single person, say, and its shape can illuminate his or her character. One of the most famous of all interactions is Michelangelo's image on the Sistine Chapel ceiling showing God creating Adam, the fingers of their two outstretched hands parting as God withdraws from his creation.

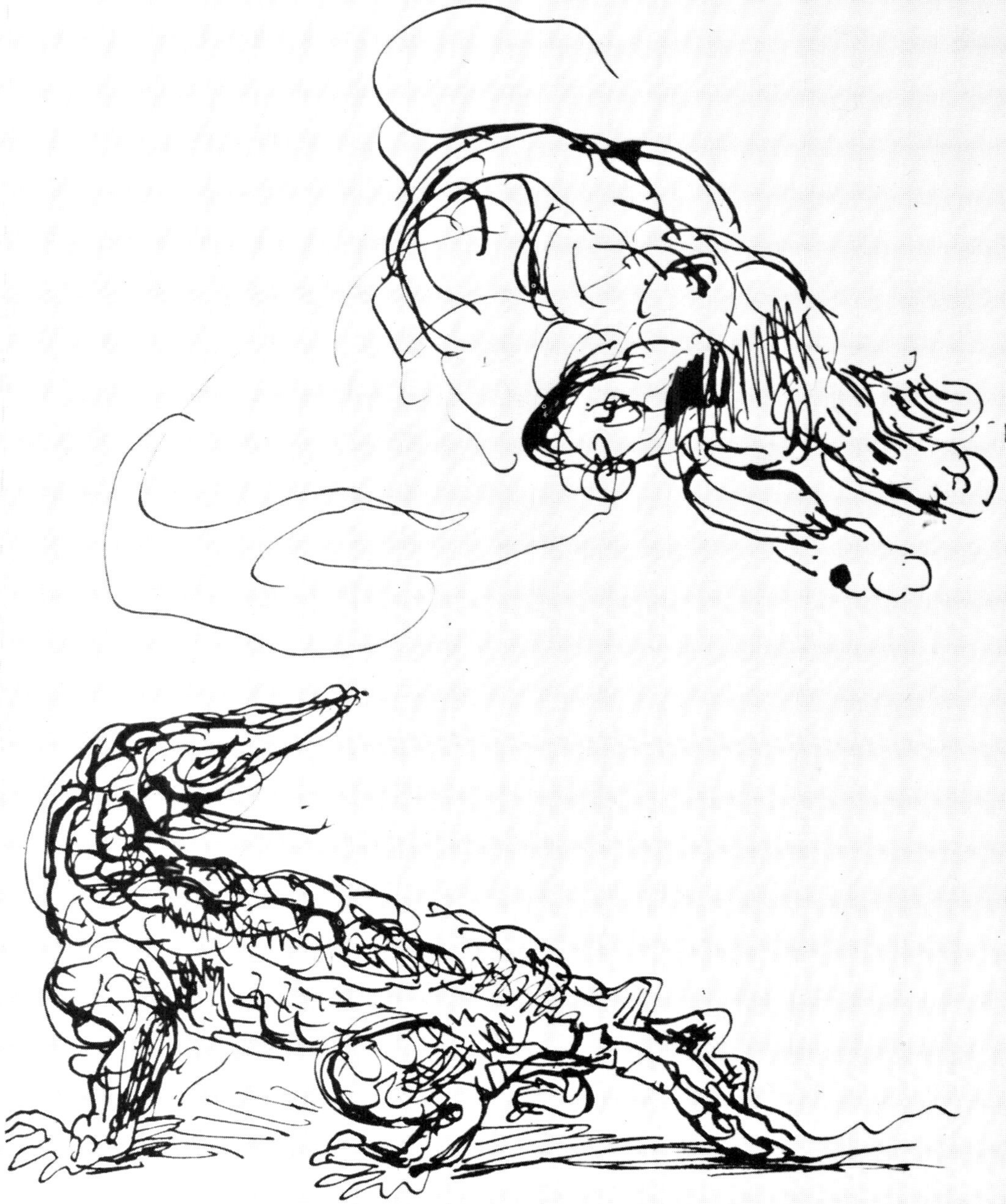

174 *Eugène Delacroix: 'Tiger and Alligator'; pen sketch of a fantastic encounter.*

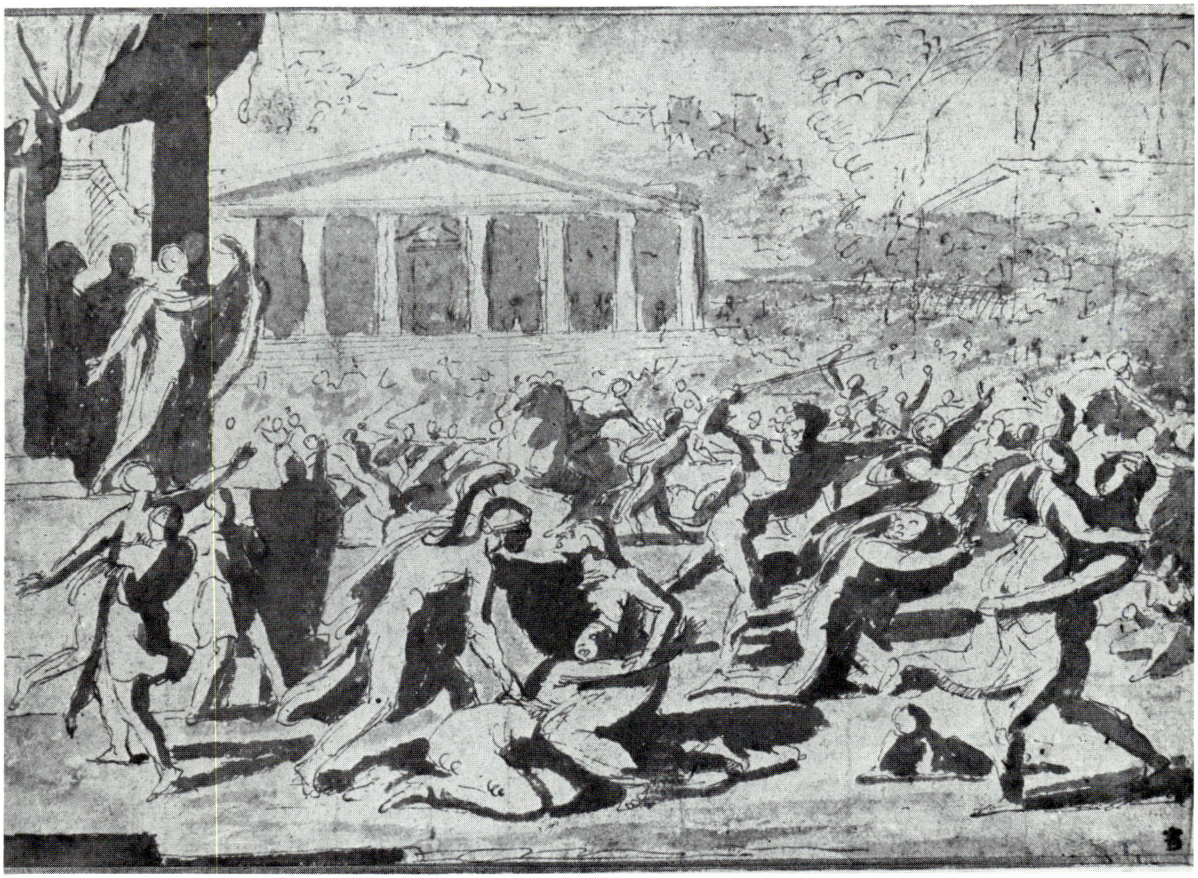

175 *Nicholas Poussin: 'Rape of the Sabines'; pen sketch.*

You will recognize how groups of figures also make sequences, passing a sense of unified movement through all of them across and into the depth of the picture by bridgings and overlaps. Poussin does this very vividly. You can see how he imagines the series of figures in the foreground of *Rape of the Sabines* as a human chain of volumes, linked to each other by modelling and cast shadow. You only get the real feeling for such sequences when you have actually spelled them out to yourself, filling out each figure and transition with your own memories and responses.

In Rubens' drawing, *Soldiers Carousing*, the most obvious features are the extraordinary sense of boisterousness and ribaldry the figures convey, and the way their attention is focused on the action taking place towards the left of the drawing. This is not in Rubens' usual polished, flesh-conscious style; it is immediate and abrupt, suggesting that Rubens was probably working, if not actually in the bar, at least from a very recent memory of a bar scene. He was probably doing what I suggested you do – sketching from life.

It is relatively easy to work out what is meant to be happening in both these drawings. They tell their story directly. Poussin's came out of his imagination, Rubens' from a specific visual experience. But both are equally artistic inventions. Both artists had to employ a language of glyphs to convey to you their meaning. The two drawings

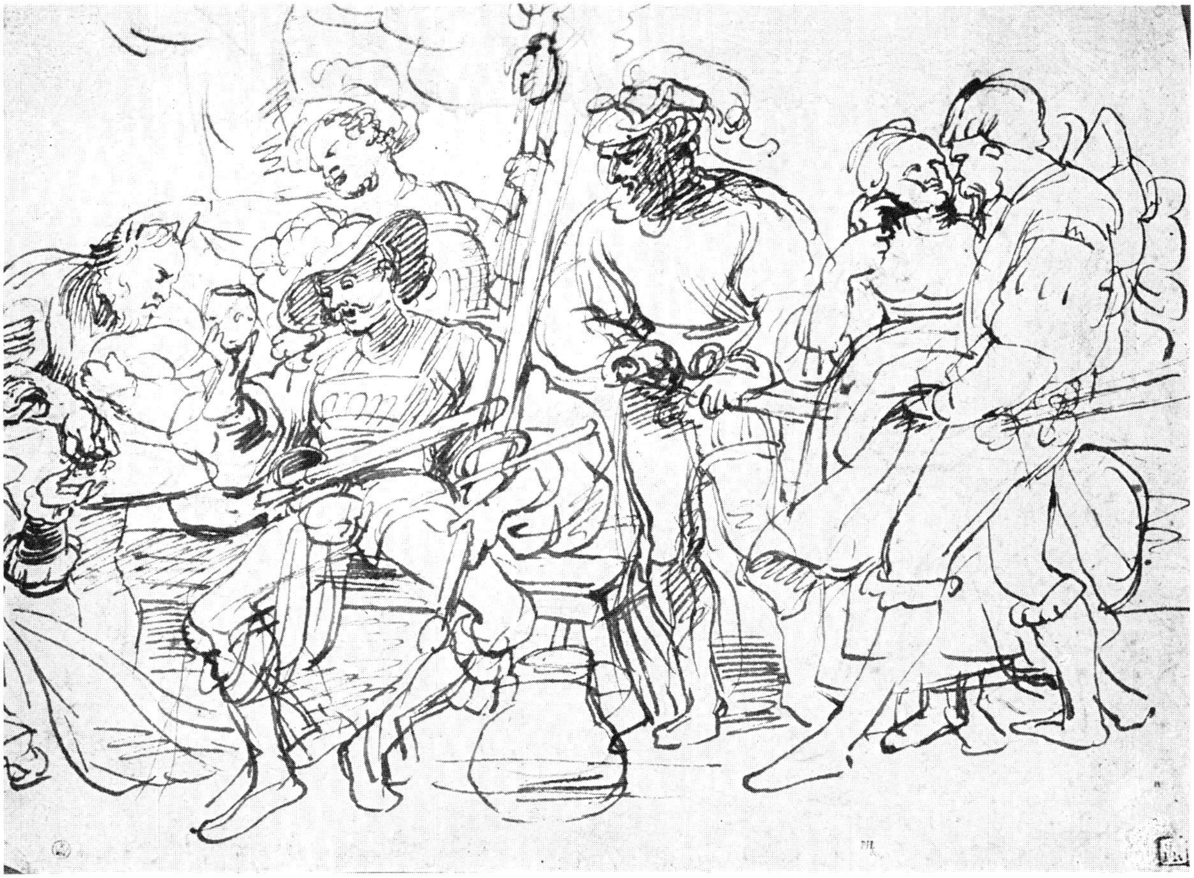

176 *Peter Paul Rubens: 'Soldiers Carousing'; pen sketch.*

also share a common purpose: to reach beyond the surface arrangement of the drawn shapes to refer you to something going on, a dramatic interaction, to which all the figures contribute. It is something the artist could not state directly on to the paper, but could only imply by appealing to your memory and imagination.

Just as you need to compose your single figures out of glyphs which convey a sense of individual expression, so you need to compose your dramas out of expressive figures, each one demonstrating different postures and gestures which contribute to the whole. The best basis for you to develop graphic interaction-dramas is to treat your figures very sketchily at first, perhaps as little more than pin-men or clusters of rough strokes. You may feel you need to work out your ideas through a series of preparatory rough designs on separate sheets of paper. The important thing is to invent different postures and gestures for each of the figures, all of which can contribute to a final image.

This can be very taxing; and you should not expect to think of all of them at once. You may need to scour your notebooks and your memory to recall relevant visual possibilities. You might think two figures should be easier to combine than three or more. But this is not necessarily the case. You can often make your dramatic idea much clearer by a contribution from additional figures and from marks which are traces of bodily action.

When you feel ready, you can begin to clothe or flesh out your rough figures with those glyphs and three-dimensional techniques we have studied in earlier sections. But, as we saw with individual figures, you will find that as you gain experience you gradually become able to express your first thoughts in terms of valid sets of glyphs. It is not that your first thoughts ever arrive fully formed. But the very nature of drawing means that you may be able to add second and third thoughts on top of first thoughts and find they can work together rather than obliterate each other.

You can approach your drama from two different directions. You can illustrate a story or event – either a well-known one or one you composed for yourself. Or you can begin by assembling figures with different postures and gestures to explore the possible kinds and meanings of interactions in both graphic and human terms.

The second can be especially interesting. You can produce images which are convincing, but remain mysterious. Goya's tormented creatures in *Disparate Furioso* are undergoing a hideous experience that we can easily recognize. Their bodily expressions are rooted in everyday experience. But the total image to which their interaction adds up cannot be explained in terms of any simple story. What they illustrate is something that does not exist in any other form. It is a complex of feelings we can only reach through the linking together of bodies with glyphs, expressive gestures in space with lines and shadows.

Here we reach a level of figurative art which is open to limitless exploration. It is the place where we can complete the circle of this book and return through figuration directly back to the techniques of mark-making and direct graphic expression described in the earliest sections.

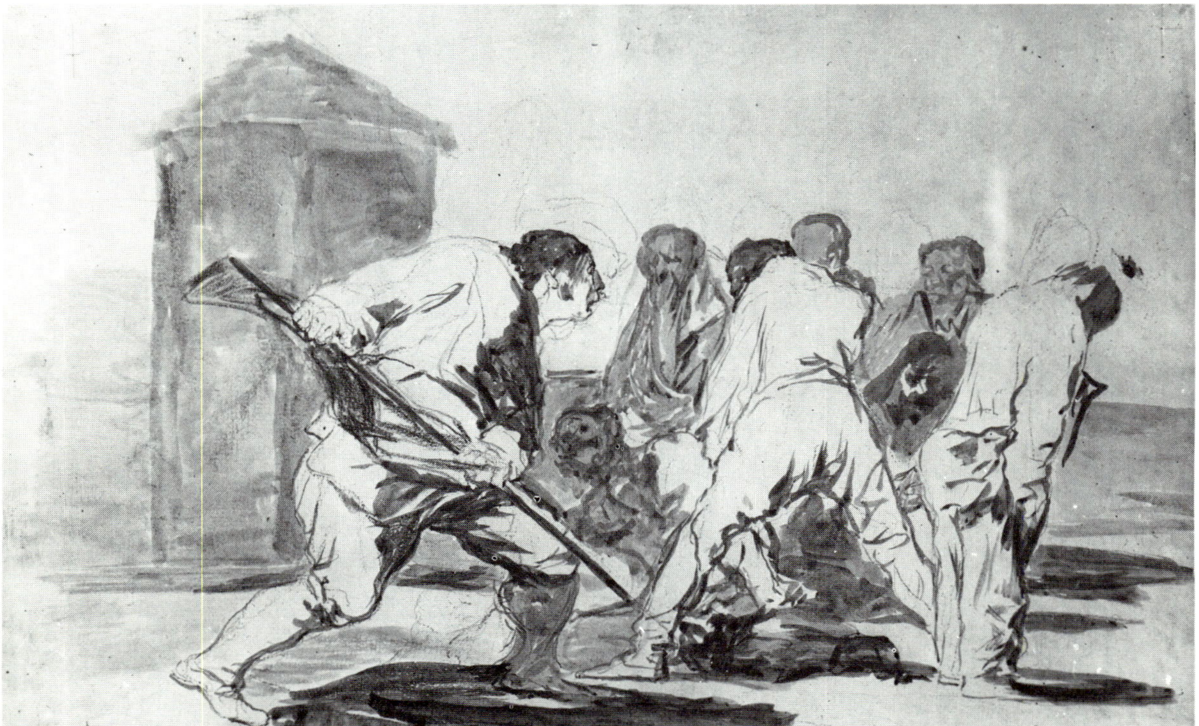

177 Francisco de Goya: 'Disparate Furioso'. Chalk and brush with wash drawing of a scene of gloomy violence.
178 Utamaro: 'Girls Picking Persimmons'. Woodblock print conveying a strong sense of action through its beautiful clusters of lines. The movement of the lines expresses the movements of the bodies, creating of them a unified image.

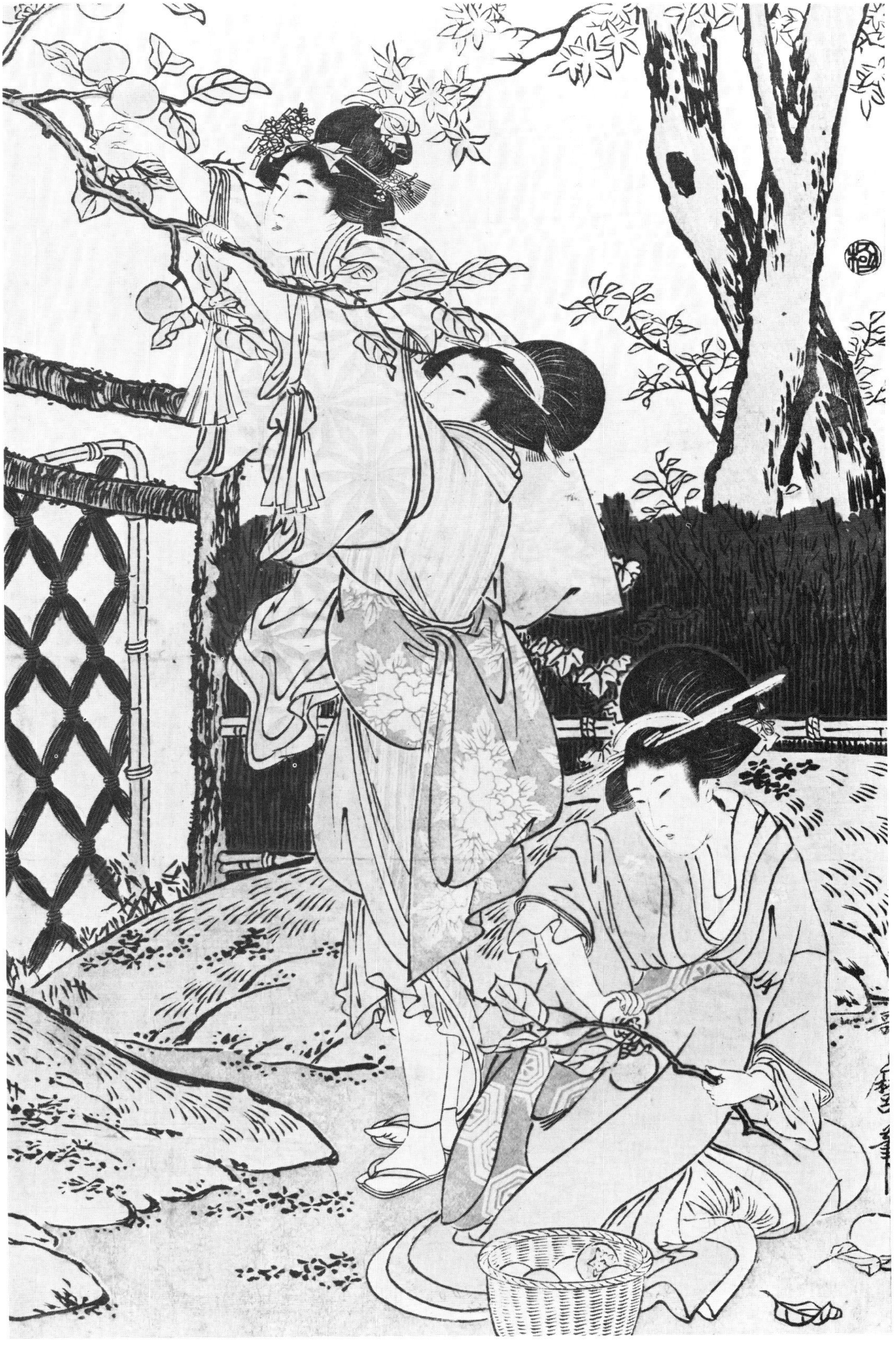

List of Illustrations

Measurements are given in inches and centimetres, height before width

The following pictures, which are not listed below, are by the author: 5, 7, 9, 10, 11, 13, 15–19, 23, 25, 26, 30, 31, 34, 35, 38, 39, 42–4, 46, 48, 53, 55–8, 60b, 62, 66, 67, 69, 70, 72, 73, 75, 78–80, 83, 84, 86, 94, 101, 110, 117, 121, 123, 124, 126, 127, 129, 131, 134, 137, 144, 146, 149, 152–4, 156, 158, 159, 168, 171. Ills. 57 and 79 are also by Piers B. Rawson.

Jacket front: Henry Moore
Nude Study of a Seated Girl, 1927. Red and black chalk with watercolour, $16\frac{3}{4} \times 13\frac{3}{4}$ (42.5 × 34.9). Whitworth Art Gallery, University of Manchester

1 Henri Matisse (1869–1954)
The Plumed Hat, 1919. Graphite pencil, $21\frac{1}{4} \times 14\frac{3}{8}$ (54 × 36.5). Collection The Museum of Modern Art, New York; gift of the Lauder Foundation, Inc. © SPADEM

2 Rembrandt van Rijn (1606–69)
Cottages beneath High Trees in Bright Sunlight, *c.* 1657–8. Pen and brush in bistre with wash and white body colour, $9\frac{3}{4} \times 7\frac{1}{2}$ (24.7 × 19.2). Louvre, Paris

3 Leonardo da Vinci (1452–1519)
Star of Bethlehem and other Plants, *c.* 1503–14. Pen and ink over red chalk, $7\frac{3}{4} \times 6\frac{1}{4}$ (19.8 × 16). Royal Library, Windsor Castle. Reproduced by gracious permission of Her Majesty the Queen

4 Edgar Degas (1834–1917)
Mounted Jockey, 1882–6 (Notebook 37, p. 194). Black crayon, $6\frac{1}{3} \times 3\frac{7}{8}$ (16.2 × 9.8). Bibliothèque Nationale, Paris

6 Tao Chi (1641–before 1720)
Landscape. Ink with colour on paper

8 Jackson Pollock (1912–56)
Untitled, *c.* 1950. Ink on Japan paper, $17\frac{1}{2} \times 22\frac{1}{4}$ (44.4 × 56.5). Collection The Museum of Modern Art, New York; gift of Mr and Mrs Ronald Lauder in honour of Eliza Parkinson Cobb

12 Unknown Chinese artist
Head of Bodhidharma, 14th century. The Cleveland Museum of Art, Ohio

14 Henri de Toulouse-Lautrec (1864–1901)
Odon Tapié de Celeryan at the Age of Ten. Charcoal on white paper, $2\frac{1}{2} \times 17\frac{3}{4}$ (65 × 45). Private collection, New York

20 Piet Mondrian (1872–1944)
Church in Domburg (façade), 1909. Ink on paper, $16\frac{1}{3} \times 11$ (41.5 × 28). Haags Gemeentemuseum, The Hague (Inv. T.110–1971)

21 Piet Mondrian (1872–1944)
Church in Domburg, 1914. Ink on paper, $24\frac{7}{8} \times 19\frac{5}{8}$ (63 × 50). Haags Gemeentemuseum, The Hague (Inv. T.127–1971). © SPADEM

22 Unknown Chinese artist
Bodhidharma, (?) 14th century. Brush. The Cleveland Museum of Art, Ohio

24 Joan Miró (1893–)
Samedi 19 octobre, 1963. Page of a diary

27 False-necked stirrup jar with stylized octopus design from Crete, *c.* 1500 BC. Late Marine style. Heraklion Museum, Crete. Photo Peter Clayton

28 Titian (Tiziano Vecelli) (*c.* 1487/90–1576)
The Bloody Deed of a Jealous Husband. Study for a fresco in the Scuola del Santo, Padua. Pen on white paper, $7\frac{3}{8} \times 7$ (18.8 × 17.7). Ecole des Beaux-Arts, Paris

29 Cave painting of buffalo from Lascaux, Dordogne, France, *c.* 20,000 BC. Photo Caisse National des Monuments Historiques et des Sites

32 Jalayrid
Muslim calligraphy, Persian, *c.* 1400. Photo Piers B. Rawson

33 Huang T'ing-Chien
Chinese calligraphy of a poem. Brush and ink

36 Tao Chi (1641–1717)
Landscape, from an album of 8 leaves. Ink and colours on paper, $8 \times 10\frac{7}{8}$ (20.3 × 27.5). British Museum, London (OA Add. 349/1965 7–24 011)

37 Le Corbusier (1887–1965)
Page from *The Modulor*, 1954

40 Rembrandt van Rijn (1606–69)
Child Learning to Walk (seen from behind), *c.* 1650–8. Pen and sepia, 9 × 15 (22.8 × 38.1). British Museum, London (PD 81/1912.4.16.2)

41 Paul Klee (1879–1940)
Polyphonic Synthesis with a Linear-Active Subject. Pencil. © ADAGP Paris & Cosmopress Geneva 1983

45 Jean A.-D. Ingres (1780–1867)
Two Nudes, Study for The Golden Age, 1842. Graphite on cream woven paper, backed, traced with a stylus after mounting, $16\frac{3}{8} \times 12\frac{3}{8}$ (41.6 × 31.4). Courtesy of the Fogg Art Museum, Harvard University; bequest Grenville L. Winthrop (1943.861)

47 Example of Chinese calligraphy. Photo Piers B. Rawson

49 Pablo Picasso (1881–1973)
Guernica, 1937 (detail). Oil on canvas, whole = $11'5\frac{1}{2}'' \times 25'5\frac{3}{4}''$ (349.3 × 776.6). Picasso Museum, Barcelona. © SPADEM

50 Photograph of a hand. Photo Eileen Tweedy

51, Rembrandt van Rijn (1606–69)

52 Details from two figurative drawings

54 Architectural plan of the bazaar at Kashan (segment)

59 Kasimir Malevich (1878–1935)
In Suprematist Space, 1920. Lithograph $46\frac{3}{8} \times 30\frac{3}{4}$ (118 × 78)

60 Medieval woodcut of 'Hyginus', illustration to a book by Lucianus, 1488

61 Paul Klee (1879–1940)
Sailboats in Gentle Motion, 1927. Pen and ink on paper. Private collection, Berne. © ADAGP Paris & Cosmopress Geneva 1983

63 Eugène Delacroix (1798–1863)
Moroccan Rider Fording a River. Pen. Louvre, Paris

64 Greek cup (interior), 520–510 BC. *Rider*. British Museum, London

65 Greek cup, *c.* 485 BC. *Young Girl Washing Herself*. Musées Royaux, Brussels

68 Circular shell gorget with decoration representing an eagle and a puma. Mould Culture, Bell County, Texas, 1300–1700. Maximum diameter $5\frac{1}{2}$ (13.9). Photo courtesy of the Museum of the American Indian, Heye Foundation (22/7574)

71 Henry Moore (1898–)
Madonna and Child, 1943. Pen and ink with wash, $8\frac{7}{8} \times 7\frac{7}{8}$ (22.5 × 17.5). The Cleveland Museum of Art, Ohio; the Hinman B. Hurlbut Collection

74 Jasper Jones (1930–)
Diver, 1963. Charcoal and pastel on paper and mounted on canvas, $86\frac{1}{2} \times 71$ (219.7 × 180.3). Private collection, New York

76 Kurt Schwitters (1887–1948)
Merz: Santa Claus, 1922. Collage of papers and cloth, $11\frac{1}{4} \times 8\frac{1}{4}$ (28.4 × 20.8). Collection The Museum of Modern Art, New York; Purchase. © ADAGP Paris & Cosmopress Geneva 1983

77 Henri Matisse (1869–1954)

Acrobats, 1952. Painted, cut and pasted paper, and charcoal, $83\frac{5}{8} \times 82\frac{1}{2}$ (213 × 209.5). Private collection. © SPADEM
81 British Ordinance Survey map. Information code
82 Paul Klee (1879–1940)
Diagram. Pen. © ADAGP Paris & Cosmopress Geneva 1983
85 Thiery's figure
87 El Lissitzky (1890–1941)
Study for a page from 'A Suprematist Story About Two Square in Six Constructions', 1920. Watercolour, pencil on cardboard, $10\frac{1}{8} \times 8$ (25.7 × 20.3). The Sidney and Harriet Janis Collection; gift to the Museum of Modern Art, New York
88 Agnes Martin (1912–)
Untitled, 1960. Pen and ink, $11\frac{7}{8} \times 12\frac{1}{8}$ (30.2 × 30.6). Collection, The Museum of Modern Art, New York; acquired with matching funds from the Lauder Foundation and the National Endowment for the Arts
89 Viktor Vasarely (1908–)
Plate from *Kinetic Album no. III*, 1959
90 Jim Dine (1935–)
Untitled (5-Bladed Saw) from *'Series of Seven Tool Drawings'*, 1973. Charcoal and graphite, $25\frac{5}{8} \times 19\frac{7}{8}$ (65.1 × 50.2). Collection, The Museum of Modern Art, New York; purchase
91 Joan Miró (1893–)
Brush drawing
92 School of Rembrandt van Rijn (17th century)
Woman and Child. Pen and ink on paper, $6\frac{5}{8} \times 5$ (16.9 × 12.6). Rijksmuseum, Amsterdam (Inv. A.2059 v.)
93 Chinese Tangrams. From a Chinese 19th-century Tangram woodcut book
95 Jean Arp (1887–1966)
Arrangement According to the Laws of Chance, 1916–17. Torn and pasted papers, $19\frac{1}{8} \times 13\frac{5}{8}$ (48.6 × 34.6). Collection, The Museum of Modern Art, New York; purchase
96 Pottery from Susa, Tanzania, 4th millennium BC
97 Drawing on cloth from an Egyptian Book of the Dead, New Kingdom. Mummy bandage, *c.* $2\frac{1}{2}$ (6.3) wide. Gulbenkian Museum, University of Durham
98 Paul Klee (1879–1940)
Lady Apart, 1940. Brush and ink, $16\frac{3}{8} \times 11\frac{5}{8}$ (41.6 × 29.5). Collection, The Museum of Modern Art, New York; A. Conger Goodyear Fund. © ADAGP Paris & Cosmopress Geneva 1983
99 Matthew Paris (13th century)
Virgin and Child. MS ROY.14.C.VII. British Museum, London
100 Drawing to advertise a house for sale, 1981
102 Edgar Degas (1834–1917)
A Ballet Dancer in Position Facing Three-quarter Front, 1872. Soft black graphite accented with black crayon, heightened with white chalk on pink paper, $16\frac{1}{8} \times 11\frac{1}{4}$ (40.9 × 28.5). Courtesy of the Fogg Art Museum, Harvard University; bequest Meta and Paul J. Sachs
103 Auguste Rodin (1840–1917)
Two Nudes. Pencil and watercolour. $12 \times 7\frac{5}{8}$ (30.4 × 19.5). Graphische Sammlung Albertina (Inv. 23.782)
104 Hans von Marées (1837–87)
Cheiron and Achilles. Red chalk, $22\frac{5}{8} \times 16\frac{7}{8}$ (57.5 × 43). Staatliche Graphische Sammlung, Munich
105 Antoine Watteau (1684–1721)
Head of a Man in a Turban. Black and red chalks heightened with body-colour, $84\frac{1}{4} \times 62\frac{1}{4}$ (214 × 158). Royal Library, Windsor Castle (RL. 3948). Reproduced by gracious permission of Her Majesty the Queen
106 Giorgio Morandi (1890–1964)
Still-Life, 1936. Pencil on paper $9 \times 6\frac{1}{3}$ (23 × 16). Private collection, Milan
107 Jacques Lipchitz (1891–)
Girl with Braided Hair, 1914. Pencil, $7\frac{7}{8} \times 6\frac{1}{4}$ (19.9 × 15.8). Collection, The Museum of Modern Art, New York; Mr and Mrs Milton J. Petrie Fund
108 Paul Cézanne (1839–1906)
Pistachio Tree in the Courtyard of Château Noir, *c.* 1900. Watercolour over pencil sketch, $21\frac{1}{4} \times 16\frac{7}{8}$ (54 × 43). Collection of The Art Institute of Chicago
109 Claude Lorrain (Gelée Claude) (1600–82)
Campagna Landscape. Pen and bistre with wash, $12 \times 8\frac{1}{2}$ (30.4 × 21.6). British Museum, London (PD 29/007.202)
111, 113 Anonymous Persian (16th century)
Balquis, Queen of Sheba (with the hoopoe which carried her love letters to Solomon), *c.* 1590. Ink and brush on paper with colour, $3\frac{7}{8} \times 7\frac{1}{2}$ (9.9 × 19.2). British Museum, London (OR 1948 12–11 08)
112 Utamaro (1753–88)
Reclining Lovers with Fan, from 'The Poem of the Pillow', 1788. Coloured woodcut, $9\frac{3}{4} \times 14\frac{3}{4}$ (24.8 × 37.4). Victoria and Albert Museum, London (E.98–1954)
114 Ernst Barlach (1870–1938)
Pair of Furies, 1922. Charcoal, $13\frac{1}{2} \times 10\frac{1}{3}$ (34.5 × 26.2). Nachlass, Güstrow
115 Jacopo Tintoretto (1518–94)
Figure Study of a Man. Charcoal on grey-blue paper, $12\frac{3}{8} \times 8\frac{3}{4}$ (31.4 × 22.3). Courtesy of the Fogg Art Museum, Harvard University; bequest Charles Alexander Loeser
116 Egon Schiele (1890–1918)
Seated Girl with Orange Garters, 1917. Black chalk, gouache and watercolour, $18 \times 11\frac{3}{8}$ (45.7 × 29). Private collection. Photo courtesy Marlborough Fine Arts Ltd, London
118 Pieter Breughel (*c.* 1525/30–69)
Summer, 1568. Pen and ink, $8\frac{5}{8} \times 11\frac{1}{4}$ (22 × 28.6). Kunsthalle, Hamburg (Inv. 21758)
119 Eugène Delacroix (1798–1863)
Horses, page of studies. Pen on paper. Louvre, Paris
120 Titian (Tiziano Vecelli) (*c.* 1487/90–1576)
Study of Trees. Pen and bistre, $8\frac{1}{2} \times 12\frac{1}{2}$ (21.6 × 31.7). Metropolitan Museum of Art, New York; Rogers Fund, 1908 (Inv. 08.227.38)
122 Albrecht Dürer (1471–1528)
Head of an Apostle, 1508. Brush, heightened with white, on green-grounded paper, $12\frac{1}{2} \times 8\frac{1}{3}$ (31.7 × 21.2). Graphische Sammlung Albertina (Inv. 4836.D.87)
125 Luca Cambiaso (1527–85)
Allegory. Pen and iron gall ink with brush and brown ink on buff-laid paper, $10\frac{7}{8} \times 96\frac{5}{8}$ (27.5 × 24.4). Courtesy of the Art Institute of Chicago; gift of William F. E. Gurley, Lenora Hall Gurley Memorial Collection (22.15)
128 Jean Baptiste Camille Corot (1796–1875)
Landscape with Trees. Charcoal, $14\frac{1}{2} \times 21\frac{1}{2}$ (36.9 × 54.7). Private collection, New York
130 Rembrandt van Rijn (1606–69)
Portrait of a Syndic, *c.* 1662–5. Reed pen and bistre with white body colour, $9\frac{3}{4} \times 7\frac{1}{2}$ (24.7 × 19.2). Louvre, Paris
132 Kuo Hsü (?17th century)
Boy on a buffalo's back playing common flute. Drawing on paper, $11\frac{3}{4} \times 9\frac{7}{8}$ (29.9 × 25). Nanking Museum
133 Aristide Maillol (1861–1944)
Reclining Nude, *c.* 1932. Red crayon, $21\frac{1}{8} \times 30\frac{5}{8}$ (53.8 × 77.8). Collection The Art Institute of Chicago; gift of Mr and Mrs William N. Eisendrath Jr. (40. 1044)
135 Jan van Eyck (*c.* 1385–1441)
Portrait of Cardinal Nicolo Albergati, *c.* 1430. Silverpoint on prepared paper, $8\frac{1}{3} \times 7$ (21.2 × 18). Staatliche Kunstsammlungen, Dresden (Inv. C 775)
136 Nicholas Poussin (1594–1665)
Three Nymphs, *c.* 1633–5. Pen and bistre over black chalk, $5\frac{1}{8} \times 5\frac{3}{4}$ (13.1 × 14.6). Reproduced by gracious permission of Her Majesty the Queen. Photo A. C. Cooper Ltd
138 Oskar Schlemmer (1888–1943)
Study for the 'Triadic Ballet', 1922. Gouache, ink and collage of

photographs, $22\frac{5}{8} \times 14\frac{5}{8}$ (57.5×37.1) (irregular). Collection The Museum of Modern Art, New York; gift of Lily Auchincloss

139 Antonello da Messina (*c.* 1430–93)
Portrait of a Young Man. Charcoal on brown paper, $12\frac{7}{8} \times 10\frac{1}{2}$ (33×26.9). Graphische Sammlung Albertina (Inv. 17611)

140 Georges-Pierre Seurat (1859–91)
Seated Woman, 1884–5. Conte crayon, $18\frac{7}{8} \times 12\frac{3}{8}$ (47.9×31.4). Collection, The Museum of Modern Art, New York; Abby Aldrich Rockefeller Bequest

141 Paul Cézanne (1839–1906)
Still-life with Candlestick, 1881–4. (Page XVII from sketchbook CBS III). Pencil, $8\frac{1}{8} \times 4\frac{7}{8}$ (20.7×12.5). Kupferstichkabinett, Basle (Inv. 1935.185)

142 Eugène Delacroix (1798–1863)
Landscape. Wash, from a page of a sketchbook. Louvre, Paris

143 Fernand Léger (1881–1955)
Face and Hands, 1952. Brush and ink, $26 \times 19\frac{3}{4}$ (66×50.2). Collection, The Museum of Modern Art, New York; Mrs Wendell T. Bush Fund. © SPADEM

145 Pablo Picasso (1881–1973)
Mlle Léonie, 1922–12. Pen and ink, $12 \times 7\frac{3}{4}$ (30.5×19.7). The Museum of Modern Art, New York; anonymous extended loan (1982. 55). © SPADEM

147 Henri Matisse (1869–1954)
Woman nursing her knee . . . a foot, *c.* 1909. Reed pen and ink, $11\frac{1}{2} \times 9\frac{1}{4}$ (29.4×23.5). Courtesy the Art Institute of Chicago; gift of Mrs Emily Crane Chadbourne (26.1533). © SPADEM

148 Tung Ch'i-Ch'ang (1555–1636)
Landscape (detail). Ink. The Cleveland Museum of Art, Ohio

150 Michelangelo Buonarroti (1475–1564)
Two Studies of a Crucified Man, sketches for Haman of the Sistine Chapel ceiling, *c.* 1504. Pen and brown ink over a light sketch with a stylus, $9\frac{7}{8} \times 6\frac{1}{3}$ (24.9×16). British Museum, London (PD W.12/59.L.25.555)

151 Raphael (Raffaello Sanzio) (1483–1520)
Study for 'Fire in the Borgo', *c.* 1514. Uffizi Galleries, Florence. Photo Alinari

155 Kuo Hsi (?copy after) (*c.* 1020–90)
Chinese Winter Landscape (far left detail of scroll painting) 22″ × 33′4″ (whole scroll) (55.8×1016). Toledo (Ohio) Museum of Art; gift of Edward Drummond Libbey (Inv. 27.151)

157 Albrecht Dürer (1471–1528)
Drawing Machine. Pen and ink

160 Raphael (Raffaello Sanzio) (1483–1520)
Male Nude 'David' (after Michelangelo), *c.* 1504. Pen and brown ink with faint traces of black chalk, $15\frac{1}{2} \times 8\frac{5}{8}$ (39.3×21.9). British Museum, London

161 Théodore Géricault (1791–1824)
Study for 'The Raft of the Medusa', *c.* 1819. Black crayon on white paper, $8 \times 11\frac{1}{3}$ (20.5×28.9). Musée des Beaux-Arts, Besançon (Inc. D 2153)

162 Pablo Picasso (1881–1973)
Minotaurs caressing a Girl, 1933 (Vollard Suite). Combined technique $11\frac{3}{4} \times 14\frac{1}{2}$ (29.8×36.8). © SPADEM

163 Buddhist head of a deity, Japan, 8th century. Shosoin, Nara, Japan

164 Otto Dix (1891–1969)
Café Couple, 1921. Watercolour and pencil, $20 \times 16\frac{1}{8}$ (50.8×41). Collection, The Museum of Modern Art, New York; purchase

165 Henri de Toulouse-Lautrec (1864–1901)
Aux Ambassadeurs, (*Mlle Bélanger*). Pencil, $10\frac{1}{8} \times 7\frac{3}{4}$ (25.9×19.7). Graphische Sammlung Albertina (Inv. 24.170)

166 Pablo Picasso (1881–1973)
Head of a Woman, 1938. Pen and indian ink, $17\frac{7}{8} \times 9\frac{5}{8}$ (45.5×24.5). Musée Picasso, Paris (Inv. MP 1203). © SPADEM

167 Henri Gaudier-Brzeska (1891–1915)
Standing Nude. Pen. Collection, The Museum of Modern Art, New York

169 Luca Signorelli (*c.* 1441/50–1523)
Male Nudes being Bound. Study for fresco in Orvieto Cathedral. Black and red chalk, $11\frac{1}{4} \times 8\frac{1}{2}$ (28.5×21.5). Uffizi Galleries, Florence (Inv. 1246E). Photo Alinari

170 Henri de Toulouse-Lautrec (1864–1901)
Yvette Guilbert Taking a Curtain Call. Crayon and watercolour, $16\frac{1}{3} \times 9$ (41.6×22.9). Rhode Island School of Design Museum of Art (New York)

172 Chinese woodblock print, *Group of Trees*, 17th century

173 Rembrandt van Rijn (1606–69)
Child Learning to Walk (seen from the front). Red chalk on grey paper, 4×5 (10.4×12.9). British Museum, London (PD 1910–2–12–187/446)

174 Eugène Delacroix (1798–1863)
Combat between a Tiger and an Alligator. Pen (from a page of studies). Louvre, Paris

175 Nicholas Poussin (1594–1665)
Study for 'The Rape of the Sabines', *c.* 1630s. Pen and brown ink with brown wash, $6\frac{1}{2} \times 8\frac{1}{2}$ (16.4×21.9). Reproduced by permission of the Chatsworth Settlement Trustees. Photo Courtauld Institute of Art, London

176 Peter Paul Rubens (1577–1640)
Soldiers Carousing in front of a Farmhouse, *c.* 1635–40. Pen on brown paper, $10\frac{5}{8} \times 14$ (27.1×35.8). Collection Fondation Custodia (coll. F. Lugt), Institut Néerlandais, Paris (Inv. 2535 recto)

177 Francisco de Goya (1746–1828)
Disparate Furioso, No. 6 from a set of etchings, 'Disparates', *c.* 1815–24. Sanguine wash with traces of red chalk, $9\frac{5}{8} \times 10$ (24.4×25.4). Prado, Madrid. Photo Mac, Barcelona

178 Utamaro (1735–1806)
Girls Picking Persimmons, *c.* 1790. Coloured woodcut, $14\frac{7}{8} \times 9\frac{5}{8}$ (37.8×24.4). Victoria and Albert Museum, London (E 1069–1963)

Photo credits for pictures not included in the above list: Piers B. Rawson 9, 10, 17, 35, 66, 72, 80, 101, 153, 168; M. Smith 131

Index